D1103422

Also by Alexander Piatigorsky

THE BUDDHIST PHILOSOPHY OF THOUGHT

MYTHOLOGICAL DELIBERATIONS:
LECTURES ON THE PHENOMENOLOGY OF MYTH

ALEXANDER PIATIGORSKY

Freemasonry

The Study of a Phenomenon

THE HARVILL PRESS

LONDON

I dedicate this book to my dear friends Christopher MacLehose,
Andrew Nurnberg, Tudor Parfitt and Charlotte Elizabeth Rickets,
who all helped me, at various stages of my work, with their
enthusiasm, encouragement and love.

First published in Great Britain in 1997 with the title
Who's Afraid of Freemasons? by Harvill

This edition first published in 1999 by
The Harvill Press
2 Aztec Row
Berners Road
London N1 0PW

www.harvill.com

1 3 5 7 9 8 6 4 2

Copyright © Alexander Piatigorsky, 1997

Alexander Piatigorsky asserts the moral right to be
identified as the author of this work

A CIP catalogue record for this book
is available from the British Library

ISBN 1 86046 265 0

Printed and bound in Great Britain by Biddles Ltd,
Guildford and King's Lynn

CONTENTS

E. The foundation sacrifice of warriors in 12 c. B.C. China.

F. Core-plot of the Japanese legend:

(I) A bridge is repeatedly washed away by the flooding of a river.

(II) A knowledgeable person suggests that a human sacrifice is necessary, and recommends

(III) a victim, possibly a stranger, and advises how to choose a victim.

(IV) The adviser turn out to be, himself, sacrificed.

(V) He warns his daughter not to speak out in the future.

G. Core-plot of H. Ibsen's Master Builder:

Solness, the master-builder commits suicide (?) by throwing himself from the tower of his building.

C. Some elements of mythology and Cult of Melkart:

(I) Melkart, the founder (builder) of Tyre,

(II) who erected the twin pillars of his shrine (as the priest),

(III) the city-god of Tyre,

(IV) was maimed,

(V) and murdered.

(VI) His wife burned his body on the funeral pyre,

(VII) buried him,

(VIII) and avenged his death by killing and dismembering the body of his murderer.

(IX) Each year he is murdered and then resurrected.

(X) After his death he becomes King (god) of the underworld and

(XI) the 'Master of the Furnace'.

(XII) The sacrifice of the first-born boys in the fundament of the temples and fortresses was the central feature of his cult.

to A
to A (II)
to A (V)

B. Core-plot of the Biblical Passages

(I) Hiram the Brassworker,

(II) working for the temples of Melkart in Tyre,

(III) the son of a widow,

(IV) when Solomon's Temple was completed,

(V) cast the twin-pillars at the porch.

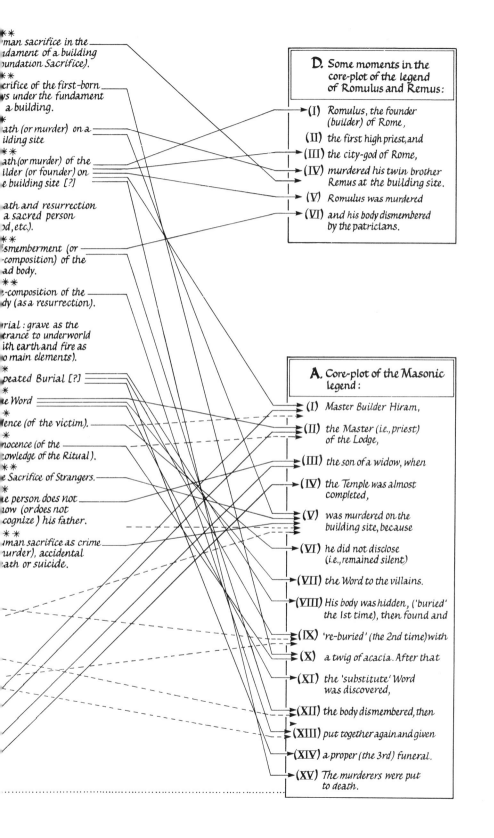

man sacrifice in the
ndament of a building
undation Sacrifice).
**

crifice of the first-born
ys under the fundament
a building.
*

ath (or murder) on a
ilding site
**

ath (or murder) of the
ilder (or founder) on
e building site [?]

ath and resurrection
a sacred person
od, etc.).
**

smemberment (or
-composition) of the
ad body.
**

-composition of the
dy (as a resurrection).

rial : grave as the
trance to underworld
ith earth and fire as
o main elements).
*

peated Burial [?]
*

e Word
*

lence (of the victim).
*

nocence (of the
nowledge of the Ritual).
**

e Sacrifice of Strangers.
*

e person does not
now (or does not
cognize) his father.
**

uman sacrifice as crime
murder), accidental
ath or suicide.

D. Some moments in the
core-plot of the legend
of Romulus and Remus:

(I) Romulus, the founder
(builder) of Rome,

(II) the first high priest, and

(III) the city-god of Rome,

(IV) murdered his twin brother
Remus at the building site.

(V) Romulus was murdered

(VI) and his body dismembered
by the patricians.

A. Core-plot of the Masonic
legend :

(I) Master Builder Hiram,

(II) the Master (i.e., priest)
of the Lodge,

(III) the son of a widow, when

(IV) the Temple was almost
completed,

(V) was murdered on the
building site, because

(VI) he did not disclose
(i.e., remained silent)

(VII) the Word to the villains.

(VIII) His body was hidden, ('buried'
the 1st time), then found and

(IX) 're-buried' (the 2nd time) with

(X) a twig of acacia. After that

(XI) the 'substitute' Word
was discovered,

(XII) the body dismembered, then

(XIII) put together again and given

(XIV) a proper (the 3rd) funeral.

(XV) The murderers were put
to death.

LIST OF ILLUSTRATIONS

Frontispiece from *Mahhabone or The Grand Lodge Door Open'd*, 1766
Courtesy of the Grand Lodge Library and Museum, London

Frontispiece from *The Three Distinct Knocks*, 1776
Courtesy of the Grand Lodge Library and Museum, London

Three tracing boards from Ivanhoe Lodge, No. 631, by
   Arthur L. Thistleton, 1836
Courtesy of the Grand Lodge Library and Museum, London

Two tracing boards from the Royal Naval Lodge, No. 59, by J. E. Godwin
Courtesy of the Grand Lodge Library and Museum, London

The Great Hall at Syon House, Robert Adam, 1762
By kind permission of His Grace the Duke of Northumberland

Print by Albrecht Dürer from *Perspectiva Corporum Regularium*,
   by Wenzel Jamitzer, 1568
Courtesy of The British Library

Brass of Erasmus Williams by Haydocke, *c.*1608
The Society of Antiquaries

Emblem from *A Collection of Emblemes*, by George Wither, 1635
Courtesy of The British Library

Title page of *The History of the World*, by Sir Walter Ralegh, 1614
Courtesy of The British Library

Title page of *The Christian Zodiack*, by Jeremias Drexel, 1633
Courtesy of The British Library

LIST OF TEXT FIGURES

AUTHOR'S NOTE

I am deeply thankful to all those informants, interviewees and interlocutors, Masons, ex-Masons and non-Masons who patiently bore my imposition on their time. I apologize to them in advance for all abbreviations and inexactitudes that appear in the transcripts of my conversations with them.

Finally, I am most grateful to the small community of the Harvill Press, and to Mr Euan Cameron, for their work and patience.

Imprisoned by you in the mood, doubtful, loaded by you, with distressing embarrassment, we are, we submit, in no position to set anyone free.
W. H. Auden "Caliban o the Audience", *The Sea and the Mirror*

Preface

The Title, Two Meanings and Three Paradoxes

"This mystical key must be delivered personally, and to none but those who . . ."

J. Browne, Past Master of Six Lodges

The sub-title of this book, The Study of a Phenomenon, combines two meanings, making use of a convenient ambiguity in the word "phenomenon". In the first place, following the more philosophical sense of the term, it says that the book is about Freemasonry as an object of thought: about what Masons think of Masonry and of themselves, about what other people think of them, and about what I, the author, think of what Freemasons and what other people think on the same subject. In other words, it is about the perceptions of the thing called Freemasonry.

Secondly, the book looks at the thing itself as an object of life: Masons, their Lodges, rituals, signs and symbols, habits, language, speeches, history and, once again, thoughts and ideas, which constitute the raw material of thinking. This second aspect of the title refers to Freemasonry simply as a fact or sum of facts.

Discriminating between these two meanings seems to me to be of the utmost importance, and I have endeavoured throughout to make it as clear as possible from which angle I am approaching the subject, though life and thought being hopelessly intertwined it is not always easy.

Here is a small illustration. Let us take, for example, the statement: "Freemasonry is a secret religious organization with a world membership exceeding seven million men."

This reveals two things about Freemasonry – its social definition as an organization and the statistics concerning its membership – which can be classified as factual, irrespective of whether the facts are correctly given or not.

To describe it as a "religious" organization, however, depends entirely on one's view of Masonry and of religion, or on one's own critique of other people's thinking about them. To one person

Freemasonry is a religion, to another it is definitely not, to a third it is a pseudo- or quasi-religion, whereas a fourth may assert that the question of religion is irrelevant to our understanding of Freemasonry since it is a purely social phenomenon.

In the light of my distinction, even such an apparently self-evident feature as "secrecy" can be thought of in quite a few different ways, including its complete denial, depending on one's approach.

I have attempted to concentrate more on the phenomenological aspect of Freemasonry than the factual side, for not only am I reluctant to add to the already gigantic number of publications devoted to its description, but I really do wish to present it as a type of self-awareness and not as a mere historical event or a plain fact of social life. I want to see Masonry as it sees itself, first; as it is seen by others, second; and as it sees those others, third.

I treat the opponents of Masonry in the same way. Who or what the opponents are is for me a minor concern. What really matters is their *conscious* attitude to Masonry and to themselves as relating to Masonry. So, for instance, when an anonymous American critic said in 1883 that "Masons are enemies of God and the Government of the United States", or when David Yallop in 1983 wrote that "Bugging telephones is a Masonic habit" I do not discuss whether these assertions are right or wrong factually, but simply accept them as symptoms of their authors' thinking.

Masonry is a "theatre for itself", and my place is not on stage with the Masons, nor sitting with the audience, but in the wings as an observer. I play the role of a sympathetic but neutral commentator, uncommitted to either of the parties. I do not think that the world would be any better off without Masonry, nor is it my main hope that this work will make Masonry much more comprehensible to the world. My aim foremost is to explain my own understanding of this strange anachronism which still flourishes in our society.

Yet in presenting Freemasonry as a phenomenon – where Freemasons', other people's and my own thinking converge on one object of observation – I have to start with the *fact* of this observation. Only afterwards will I move on to the thinking that underlies both the observation and the facts observed.

So, what is it about Freemasons? There are, certainly, a great many of them still around and they manage to irritate or alarm a lot of people. Throughout the period of my own preoccupation with Masonry, I have developed my own very basic research method which seems to work quite well. Whenever I have travelled by plane, I have never permitted myself a drink before asking at least one fellow passenger what he or she knows or thinks of Freemasonry. Out of the 120 English-speaking passengers I have interviewed during my last forty flights (leaving aside three people who actually were Freemasons), twenty-six did not even know the word; thirty-one knew the word and its basic meaning, but had never heard, read or thought any more about the matter. Of the rest, thirty-three had some vague idea but no opinion whatsoever on the subject; and thirty had both an idea and an opinion. This amateurish exercise at least proves that present-day Masonry is not a product of my (or Masons') imagination, and that a creditable percentage of the non-Masonic population has some degree of knowledge about the institution. They may be surprised to discover that there are as many as 700,000 Masons in Great Britain,[1] and that it remains the largest and oldest international non-denominational religious organization in the world:[2] 273 years of uninterrupted and well-documented historical existence since the foundation of the Grand Lodge of England in 1717.

Why do Masons irritate or alarm people? Out of the thirty interviewees who were able to say something definite about Masonry, sixteen were against it for one reason or another; nine were slightly disapproving, and five spoke of it with a certain sympathy.[3] And of those sixteen who were against Freemasonry, only five opposed it because of what they knew about it, while eleven felt that they did not know enough: in other words they were put off because of Masonic secrecy. This is the feature that most irritated my interviewees.

But who can speak of secrecy when the minimum bibliography on Masonry amounts to some 60,000 titles? This is the first of the Masonic paradoxes: secrecy which is no secrecy at all, and paradoxes which are not invented by ourselves tend to irritate us very much.

The second paradox is this: Freemasonry has existed almost unchanged since the beginning of the eighteenth century, quietly defying history and the march of time, while simultaneously being more obsessed with its own history than any other institution in the world. From the start, the Craft (as it is often referred to) has assiduously recorded its existence year by year, month by month, day by day, constantly defining its own past,[4] while remaining almost unaffected by the history of mankind in general.[5] The whole corpus of Masonic historical literature rivals in size – if not exceeds – the collection of works devoted to the history of any major country during the same period (1717–1990).

So why does Freemasonry persist, and to what end? The range of opinion on this point is very wide. Among Masons themselves, views vary from "the reason is to be enlightened by the divine unfathomable light" (William Preston), through "our scope is spiritual perfection and moral self-improvement" (G. Oliver), to "our utmost pleasure is enjoying the good conversation" (Martin Clare).[6] Among those opposed to Masons the spectrum is equally wide: from the quite innocuous "a children's game which children themselves are not able to understand" (J. Weiss), through "an extreme case of institutional nonsense and religious incongruity mixed with blasphemy" (an American anonym), to "a hidden aspiration to achieve their malevolent power over the whole world" (John Quincy Adams).

The two Masonic paradoxes, its unveiled secrecy and its anti-historical history, do not arise out of our ignorance of Masonry or out of Freemasonry's incomplete knowledge of itself. They are inherent in the nature of Freemasonry as a religious phenomenon and are exacerbated by an incomplete understanding of it as such by Masons and non-Masons alike. To understand Masonry – and this applies to the understanding of any religious phenomenon – is to understand oneself with respect to Masonry. The average contemporary writer on Masonry reflects, on the whole, the general attitude to Masonry in that he usually reacts to it either positively or negatively, and with or without adequate information. Yet what is needed, more than reaction or even knowledge, is understanding.

Why then do I try to understand it? I have a personal interest in religious symbolism in general, but why should I wish to understand Masonry, one of the most symbolic of all contemporary religious phenomena, in particular? The answer is that it is not only of historical but also of historic significance. We have already entered an epoch marked not by confrontation between the forces of religion and atheism, as was the case with the previous period, but by a conflict between an increasing indifference to religion and religious fundamentalism within almost all established religions of the world.[7] It is in the context of this conflict that Masonry is becoming objectively more and more important in that it provides a kind of religious "third force", the force of esoteric religious symbolism. No third force can be popular – public opinion by its own nature tends to polarization – and this is, again paradoxically, one of the additional factors in the growing aversion to Masonry in Europe and America among non-Masons. It serves, as ever, as a handy scapegoat; in irreligious societies for its religious esoterism, and in religious ones for its alleged irreligion. The fact that the number of Masons in the world is growing – along with their unpopularity – is perhaps not entirely causally unconnected.

xv

Caught in the religious context between the Scylla of progressivism and the Charybdis of fundamentalism, Freemasonry seems to be entirely out of tune and out of time.[8] And neither Masons themselves nor their opponents at either extreme of the religious spectrum are able to see that it is just this out-of-tune-ness and out-of-time-ness that save Freemasonry from oblivion and contribute to its perpetuation. What I am offering in this book is not a bare, factual description of Masonry, but an attempt to *think* the idea of it, to reformulate it.

Notes

1 The latter figure is under dispute. The minimum estimate is 350,000, the maximum is 750,000 (700,000 according to an extremely anti-Masonic article in the *New Statesman*, July 1985).

2 My reasons for calling it a religious organization, even though it does not formally claim to be such, are explained in detail in Chapter 3.

3 For the sake of comparison, I offer my equally amateurish statistics concerning Jesuits: I interviewed one hundred of my students, of whom six knew nothing, twenty-nine knew the meaning of the word and nothing more, twenty had some vague historical idea, but no opinion, and forty-five had a definite opinion, which in thirty-nine cases was negative, four neutral, and two positive.

4 It is enough to note that the central historiographical body of British Masonry, *Quatuor Coronati Lodge* (No. 2076), alone published, during the first hundred years of its history, ninety-nine volumes containing materials related to the history of Masonry, its own history and the current records of the Lodge. See C. Dyer, 1966, p. 3.

5 Kenneth S., an elder of the Presbyterian Church, says: "For the last two hundred years Masonry has changed doctrinally, organizationally, and in any other way, much less than my Church, the Church of England, the Catholic Church or the Society of Jesus." The concept of history implies a dynamic, a process of development. We expect historical records to reflect this process. The records of Freemasonry, however, reveal an essentially static organization amid a changing world.

6 Douglas Knoop, G. P. Jones and Douglas Hamer, Eds. *Early Masonic Pamphlets*, Manchester University Press, Manchester, 1945 (E.M.P., 1945), pp. 328–9.

7 Traditionally, aetheists opposed themselves ideologically to religion as an *institution*, and therefore considered themselves outside it, as did many fundamentalist movements. Whereas nowadays both strands can be found inside organized religion – "atheistical" Anglicans and Catholics, for example, and some extreme Hindu fundamentalist sects.

8 I cannot help observing, in this connection, the rapidly growing tension between two far more general tendencies in modern religion, which I call "intensive" and "extensive", or "centripetal" and "centrifugal". The former tries to resolve the problems and exigencies of an external and non-religious character within religion itself; for example the Church of England. The latter tries to resolve the religion's own inner contradictions by extending the sphere of application of

religious norms to the world outside religion; for example, fundamentalist Islam and some extreme Hindu movements. The very word "secularization", so misused and misunderstood, is, in my opinion, much more about secularization of religion itself, than about "de-religionization" of society.

INTRODUCTION

CHAPTER 1

Secrecy, Privacy and Provocation

*And first, give me leave to ask you whether there is Anything or Nothing
in this Affair of Masonry?*
A letter of a Gentleman in the country to his Son in the Temple,
1726

NEWS IN BRIEF
Masons' Oath
*Freemasons will no longer have to face having their tongues cut out
and their throats slit if they break their oaths.*

*The United Grand Lodge, the society's governing body, said yesterday
that it would remove references to physical penalties in candidates'
obligations.*

*The Grand Master, the Duke of Kent, has said that such references
contributed to the society's reputation for secrecy and idolatry.*
Independent, 13 June 1986.

The three sentences quoted above summarize in themselves the three
aspects of what can be called the problem of Freemasonry in Britain.
The first represents public opinion and reflects the position of the
Independent, which accepts that Freemasons have, until now, had "to
face having their tongues cut out and their throats slit if they break
their oaths". It maintains the possibility (despite its half-ironic tone) of
cruel physical punishment of the Brethren by their equals or superiors.
The second sentence represents the official attitude of the Grand Lodge
concerning the removal of any references to such cruelty, but not necessarily to the cruelty itself. The third sentence seems to be more complex
in its meaning, for it reflects both the internal position of the Grand
Master as a Mason and his stand, not on the references themselves, but
rather on the general public's reaction to them as something likely
to exacerbate Freemasonry's reputation for secrecy and, even worse,
idolatry.

The first and third sentences in this news item are, in fact, two different commentaries on the second sentence, which can be seen as a
primary text. Each of the three sentences represents a different position:
the first represents the external non-Masonic position; the second the

internal Masonic position; the third is a combination of both, for the Duke of Kent at one and the same time is a senior figure in the Society of Masons and in modern English society.

What then is my own position as the author of this book? Not being a Christian, a practising Jew, or a Muslim, I cannot represent that religious sector of the public which accuses Masonry of idolatry. Not being a Mason, I am not worried, as the Duke of Kent was, about the reputation of the Craft in the eyes of public opinion which accuses Masonry of both idolatry and secrecy. And finally, not being a native member of British society (I am a foreigner), I do not blame Masonry for being secret, for I like secrecy; as to whether I like idolatry, I have not yet decided.

This said, it becomes clear that the only position left to me is that of the third commentator: I will comment on the decision of the Grand Lodge after the commentaries have been made by the *Independent* and the Duke of Kent. An advantage of being third in line is that I am entitled to comment not only on the primary text, but also on any other commentary related to it. However, as any commentator, I must confine myself entirely to what there is in the text concerning Masonry, be it a speech, an article or a book by anyone either for or against it. Only having respected that limiting condition can I bring to it my own interpretation.

Encompassed in these three sentences I have quoted is the core of the problem of Freemasonry.

Let us start with the question of secrecy, for it is a breach of the oath of secrecy that is to be punished. The strange thing about Masons is that they have never kept secret the fact that they have secrets. More than that, from the time of the establishment of the Grand Lodge of England, they widely publicized the fact in dozens of pamphlets, poems, songs, even in the prologues and epilogues of theatrical benefits and were ". . . always immodestly boasting of their foolish secrets", as one of their earliest opponents complained. Masonic secrets have been exposed to those outside Masonry in hundreds of books, written mainly by ex-Masons, pseudo-Masons, quasi-Masons, Masonic impostors, Masonic traitors and sometimes by "honest opponents" of the Fellowship.

But even being exposed, the secret remains a secret if its understanding is secret by definition, or, as the Revd George Oliver (1782–1867), *enfant terrible* of Masonic historiography, put it: "You cannot divulge the secrets of nature except to those who can understand them, that is, to those who are inside the Science of Nature, such as physicists and natural philosophers. The same applies to the secrets of Masonry." From this it follows that Masonic secrets, in this sense, have no meaning outside the Lodge, while within it their meaning is solely symbolic.

This also explains why the description of Masonic rituals in this book, as anywhere else for that matter, does not amount to revealing their secrets. The secret does not reside in the possession of factual information about the words, actions, gestures and so forth, or even in the explanation of their meaning in terms of how they derive from, or fit into, the Legend of Hiram the builder, which is not at all secret. It resides in the understanding of their meaning within the unique context of ritual enactment within the Lodge. Every detail of the rite of the Catholic Eucharist may be made public – indeed, it must, since it is by nature exoteric – together with any commentaries, but full understanding of its meaning is available only to communicants. In the same way full understanding of the meaning of Masonic rituals, and more than this, of the meaning of their secrecy is open only to Masons.

The meaning of the term "secrecy", as used by Freemasonry, has therefore been almost universally misunderstood. The key is to understand the essential difference between what the terms "symbolic" and "secret" mean to Masons. If Masonic secrets are symbolic, then the Oath is also symbolic, together with any punishment, however dire, for breach of this Oath.

Thus, a non-Mason cannot say: "There is no way I can get to learn these secrets", for in fact if he wishes to he could – although, out of context, he would not be able to understand them. It is this factor that not only "contributes to a reputation of secrecy..." in the Grand Master's words, but in my opinion contributes to the constant tension, not only between Freemasonry and the whole body of public opinion, but primarily within the "collective consciousness" of society itself.[1] The tension arises from the conflict between the public's knowledge of Masonry, and its incomprehension of what is known and of any possibility of comprehending it. This tension is passively exacerbated by the institution itself, for Masonry cannot help feeling that this is the price it has to pay for its comfortable autonomy and separateness from the rest of society, and this price cannot be too high.[2] At the same time, it is that very tension which continuously generates Freemasons' awareness of themselves as people whose knowledge is not common, is not to be shared with others (or even, depending on which level they are, with other Masons), but is entirely exclusive.

The second aspect of our problem is more specific and would be of concern only to those "monotheistic" non-Masons who are worried about the purity of Christianity in Britain (and, even more so, in

America). It may also disturb some Christian Masons who have doubts about the un-Christian character of Masonic rituals and symbolism. Unfortunately, the very term "idolatry" is always used as an expression of Christian critique; it can't be used as a term of religious self-awareness in general (try to imagine an African tribesman saying: "By the way, did I mention that I am an Animist?").

In the present climate of Christian tolerance, the accusation of idolatry does not sound particularly defamatory, even in the mouth of a theologian or clergyman. To the majority of the Christian population in Britain and America, with the exception, of course, of strict fringe religious groups, this word does not carry any serious religious or philosophical meaning, while to the majority of atheists and agnostics it has little more than a metaphorical sense. In spite of all this, however, idolatry retains a certain significance even for those in our society who would never confess that it does, not least many Freemasons, for our society still remains, to an extent at least, Christian.[3] On the whole, public opinion now is not explicitly aware of itself as reflecting Christian views, but, rather, regards itself as *public*. As such it is heavily loaded with a contemporary partiality towards *openness*. Masonry, on the contrary, regards itself first of all *historically*, and most Masons do not realize that what in 1723 (the year of publication of the first official Masonic Constitutions) was seen by public opinion as the "spiritual eccentricity" of gentlemen of leisure, is today viewed by public opinion as a scandalous breach of a very important social convention. So it is that something that 260 years ago aroused some theological doubts but remained socially acceptable, is now seen as socially unacceptable. For, indeed, the "idolatrous cruelty" of the afore-mentioned punishment, intended in one sense as an allegory, is totally inhuman in the eyes of a modern, secularized public.[4] Public opinion, however, is quite unable to think allegorically.[5]

But there is one further point of importance, a point so obvious that one may only wonder why it has so seldom been paid any attention. It is Masonic privacy. Speaking about Masonry one should not forget that, despite its absolute centralization (I am now speaking of England and of the three Degrees of the Craft only), the whole of Masonic life takes place in private Lodges. A Lodge, once established and warranted (from the Grand Lodge of England or a provincial Grand Lodge), is entirely self-sufficient. Whatever goes on there is the result of private and voluntary agreement. Everything that goes on there is secret because it is private, not the other way around; this includes, in addition to the secrets concerning rituals and signs, which are secrets because they are symbolically secret,[6] all the official transactions, unofficial speeches, conversations and remarks made in the Lodge. In the last instance they are not bound by a Masonic Oath of Secrecy; a Mason is *obliged* to keep such things secret by an unwritten "law of privacy".[7] This is what makes Masonry a kind of "sub-culture", more separated from the rest of society than any club in the world, however exclusive it might be. Public opinion, Orwell's "funny animal", his "powerful phantom", would rather tolerate an open disagreement than indifference or aloofness, which is what Masonry has so often offered to the world outside.

Nowhere is this Masonic aloofness demonstrated more clearly than when enemies attack Freemasonry as a whole because some of its Brothers have misbehaved. For example, when I asked John Hamill, then the Master of the famous *Quatuor Coronati*, Scholarly Lodge of English Masonry, what was their reaction to the anti-Masonic campaign inspired by the criminal activity of some members of the notorious Italian Lodge "Propaganda 2", he said: "we never sued them [our opponents] for libel. We do not refute their accusations; we only *correct* their factual mistakes, from time to time. In the days of the P2 scandal, we simply informed the media, when asked, that P2 is not a regular Masonic Lodge and that even as an irregular one, it was struck off the list of Masonic Lodges in Italy, at least four years before the scandal."[8]

"There is one other provocative point about Masonry," said Rabbi Samuel D. K., a Mason and insurance broker (an immensely suspicious combination in the eyes of an anti-Mason). "Look, a Jew, even if he is an uncircumcized atheist or a Reformist, and however good for nothing as a Jew, is still a damned Jew, is he not? A Catholic priest, even twice excommunicated, remains a priest. Not so a Mason. There can be no universal criterion of one's Masonry, for there are too many jurisdictions in the world. Our enemies do not want to know that. They want to treat us all alike, like anti-Semites who want to treat the whole of Jewry as one Jew. But you know, it is extremely difficult with Masons. As a Mason I am more private than as a Jew."

This is indeed so; what is more, in his last sentence the Rabbi put his finger on a very sensitive spot concerning public opinion and Masonry: one can be a crypto-Catholic, one can even be a crypto-Jew, but one cannot be a secret Mason.[9] This is so because the very secrecy of Masonry is its privacy, and it is this privacy that contributes to the atmosphere of provocation surrounding Freemasonry.[10]

One more point about our perception of Freemasonry. One may look upon Freemasonry as good, bad, or indifferent; as interesting or

uninteresting. One can ignore it altogether for that matter. But if perceived, its very perception can be seen as the touchstone of our notion
of *freedom* – our own individual liberty and freedom in general.

The theatre, the audience, and the wings are not superfluous meta-
phors for our understanding of Masonry. Our very idea of freedom is
always far more negative than we would ever care to admit. Negative,
not only with respect to that which lies outside our field of conscious
experience and observation, but also with respect to that which is inside
it and of which we are not sufficiently conscious. When George D., a
well-known cleric of the Church of England, says "We ought to free the
healthy body of the Church from all its Masonic outgrowths", he is as
unfree within his Church as is Vitaly K., a Russian journalist who recently
said that "the Russian people of today should free themselves from all
symptoms of Judaeo-Masonic disease", within his own Russian people.
Neither the cleric nor the journalist knows that Caliban simply cannot
just "set them free", for they are "the audience", and an audience is
a collection. It is "we" and not "I" and freedom cannot be either
collective or merely negative.[11] But if even Masons themselves stick to
a negative and deterministic understanding of freedom ("Freedom is
defined to be a state of exemption from the control or power of
another"),[12] what can be said of those who are battling against them?
It is from the point of view of a positive individual freedom that one
should now tackle Masonry as a theme, a problem, and a phenomenon
of religious consciousness.[13] Any ideology can only pretend to be about
freedom. This is particularly so in the case of an "ideology of freedom",
an ideology in which the central idea is to "set somebody else free".
Masonry has never been, in this sense, an ideology, for it meant and
still means to be an association of those and only those who had already
been freed, or become free, before they began to be associated with
one another in the Masonic manner. That is why Masonry (or being a
Mason) cannot nor does it need to free anybody.[14]

Notes

1 I do not use here the term "collective consciousness" in the sense in which
C. G. Jung used it. What I mean here is what the majority of those who have
pronounced on the subject of Freemasonry regard as their opinion on the subject.
My task then will be to interpret what they say or write, as a kind or type of *thinking*.
But about that further, in the chapter on method (see Chapter 3).

2 My friend Geoffrey K., a prominent Mason, remarked on the decision of the
Grand Lodge referred to in the *Independent* article: "It is totally silly, it is an open

bowing to pressure. Let them [the Grand Lodge] do what they want, but I will never agree with it." Kevin R., the only Mason schoolteacher I have ever met, said: "They did it because they are afraid of the *cowans* [non-Masons] on the street. What a disgraceful capitulation!" Still, the uneasiness felt by some prominent Masons as regards the content, character and implication of the Masonic oaths is shared by many rank and file members of the Craft and cannot be accounted for merely by the need to court favourable publicity or by the "humanist" flavour of the present age. John Fellows, a learned American Mason, writing at the beginning of the previous century, could be hardly suspected of being a "wet" Mason when he says that "the false construction put upon these oaths, has implicated the order in the foulest deeds . . . The only means, therefore, of avoiding this evil, and of wiping away the stain at present attached to the Society, is a total abandonment of the oaths." (J. Fellows, *The Mysteries of Freemasonry, or an exposition of the Religious Dogmas and Customs of the Ancient Egyptians, etc.*, London, Reeves and Turner, 1866 (J. Fellows, 1866), p. iv.)

3 When C. S. Lewis said that "Christian civilization in England ceased to exist at the beginning of the twentieth century", he meant Christianity as the *form of existence* of society. Though, as the *religion* of society it, of course, still continues to exist.

4 Once again, the term "secularization" here means not so much a decline in the religiousness of society (that is, its "de-Christianization"), as the decline in the religiousness of religion itself. The Church has become increasingly secular, and the very fact that nowadays theologians and churchmen are considerably more bothered about Freemasonry than they were at the beginning of the eighteenth century demonstrates that at that time the Church was too strong to care.

5 That is exactly what the Grand Master, in uttering those words, purported to do. As a result, "the audience remained dissatisfied and the actors embarrassed," as Peter R., an Anglican Minister and Mason, said, adding: "Yet who said that we Masons are good actors, and that the world is a good theatre?"

6 There is a marvellous passage in the Minutes of the Lodge of Hope No. 302 of Bradford: "March, 1805, John Wilkinson, for forfeiting the rights of Masonry by listening to and practising [during a magistrates' investigation] the *commands of justice* was by mutual consent expelled from the Lodge." M. S. Herries, *The Mother Lodge of Bradford*, Bradford and London, 1948 (M. S. Herries, 1948), p. 23.

7 "Whatever the subject of conversation," James C., a Mason and lawyer, explained to me, "you cannot refer to your own or somebody else's words spoken *in the Lodge* and use them in any way *outside* the Lodge (for instance, in court), for their use and meaning inside the Lodge might well be *special and private*." Geoffrey K. comments: "The greatest and indeed the only secret of Masonry is the secret of its fellowship (or *fellowships*). Taken outside the situation of fellowship, the secret has no meaning at all. That is to say that it cannot have any *real* meaning to an outsider."

8 A Regular Lodge is a lodge which is under the jurisdiction of a Grand Lodge recognized by the Grand Lodge of England. In his recently published book, Hamill slightly changes the tenor when speaking of these subjects: ". . . in 1984 the Grand Lodge began to reconsider its traditional 'no comment' policy on questions about Freemasonry from outside, instituting a new policy of *limited comment* . . . so that non-Masons could better judge for themselves the accuracy, or otherwise, of reports appearing in the media." (John Hamill, *The Craft*, London, Crucible, 1986 (J. Hamill, 1986), p. 60.)

9 I have seen quite a few distinguished persons in Moscow who were very active crypto-Catholics (two of them became Jesuits), and they told me that the Church entirely accepted and strongly encouraged their being so. I knew a lot of Jews (old and young) who not only were Jews but regarded themselves as Jews, while hiding (sometimes quite successfully) this fact from "all persons whom it may concern" in Moscow. In both these cases we deal with the existence of a *Body* which traditionally has taken upon itself the spiritual and moral responsibility for a partial apostasy of its members. Masons must never *volunteer* the information but, if asked, they must always admit that they are Masons. And once you cease to be a Mason (voluntarily or otherwise) all connection with Masonry is severed. The connection is symbolic; the secrecy symbolic. There is no such thing as an "essential" Mason, unlike a Catholic or a Jew in the eyes of their respective religions.

10 It is this Masonic provocativeness that very often, as in the case of anti-Semitism, results in the curious phenomenon of the inverse formulation of evil. That is, when instead of saying "Masonry (or Jewry) is evil", one says "Evil is Masonry (or Jewry)". On this phenomenon I shall embark further in Chapter 3.

11 "Free *from* what? . . . But your eye should clearly tell me: free *for* what?" F. Nietzsche, *Thus Spake Zarathustra*, trans. by R. J. Hollingdale, Harmondsworth, Middlesex, 1977 (1961), p. 89.

12 *Encyclopaedia of Freemasonry*, London, 1923, Vol. I, p. 281.

13 Though accepting the negative aspect of freedom and defining it as an "independence of everything empirical," Kant introduced a purely religious and positive concept of freedom as "Man's absolute autonomy". See I. Kant, *Religion Within the Limits of Reason*, trans. by T. M. Greene and H. H. Hudson, London, 1934, p. 38.

14 In one of his articles published a couple of years ago, Bernard Levin draws a clear parallel between anti-Masonry and anti-Semitism. He puts his finger on the very core and essence of a classical populist prejudice, nowadays shared by a lot of half-baked intellectuals on both left and right of the political spectrum in Britain: the hatred of any particular (and especially, peculiar) self-expression. The crucial historical difference between Jews and Masons in this country is that only a minority of the former were free to settle here, and were lucky enough to become emancipated (however partially) by Oliver Cromwell in the seventeenth century, but the latter were from the start free and themselves emancipators. Note the difference between "to free" and "to emancipate": you can free only yourself, but you may emancipate someone else. The "symbolic" freedom of Masons may be as irritating to populists as the "civic" freedom of already assimilated Jews.

CHAPTER 2

Freemasonry as Theme and a "Thing Apart"

It's a thing rather to be hoped than wished for.
William Hutchinson

The theme of this work is both subjective and objective, as any true theme must be. On the one hand, the theme is everything I myself bring into my chosen subject, all of that which, when the subject has already been singled out, has shaped it and endowed it with the contours of my thinking and feeling, adding to it the special flavour of my aspirations and dreams. Positive knowledge plays a minimal role here. The theme feeds on my intentionality, arousing my concrete intention not only to explain to others and to myself how and what I think of Freemasonry and its enemies, but to answer the question of why I chose it as the subject of my work. On the other hand, my own inclinations, predilections, prejudices and superstitions can be seen as connected with, or rooted in, the objective circumstances of my own background, upbringing and biography – as far, of course, as I can be aware of them. One thing, however, seems to me to be an absolute condition for forming a theme: you cannot be negative about it, for an entirely negative approach is always a self-blinding one.[1]

As a phenomenon Freemasonry is of great importance, significance and vitality. This is so, not only on account of its being the largest non-denominational organization in the United Kingdom – one adult male in twenty is a Mason – but also, and probably most crucially, on account of its being as a body the most representative and typical of the very character of British civilization as it is now, and even more importantly, as it has always been.

There are three main features of British Freemasonry which, from the time of the founding of the Grand Lodge in 1717 up to the present day, have made it unique in the modern history of the world.

The first is that Freemasonry concentrates in itself all that was and still is typically and specifically British, yet at the same time it attenuates its Britishness to such an extent that, paradoxically, it is often cancelled out within the Lodge. Being the most British of all British institutions, embodying and sometimes even caricaturing the most prominent trends of British behaviour and psychology, Freemasonry from the very start was avowedly cosmopolitan both in its philosophy and in its practice. And if, as tradition has it, one of the most typical of British characteristics is social snobbery, Masonry itself has indeed exemplified this. Yet is it not, at the same time, an exclusive club into which, both in theory and practice, a man of any social station could be admitted? The celebrated British individualism became coupled in Masonry with a peculiar kind of egalitarian collectivism quite impermissible in any exclusive club. In short, while being British to the very marrow, it has consciously created so many exceptions from and anomalies within its Britishness as to accommodate quite comfortably all possible candidates. This is particularly surprising in view of the fact that when it was founded the institution had not a single non-British member or candidate (the first Jew was admitted some twenty-five years thereafter), and especially since the founding fathers of the Grand Lodge in London did not anticipate the enormous spread of Masonry all over the world within less than half a century of its inception.

The second feature is that the whole milieu in which the formation and development of British Masonry took place was not only extremely Protestant and Anglican, but also exceedingly theological. It would not be an exaggeration to say that it is simply impossible to imagine that germinative period of the Fraternity, their meetings, dinners, and traditional discussions, without the presence of the learned doctors of the Divine Science arguing, pronouncing and perorating on behalf of Freemasonry from the point of view of the strictest Christian Orthodoxy. However, what we see now as the final product of their Masonic activity – the clauses in Constitutions, the rules and regulations, the apologetic pamphlets, etc. – seems to be in flagrant breach of the dogmas, rules, and rituals of almost any Christian denomination or sect in existence then or now. The fundamental Masonic idea of "religion in general" (I'm not speaking now of Masonic religion or Freemasonry as a religion), if looked at from outside through the eyes of an observer equally unconnected with both Masonry and Christianity, seems to have been an invention which, though undoubtedly quite congenial to the free-thinking spirit of the time, has remained totally alien to the spirit and letter of the Anglican Church. But its religious universalism knows no equal even today. If the percentage of non-Christians among Freemasons of the whole world does not now exceed fifteen per cent, at the end of the eighteenth century in England it could have been no more than one or two per cent. So, we have no reason whatsoever to suppose that Masonic religious universalism was invented to make the Fraternity more popular. On the contrary, there was even then an inherent danger that it would bring them into conflict with the established Church.

So, a religious anomaly it was and still is, but, as James Dewar aptly remarked: "The British like anomalies and know how to make them work."[2]

The third feature can be conventionally called "sociological" or, more precisely, "socio-psychological", and it characterizes not so much the Institution itself as its members taken individually (see Appendix A). As I have had ample opportunity to establish from my conversations with Freemasons, most of them quite consciously regard Masonry as *something apart*. Apart from not only their work or family life, but also from their social or political position, hobby, and even religion. A man's awareness of being a member of a Lodge seems to be essentially different from his awareness of being a postman, or a broker, or a policeman, or a parishioner, or a member of a trade union, corporation or political party. He simply feels it as different; all this, of course, from *his* point of view, not mine.[3] I see in this "apartness" of the British Freemason a kind of philosophical stance, though few Masons would make such a claim. This position connects him, on the one hand, with the way of living and of thinking of his fathers and grandfathers either literally, as a member of successive generations of Masons, or by adoption into the Masonic heritage. Thus, it limits his thinking, confining it to an historical standard and type, and strengthens his inbred or acquired traditionalism. On the other hand, it makes his thinking and his self-awareness less dependent on the changing circumstances of the present time, affording him an additional dimension of personal freedom. As one of my Masonic acquaintances put it: "When I am at my Lodge meeting, I feel very strongly that what I speak and how I think there is not entirely the same as I think when I am alone. But when I am in the office with my colleagues and my boss, or when I am at a branch meeting of my trade union, I feel even more strongly that whatever the circumstances, I can act or speak as if I were acting or speaking in my Lodge. My being in the Lodge gives a great support to my remaining myself and true to myself anywhere else."

Freemasonry is, in fact, a perfect paradigm of the crystallization and materialization of European, and particularly British, historical consciousness – by which I do not mean a philosophical category or a psychological trend. In the context of this book, historical consciousness means an indication of the degree to which our present thinking and language depend on the modes and patterns of the thinking and language of the past, and the degree to which we are aware of this dependence. Even Masonic individualism and elitism are less important features than this. And when I hear the opponents of Masonry claim that "they mostly invented their history",[4] I see in this very accusation a powerful proof of my point; of course they did! for that was their *conscious* historical creativity at work. This creativity came in a sudden burst at the beginning of the eighteenth century, as they sat at their leisure in their favourite haunts in Covent Garden and Drury Lane, seeking, amongst other things, for a meaning as to why they were sitting there.

From its very inception, British Freemasonry tended to serve as an instrument for solving or at least easing the endemic British tension between individual desire and public responsibility. Whereas the early development of the Lodges in, for instance, France and Russia suggests no such tension, for in both these countries (one ruled by an absolute monarchy and the other by semi-oriental despotism) any personal desire for drastic and radical changes in the political régime and social structure coincided more or less completely with a Freemason's public duty, as they understood it. Unlike their British counterparts, the French and Russian Lodges in the eighteenth and nineteenth centuries understood this duty in terms of the centrifugal principles of societal change. This outward-looking tendency, which found its outcome in the theory and practice of Enlightenment, became embodied in the kind of open cultural activity considered to be necessary for the progress and welfare of those outside the Lodges. Most of the French materialists of the period of the Encyclopaedia were Masons and regarded their membership as a social obligation arising from their avowed task of enlightening the people on matters of politics, philosophy, religion and science. (When the police in Russia under Catherine the Great arrested the leader of Masonic enlightenment, Nikolai I. Novikoff, and closed down his publishing house, they found dozens of "subversive" books in thousands of copies, of which only a very few were on the subject of Freemasonry itself.) In Britain, on the other hand, all the intellectual activity of Freemasonry, and almost all its charity, was centripetal and directed towards preserving and developing the Fraternity itself.

The English Freemasons of the eighteenth century regarded the Craft as a place where they could go on living as they were accustomed to do, but where their private mode of life would assume an additional religious and ethical quality and acquire a framework other than that which embraced State, Church, family, etc. The focus of activity remained inward within Masonry itself.

In the seventeenth and eighteenth centuries, the Scots were caught

between an unbridled hedonism and the severest Presbyterian predestinarianism. This odd combination was brilliantly embodied in the writer
James Hogg,[5] also a Mason (like his near contemporaries Robert Burns
and David Hume), and marked the consciousness of the period. Freemasonry served (in its own reasoning too) as a palliative rather than as
an antidote. However strange it might seem, it offered a middle position
to those in Scotland, as did – though in a different way and in a totally
different context – the Catholic Romanticism of the beginning of the
seventeenth century in England. For, instead of trying to resolve this
contradiction radically, the Craft produced a tolerant and liberal
environment within which a person could remain the person he actually
was while gradually acquiring an improved social condition and a more
informed intellect.

And what was the condition of Masons at that time? Many were
probably heavily in debt. Debt was a disease that plagued the members
of the Brotherhood, both in England and in Scotland, for at least one
hundred years after its foundation in 1717. To mention only three of
the luminaries of the Fraternity – its first legislator and historiographer
Dr James Anderson; the first champion of its expansion, Thomas Dunckerley; and its most brilliant preacher and theologian, Dr Dodd – it would
not be superfluous to note that the first spent some time in prison for
debt,[6] the second died in penury, while the last went to the gallows
for forgery carried out to relieve his debts. This, rightly, did not diminish
the esteem with which the Masonic historians have treated him.[7] I say
this only to stress the point already made, that irrespective of what
Masons in Britain themselves have asserted, their religious and ethical
conceptions implied and still do imply, as does their idea of charity, a
use and application which is almost wholly internal to Masonry. Much
of the latter was expended in trying to rescue (not always successfully)
Masons and their families from pecuniary difficulties.

Notes

1 A professional historian may or may not have a theme. Lord d'Acre (Hugh
Trevor-Roper) seems to have had one while Sir Louis Namier did not. On the idea
of theme I follow Robert Graves and his Theme in *The White Goddess*, where he
treats it as the projection of the heart into its object.

2 James Dewar, *The Unlocked Secret, Freemasonry Examined*, London, William
Kimber, 1966, p. 23. This book is, I believe, one of the most serious and honest
"expositions" of Freemasonry.

3 This is the *emic* viewpoint; my speculations that follow are *etic* (see p. 21–2).

4 This was said by a teacher of history from Oxford. The same Oxonian don remarked very sharply: "Masons originated in the seventeenth century, and in the beginning of the eighteenth they represented, in Britain at least, the type of persons who never outgrew the seventeenth century and did not wish to." I think he was quite right, in his own way.

5 James Hogg (1770–1835) the controversial Scottish writer whose best-known book was entitled *The Memoirs and Confessions of a Justified Sinner.*

6 *The Constitutions of Freemasons, 1723* with an Introduction by L. Vibert, London 1923 [1723 (1923)] p. vii.

7 "On an evil hour, to the universal sorrow ... of all his friends he forged a cheque on Lord Chesterfield, his former pupil, for £4,200 ... and being capitally convicted of the forgery ... suffered the extreme penalty of the law." Dr S. Johnson said of poor Dr Dodd: "He was at first what he endeavoured to make others, but the world broke down his resolutions ..." G. Oliver, *The Revelations of a Square,* London, 1855 (G. Oliver, 1855), p. 182. It is worth noting that having highly placed and influential friends did not save Dr Dodd from the "extreme penalty".

CHAPTER 3

Method, Phenomenology and Religion in General

No mortal can more,
The Ladies adore,
Than a Free and Accepted Mason.
From a Masonic song

Since I have adopted a particular methodological approach to my subject I had better explain it a little. It is commonly thought that a methodology should serve as an aid to explaining one's material as simply and clearly as possible. In the case of Freemasonry, however, I have set aside this requirement as inappropriate and restricting, because I believe that only a simple phenomenon can be explained simply; if a phenomenon is complex it has to be explained in a complex way. For example, an explanation of a religion – and I regard Freemasonry as something religious enough to be called a religion, the reasons for which I will set out in detail later on – should not only in its content but also in its form follow the character and pattern of the religion itself. This is particularly essential when one is involved in the observation or description of religious texts or actions (ritual, etc.) which are intentionally complex in themselves.[1]

Even the simplest formal scheme of the phenomenon of religion must reflect the complexity of religion itself, and must therefore exhibit a considerable degree of methodological complexity. Practically no known religion in the world can be described as consisting of fewer than three components: ritual, myth, and teaching.[2] Moreover, if we turn from the composition of religion to our religious self-awareness, we invariably find ourselves faced with the intricacy of our motives, beliefs and considerations.

The same comments apply to clarity of explanation. Very often (though, of course, not always) the observer of religion tries to account for the opaqueness or incomprehensibility of a religious text, belief, or ritual, by the objective difficulty in understanding it, that is, the difficulty in understanding the technical terminology of a religion, or the symbolic language of its ritual. But we often deal with texts the conscious intention of which is to preserve and perpetuate the archaic character of the language of the past. This is definitely the case with at least some of the Masonic Constitutions.[3] This intention – if not actually to make things more difficult to understand, certainly not to make them easier – derives from the particular nature and character of a given religion at the time of the creation of the text under consideration, and as a result clarification can only go so far. Some things are just not meant to be immediately transparent.

So, I cannot speak of religion as something simply and clearly explainable for the simplest and clearest reason that religion is not only for me an external object of investigation. The opposition of what is "observable" in religion to that which is "unobservable": for example, the opposition of "temple" to "belief in God", can be applied here only on a very limited scale. And this is so not only on account of the subjective and psychological character of this kind of opposition, but, first of all, because of the fact that when I say "this building is a temple" ("temple" = "observable"), it implies a working of my thought which is essentially different from the process implied by the sentence "this is a building".

This difference in type between the operation of thought in a religious context and in a non-religious context is my most important methodological point: my *awareness* of such a difference in my thinking on matters religious presupposes that it may be inherent in religion itself.[4] This also implies that one and the same situation, one and the same thing (in this case a building), may have at least two thinkable existences: religious and non-religious. Yet although this distinction exists in both the observer's mind and in the religion he observes, the former is usually unaware of its existence in the latter.

All this, of course, does not mean that religion itself is primarily only about thinking. What I hope to show is that if I, as investigator, think about a religion, I ought to be aware of this religion as a "thinking subject" too, and not just as an object of my thought.

It is important, too, that a study of religion should include the investigator's awareness of himself as a thinking subject from the point of view of any religion. He should concede to the religion he investigates that he, together with his methodology of investigation, is himself a part of a structure of religious consciousness which is different from and broader than both the religion he investigates and his own religion, or non-religion. As I have already emphasized, no religion can be understood entirely from outside, nor can the historicity of any religious phenomenon be understood when the observer tries to place himself outside history (and if we choose to stay outside history then we have no right to exercise an historical approach at all).[5]

The investigator of religion should take into consideration not only the fact of his own religiousness, be it understood either in a positive or in a negative way (the latter would be the case with "scientific", "positivist" or even "atheistic" standpoints), but also the fact that the religious phenomenon under investigation may be open to influences from the investigation itself. Speaking historically, one may note that describing and analysing religion began long before the invention of any "scientific" concepts of investigation, at a time when the role of investigators was still played by theologians and religious philosophers – those who consciously and intentionally included themselves in a given religion. In this connection I would like to point out that the very concept of theory within religion later gave way to theory *of* religion.

From this it follows that religion itself may use the language of those who describe or criticize it as well as the rules of their communication with and about religion. It can be illustrated by one of the speeches of a recent Archbishop of Canterbury who, while trying to convince some "progressive" Bishops that the essential core of Christian theology still exists, was in fact trying to convince those outside the Church that they (the Bishops) still believe in that core, and that is why he used the language of the external critique, not of his own theology. More or less the same can be said about the remarks quoted earlier of the Duke of Kent. All this leads one to think that the language of a particular religion or religion in general very often does not coincide with the language of its communication with the world outside, resulting in the extremely strange phenomenon of "mixed language" within a religion.

So when we look at a religious phenomenon not only must we try to put it into a proper, that is, more or less objectively verifiable historical context, but our investigation should also be subject to the same procedure. The *study* of a religion should be intentionally contextualized historically as consciously as is the attempt to contextualize a religion itself. And to understand Masonry within its own conceptual framework we have to take into account the very deep gulf between the religious perceptions in our time and those prevalent at the time of the formation of the Grand Lodge of England, in 1717.

Our present-day cultural perception of religion – cultural, because we are aware of it within our culture, not the reverse, being aware of our culture within religion – is marked by three predominant tendencies.

The first tendency is to perceive religion as a reflexive concept. This means that we almost invariably consider our own, or other people's religion first of all as a type of thinking.

This reflexive attitude is closely tied up with our current use of the term "religion", a use which creates its own context within which everything uttered by anybody about religion actually becomes a statement about one's own conceptualization of religion as a phenomenon. Questions like "is Masonry a religion?" or assertions like "Masonry is a religion" show how our perception of religion acquires a kind of religious meaning of its own. It seems that some authors (and readers too) may indeed think that Masonry or Buddhism (or, at least, something in Buddhism) depends entirely on what or how they think of it. Instead of being something one consciously brings to religion while at the same time respecting the fact that it has an objective existence of its own, thinking about religion assumes almost the ontological status of religion itself. This has become so because this reflection is not aware of itself as "mere thinking" – as no more than a "psychological subjectivity", one side of the coin – and, therefore, it cannot think of religion as an "objectivity". A brilliant example of such "unconscious" thinking on one's own religion was recently demonstrated by the previous Bishop of Birmingham, who insisted on the necessity to revise and purify a sacred text, the Holy Bible, because some of its passages could be interpreted as anti-Semitic and therefore incompatible with Christianity as he understood it. It is evident that for him there can be no objectivity in the fact of Revelation, as for the Bishop of Durham there can be no objectivity in the Resurrection, or for Don Cupitt in the Incarnation, etc. In this way the world of religion, denied an independent life, becomes completely reduced to the mental world of those who think about it.

The second and wholly opposite tendency in the modern perception of religion is the tendency to think of any religious phenomenon as an absolutely external object, something which is ascribed to another person, or another ethos, or another culture, or another type of mentality, etc. One's thinking about a religion is opposed to it just as *thinking* is opposed to objects, for religion is not supposed to think at all. As one of the currently fashionable writers on religion said of the modern Chinese: "Their religion persists in their searching for new cults and new cult objects. They are not aware of this, but I am." According to this view, one's own religion would figure as "thinking" and that of another person as "non-thinking" – as "acting", "behaving", etc., and as observable par excellence. This attitude is simply an arrogant unwillingness to countenance any mode of consciousness other than one's own, and can be detected in the ordinary man no less than in the ordinary anthropologist or sociologist of religion.

The third tendency is the tendency to think of one's own religion as a matter of one's choice between religions. What really matters here is not so much the actual availability of information *about* religion as the idea that in the final analysis what one deals with is neither a religion, nor, least of all, *the* religion (as in the "one and only true religion"), but religion in general – which has diverse concrete, historical manifestations. One tries to find a religion which would accommodate one's own personal philosophy without too much conflict of interest. One may even try to combine two or more religions for that purpose. "Practically, I am half-Christian, half-Buddhist," said the late R. D. Laing, one of the leading psychiatrists of this country.

One of my ex-pupils, presently a lecturer in religious studies, put it quite bluntly: "My father, a Scottish Presbyterian, was a deeply religious man, but I found his religion too inhuman and restrictive, and became a convert to Catholicism which, though restrictive, is far more human. Now I am thinking of becoming a priest, but I do not like the idea of living without my wife. So in principle I have decided to become a Catholic of the Eastern Rite where celibacy is not obligatory."

I have used the term phenomenon more than once and will employ the concept of phenomenology from time to time, so I had better offer a brief definition and explanation of these words as they appear in the book. A religious "phenomenon", in the context of my methodology, refers to the fact of my own awareness of something as a religion, an awareness which takes into account that this religion is aware of itself and may also be aware of myself as its investigator. Therefore, the fact of my awareness of a religion merges with the fact of its own self-awareness as well as with the fact of my own self-awareness, however indigestible this may sound.[6] When I am investigating Freemasonry, I am aware that my point of view concerning religion may in one way or another be understood or accepted, or related to the Masonic religion by Freemasons themselves; and even if it is refuted, it still remains within the boundaries of their own religious consciousness.

The phenomenological method in the study of religion depends on the application to religious phenomena of the principle of discrimination between two basic, and equally necessary, approaches – *emic* and *etic*. This distinction, introduced into modern social sciences in the late 1950s by the outstanding American linguist and priest Kenneth Pike, is of fundamental importance to our attempts to understand any religious phenomenon, as well as our own understanding of these attempts. The division is a relative, not an absolute one; within a given religion some statements reflect an emic position and some an etic. The former represents the inner perspective, when something is allowed to speak for itself, and the latter an external viewpoint, descriptive, analytical or critical. The division corresponds roughly to the subjective and objective positions with regard to the object of investigation. So, when a religion, through its sacred texts and exegetics, oral or written, its general literature, if it has one, its spokesmen and apologists presents its own self-description and standpoint, and this is given primary place, the approach is emic. When an individual or group of individuals present their own opinions or critique of a religion from an external point of view this is to take an etic approach.[7] A person within a given religion may adopt either stance (consciously or unconsciously) and so may an outside observer. Any balanced analysis will involve a combination of both, but since I try in this book to apply a phenomenological rather than a positivist methodology, the initial focus is on the emic side – Freemasonry speaking for itself as the starting point – with my own etic interpretations and conclusions taking second place. These two perhaps rather elusive perspectives can be illustrated in the following way: when one observes a complex phenomenon, one can see in the complexity of its various elements, what exactly it is that makes them different and the principle which organizes or unites these elements into one structure or system. So, for instance, when an American acquaintance of mine, Dr Spence Morgan, says that "Freemasonry is a conglomeration of Christian, Gnostic and pagan beliefs and rituals", he establishes the difference between those particular beliefs and rituals, as well as between "belief and ritual" in general according to his own view. This may or may not coincide with any differences formally accepted by Masonry. In giving his personal critique he is speaking etically. But when we read in a famous Masonic Handbook of the nineteenth century that "Masonry is a peculiar system of morality veiled in allegory and illustrated by symbols" and "by no means a religion" (as John Hamill added in his recent book), this is an official, institutional definition of Masonry established by and within the phenomenon itself and, as such, represents the emic level. An observer who applies the distinction between "emic" and "etic" would not find the individual opinion of Masonry as a "syncretic religion" and its own self-definition as a "system of Morality, and no religion at all", mutually contradictory. He would regard these two definitions as belonging to two different levels in his descriptions of one and the same phenomenon: Masonry.

To me this book is a kind of "essay in self-awareness" more than an objective investigation of facts. That is why it is so important here to stress the methodological distinction between a bald description of facts and an understanding of these very facts. And it is in connection with understanding that I feel it necessary to introduce the notion of *hermeneutics* or the science of understanding. So, for instance, to know what the word "Freemasonry" means it is enough to look in the *Oxford English Dictionary*, but to understand it more fully, not merely at a linguistic level, would mean, among very many other things, knowing *why* they – lawyers, plumbers, doctors, policemen, publicans – call themselves "Freemasons". If you employ a hermeneutic approach, you must, temporarily at least, suspend your accumulations of factual knowledge, and try to understand why one of the Masonic (or non-Masonic) historiographers chooses to think that the original meaning of the term "Freemason" was "a *free* [that is, independent and 'born free'] mason", while to another it was "a mason not belonging to a guild", and to the third it was "a mason who worked with a special kind of stone called 'free-stone' ". In which case, it is clear that the "historical truth", or the possibility of several conflicting historical truths, would not matter too much. Hermeneutics makes us understand the conscious *uses* of facts, whether cultural, historical or religious uses, which are quite as much facts in themselves.

An understanding of a religion is neither more nor less subjective than a factual knowledge of it. But there can be no understanding of any religious phenomenon without the underlying idea that this phenomenon may have an objective meaning irrespective of whether or not it is known by the phenomenon itself or by its investigator, so it cannot simply be reduced to someone's understanding of it. So, for instance, in the case of the lasting debate on whether or not Freemasonry is a religion, a phenomenologist would have to admit that there might be something in Masonic rituals and symbols which allows for their interpretation as religious. And, as Franco Micchelini-Tocci, an Italian historian of religions and a hermeneutist, put it: "Is it not possible for a very ancient esoteric tradition to choose to continue through the esoteric rituals of Masonry? And is it not possible that neither we nor Masons themselves know anything about it?"

Two notions play an important role in our phenomenological approach to Freemasonry as a religion, namely, the *subjective* religious situation and the *objective* religious situation. The subjective religious situation of Freemasonry includes in itself all that Freemasons say or write of Masonry as a religion, if they regard it as such, or if they do not regard it as a religion, about themselves in relation to one or another religion, or religion in general. It also comprises what they say or write about the meaning of their ritual and the legend connected with that ritual. While describing a subjective religious situation we ought not to be asking for consistency in reasoning or unanimity in opinion. So, for example, when one Mason says that Freemasonry is "no religion at all", another that it is "a peculiar case of a combination of ethics and religion", and the third that it is "a charitable institution, the only religious element in which is its ritual of Master Mason", we should content ourselves with stating that these three sentences might describe the subjective religious situation of Freemasonry here and now.

The objective religious situation comprises all that a person investigating a given phenomenon as a *religion* has to say about it as a religion, as well as the ways and means of his description. This, however, is not to say that the description of a subjective religious situation will not be similar to or even the same as the description of an objective religious situation with respect to the same phenomenon or that it may never be made by the same investigator. They may often coincide with one another. But the investigator ought to be acutely aware of that distinction, knowing all too well that even such a seemingly simple question as "are you a religious person?" and the answers "I am" or "I am not" have already implied the possibility that in his question the investigator used the term "religious" in a sense different from that in which the term figures in the answer. Moreover, the situation will invariably be complicated by the fact that the person who is asked about his religiousness may express in his answer not only an opinion generally accepted in his religion, but his own opinion too, which may or may not conform with the orthodox view.

The reaction to outside criticism of any religion, particularly a religion whose *religious* status seems to be in some doubt either to the world, or to itself, or both, very often reveals a large variety of subjective religious situations unrecognized and unformulated by the religion as a whole. And it is usually in such a context that we meet with the phenomenon of alternative religion. As a term of description, alternative religion can be used in both objective and subjective senses; either when I describe a religious situation or when the latter describes itself. It applies when a religion is opposed, within one society, culture, or state, either to another religion or group of religions, or to the predominant form of religiousness, or to the broadly accepted ideology, be it religious, secular or even atheist. In the last case it will figure as an alternative to non-religion.

I have allowed myself another bout of methodology, at the risk of boring the reader, but I think the notions outlined above would help us to understand better the situation of the Freemasons as seen (and understood) by the non-Masons in this country. Let us take one very curious example: Bernard Levin, writing in *The Times*, compared the Masons to the Jews, attacking a tendency inherent in almost all anti-Masonic and anti-Semitic propaganda to present both of them jointly as a "malicious, malevolent and subversive" whole.[8] In doing this he treats Jews and Freemasons as two groups distinguished from the rest of the British population by virtue of their specific historical destiny which is to be lumped together for vilification by their enemies for at least two centuries. To this may be added that while so many other locally despised and persecuted religious sects such as the Cathars and the Knights Templar in medieval France or the Zorastrian Gebres and the Bahais in modern Iran are despised or persecuted separately and for different reasons, the Jews and Freemasons are usually treated in tandem. So, not only will the individual wrongdoing of a single Jew be regarded as typical of Jews as a whole, but a case of Masonic misbehaviour has, as its sub-text, the implication that somehow there must be a Jewish connection making it a Jewish-Masonic affair. Why is this so? It cannot simply be explained by their status as minority groups, for the Jews in Britain are, for the most part, both English-speaking and thoroughly assimilated; and Freemasonry, though cosmopolitan in its philosophy, finds at least eighty-five per cent of its membership among the English, Welsh and Scots, with only a tiny proportion of Jews. Associating them on the basis of specifically Jewish elements in the Masonic teaching and ritual is even more unlikely.[9] For a start, most conspiracy theories are just not sufficiently well-informed about the background to the ritual to be able to identify these elements. If they were, they would be aware that their presence militates against any objective connection as there has been no ritual proper in Judaism, nor any priesthood, since the time of the destruction of the last Temple; while every Freemason, and any remotely knowledgeable critic, would readily acknowledge, even if he does not regard Freemasonry as a religion, that the Ritual is the centre and focus of all Masonic activity. What, then, is left that could be considered as a feature common to them both, a feature that has made so many people, though mostly unconsciously, assimilate one to another and even identify them as a single evil?

The answer which I would venture to give is that both the objective and subjective religious situations of Freemasons and Jews are marked by a very high degree of uncertainty. In spite of his claim, I do not think that Mr Levin seriously believes that people who do not like the Jews do not like them because they are Judaists. Nor do I think that he believes that those who do not like Freemasons do so because the latter have a queer sort of religion. The criteria of Jewishness, if you try to describe them in terms of the subjective religious situation, are a motley mixture of religious self-awareness, ethnic self-identification, scriptural references and commentatorial interpretations and the observation, in varying degrees of certain customs and traditions. Still one may be assured that even when an individual Jew is not a practising Jew he remains one not only in his own eyes, but in the eyes of everyone else (unless he conceals his Jewish origins). At the same time, Jewry as a general term implies, first and foremost, Judaism, the faith. If looked at from this angle the connection of Jewry with Judaism is infinitely more necessary and relevant than that of, say, "Englishness" with Anglicanism. For a person who calls himself a Jew while being an atheist or agnostic demonstrates a kind of self-awareness where his religion, Judaism, figures as an historical point of departure, and the deviations from the primary religious principle, atheism or conversion to another religion included, figure as no more than versions or varieties in the manifestation of that principle. In the case of a Freemason, however, the religion of a Freemason may be either any known religion in the world or any individual religious conviction, so long as it includes a belief in the existence of a Superior Being, combined with some specifically Masonic religious ideas and practices. In both cases, though in Freemasonry considerably more than in Jewry, it can be seen that religious uncertainty and ambiguity, which on the one hand gives one a greater possibility of choice and on the other produces a certain tension in the relations between Freemasonry and Jewry and the public at large, with their natural need to identify the religion of others in the same unequivocal way in which they are accustomed to identify their own religion.

To define descriptively at least, if not theoretically, what I mean when I use the word "religion": it denotes any action, speech, thought (as far as this thought is fixed in speech, or in a text) or situation in which a relation is sought for, established and expressed in one way or another between the "natural" and the "supernatural". The latter embraces all beings, entities, things, forces and agencies of which humans are aware as *different*, or with respect to which they behave as if they belonged to a class absolutely different from their own.

Perhaps it would be better simply to focus on this sense of difference or essential "otherness" experienced by the various orders of beings with respect to one another, since the phenomena or beings we class as either natural or supernatural by no means always correspond to the classifications made by non-Judaeo-Christian religions.

It is, then, a defining characteristic of religion that it not only generates such distinctions between classes of beings or events, but fixes them in its symbols, texts (written or oral), and actions, i.e. rituals. These fixations themselves serve as objects or processes by means of which one order or class of beings is related to another.

When a Freemason in the making says "I *am* Master Hiram" in the Initiation Ritual, he connects himself with Hiram, the central figure of Masonic legend, as another kind of being, whom he will become as a result of the ritual that is being performed at that time. Likewise, when a Christian says "I believe in God . . ." he refers to that which is a consequence of his being related to Jesus Christ through the ritual of the Eucharist, or other Christian rites. And, when a Freemason states that he believes in the existence of a Superior Being, it is only through the subsequent ritual of Master Mason, by means of which he will "become Hiram", that his belief in a Superior Being assumes its concrete religious meaning. In both cases a believer, as an ordinary human being, is related through the rituals and symbols of his religion to a being belonging to a class or order other than his own, and this and this only makes an ordinary man a believer, and makes his ordinary words and thoughts a *religious* belief.

Having introduced the idea of "natural" versus "supernatural" as a particular case and concretization of the more general idea of "otherness", it should be made quite clear that these notions are based on the practical uses of the terms in everyday language. My definition of religion only hopes to demonstrate how the natural, the supernatural and otherness are empirically applied in descriptions of what goes on *within* religion. Several other related oppositions are also part of our habitual language of description of religious phenomena in the sense of an inner division made also by religion itself, for example sacred and profane, pure and impure, and so forth.

The opposing pair of natural and supernatural within religion brings us to the idea of naturalness as applied to a religion as a whole, viewed from the outside. The notion of the naturalness of religion in general arose as a modification of the idea of "humanness": religion as that which all human beings possess as part of their nature. This was complemented by the development of religious awareness of the natural (non-human) world as a creation and of its Creator, together with human reflection and philosophizing upon them, which gave rise to a slightly different aspect of religion and thinking about it as a natural phenomenon.

This notion of "naturalness" in connection with religion, so important in the critique of Freemasonry as well as in its own self-awareness, became crystallized in the Protestant thought of the seventeenth and eighteenth centuries, with its need to provide a rational and scientific account of the character and function (and even origins) of religion in general, and of Protestantism in particular. It was later taken up and expanded by the evolutionary, sociological and psychological schools – in the academic study of religion which rose to prominence towards the end of the nineteenth and beginning of the twentieth centuries. It is their concepts and attitudes which have permeated almost all modern investigation of religion. Let us take, for example, two of the foremost theorists in the sociology of religion and of Protestantism in particular, Max Weber and Emil Durkheim. The former wrote in 1915: "The only way of distinguishing between 'religious' and 'profane' states is by referring to the extraordinary character of religious states."[10] The "extraordinariness" to which religion is historically and logically reduced is opposed by Weber to the process of scientific rationalization: ". . . the irrational elements in the rationalization of reality have been the *loci* to which the irrepressible quest of intellectualism for the possession of supernatural values has been compelled to retreat."[11]

What has been stated here exemplifies that habitual Protestant dualism which no system of sociology of religion has yet escaped – the opposition between religion and our thinking about it. Intellectual reflection, together with the object it returns to, religion as such, form the concept of *natural* religion in one of its several senses. For the spontaneous, "extraordinary" and supernatural state which is not natural and does not "know itself" is one thing and one's subsequent thinking on that state quite another. It is their coming together in the experience of one person via the use of particular rituals and symbols that brings about "beliefs" in religion, and it is their separation from one another that brings about "conceptions" in the sociology of religion. The source for this description of religion in terms of "beliefs" and "conceptions" remains, however, the same: Protestantism.

Emil Durkheim wrote in 1912: "All known religious *beliefs* . . . present one common characteristic: they presuppose a classification of all the things, real and ideal, of which men think, into two classes or opposed groups . . . 'profane' and 'sacred'."[12] And then he makes this statement more precise by adding that ". . . there is nothing left with which to characterize the sacred in its relation to the profane except their heterogeneity" [i.e. their difference from one another].[13] So the "sacred", which is "extraordinary" in Max Weber, is simply "heterogeneous" or different from the profane in Emil Durkheim, and in both it is about *beliefs* and, therefore, about thinking. This is one entirely etic version of natural religion derived from seventeenth-century Protestant thinking which continues to generate the concepts of the sociology of religion up to the present day.

But what if I do not share the Protestant way of thinking and do not want to assume that this naturalistic approach should be taken for granted? What if my classifications take a different course and I assume that one's thinking about God is as supernatural as God Himself,[14] and that one's naturalness (including all other kinds of thinking) is tantamount to non-religion or irreligion in general?[15] In other words, how to escape from the tyranny of the concept of natural religion and the Protestant approach to thinking on religion? And who *has* been able to escape it?[16]

Any definition of religion based on the dualism of "sacred/profane", or "supernatural/natural", or "God/man", can usefully be applied to some concrete phenomena, which have already been empirically perceived by us as religious – but with one necessary provision: that we regard this and all suchlike dualisms first of all as oppositions of our own thinking on religion, and only in the second place as possible oppositions inherent in the thinking of those whose religion we are investigating. For our own culturally conditioned thinking on religion tends, quite uncontrollably sometimes, to present any religion other than our own entirely in terms of thoughts, concepts and notions which we objectify as particular religious principles, beliefs and convictions.

There is yet another dualism in operation, also a by-product of the Reformation, that of "religion/non-religion", which should not be confused with that of "religious/secular". It implies a division which seems to be possible only as a result of some conscious work done within a religion and by religious thinking. So when a Quaker says that "Freemasonry is not a religion, while the Church of the Latter Day Saints is", what he really means is that there is a division into religion and non-religion in *his* religion, and that from the point of view of that division the Mormons, though not belonging to his (true) religion, do belong to *a* religion, while Masons do not. If some Masons do not consider the Craft to be a religion, emically speaking it should not be regarded as a religion for them since their self-awareness tells them otherwise. There are nevertheless a great many members of the institution who do regard it as "something definitely religious" and this view must also be recognized. The trouble is that Masonry quite clearly possesses two contradictory lines of self-description giving it an inherent ambiguity about which I will have more to say later when comparing Masons to Jews.

In applying the broadly phenomenological principle taking as primary the religious self-awareness of those who are the subjects of an investigation, it must still be admitted that Masons who do regard Freemasonry as a religion and those who do not – the priests and theologians of the Church of England who regard it as a natural religion with some "unnatural" Gnostic elements; Quakers who do not regard it as a religion but regard the Mormon Church as one among a number of Christian denominations – all use the term "religion" in another sense of the expression "natural religion", slightly different from the intellectualism of Weber and Durkheim. The concept they, in all probability, unconsciously use is its precursor, and was first formulated by the diplomat and writer Lord Herbert of Cherbury (1582–1648), who outlined the religious outlook subsequently known as Deism in his treatise *"De Veritate"* published in 1623. In it he lists the five elements of religion "common to all Man":

1. There is a God;
2. He should be worshipped;
3. Ethics (piety, virtue, etc.) is essential in terms of one's relation to God side by side with worship;
4. There is an afterlife (in any form);
5. That afterlife is a place and time for reward and punishment for one's virtues and sins, and depends on the will of a God.

Lord Herbert regarded any religion that includes all or most of these elements as natural to man. This Deist philosophy became the fashion among enlightened sceptics of the seventeenth and eighteenth centuries.[17]

But, to go back to the as yet unsolved problem of my descriptive definition of religion as the establishing of relations between the natural and the supernatural: wouldn't it be as much influenced by my own religious "complex" as other people's by theirs? Wouldn't my tentative definition suffer from the same fallacy as all the others for the simple reason that, whatever kind of religious practice it might describe, this practice is already formulated in terms of religious thinking? So all that is left, again, are my thoughts and concepts objectified as beliefs and convictions. However, being aware of this, I may make a small step further and ask: can my thinking about any religion I am describing and that same religion which I am unable to describe as anything but thinking, be, from a certain point of view, regarded as two aspects of one and the same phenomenon?

This is a desperately difficult question, upon the answer to which

31

depends not only practically the whole methodology of so-called religious studies in the West, but also, and far more importantly, the character and direction of the religious self-awareness of Western man himself. For one's preoccupation with religion, however non-religious or irreligious one might be, reveals both a certain type of underlying intention and the *theme* of one's thinking; and I am inclined to think that the intention is religious and the theme is religion.[18] The fact that I am interested in Freemasonry as a religion in the first place, and not as a social, cultural, or psychological phenomenon, I regard as indicative of, or at least related to, my own religious self-awareness. For me no religion can be reduced to or more than partially interpreted in terms of any social, cultural, or psychological phenomena. In saying this I mean that one religious phenomenon can find its explanation only in another religious phenomenon, though the latter may belong to a different level of abstraction or to a different religion, or, finally, to a different time. So, for instance, in speaking of the beliefs of a certain religion, I would be, first of all, inclined to understand them on the basis of the rituals and symbols of the same religion, and not on the basis of contemporary or prior economic conditions, or the character of the prevailing culture or power structures. In doing this I assume that religion, as an intention and theme of human consciousness, is more primary and all-embracing than science, art, or that which we call "culture" in general.[19]

Notes

1 Complexity of intention here means that the text or ritual in question implies, or explicitly states, a conscious effort to perform and to understand on the part of the initiate, and a conscious necessity to interpret and to instruct on the part of the teacher or priest.

2 See W. B. Kristensen, 1960; Introduction (by H. Kraemer) and pp. 1–7.

3 Many of these texts need deciphering, some of them even need decoding.

4 Which is not to say that to a non-religious person, entirely divorced from any religious context – someone who is not engaged in examining some religious phenomenon and becomes drawn into that context by his intention – a temple may not be just another building.

5 It is a widespread illusion among historians that when they study history they study only facts and are able to exclude their own standpoint from the historical process. They forget that they, too, together with their standpoint, are also historical facts and cannot be left out of the picture.

6 H. Kraemer writes: "The phenomenologist must not try to understand 'the essence of religion'. That is a philosophical concern. His special task is to enter

32

into the mind of the believer." See in W. B. Kristensen, 1960, pp. xxi-xxii.

7 While the emic position is more likely to have a collective character, since it derives from an impersonal (in that sense, objective) tradition, an etic viewpoint even when presented as the expression of a particular individual may also reflect a collective background – a cultural milieu for example – which the individual may or may not be aware of belonging to when he makes his observations. This collectivity would be etic, of course, relative only to the object of investigation; it would be emic in relation to the observer. This shifting of perspectives is not easy to maintain a firm grasp of and is the source of much confusion.

8 "The Latest of Them", *The Times*, 21 April 1988.

9 A more detailed treatment of this problem is given in Chapter 12.

10 From *Max Weber* ed. by H. H. Gerth and C. Wright Mills, Oxford, 1946 [M. Weber, 1946 (1915)], p. 280.

11 *Idem*, p. 283.

12 Emil Durkheim, *The Elementary Forms of Religious Life*, trans. by J. Swain, Glencoe, 1961 [E. Durkheim, 1961 (1912)], p. 52.

13 *Idem*, p. 53.

14 This, in fact, is a point of view shared by very many exponents of the teaching of the Upanishads in ancient India, where one's *knowledge* of one's self (*atman*) being *one* with and the same as the Self of the Universe (*Brahman*) is regarded as tantamount to this *one-ness* and entirely non-natural.

15 Or alternatively, as we see it in some of the teachings of the Upanishads, religiousness together with all rituals is regarded as *natural* and, as such, is opposed to the Highest Knowledge of Brahman.

16 It is amazing how difficult it is to get rid of this attitude which permeates the thinking of modern scholars. And it is particularly difficult when the sociologist of religion deals with a "natural" classification of its content: "Going to church, believing, and acting ethically are generally recognized as components of being religious. However, simply because a person is religious in one of these ways is no guarantee that he will be religious in others." In this quotation we definitely deal with what could be called "religiousness" but by no means religion. At the same time, and quite unnoticed by the person who wrote it, this is a kind of religiousness based on the notion of natural religion and, as such, perfectly applicable to the average Freemason. He, indeed, is the man who frequents the Lodge, believes in the existence of a Superior Being, and is supposed (at least in principle) to behave ethically. R. Stark and C. Y. Glock, "Dimensions of Religious Commitment" in *Sociology of Religion* ed. by R. Robertson, Harmondsworth, 1969, p. 253.

17 David Hume subsequently worked out a third notion of natural religion which I would call "theological". According to this notion the perception of nature by a rational being inevitably impels him to regard this nature as effect, and the deity who created it as cause; in other words, the classical argument from design.

18 This, of course, poses another, and very interesting, problem, namely the problem of the relation between (a) one's intentional attitude to a concrete religion, or religion in general, and (b) that very intentional attitude, seen from the point of view of a concrete religion. I will demonstrate this problem with an example from the history of Russian Freemasonry:

a) In 1916 most of the members of the Russian Lodges considered themselves Christians and preservers of the *humanist* strain in the Christian teaching.

b) (i) From the point of view of the Russian Orthodox Church Hierarchy, Freemasons were anti-Christian, anti-Orthodox Church, anti-clerical in general, Gnostic theologically and, therefore, together with Jews and Socialists, preparing the Revolution and paving the way for the Antichrist.

(ii) From the point of view of Maxim Gorky – who regarded himself as a Gnostic and who was very close to both Masonic and Theosophical circles in Russia and abroad – Christianity in general and the Russian Orthodox Church in particular, should be destroyed in order to give way to a new universal religious order. That is why, in his opinion, the totally atheistic revolution was so spiritually necessary and inevitable, whether or not those who planned and carried it out were aware of its *final purpose*. In the light of this Gnostic conception he regarded Freemasons as one of the most useful forces of destruction of the "old religious order".

19 Both Weber and Durkheim were so preoccupied with the problem of how modern societies would manage *without* religion, that they simply overlooked the fact that they could not. And least of all were they able to predict (and account for) that upsurge of interest in religion during the two subsequent decades, which itself can undoubtedly be regarded as a symptom of a forthcoming growth of religiosity and as the shape that religiosity came to assume in the 1960s and 1970s. It is impossible to over-estimate the effect which is usually produced on the sociologist of religion, himself self-avowedly religiously uncommitted, by his own religious background. So, for instance, both Weber and Durkheim, when they spoke of religions, mainly meant beliefs that could be accounted for by their predominantly Protestant ideology of which each was aware as the basis of his own non-religious and non-ideological conception. Or, slightly metaphorically speaking, one might see in their conceptions the way in which Protestantism as a religion chose to express itself as a scientific ideology.

HISTORY

"The origins of Freemasonry are wrapped in mystery."
Frances A. Yates

But any "origins" are exempt from history, being mere symbols of that which history preserves or forgets.
Alexander Piatigorsky

CHAPTER 4

The Beginnings of Official Masonic History

Anderson's Constitutions 1717–38 and the Founding of the Grand Lodge

Why official? And what is history? In my attempt to produce the shortest possible account of the first twenty-one years, 1717–38, of the existence of Freemasonry under the aegis of the Grand Lodge of England I am following in a simplified form the phenomenological approach outlined in the previous chapter. I intend, first of all, to rely primarily on what Masons have actually said, as it reveals their own conscious intentions. And, secondly, I treat as equally significant both the facts described in a particular account and the fact of their description. A historical phenomenon is not just a matter of bare facts, it is also a fact of consciousness – it must be known, perceived, articulated and recorded in a particular way. So the history of Masonry, for the purposes of this book, is mainly what Masons themselves have told us, and continue to tell us, about the origins and development of their institution.

The sources they have used are, in the first place, official Masonic records such as Constitutions, Minutes and Records of the Lodges. A source is called official when it is issued by, or in the name of, a body of men (the Lodge). It remains official even if it had actually been written by a single individual and was submitted for approval by the Lodge before being issued in the name of the Lodge, and even if it contradicted other official sources.

Masonic historians, while relying chiefly on these official records, also used a lot of individual "non-official" Masonic sources. If these internal versions of Masonic history are regarded as representing a Mason's point of view, and hence as "subjective" accounts, the non-Masonic position (including mine) is "objective" only in relation to the Masonic one. From any other standpoint a non-Masonic position will be equally subjective.

Since I wish to let the Masons speak for themselves, at least as a starting point, my brief history commences with the version compiled by Dr James Anderson, the first official Masonic historian, interspersed with some material from other early accounts.

Anderson was a contemporary to all the events he describes,

personally witnessed most of them, and was an active participant in quite a few. His history, though not always true, or truer than others, was the only history of that period recognized by the Grand Lodge.[1]

According to Anderson, there were in London in 1716, among a number of other somewhat moribund Masonic Lodges, four particular Lodges, namely: the Lodge that used to meet at The Goose and Gridiron Ale-house in St Paul's Churchyard; the Lodge at The Crown Ale-house in Parker's Lane near Drury Lane; the Lodge at The Apple Tree tavern in Charles' Street, Covent Garden; and the Lodge at The Rummer and Grapes tavern in Westminster [p. 109]. William Preston (1742–1818), almost two generations later, writes in his *Illustrations* that they were, "the only four Lodges in being in the South of England at that time . . ."

There is no way of knowing who is right. These four Lodges met in February, 1717, at The Apple Tree Tavern and "having voted the oldest Master Mason then present into the chair, *constituted themselves a Grand Lodge* (pro tempore in *due Form*) [Idem].[2] Furthermore on St John the Baptist's day, 24 June 1717, Mr Anthony Sayer, gentleman, was elected the *Grand Master of Masons* for the ensuing year. He appointed Captain J. Elliot and Mr Jacob Lamball, carpenter, as *Grand Wardens*, and commanded the Brethren of the four lodges to meet him and his Wardens *quarterly* in communication". It was also agreed at this meeting that "the privilege of assembling as Masons . . . hitherto unlimited . . . should be vested in certain lodges . . . and that every lodge . . . except the four old lodges . . . [i.e. these very four] should be legally authorized by . . . a warrant from the Grand Lodge . . ."[3] Some other Masonic authors, whose information is mainly derived either directly from Anderson's *Constitutions* of 1738 or from the *Constitutions* as given in Preston's *Illustrations*, add to that very modest list of the first participants the names of Dr Desaguliers, G. Payne, Gofton, Cordwell, De Noyer, Vraden, King, Morrice, Calvert, Ware and Madden, who were the Masters and Wardens of the four *existing* Lodges.[4]

However, even these few facts are given to us not by the actual participants but by Dr Anderson twenty years after they were said to have taken place. His first serious critic, the great Masonic historiographer, Robert Freke Gould, writes: "The only official account we possess of the foundation of the Grand Lodge of England in 1717, and the first six years of its history, is contained in the 2nd edition of Dr Anderson's *Constitutions*, published in 1738 . . ." The account starts with the celebrated words: "After the Rebellion was over, A D 1716, the four Lodges in London thought fit to cement under a Grand Lodge . . ." [p. 109][5].

Anderson, therefore, is the only source and he was writing well after the event.

A later commentary, written in 1756 by the most brilliant deviant of Freemasonry, Lawrence Dermott (1720–91) in his *Ahiman Rezon*[6] states: "About the year 1717 some joyous companions who had passed the degree of the Craft, though very rusty, resolved to form a Lodge for themselves, in order, by conversation, to *recollect* what had been formally dictated to them or, if that should be found impracticable, to substitute something new, which might for the future *pass for* Masonry among themselves."[7] But why should they need to recollect? "Because", Anderson states, "in the South the Lodges were more and more disused when ... some few years after 1708 ... Sir Chr. Wren neglected the offices of Grand Master (which, according to Anderson, he had been at that time) ..." [p. 108]. So there seems to have been a gap in the Masonic memory of, say, some eight to nine years.

Now, let us suppose that all we know has been taken from these two sources – for factually Dermott and Anderson do not contradict one another; theirs was disagreement only in tone and in interpretation – and ask ourselves what the meanings of three words: "Lodge", "Mason", and "Degree" were at that time.

The first term is undoubtedly the most crucial, for the *theme* of Masonry is not about individuals but about a fundamental Masonic historical self-awareness which comprises (and did so 270 years ago) the idea of a Mason's connection with his past or, more precisely, with the past of a Mason's own particular culture as well as with the past of human culture in general;[8] that is its primary basis. The Lodge, then, is the place where this idea assumes its visible and audible form, its concrete image, the only place where Masons meet as Masons. A Lodge does not exist as a Lodge without being a place of meeting, and a meeting, when it takes place in any house, apartment or room, becomes a Lodge. According to pre-Grand Lodge tradition, any five, six or seven persons who have passed an initiation (still unspecified at that time) could institute their own Lodge, wherever these might happen to be. So, the building itself does not matter, and indeed some Lodges throughout their history moved quite frequently from one ale-house or tavern to another, and even when they settled down more or less permanently in a place of their own, that place was still seen as no more than a temporary material framework for the *symbolic locus of a Lodge*. According to Anderson's *Constitutions*, 1723, [p. 51], "A Lodge is a place where Masons assemble and work; hence that Assembly, or duly organiz'd Society ... call'd a Lodge, and every Brother ought to belong to one . . ." The same applies to the Grand Lodge, which is the place where ". . . the Masters and Wardens of Lodges . . . meet the Grand Officers Quarterly . . . at the place that Grand Master should appoint in his summons . . ." [p. 110]. That is why we see so very often the expression "the Lodge assembled at such and such place", but not that "the meeting took place *in* this or that Lodge".[9] However strange it might sound, even the Grand Lodge had no fixed or permanent place and was treated as the symbolic centre rather than the actual location of the Masonic leadership.[10]

Those who, probably from the beginning of the sixteenth and definitely from the beginning of the seventeenth century in England, were accepted into the Lodges of working or "operative" Masons were also referred to as honorary members.[11] They were also known as *accepted* or *speculative* Masons, the latter because they had nothing to do with the actual craft, art, and profession of stonemasonry. It goes without saying that the term "operative" would not have been used prior to the appearance of the non-operative or speculative Masons, and that the term "accepted" refers to the act of accepting some individuals who did not work as stonemasons into a Masonic Lodge. This point is extremely important because, in the case of working Masons, the admission to a Lodge was, in principle at least, *non-individual;* all persons following that profession were eligible for admission. The criteria for "Acception", however, being selective, were mainly individual and we have no positive information as to what they might have been.

Speaking of the individual Masons, members of the four old Lodges, their "Mason-ness" consisted in their (a) attending the monthly, quarterly, or annual Lodges, followed by dinners with not yet entirely regularized speeches and toasts (or "healths"); (b) taking part in the annual ceremonies if, at that time, there were any; (c) taking part in the rituals and other ceremonies connected with the admission of candidates, and their subsequent "moving" and "raising"; (d) paying the membership fees. Nothing else is known of them, and even the little that is known is second-hand. So, the minimum of Mason-ness can be reduced to something like "one's initiation into it at a Lodge, and one's attending that Lodge at least once".[12] But what were they doing during the intervals between one Lodge meeting and another? Nothing, so far as we know. For, and it transpires from the few surviving private letters, unrelated to Masonic affairs, that even at that almost prehistoric time, Masonry did not in any conceivable way mark one's behaviour, style or speech, when one was not in the Lodge.

The word "Degree" means, in the case of accepted or speculative

Masonry, in imitation of the customs and terminology of operative Masonry, that when a candidate was initiated he was given the first Degree, or that of *Apprentice*. He then moved, either immediately or after some time, to the second Degree, that of *Fellow* or Brother. The third Degree, that of Master, did not exist in the speculative Lodges at the beginning of the eighteenth century. The word Master, at the time, simply meant "the Head of a Lodge", which position did not require, as it subsequently did, an especial ritual, and was usually held by a Fellow. "Passing the Degree" in our quotation from Dermott meant, therefore, either the ritual of initiation of a candidate, or his "being moved" to become a Fellow, or both. It might be supposed then that a Lodge was a meeting of those already initiated, the chief function of which was to initiate new candidates by means of special rituals which copied those of the old operative Lodges (given that the terms "operative" and "speculative" themselves came into regular use much later). This supposition of mine is useful as no more than a working hypothesis which may, later on, be partly or entirely disposed of. So the very meaning of Masonic ritual was confined to the fact of admission into a Lodge, and that which went on within a Lodge for those already admitted amounted to not much more than the "conversation of joyous companions". The chief task of the Grand Lodge, if we formulate it as we have just formulated the function of the ordinary *Particular* (or *Private*) Lodges, was "to spread Masonry by warranting the establishment of new Lodges" which can then be thought of as "collective candidates".

To return to the history of the Grand Lodge: on 24 June 1718, there were "Assembly and Feast at the same place (i.e., the Apple Tree Tavern). Bro. Sayer proclaim'd aloud our Bro. George Payne as a Grand Master of Masons ... and Mr John Cordwell, City Carpenter, and Mr Thomas Morrice, stone-cutter, Grand Wardens ..." [p. 110]. After Payne was elected the second Grand Master, he asked the Brethren to seek for, find and bring to the Grand Lodge all old writings and records of the previous Masonic Lodges. As a result, several copies of the so-called "Gothic Constitutions" or old manuscripts containing the legends, charges and regulations of operative Masons of, supposedly, the sixteenth and seventeenth centuries, were made available. This was the first attempt on the part of the Grand Lodge of England to begin to describe its prehistory, for its actual history was still all too short even to start describing itself – there was barely a generation of Masons in London.[13]

But if it really was the intention of George Payne to use one or several of the old Masonic manuscripts, and not only an intention attributed to him by Anderson, then we may see in it the beginning of a tendency, widespread a little later, to graft the earlier legends, rules and rituals of the operative Masons, passed down in the Lodges, onto the young sapling of their Institution. And if Anderson did not invent this episode (as he did quite a number of others), Payne emerges as a man who felt it necessary for Masons to know who they had been in the past before becoming what they were at the beginning of the eighteenth century.

The third Grand Master, for 1719, was Dr John Theofilus Desaguliers (1676–1740), Fellow of the Royal Society, priest and "experimental philosopher", in the language of that generation. He is referred to by Anderson as the person who established, renewed, or revised, some of the rules of Masonic conviviality, and who set down how their Freemasons' toasts or Freemasons' healths should be performed. He was also described as the First Grand Master under whom "Dukes and Lords were admitted into Masonry". In the same year it was decided that the Grand Wardens should not, as had been the custom previously, be elected together with a Grand Master, but appointed by Grand Masters personally. It is probably at the time of his Grand Mastership that the two "Craft Degrees", later called by Anderson "Entered Apprentice" and "Fellow Craft", were moulded into something broadly approaching the form in which we have them today.[14]

Practically nothing else is known about his Grand Mastership.

In 1720 George Payne was elected Grand Master for the second time. It was under him that the Cooke Manuscript was found and the 39 General Regulations (so-called Ancient Regulations) completed which, three years later, were incorporated in the first of Anderson's *Constitutions* of 1723.[15] It is to the end of his Grand Mastership, somewhere between January and May of 1721, that the Masonic tradition has ascribed the destruction of several invaluable manuscripts, including the Stone Manuscripts, "by some scrupulous brothers that those papers might not fall into strange hands" [p. 111]. This event, even if it actually happened, started what I would call a "fiction line" in the Masonic historiography. For, whether the "Antient" MSS were in fact destroyed or had simply never existed, the absence of any documents or records would account for the necessity to produce pretty quickly a "new" version of what such documents ought to have contained. Here ends that part of the tale told by Dr Anderson, and another part starts which can pass for something like a proper history – for one source, or one eye-witness, however credible, does not make history, nor does one man's tale.[16]

It is said to be since that time that the customary yearly routine of

Masonic meetings was established, a routine that assumed its standard form and style of description under Anderson's pen. But it is by no means impossible that this idealized formula of Anderson's influenced the form meetings actually took several years thereafter. This formula exists in two main versions, one used in the description of the *Annual Assembly and Feast*, when a Grand Master, newly chosen by all Grand Officers of the Grand Lodge – the Grand Master Elect – is proclaimed by a previous Grand Master; and the other used in the description of a Quarterly Lodge, or Communication, with its regular transactions, of which one, usually the last before the next Annual Assembly, is devoted to the proposal of a new Grand Master, and his election. So we read: ". . . At the *Grand Lodge* in *Ample Form* [i.e., with Grand Master present] on Lady-Day 1721, at the said place [the Apple Tree Tavern] Grand Master Payne proposed for his successor . . . John Duke of Montagu, Master of a Lodge; who being present was forthwith saluted Grand Master Elect, and his health drunk in *due form* [after a manner previously established by Payne] . . ." [p. 111]. And further: "*Assembly and Feast* at Stationers Hall, 24 June 1721 . . . Payne Grand Master with his Wardens, the former Grand Officers, and the Masters and Wardens of *12* Lodges, met the Grand Master Elect in a *Grand Lodge* at the *King's Arms Tavern,* St Paul's Churchyard, in the morning; and having forthwith recognized their choice of . . . Montagu, they made some new Brothers, particularly . . . *Philip Lord Stanhope,* now *Earl of Chesterfield*; And from thence they marched on foot to the Stationers Hall Ludgate Street . . .

"Brother Payne, the Old Grand Master, made the *first procession* round the Hall, and then return'd, he proclaim'd aloud John Montagu Duke of Montagu Grand Master . . . and install'd him in *Solomon's Chair* . . . Montagu, immediately call'd forth, as it were carelessly, *John Beal,* M.D., as his Deputy . . . , whom Payne invested, and install'd him in *Hiram Abiff's Chair*[17] on the Grand Master's Left hand. In like manner his Worship call'd forth and appointed Mr Josiah Villeneau and Mr Thomas Morrice, Grand Wardens, who were . . . invested and install'd by the last Grand Warden. And . . . after Grace had been said they sat down to an elegant repast according to ancient Masonic Usages, and regaled themselves with all cheerfulness.

"Then Montagu . . . with his officers and the old officers, having made the 2nd procession round the Hall, Brother Desaguliers made an eloquent oration about Masons and Masonry . . ." [pp. 112–13][18]

The formula describes when and where they met, who participated in the meeting, where they marched from, who proposed whom to be Grand Master, where and how they dined, etc. This model was meticulously followed by Anderson throughout the whole period even, I dare suggest, when the events did not quite coincide with the model. Although this particular occasion was not written up until some seventeen years later, Anderson's version of the event is corroborated in part, for the first time, by the diary of a Dr W. Stukely, in an entry dated 24 June 1721. It states that at the Annual Feast of the Grand Lodge at Stationer's Hall, "Dr Desaguliers pronounc'd an oration".[19]

Three very important events marked the period of the Duke of Montagu's rule. The first was Dr Anderson's appearance for the first time on the scene of Masonic history, not as a historiographer, but as an active participant in the work of the Grand Lodge.[20] On 25 September 1721, at the meeting of the Grand Lodge, which was held "in ample form at *The King's Arms* . . . his Grace's Worship and the Lodge *finding fault* with all the copies of the old Gothic Constitutions order'd Brother James Anderson, A.M., to digest the same in *a new and better method*", [p. 113–4].[21] The description of this very significant episode is somewhat elliptical; it is not explained what exactly was wrong with the old manuscripts. In any case, the expression "in a new and better method" indicates that the "Gothic Constitutions" were regarded as somehow inadequate for use by the Grand Lodge as its own Constitutions. Entirely new work had to be done to produce a canonical text which, while not contradicting the old ones, and using them as its historical basis, could serve as a standard law book for an entirely new association of persons.

The second event of great and often under-estimated importance was the publication, in August 1722, of the so-called "Old Charges", in five successive issues of the *Post Man*, and the *Historical Account.* This newspaper version was subsequently printed as a pamphlet by J. Roberts. (Reference *Early Masonic Pamphlets* by Knoop, Jones Hamer, Manchester University Press 1945, p. 71.) The preface to the pamphlet, known as *The Old* [or *Roberts'*] *Constitutions,* gives the following reason for publishing the document: "it had seen the world but in fragments, but is now put together".

It is not clear why the Charges, and then the Constitutions, were referred to as "Old".[22] Possibly, as the title implies, it is because they were taken from an older manuscript, or series of manuscripts, than those perused and recommended by the Grand Lodge in commissioning Anderson to prepare another version. Or it may have been because J. Roberts himself, anticipating the publication of Anderson's *Constitutions*, wanted to diminish its impact by establishing the antiquity and therefore superiority of his sources. He may even, as A. E. Waite speculates, have seen a draft copy of Anderson's text, or got wind of its content, and wished to put his (and his supporters', if any) own slant on the proceedings.[23]

Whatever the reason, from Anderson's point of view it must have been a momentous and perhaps not entirely welcome event. *Roberts Constitutions* was the first Masonic text in the world to have been published. Someone had stolen a march on him. It is highly unlikely that he would not have been aware of its existence before publication, although at that time the text of his own *Constitutions* was not yet ready for printing. Moreover, he could not have been unaware of the essential differences between these two Books of Constitutions, as well as of the difference between the two streams of Masonic opinion at that time, specifically Christian and generally Deist. *The Old Constitutions*, representing the former, starts with a Prayer: "The Almighty Father of Heaven, with the Wisdom of the Glorious Son, through the goodness of the Holy Ghost, Three Persons in One Godhead, be with our beginning, and give us His grace so to govern our lives that we may come to His bliss, that never shall have end. Amen."

Waite comments: "If it was intended as a counterblast beforehand to the Clause on God and Religion [in Anderson's *Constitutions* of 1723], we may question whether its silent protest ... could have been exchanged more profitably for forms of denunciation ... or of clerical debate".[24] The problem, as I see it, is whether this prayer and, particularly, "be with our beginning" could be thought of as referring to any concrete Masonic Body existing at that time. Or did it simply represent the conviction of some individual orthodox Christian Masons, belonging to one of the Lodges under the Grand Lodge?

The Old [or *Roberts'*] *Constitutions*, though the first to appear in printed form, was of similar pattern and style to very many others, written before or after 1723 and published after that date, whereas Anderson's *Constitutions* of 1723, though partly following the scheme of *The Old Constitutions*, remains unique and the first of its kind. Before I begin to deal with the latter I will look more closely at *The Old Constitutions* and, after having considered the scheme of its content, compare it with Anderson's.[25]

The editor starts his preface (I am following the pamphlet version) by referring to the already prevalent negative attitude of some sections of society to Masons: "If anything could have escaped the censure of this litigious age; if the most innocent and inoffensive set of men in the world could be free from satyre and sarcasm, one would have thought the Ancient and Noble Society of Free-Masons should have been the men." After that he mentions the fact that quite a few persons belonging to the higher social strata of society had joined the Craft, stressing its aristocratic connections and, by implication, the plebeian nature of anti-Masonry. This antithesis will, very soon, begin to be a feature more or less common to all Masonic prefaces.

There follows a very significant, and among Masonic writers at that time fashionable, reference to the Manuscript itself. The editor warns the reader that due to the fact that the Manuscript is worn out, there are some lacunae and parts are unreadable. In other words, he implies that the Manuscript is both *genuine* and very old. This is emphasized by his only note found at the beginning of the last paragraph of the text itself: "Additional Orders and Constitutions made and agreed upon at a General Assembly held at ... the 8th day of December, 1663", which suggests that the rest of the text belonged to an even earlier date.

The first part of the Constitutions is a "History of the Society of Freemasons" (all headings are those of the editor), and describes the evolution of the science (i.e. masonry and architecture) and the sciences (i.e. all other sciences and crafts):

... You ask me how this science was invented; my answering this, that before the General Deluge, which is commonly called Noah's Flood, there was a man called Lamech ... who had two wives ... Ada and Zilla; by Ada he begat Jaball and Juball; and by Zilla he had Tuball ... and a daughter called Naamah ... Jaball found out Geometry, and he divided flocks of sheep and lands ... and he first built a house of stone and timber. Juball found out music; Tuball found out the smith's trade ... also of gold, silver, etc. Naamah found out the craft of weaving ... And these children knew that God would take vengeance for sins ...

Afterwards, the Manuscript goes on, before the vengeance for sins was manifested, there were the two *Pillars of Stone* ...

... undestructible ... either by Fire or Water, wherefore they [i.e. "pre-Noachida"][26] did write these *sciences* that they have found, ... two pillars that might be found after that God had taken vengeance; the one was marble, that would not burn, the other was brick that would not drown in water ... It resteth now to tell you how these stones were found, whereon the said sciences were written, after the said deluge: It so pleased God Almighty, that the said Hermames [i.e. Hermes], whose son Lunie was, who was the son of Sem, who was the son of Noah; ... found one of the two Pillars ... and the sciences written thereon, and taught them to other men. And at the Tower of Babylon, Masonry was

much made on; for the King of Babylon, who was Nemroth, was a
Mason, and when the City of Ninevah, and other cities of the East
should be built, he sent thither three score masons . . . and when they
went forth, he gave them a *Charge* after this manner: that they should
be true one to another, that he might have worship by them in sending
them to his cozen the King. He also gave them Charge concerning their
science [i.e. Masonry]. And then was it *the first time that any Mason had
Charge* . . . Also Abraham, and Sarah his wife, went into Egypt, and
taught the Egyptians the Seven Liberal Sciences; and he [i.e. Abraham]
had an ingenious scholar called Euclydes, who perfectly learned [them]
. . . It happened in his days the Lords and States of the Realm [of Egypt]
had so many sons unlawfully begotten by other men's wives, that the
land was burthen'd with them, having small means to maintain them
withal; the King . . . caused a Parliament to be . . . summoned for redress
. . . Whereupon Euclydes came to the King, and said thus, my Noble
Sovereign . . . I will teach [those Lords' sons] the Seven Liberal Sciences,
whereby they may live honestly like gentlemen . . . And there Euclydes
gave them these Admonitions following:

I. To be true to their King.
II. To be true to the Master they serve.
III. To be true and love one another.
IV. Not to miscall one another, etc.
V. To do their work so duly, that they may deserve their wages at
their Master's hands.
VI. To ordain the wisest of them Master of the rest of their work.
VII. To have such reasonable wages, that the workman may live
honestly and with credit.
VIII. To come and assemble together in the Year, to take council
in their Craft how they may work best to serve their Lord and
Master . . .

. . . The Masonry was heretofore term'd geometry, and so thence the
children of Israel came to the land of Bethest, in the Country of Jerusalem, where they began a Temple . . . And King David loved Masons well
. . . for he gave them a *Charge*, as Euclydes had given them before in
Egypt . . . and . . . King Solomon finished the Temple that his father
began; he sent for Masons of *diverse nations*, to the number of four and
twenty thousand, of which number four thousand were elected
and created Masters and Governors of the Work. And there was a King
of another region . . . called *Hiram*, who loved well King Solomon, and
he gave him timber for the Work; and he had a son called Amon, and he

was Master of Geometry . . . and Chief Master of all Masons . . . that belong'd to the Temple as appears by the Bible in Lib. Regum Cap. Y. and King Solomon confirmed all . . . that King David had given in *Charge*; and then Masons did travel divers countries . . . to augment their knowledge in the said Art, and to instruct others. And it happened that a curious mason named Memongrecus, that had been at the building of the Solomon's Temple, came into France, and taught the Science of masonry to the Frenchmen; and there was a King of France called Carolus Martel, who loved greatly Masonry, and . . . who learned of Memongrecus the said Sciences, and became one of the Fraternity; . . . He confirmed unto them a large *Charter*, and was yearly present at their Assembly . . .

The Knowledge of Masonry was unknown in England until St Alban came thither, who instructed the King in the said Science . . . and also in Divinity, who was a pagan: St Alban . . . was knighted, and made the King's Chief Steward . . . He greatly cherished . . . Masons, and truly paid them their wages weekly, which was 3*s.* 6*d.* the week. He also purchased for them a *Charter* from the King to hold a *General Assembly* and *Council* yearly. He *made* many masons, and gave them such a *Charge* as is hereafter declared.

. . . After the martyrdom of St Alban . . . a certain King invaded the land and destroy'd most of the natives by fire and sword . . . and Science of Masonry was much decay'd, until the reign of King Athelston . . . who brought the land to peace and rest, from insulting Danes. He began to build many Abbies, monasteries . . . castles and divers Fortresses . . . He loved masons more than his father; he greatly study'd Geometry, and sent into many lands for men expert in Science. He gave them a very large *Charter*, to hold a yearly *Assembly*, and power to correct offenders in the said Science; and the King himself caused a General Assembly of all Masons . . . at York . . . and delivered them the said Charter to keep; and when this assembly was gathered together, he caused a cry to be made, that if any of them had any writing that did concern Masonry, or could inform the King of any . . . matter that was wanting in the said *Charge* already delivered, that they should show them to the King, or recite them to him; and there were some in English, some in Greek, and some in French and other languages, whereupon the King caused a Book to be made . . . and from that time unto this day Masonry hath been much respected and preserved, and divers new articles have been added to the said Charge . . . saying thus by way of exhortation, My loving and respected Friends and Brethren, I humbly beseech you, as you love your Soul's eternal Welfare, your Credit, and your Country's

Good, to be very Careful in Observation of these Articles . . . I will, by God's Grace, begin the Charge.

I. I am to admonish you to honour God in his holy Church that you use no heresy, schism and error . . . etc.

II. To be true to our Sovereign Lord the King, his heirs and Successors . . .

III. You shall be true to your Fellows and Brethren of the Science of Masonry, and to do unto them as you would be done unto.

IV. You shall keep secret the obscure and intricate parts of the Science, not disclosing them to any but such as study and use the same.

V. You shall do your work truly and faithfully, endeavouring the profit and advantage of . . . the owner of the said work.

VI. You shall call Masons your Fellows and Brethren, without addition of "knaves" or other bad language.

VII. You shall not take your neighbour's wife villinously [*sic*], nor his daughter, nor his maid or his servant to use ungodly.

VIII. You shall not carnally lye with any woman that is belonging to the house where you are at table.

IX. You shall truly pay your meat and drink, where you are at table.

X. You shall not undertake any Man's work, knowing yourself unable or unexpert to perform and effect the same.

XI. You shall not take any work to do at excessive or unreasonable rates, to deceive the owner thereof . . .

XII. You shall so take your work, that thereby you may live honestly, and pay your Fellows the wages as the Science doth recognize.

XIII. You shall not supplant any of your Fellows of their work . . . altho' you perceive him or them unable to finish the same.

XIV. You shall not take any Apprentice to serve you in the said Science of masonry under the term of seven years; nor any but of good and honest parentage.

XV. You shall not take upon you to make any one Mason without the Privity or Consent of six, or five at least of your Fellows, and not but such as is Freeborn, and whose Parents live in good Fame and Name, and that have his right and perfect Limbs, and able of Body. . .

XVI. You shall not pay any of your Fellows more Money than he or they have deserv'd.

XVII. You shall not slander any of your Fellows behind their Backs.

XVIII. You shall not, without very urgent Cause, answer your Fellow doggedly or ungodly, but as becomes a loving Brother . . .

XIX. You shall duly reverence your Fellows, that the Bond of Charity and mutual Love may continue . . .

XX. You shall not (except in Christmas time) use any lawless Games, as Dice, Cards or such like.

XXI. You shall not frequent any Houses of Bawdery, or be a Pander to any of your Fellows.

XXII. You shall not go out to drink by Night, or if occasion happen that you must go, you shall not stay past Eight of the Clock, etc.

XXIII. You shall come to the Yearly Assembly, if you know where it is kept, being within Ten Miles of the Place of your Abode, submitting your self to the Censure of your Fellows.

XXIV. You shall not make any Mould, Square, or Rule to mould Stones withal, but such as are allowed by the Fraternity.

XXV. You shall set Strangers at Work, having Employment for them, at least a Fortnight, and pay them their Wages truly, and if you want Work for them, then you shall relieve them with money to defray their reasonable Charges to the next Lodge.

XXVI. You shall truly attend your Work, and truly end the same, etc. All these Articles and Charge, which I have now read unto you, you shall well and truly observe, perform and keep to the best of your Power, and Knowledge, So help you God, and the true and holy Contents of this Book.

And moreover I, A.B. do here in the Presence of God Almighty, and of my Fellows and Brethren here present, promise and declare, That I will not at any Time hereafter by any Act or Circumstance whatsoever, directly or indirectly, publish, discover, reveal or make known any of these *Secrets, Privities or Councils of the Fraternity or Fellowship of Free Masons,* [my italics] which at this time, or at any time hereafter shall be made known unto me. So help me God, and the true and holy Contents of this Book.

This Charge belongeth to Apprentices

Imprimis, You shall truly honour God and his Holy Church, the King, your Master, and Dame . . .

II. You shall not purloyn or steal, or be Privy or Accessary to Purloyning or Stealing . . .

III. You shall not commit Adultery or Fornication in the House of your Master, with his Wife, Daughter or Maid.

IV. You shall not disclose your Master's or Dame's Secrets or Councils, which they have reported unto you, etc.

V. You shall not maintain any disobedient Argument with your Master, Dame, or any Free-Mason.

VI. You shall reverently behave yourself towards all Free Masons, etc.

VII. You shall not haunt or frequent any Taverns or Alehouses, or so much as go into any of them, except upon your Master's or Dame's errand, etc. . . .

VIII. You shall not commit Adultery or Fornication in any man's House, where you shall be at Table or Work.

IX. You shall not marry, or contract your self to any Woman, during your Apprenticeship.

X. You shall not steal any Man's Goods, but especially your Master's or any of his Fellow Masons . . .

Additional orders and Constitutions made and agreed upon at a General Assembly held at — the 8th Day of December, 1663

I. That no Person, of what Degree soever, be accepted a Free Mason, unless he shall have a Lodge of five Free-Masons at the least . . .

II. That no person hereafter shall be accepted a Free Mason, but such as are of able Body, honest Parentage, good Reputation, and Observers of the Laws of the Land.

III. That no person hereafter, which shall be accepted a Free Mason, shall be admitted into any Lodge or Assembly, until he hath brought a Certificate of the Time and Place of his Acception from the Lodge that accepted him . . .

IV. That every person who is now a Free Mason, shall bring to the Master a Note of the Time of his Acception . . .

V. That for the future the said Society, Company and Fraternity of Free-Masons shall be regulated and governed by one Master, and as many Wardens as the said Company shall think fit to chuse at every yearly General Assembly.

VI. That no Person shall be accepted a Free Mason, unless he be One and Twenty Years old or more.

VII. That no Person hereafter be accepted a Free Mason, or know the Secrets of the said Society, until he shall have first taken the Oath of Secrecy here following, (viz.)

I A.B. do in the Presence of God Almighty, and of my Fellows and Brethren here present, promise and declare, That I will not at any time hereafter by any Act or Circumstance whatsoever, directly or indirectly, publish, discover, reveal or make known any of the Secrets, Privities or Councils of the Fraternity or Fellowship of Free Masonry, which at this time, or at any time hereafter shall be made known unto me. So help me God, and the true and holy Contents of this Book.

I have thought it essential to reproduce a good part of the text, not because of its importance as history, but because of the enormous importance of its appearance in 1722 as the first officially published Masonic Constitutions.

I will now make a very elementary analysis of this text as I see it, bearing in mind the context of its appearance and its relation to other Masonic circumstances which preceded, followed or were contemporary to its publication.

REMARKS ON THE CONTENT OF THE OLD CONSTITUTIONS

1) The author's address to the *Noble Society of Freemasons* stands outside the text itself: it is *Accepted* Freemasons and, by implication, those belonging to the Grand Lodge of England who are addressed, though the Grand Lodge is not mentioned. Moreover, the emphasis is put on the public outside Freemasonry, so that in a way the author seems to speak *about* Freemasons more than *to* them. As for the text of *The Constitutions* itself, it is not presented as the Constitutions of contemporary speculative Freemasons but of some order of Masons pre-existing from time immemorial. Unlike later Masonic works, its editor does not mention himself in connection with any of the circumstances described in the text other than those pertaining to the preface.

2) The author's reference to the Manuscript as an old and worn-out *vellum* implies that it was written not even in the seventeenth century, but at least a century earlier. When he refers to an addition made in 1663, he does not specify whether it was on the same vellum or not.

3) Unlike the Additional Orders, the charges which make up the Second Part of the Constitutions do not mention the custom of *acception* of non-working members – it is entirely about working Masons, addressing them as "Fellows" and "Brethren".

4) The text relates the history of Freemasonry from the time of Noah's flood to that of the King Athelstan when the first Charge was given to English Masons. As with Anderson, it is hard to know what on earth anyone could make out of such an implausible tale. One may, of course,

argue that it could have been written at some time in the sixteenth century to serve the needs of simple working Masons, but why, then, should it be republished in the eighteenth century to serve the needs of a new and non-working Freemasonry among which there were at least three Doctors of Divinity, and not less than a dozen persons with Oxford or Cambridge behind them? I do not know who J. Roberts was, but his seriousness in endeavouring to endow the New Masonry with an ancient and noble past is, as it transpires from the preface, quite genuine. How could he fail to be aware that all this is anachronistic nonsense? My answer is this: he could not; and more than that, I assume that what mattered to him and to his actual and potential readers was the antiquity of the legend, not any real history. The "historical" tale was meant from the start to be an ancient legend, not an ancient history. Whether this also holds for those to whom the manuscript itself was allegedly addressed in the seventeenth century is unknowable, though I am pretty certain that by the beginning of the eighteenth century, the historical legend had already become separated from historiography and had become quite another phenomenon – that of an historical convention. One step further and one is embroiled in opaque complexities of Masonic allegory and symbolism, but that is still to come. So far we deal with a Body, the Grand Lodge of England, whose claims to antiquity are "confirmed" by the antiquity of the legendary past of another Body, the "working Masons", to which the former is related by "adoption", and also, though to a much lesser extent, by the antiquity of the document.[27]

5) The Charges which constitute the second part of the text, and which are "historically" referred to in the first, regulate the relations of a Mason to the person for whom he works together with all other persons. The references to any Masonic body are very scarce. The Lodge is mentioned only once (Charge XXV), and only in connection with payment of new Fellows. The whole profession or Science of Masonry to which Charges, or Charters, are given by Kings is no more than vaguely manifested in "Yearly Assemblies".

6) No rituals, or passwords, or signs are described or mentioned.

7) The two oaths of secrecy do not contain, or allude even indirectly to what was to be kept secret. Still, the very form of these oaths suggest that there were two kinds of secrets: the first, the "obscure and intricate parts of the Science", is possibly related to things secret by definition,

such as rituals, signs, etc., and the second related to all professional, personal and other businesses discussed between Masons, and called here "privities" and "counsels".

8) The Christian character of Masonry revealed in the Prayer quoted above is reiterated in the Charges, so that we may assume that these Charges were Christian and given to Christian working Masons only. This, however, is neither specified nor mentioned in the editor's preface addressed to the contemporary non-working Masons and the public at large.

9) One may assert that none of *The Old Constitutions* – neither its historical part, nor the Charges, nor its religious content – is related to the *new* Masonry in any way other than via the editor's preface.

10) *The Old Constitutions* is the first printed Charter of working Masons that appeared in the context of the new, speculative, Masonry, endowed with an unambiguously ideological function. All subsequent publications of various Masonic MSS, though they retained that function, were made in a considerably more scholarly and less apologetic way.

Around the time of the beginning of Masonic polemics in 1722–3 a French book called *Long Livers* ("A curious history of such persons of both sexes who have liv'd several ages, and grown young again") (1715)[28] written by de Longeville Harcouet and translated by Eugenius Philalethes (the name is probably a pseudonym of Robert Samber, a contemporary Masonic author) arrived on the scene. In his Dedication the translator greeted "the Grand Master, Masters, Wardens and Brethren of the most Antient and Honourable Fraternity of the Freemasons of Great Britain and Ireland". This is the first text written by a Mason where British Masonry figures as a whole body and where it is described as unambiguously Christian ". . . because ours is the true language of the Brotherhood which the primitive Christian Brethren as well as those who were from the Beginning, made use of, as we learn from the Holy Scriptures, and an uninterrupted tradition").[29] I am inclined to think that the author of the Dedication expressed the position of those early Masons who, probably, even before entering the Society, had genuinely believed in its Christian character, and had identified their own Christianity with the "religion of Masons". (He wrote: "A multitude of Gods is utterly inconsistent with the idea of divinity; it is the same as the multitude of the First Beings, nonsense the most blasphemous and enormous" and further: "... I speak in Brother St Paul's style ... so worship we the God of our Fathers who, we know, is but one as is our Faith").

Thus, in one way or another, Masonry became public in 1722 and the very fact that the two Books of Constitutions were compiled almost simultaneously not only reflects an already marked divergence of opinions among Masons but also the possible existence of several different groups based on several different Lodges. When Gould writes that "... there is not a scrap of evidence that Payne, Desaguliers, and Anderson ... took part in the formation of the Grand Lodge in 1717 ... though all three had a share in the compilation of the *First Book of Constitutions*",[30] he exposes this divergence: the compilers of the first Book might have been philosophically opposed to the founding fathers of the Grand Lodge as innovators to the orthodox even though the time span is extremely short. This may have something to do with the fact that all three belonged to the most aristocratic of the four Lodges, Lodge No. 4.[31]

Meanwhile, however, the committee of fourteen previously appointed by the Grand Lodge gave its approval, at a meeting at The Fountain in the Strand, 25 March 1722, "after some amendments", to Anderson's manuscript in the form ready for printing. And it was Lodge No. 4 which, according to Anderson, triggered the first major Masonic controversy, for "... Montagu's good government inclin'd the *better sort* to continue him in the Chair another year; and therefore they delay'd to prepare the Feast" [p. 114]. The decision to postpone the annual Assembly and Feast, however irregular it may have seemed, was probably motivated by their lack of unanimity over the choice of a future Grand Master. Preston even insists that Montagu decided to resign his Office in January 1722, while Albert Calvert, a Masonic historian, stresses that the indecision over the procedures at the Grand Lodge was due to an absence of regulations concerning "the proposed precedent".[32] As we shall see, it is the young, petulant and adventurous Philip, Duke of Wharton, who, only recently "made a Brother, tho' not the Master of the Lodge, and being ambitious of the Chair", decided that the best way of establishing a precedent was simply to create one there and then. "He got a number of others to meet him at Stationers Hall, 24 June 1722, and, having no Grand officers, they put in the Chair the oldest Master Mason [who was not the present Master of a lodge, also an irregularity] and without the usual proper ceremonials, the said old Master proclaim'd aloud Philip Wharton, Duke of Wharton, Grand Master, and Mr *Joshua Timson*, Blacksmith, and Mr *William Hawkins*,

Mason, Grand Wardens; But his Grace appointed no Deputy, nor was the Lodge opened and closed in *due* Form . . ." [p. 114].[33]

This nice little *coup d'état*, one may imagine, was by no means to the taste of those Anderson refers to as "the better sort". As it transpires from the *Constitutions* of 1723, 1738 and some contemporary pamphlets "the better sort" certainly means the nobility, scholars and gentry and, by implication, the members of Lodge No. 4, while those who wanted to have Wharton in the Chair, or whom he manipulated to that end, were of humbler origins.[34] At that time still a very young man, he had already earned a reputation as an adventurer, dueller and political opportunist. Because he was also a Jacobite, a number of Masonic historians have drawn the conclusion that he tried to use his position as Grand Master to influence the Society politically so that his position would be secured should another Jacobite attempt to claim the throne succeed. But even if this were the case, older Masons chose to ignore the political aspects of the situation and, as Calvert puts it, "it was the first and the last attempt to exploit Masonry in the interest of a political party."[35] We do not know to what extent, if any, the ensuing dissension in the Grand Lodge was due to political disagreements among the more prominent Masons, or was caused by their disapproval of Wharton as a person.[36] The controversy, however, was not very serious, for it was easily resolved by the Past Grand Master Montagu, "who summoned a Meeting of the Grand Lodge on 17th January, 1723, at which Wharton . . . having promised to be true and faithful, was regularly installed Grand Master . . ." [p. 114].[37] He appointed Dr Desaguliers his Deputy Grand Master, established the Office of Secretary (not yet Grand Secretary) the first holder of which was a certain W. Cowper, and it is from the beginning of 1723 that the first officially recorded Minutes of the Grand Lodge were kept. It is at this meeting that Anderson's book, by this time in print, received its final seal of approval.

The end of the Duke of Wharton's Masonic career was as disordered as its beginning. At a communication of the Grand Lodge on 25 April 1723 (where Anderson figured as a Grand Warden), the Duke of Wharton formally proposed the Earl of Dalkeith as his successor. But when the Earl was duly elected on 24 June 1723, reappointing by proxy Dr Desaguliers the Deputy Grand Master, Wharton incited his supporters to protest against both the election and the reappointment – ostensibly because the Earl of Dalkeith was absent at the time in Scotland. This meeting was the first properly recorded by Cowper.

Wharton's capriciousness and the almost permanent absence of Dalkeith failed to impede the growth of Lodges in and around London (now about thirty). Masonry was becoming more and more fashionable, and the reasons for this given by Anderson are almost exactly the same as those given by Masons now "...many Noblemen and Gentlemen of the first rank desir'd to be admitted into Fraternity, besides other learned men, merchants, clergymen and tradesmen, who found a Lodge to be a safe and pleasent *relaxation* from intense study or the hurry of business, *without* politicks or party..." [p. 115]. It was, probably, the growing interest of the public in London in Freemasonry, that prompted the Grand Lodge to "appoint the Committee to keep out *cowans*..." [p. 115]. "Cowan"[38] here means not only "non-Mason", but anyone with malicious intention to pass for a Mason or to mock Masonry.

But the highlight of the year was undoubtedly the first official Book of Constitutions, sanctioned by the Grand Lodge.

Much of Anderson's *Constitutions* of 1723 can hardly be taken as an historical source. Like *The Old Constitutions*, it is a historic fact, or rather it become one, but not before it had passed through the reappraisal of historical critique and historiographical verification. Unlike the Old Constitutions, however, it was meant not only as a presentation of the Masonic "past" to an audience of contemporary speculative Masons but primarily as a vast compendium of how Masons might regard themselves with respect to the hoped-for revival and spread of the Craft.

One may even go as far as to assert that Anderson's was a vision of a kind of "Imperial Freemasonry" that prefigured the founding of the British Empire a couple of decades later.[39]

Anderson's name does not appear in the title; the Dedication to the Duke of Montagu is signed by Dr Desaguliers, who refers to the author without naming him.[40] The Approbation of the Book in the minutes of the Grand Lodge, however, is signed by Anderson himself. All this seems strange considering that the book, though approved twice and recommended by the Grand Lodge, was at that time and thereafter the author's private property, and that Anderson speaks in this book for himself as author and not merely editor or compiler. So, his book it was in every sense, and, despite the rather vague references and allusions to various unnamed MSS which he claims to have "collected and digested", it ought to be regarded not as a retelling, or anthology, of older unpublished texts, but as an absolutely original work, with the exception of the thirty-nine regulations drawn up by Payne a couple of years earlier.[41] He had deliberately invented a new method, whereby a tradition was explicitly established linking operative Masonry with its leisurely, scholarly and aristocratic successors. Fifteen years later, in the second edition of 1738, this "new" tradition had become accepted as a part of the historical conception of Masonic history. So here is the beginning of their very own, as opposed to their working predecessors', history marked by the fact of their own telling of it, though the tale itself remained incomplete and uncompleted until 1738 when Anderson added to it a description of the history of Freemasonry since the formation of the Grand Lodge.

The function of the Anderson *Constitutions* is clearly defined first in its title – "For the use of the Lodges" [p. 1];[42] then follows: "to be read at the Admission of a New Brother when the Master or Warden shall begin . . ." [p. 2], and ". . . for the use of the Lodges in London, to be read when the Master shall order it . . ."; and then before the last part (*General Regulations*): "for the use of the Lodges in and about London and Westminster" [p. 58].

The first part of the book, the history, starts, unlike most of *The Old Constitutions*, not with Lamech, and "before the flood", but from the very Creation:

Adam, our first parent, created after the image of God, *the Great Architect of the Universe,* must have had the *Liberal Sciences,* particularly *Geometry,* written on his heart; for even since the fall, we find the principles of it in the hearts of his offspring, and which, in process of time, have been drawn forth into a convenient method of propositions . . . ; this noble *Science . . .* is the foundation of all those *Arts,* particularly of *Masonry* and *Architecture . . .* No doubt, Adam taught his sons geometry . . . for Cain, we find, built a city . . . [pp. 1–2].

Then, almost immediately, appears the first reference to Masons and to the first emblem of their Art, the Pillars.

. . . Enoch . . . prophesizing of the *Final Conflagration* at the Day of Judgement (as St Jude tells us) and likewise of the General Deluge for the Punishment of the World . . . erected two large Pillars . . . (tho' some ascribe them to Seth) the one of stone, and the other of brick, whereon were engraved the Liberal Sciences . . . Noah, and his three sons . . . all *Masons true,* brought with them over the Flood the Traditions and Arts of Antedeluvians" [p. 3].

All remotely important Biblical personages are said to be Masons or experts in Geometry and Architecture (". . . for Abraham, after the confusion at Babel . . . was called out of Ur . . . where he learned Geometry and the Arts . . ." [p. 7]), yet it is with the appearance of Moses on the scene of Masonic history that we start dealing with what could be called the Masonic nomenclature:

... And while marching to Canaan, thro' Arabica, under Moses, God was pleased to inspire Bezaleel (of Judah) ... and Aholiab (of Dan) ... with Wisdom of Heart to erect that most glorious Tent or Tabernacle, wherein the *Shechinah* (the Divine Light) resided ... And Moses ... became *General Master-Mason* ... So that the Israelites, at their leaving Egypt, were a whole Kingdom of Masons, well instructed under the conduct of their *Grand Master Moses* ... [p. 8].

Then we pass to the building of Solomon's Temple, in connection with which the word "Lodge" is mentioned for the first time:

... The Eternal God's Temple at Jerusalem, begun and finish'd ... in the short space of seven years and six months, by ... *the Prince of Peace and Architecture*, Solomon ... by Divine Direction, without the noise of workmen's tools, though there were ... no less than 3,600 Princes (*Harodim*), or *Master-Masons* ... with 3,600 hewers of stone ... or *Fellow Craftsmen,* and 70,000 labourers ... for which a great number of ingenious Masons, Solomon was much obliged to *Hiram,* or *Huram,* King of Tyre ... [pp. 9–10], ... who sent his Masons and carpenters to Jerusalem ... But above all he sent his namesake Hiram or Huram Abif, the most accomplished Mason upon earth [p. 11] ... The wise King Solomon was Grand Master of the Lodge of Jerusalem, and the learned King Hiram was Grand Master of the Lodge of Tyre, and the inspired Hiram Abif was Master of Work ... [p. 14].

Solomon's Temple marks a height that might be achieved only by Divinely inspired Architecture and Masonry ("But none of the nations, nor all together, could rival the Israelites ... and their Temple remained the constant pattern" [p. 15]). The place of Greece and Greek Architecture is not rated very highly for the real leap to the apex of that which is *humanly* achievable without Divine inspiration can be found only in Rome towards the beginning of our era:

... they advanc'd to their zenith of glory under Augustus Caesar ... who highly encourag'd ... the great Vitruvius, the father of all true architects to this day. Therefore, it is rationally believ'd, that ... Augustus became the Grand Master of the Lodge of Rome [pp. 24–5].

So, Jerusalem and Rome, Solomon with Hiram Abiff and Augustus with Vitruvius, figure as the two models of humanly perfectable architecture. The rest of the history is presented as a series of desperate attempts by mankind to reach again the perfection attained by these archetypal master Masons and to retain the memory of the two sites of the apotheosis of their craft.

The "sources" of the ancient period are summarized in rather an uncertain manner:

The old records of Masons afford large *hints* of their Lodges, from the beginning of the world, in the polite nations, especially, in times of peace, and when the civil powers, abhorring tyranny and slavery, gave due scope to the . . . free genius of their happy subjects [p. 25].

This, of course, relates to the post-Temple architecture.

The Middle Ages, marked by Gothic invasions and Islamic conquests, are treated with disdain. The English chapter of the history starts by emphasizing the period's almost total obliviousness, initially, of the Roman past. It goes on to trace the later attempts to recollect and even restore this lost architectural heritage. At first

. . . the Angles and other lower Saxons, invited by the ancient Britons, came . . . to help them against Picts and Scots [p. 28] and . . . at length subdu'd the South Part of this Island, which they call'd England . . . and being ignorant heathens, encouraged nothing but war, till they became Christians; and then too late lamented the ignorance of their fathers in the great loss of *Roman Masonry*, but knew not how to repair it. Yet becoming a *free people* (as the old Saxon Laws testify) . . . they too began to imitate . . . the Romans and other peoples . . . in erecting the Lodges [p. 29]; being taught not only from the faithful Traditions and valuable remains of the Britons . . . but even by foreign princes in whose domains the Royal Art had been preserv'd much from *Gothic Ruins*, particularly by *Charles* Martell, who . . . sent over several Masons . . . and Architects . . . into England, at the desire of the Saxon Kings . . . and [during the time of] the Danish Invasions [they built] many Gothic buildings . . . And after the Saxons and Danes were conquer'd by the Normans, as soon as the wars ended . . . the Gothic Masonry was [p. 30] encourag'd, even in the Reign of the *Conqueror* and of his son William Rufus, who built Westminster Hall, the largest one room perhaps in the world . . . We read King Edward III had an Officer call'd the King's Surveyor General of his buildings, whose name was Henry Yevele . . . [p. 31].

Anderson then introduces a "certain" unnamed Masonic record of the fifteenth century which is particularly significant because it not only describes specifically *Masonic* history, but establishes the beginning of its "written" tradition by referring to the old Charges, Constitutions, and Regulations which are directly related to Anderson's *Constitutions* as its ancestors. Finally, the record jumps at least four hundred years, to the reign of Henry VI (1422–61) when working Masons became a part of properly attested English history. The whole passage is presented as a "quotation" which should be used ". . . for the further instruction of *candidates* and younger *Brothers*", meaning those of the Grand Lodge of London in 1723. But paragraph (4) below also uses the reading as part of the initiation ceremonies of Brothers who lived at the time of Henry VI. The passage runs:

(1) That though the ancient Records of the Brotherhood in England . . . were destroy'd or lost in the wars of the Saxons and Danes, yet *King Athelstan* (the grandson of Alfred the Great a mighty architect himself) the first anointed King of England, and who translated the Holy Bible into Saxon tongue . . . built many great works, and encourag'd many Masons from France . . . who brought with them Charges and Regulations of the lodges preserv'd from the Roman times, who also prevail'd with the King to improve the *Constitution* of the English lodges according to the *foreign model,* and to increase the wages of working Masons.

(2) That his youngest son, prince Edwin . . . purchased a *Free charter* from his father, for the Masons having *a Correction* – or a *Freedom and Power to regulate themselves* . . . and to hold a *yearly Communication and General Assembly.*

(3) That . . . Edwin summoned all the Masons in the Realm to meet him in a Congregation [p. 32] at York, who came and composed a *General Lodge,* of which he was Grand Master; and having brought with them all the writings and records extant, . . . some in Latin, some in Greek, some in French, etc. from their contents the Assembly did frame *Constitutions* and Charges of *an English Lodge* . . .

(4) That when Lodges were more frequent . . . the Master and Fellows, with Consent of the Lords of the Realm (for *most great men were then Masons*) ordain'd that . . . at the *Making* or *Admission* of a Brother, the Constitution should be read.

(5) And . . . the said Record adds, that those Charges and Laws of Free-Masons have been seen and perused by our late Sovereign Henry VI, and by the Lords of his . . . Council. [p. 33]

So, Anderson modelled his *Constitutions* on the supposed Charges of Edwin, son of Athelstan, who in turn based his Charges on more ancient ones brought from the Continent. What is most interesting, however, is the fact that Anderson identifies his own work with a previous "historical" record. This became a particular feature of Masonic historiography: for example, Anderson in his *Constitutions* (and speaking for himself) refers to a Constitution of Edwin as it existed when Henry VI also "saw and perused it". Eminent Freemasons have always based their instructions and expositions on "existing" more ancient texts.

The narrative then concentrates on the first of two central episodes of practically any Masonic prehistory. The first is connected, again, with the person and reign of Henry VI and seems to be crucial to any historiographer of Masonry, whether or not he regards it as factual:

Now, though, in the third year of the said King Henry VI, while an infant of about four years old, the Parliament made an Act, that affected only the *working Masons* who had, contrary to the *Statutes for Labourers*, confederated not to work but at their own price and wages; and because such Agreements were suppos'd to be made at the *General Lodges*, call'd in the Act *Chapters* and *Congregations of Masons*, it was then thought expedient to level the said Act against the said Congregations. Yet, when the said King . . . arriv'd to man's estate, the Masons laid before him and his Lords the above mention'd Records and Charges, who, 'tis plain, review'd them, and . . . approv'd of them . . . Nay, the said King and his Lords must have been incorporated with the Free-Masons, before they could make such review . . . Nor is there any instance of executing that Act in that, or any other reign since, and the Masons never neglected their Lodges for it, nor ever thought it worth while to employ their *noble* and *eminent* Brethren to have it repeal'd; because the working Masons, that are free of the Lodge, scorn to be guilty of such combinations; and the other *free* Masons have no concern in trespasses against the Statutes of Labourers.

That Act was made in ignorant times, when the learning was a crime, and geometry condemn'd for conjuration. But by tradition it is believed that the Parliament-men were then too much influenced by the *illiterate Clergy*, who were not Accepted Masons, nor understood architecture; . . . yet thinking they had an indefensible right to know all secrets, by vertu of . . . confession and the Masons never confessing anything thereof, the said Clergy were highly offended . . . and represented them . . . as dangerous to the State . . . [pp. 35–6].

It is stated quite categorically here that by the middle of the fifteenth century there already existed two different kinds of Mason, *working* and *non-working* (the noble and eminent) and that only the former were subject to the Statutes. More than that, the passage implies that not only were there two different kinds of Masons, but two different *institutions*: The Lodge of *Free* Masons and the "General Lodges" also known as "Chapters" or "Congregations", though what exactly is meant by "working Masons, that are *free of* the Lodge" is unclear. In all probability "the Lodge" simply refers to the Lodge or Chief Lodge of the speculative Masons alleged to have had their own institutions at this early date. The ironic references to the machinations of the "illiterate" clergy who feared that their divine right of access to all secrets through the confessional was being sidestepped by the Masons is undoubtedly a jibe at those clerics who were hostile to Masonry in Anderson's time, not the middle of the fifteenth century.

The second episode is even more typical, for it does not refer to the working Masons at all, and deals with the "annual communication" (a term which only came into use at least 140 years later) of Masons at York, traditionally the Masonic capital since King Athelstan's times, which aroused the suspicions of Queen Elizabeth I:

... the learned and magnanimous Queen Elizabeth, who encourag'd other Arts, discourag'd this; because, being a woman, she could not be made a Mason ... (and being jealous of any assemblies of her subjects, whose beliefs she was not duly appriz'd of, attempted to break up the annual communication of Masons at York as dangerous to her Government. But, as old Masons have transmitted it by Tradition, when the noble persons her Majesty had commissioned, and brought a sufficient *Posse* with them at St John's Day, were once admitted into the Lodge, they made no use of arms, and return'd the Queen a most honourable account of the ancient Fraternity.) [p. 38]

The last section of the historical part of Anderson's *Constitutions*, apart from a short discourse on the Masonic history in Scotland, describes the triumph of *"Augustan Stile"* over *"Gothic Ignorance"*, and the gradual growth of Masonry, despite all the vicissitudes of the turbulent seventeenth century. Inigo Jones and Christopher Wren inaugurate a new era in Architecture, and the Glorious Revolution of 1688 brings with it official recognition of Masonry as an embodiment of enlightenment (the Sciences), beauty ("Augustan Stile"), and tolerance:

James VI of Scotland (I of England) ... revived the English Lodges and ... recovered the Roman Architecture from the ruins of *Gothic Ignorance* ... [p. 38] ... the Great Palladio has not yet been duly imitated in Italy, though justly rival'd by ... our great Master Mason *Inigo Jones* ... and the ingenious Mr Nicholas Stone perform'd as Master-Mason under Jones [p. 39] ... Charles I being also a Mason, patronized Mr Jones too ... After the Civil Wars were over, and the Royal Family restored, true Masonry was likewise restored; especially after upon the burning of London in 1666 ... [p. 40] ... King Charles II founded the present

St Paul ... conducted by Sir Christopher Wren ... and we have much reason to believe that Charles II was an Accepted Mason ... But in the reign of his brother, James II ... the Lodges of Free-Masons in London much dwindled into ignorance ... [p. 71]. But after the Revolution Anno 1688, King William [p. 72] ... (who by most is reckon'd a Free-Mason) did influence the nobility, the Gentry, the Wealthy and the learned of Great Britain, to affect much the Augustan Stile [p. 73].

Here Anderson's history of the world, architecture and Freemasonry breaks off to be taken up again on an optimistic note fifteen years later, in 1717, with the founding of the Grand Lodge of England, which takes us into the realm of more or less attested, rather than semi-legendary history.[43] The tale becomes a kind of encomium of Freemasonry and England, as well as of the current Grand Master Montagu, under whose auspices and by whose order this Book of Constitutions was initiated. There are, however, three points in the concluding paragraphs which are of considerable interest. The first is the establishing of the link between Freemasonry and the Medieval Christian Orders. The second stresses the cosmopolitan character of Freemasonry in general which asserts itself through history by means of a secret international language of Masonic signs. And the third emphasizes the universalism of English Freemasonry in particular. The two last paragraphs look as if they were intended as a "Manifesto" within the *Constitutions*. Their tenor and style will be imitated by some and parodied and ridiculed by others. They are reproduced here almost in their entirety because of their significance for the history of Masonry in the eighteenth and nineteenth centuries:

... from this ancient Fraternity, the *Societies* or *Orders of the Warlike Knights*, and of the *Religious* too, in process of time, did borrow many solemn usages; for none of them were better instituted, more decently installed, or more sacredly ... observed ... than the Accepted Masons have done, who in *all ages*, and in every Nation, have maintained [p. 46] and propagated their Concernments *in a way peculiar to themselves*, which the most cunning and the most learned cannot penetrate into ... while they know and love one another, even without the help of Speech, or when of different languages.

And now the *Freeborn British Nations* ... reviv'd the drooping Lodges of London ... with several worthy *particular* Lodges, that have a quarterly *Communications*, and an *Annual Grand Assembly*, wherein the *Forms* and *Usages* of the most ancient [p. 47] and worshipful Fraternity are wisely propagated, and the Royal Art duly cultivated and the Cement of the

Brotherhood preserv'd; so that the whole Body resembles a well Built *Arch*; several Noblemen and Gentlemen of the best rank, with Clergymen and learned Scholars of most professions and denominations, having frankly join'd and submitted to take the *Charges*, and to wear the *Badges* of a Free and Accepted Mason, under our present Grand-Master, the most Noble John Duke of Montagu [p. 48].

The second part of the Book – the Charges – is the first exposition of the principles of *non-working* Masonry. The allusions to its "working" past are rare and merely formal, as, for instance, in the clause saying, "that no Master should take an Apprentice, unless he has sufficient employment for him." [p. 51] The most important and controversial principle concerning God and Religion is formulated, as far as Anderson was concerned, with such a clarity and precision as not to leave to future generations of Masonic law-makers and historians any possibility of its reinterpretation, not to speak of its misinterpretation. This probably accounts for the fact that both reinterpreted and misinterpreted it was, and very soon, by its being far too unambiguous and plainly put:

A Mason is obliged, by his tenure, *to obey the Moral Law*; and if he rightly understands the Art, he will never be a stupid *ATHEIST*, nor an irreligious *LIBERTINE*. But though in Ancient times Masons were charg'd in every country to be of the Religion of that Country or Nation, whatever it was, yet 'tis now thought more expedient only to oblige them to that religion in which *all men agree*, leaving their particular opinions to themselves; that is, to be *good Men and true*, or Men of Honour and Honesty, by whatever denomination or persuasion they may be distinguish'd – whereby Masonry becomes the *Center of Union* and the means of conciliating true Friendship among persons that must have remain'd at a perpetual distance [p. 50].

Thus we have here two different concepts of Religion. The first is absolute, universal, and general. As a moral concept it is called "the moral law", whereas as a religious concept it is formulated as ". . . that Religion in which all men agree". The second is relative and particular. Particular, because it embraces every concrete religion in the world, the whole world of religious variety. Relative, because on the one hand it is always related to the first, just as the particular is related to the general, while on the other, it is opposed to the first, in the sense that that which differentiates is opposed to that which unites. In other words, while "the Moral Law" and that "Religion [undefined] in which all men agree" remain *summum bonum*, any particular religion, though always

"relatively good" when opposed to "stupid atheism and irreligious liber-
tinism", appears to be "relatively bad" in the context of Masonic universalism. This is very strongly stressed further on in the Charge concerning
"Behaviour after the Lodge is over and the Brethren not gone":

You may enjoy yourselves with innocent mirth . . . but avoiding all excess,
or forcing any Brother to eat or drink against his inclination . . . No
private *piques* or *Quarrels* must be brought within the door of the Lodge,
far less any Quarrels *about Religion or Nations, or State Policy, we being only
as Masons, of the Catholic Religion* above mention'd; We are also of all
nations, tongues, kindreds, and languages, and we resolv'd *against all
Politick* [p. 43].

Another point, though not so theologically controversial as Anderson's religious ideas, is the relation between Masonry and the law and
Masonry and the State. Here, an attempt can be seen to establish a link
with the clauses in the Old Charges whereby a Lodge is endowed with
the right and authority not only to resolve disputes between Masons (as
well as between a Mason who "does the work" and a Lord who orders
it – as in the Old Charges), but also to serve as a moral and judicial
intermediary between Masons and the State in general. Furthermore,
and particularly interestingly, the inner moral standards of the Lodge
tend to neutralize, if not outweigh, the Laws of the State and accepted
norms of social behaviour. All this is intended to co-exist with the absolute loyalty of the Mason to the State and the absolute obedience to its
Laws:

A Mason is a peaceable subject to the Civil Powers . . . for as Masonry
always hath been injured by War, etc., so ancient Kings and Princes
have been much disposed to encourage the Craftsmen because of their
. . . loyalty. So that if a Brother should be a rebel against the State, *he
is not to be countenanced in his rebellion* [my italics], however, he may be
pitied as an unhappy man; and, if convicted of no other crime, though
the loyal Brotherhood must and ought to disown his rebellion, and give
no umbrage or ground of political jealousy to the Government for the
time being; *they cannot expel him* from the lodge, and his relation to it
remains indefensible" [p. 50].

And at the end of the Charges:

Finally . . . and if any of the Brothers do you injury, you must apply to
your own or *his* Lodge: and from thence you may appeal to the Grand
Lodge at *the Quarterly Communication*, and from thence to the *annual*

Grand Lodge . . . never taking a legal course but when the case cannot be otherwise decided . . . [p. 56].

The Charges establish a hierarchy of Masonic degrees throughout the whole structure of the institutions with the sole exception of its senior rank, a Grand Master, whose appointment always seems to be a special case:

. . . no *Brother* can be a Warden until he has passed the part of a *Fellow-Craft* nor a *Master* until he has acted as a Warden, nor Grand Warden until he has been *Master of a Lodge*, nor Grand Master unless he has been a Fellow-Craft *before* his election, who is also to be nobly born, or a Gentle-man, or some eminent scholar, or some curious architect, etc. [p. 52].

The last part of the Book is the General Regulations, written in 1720 by George Payne, then Grand Master, and now reworked "by the author of this Book who . . . has compar'd them with, and reduc'd them to the ancient Records and immemorial Usages of the Fraternity, and digested them into this *new method* . . ." [p. 58].

Four points in the General Regulations are of particular importance for the whole subsequent history of Freemasonry in England. The first concerns the rules of admission of candidates, and states that "No man can be enter'd a Brother [the first degree also called 'Apprentice' or 'Enter'd Apprentice'] in any particular Lodge, or become its member [i.e. if he had already been accepted into some other particular Lodge], without the *unanimous consent of all the members of that Lodge*" [p. 59].

The second establishes the principle of centralization as regards each and every *new* Lodge. No Lodge can *form itself* except by a warrant from the Grand Lodge. The same applies to the dissolution, or "striking off the list" of a particular Lodge. This leaves unanswered the question of to what extent, if any, this principle could be applied to the four *old* Lodges which were not constituted by the Grand Lodge, but constituted the latter. And it is unambiguously stated here that "A new Lodge . . . should be solemnly constituted by the Grand Master . . . or his Deputy" [Postscript, p. 71].

The third proclaims the absolute authority of this Book of Consti-tutions. In the words of the Duke of Wharton, then Grand Master, "We . . . ordain that these be receiv'd in every particular Lodge . . . as the *only Constitutions* of Free and Accepted Masons . . ." [Approbation, pp. 73–4]. Yet this authority is limited by the no less absolute ". . . inherent Power and Authority of . . . every Annual Grand Lodge . . . to make new Regulations, or to alter these, provided always that the *old Landmarks* be carefully preserv'd . . ." [p. 70]. What exactly these "old Landmarks" were is not stated; moreover the last sentence laid itself open to so many interpretations that it very soon became the source of great controversy.

The fourth concerns Masonic secrets – a theme in itself – which has since assumed an immense significance in Masonic practice, history, and philosophy. The only reference to the secret Ritual appears in the clause dealing with constituting a new Lodge, where we read that ". . . the Grand Master shall ask his Deputy if he has examin'd the new Master and Wardens . . . and finds the Candidate Master well skill'd in the Royal Art . . . and duly instructed in *our Mysteries*" [p. 71]. The most interesting thing, however, is that several times throughout the text Anderson, while speaking in the first person, refers to that which cannot be spoken of or written in his book, thereby making it quite clear that the book, though itself entirely *exoteric*, has to allude to things *esoteric* by their nature, things to be spoken or enacted only in a Lodge, but which are never to be revealed in a text. From which one may safely deduce that the idea of a secret text was totally alien to Anderson's understanding of Masonic philosophy. So, for instance, at the beginning of the historical part, after mentioning ". . . the Chaldees and Magi, who preserved the good Science, Geometry," he suddenly cautions the reader, saying that "it is not expedient to speak more plain of the premises, except in a formed Lodge" [p. 5]. And a little further, after describing the ". . . Israelites . . . who were a whole Kingdom of Masons . . . under the conduct of their Grand Master Moses . . ." he concludes: "but no more of the premises must be mention'd!" [p. 8]. Speaking of "the most accomplished Mason", Hiram Abiff, who later on became the central figure of Masonic legend and the focus of the Masonic Ritual, Anderson, while abstaining from even the remotest allusion to Abiff's mystery, remarks, as he passes to the next subject, that he omits "what must not, and indeed cannot be communicated by writing" [pp. 11–13]. And finally, when describing in the Postscript the ritual of constituting a new Lodge, and quoting the words to be spoken by the Grand Master at that ceremony, he speaks of "some other expressions (used by the Grand Master), that are proper and usual on that occasion, but *not proper to be written here*" [p. 71].

REMARKS ON THE ANDERSON CONSTITUTIONS, 1723

In the Approbation appended to the Book of Constitutions we read: ". . . our late and worthy Grand Master . . . the Duke of Montagu . . . order'd the Author to peruse, correct, and digest, into a *new and better*

Method, the History, Charges, and Regulations, of this ancient Fraternity" [p. 73]. "A new method" is the key to our understanding not
only of the Book itself, but also of its author's motivations and intentions.
How do you go about describing the form of your own life here and
now (and Masonry undoubtedly was, and still is, a form of life for very
many people) in terms of that which existed at least six generations
before in an entirely different historical and cultural context? And how
do you describe the immense variety of forms of life of those who live
here and now in terms of one non-historical principle underlying all
of them?

Being a Mason is regarded by Anderson the theologian as the natural
state of man at his Creation by God, the Great Architect of the Universe.
After his fall man becomes a part of history which is, essentially, the
development of that natural quality on the human level. Only once do
we see that natural quality temporarily elevated to the supernatural level
of Divine Perfection, when Solomon's Temple was built, and then only
through Divine intervention which raised the event above the stream
of human history. But the rest of mankind patiently followed the
course of its gradual evolution culminating in the "Augustan Stile", the
acme of which coincided with the final destruction of the Temple. Then
follows a rapid decline in Architecture, precipitated by the conquests
and invasions of the *Goths*, who represent its nadir. The post-Gothic
period sees a slow ascent again towards the heights of a revival of Classical architecture, marked by the names of Andrea Palladio in Italy and
Christopher Wren and Inigo Jones in England.

Thus, the whole of civilization is reduced to the Royal Art of designing
and building; all the sciences to geometry; and the history of Mankind
to the development of architecture and geometry. Yet there is more
than that in Anderson's tale, for being a Mason presupposes a special
kind of social organization that almost always co-exists with human
society, yet at the same time is clearly distinct from it: "Lodge" is the
name of this eternal superstructure, and "Mason" or "Brother" the name
of a "man of distinction", for Masonry is the name of that mythological elite, the existence of which had always guaranteed the perpetuation of civilized societies (his "polite nations"). So that even if there
are Mason-less gaps in the history of mankind or of England, one may
be assured that these gaps are due entirely to the loss of historical
sources, for where there is history, there too must be Masonry; one does
not exist without the other. In his description of the period from the
mid-fifteenth to the late seventeenth centuries, Anderson's idea that
"all Masons are men of distinction" almost imperceptibly gives way to

the idea that "all men of distinction are Masons", coinciding with his increasing use of the word "Lodge" in connection with non-working Masonry. Moreover, the closer he gets to the time of the formation of the Grand Lodge of England, the more it becomes necessary for him to rid those in or around the Grand Lodge of all factors (and facts) of the past which limited the universal scope and character of contemporary Masonry.

Emically speaking, Anderson's history is a continuum; it relates the parallel stories of the two branches of Masonry, working and non-working, and although there is a break of some thirty years from 1688 to 1717, for him there is no difference in quality or type between his narration of the present or immediate past, and the pre-1688 "history". From an etic point of view, however, there is a difference between the chronicling of events more or less contemporary to Anderson and what goes before. Pre-1688 – what I have called the prehistory – is mostly a legend about Masonry's past which served to legitimize its genuine present, at the time of Anderson, and which has subsequently become history proper for us.

What stands between the legend and the history proper is a text – the manuscript or set of manuscripts upon which Anderson's history and *Constitutions* are based. If that text has a credible historical provenance and is not an invention, it is history proper. If, as is probable since the text does not survive in its original form, it was largely invented (if not by Anderson, then by some others around the time of the founding of the Grand Lodge, when the revivalist-cum-creative impulse in Masonry suddenly burst out) then it, or much of it, would coincide with the author of the history's present. In this respect the book, in its references to "the Old Records", is analogous to *Roberts' Constitutions* and suffers from the same complex factors. What it is extremely important to be clear about, though, is that Anderson saw himself as Masonry's first real historian, albeit one placed *within* the chain of events systematically recorded by him for the first time as Masonic history – his new method – utilizing for this purpose certain documents. Nevertheless, subsequent historians of Masonry should not only try to see Anderson as he saw himself within his tradition, but should also take into account the probability that some of the sources for that tradition, and therefore the tradition itself, are not historically valid. So, history in this instance must also include the invention of history. But in separating the history proper from the legend one must not forget that the legend and its inventors have a historical life and value of their own. It is a historical fact of Masonry that almost from the very start it needed to construct its own past, and this meta-historical tendency is as interesting and revealing about Masonry as are the hard facts of its progress through time.

In giving written expression to Masonic universalism Dr Anderson both carried out the wishes of his colleagues and superiors and followed his own personal inclinations, for he was the one man who was able to conceive of that young Society as something whose *raison d'être* and principal strength depended entirely on its being formally independent – not only from the circumstances of the age, but also from those of the previous period. This is not a critique of his *historical* method. I take him for what he was; even if he knew that he had invented his history, he could not have known that his very inventing it had its own objective aspect, an aspect far more interesting to a phenomenologist than to a historian.

After fixing itself (albeit incompletely) historically, constitutionally and in terms of routine and etiquette, and after establishing the practice and manner of its permanent and uninterrupted self-description in Minutes and Records, the Grand Lodge continued its development through the third decade of the eighteenth century. No more than the mere surface of new English Masonry was visible to outsiders, and that surface appears as a series of meetings, processions, marches, dinners, toasts ("let noble Masons Healths go round; their praise in lofty Lodge resound"), proposals, appointments, dresses, badges, jewels ("... Masters and Wardens of Lodges shall never attend the Grand Lodge without their Jewels and Clothing ..." [p. 159]), aprons ... etc. Viewed from outside, all this was mainly a phenomenon of human association with its symbolism not yet described by the participants, and its rituals not yet exposed by their opponents. In the meantime, during the Grand Masterships of the Earl of Dalkeith (who later became the Duke of Buccleuch) and the Duke of Richmond, when the number of Lodges had reached fifty, we have the appearance of anti-Masonic comment from outside in the form of parody and mock-verses, together with the beginning of a more serious internal critique centred on the shortcomings and mistakes of Anderson's *Constitutions* of 1723, and particularly its "historical" aspect. *The Knight*, a satirical poem (1723), mentions Masons in the same breath as the Rosicrucians: "And in the Rosicrucian Trade he knew all has been writ or said ... And many learned things could tell. Of Knots and Charms, and the Night Spell, which made the Devil stand as Warden ... A charm for Masons and for Sclaters.[44] that should be writ in Golden Letters ..." etc.[45] The notorious *Briscoe Pamphlet* (1724, 1725)[46] criticizes Anderson's errors and omissions very severely, and while nothing much is known about its author, he may have some connection with the author of *The Knight* since both refer to Rosicrucianism as sharing a common origin with Masonry: "Brothers of the same Fraternity, or Order, who derived themselves from Hermes Trismegistus." The pamphlet is a kind of pot-pourri whose historical solecisms and licence would far outdo both Anderson's and *Roberts' Constitutions* were it not intended as a kind of parody. When the author "corrects" Anderson, his corrections seem to be no less fantastic than Anderson's Biblical conjectures, even though he reproaches the latter for "falling into great mistakes for want of remembering the Scripture, which they read, or should read, every day". Briscoe's extreme historical naïveté is perhaps best illustrated by his comment that ". . . I am ashamed that our Author has not attempted to prove that either King Solomon, or King Hiram, were once honoured with Worshipful Distinction of the Leathern Apron . . ." The Masonic terminology of the pamphlet, however, is quite modern, for its author speaks of "Grand" and "Particular" Lodges, of "Masters" and "Fellows" as two degrees, etc., which clearly shows that he belonged to the same Masonic milieu as Anderson.

The first of a number of organizational changes took place during the Grand Mastership of Lord Paisley, when it was resolved that the Master of a Particular Lodge, together with his Wardens and the requisite number of Brethren, could create Masters and Fellow Crafts, a power previously confined to the Grand Lodge. And it is probably around that time (*circa* 1725), or a little later, that the first Lodge in Paris was established and the great expansion began. Even more important is the seemingly insignificant development of introducing the Third Degree, that of *Master Mason*, alongside the Master of the Lodge, producing a structure which seems to have been as necessary for the external spread of Masonry "all over the terrestrial globe" as a "history", however legendary, was necessary for its inner ideological consolidation. For it is in the atmosphere of growing tension between the Tories (i.e. past or potential Jacobites) and the Whigs (mainly partisans of the then dominant and mostly Protestant political regime) that English Masonry started on its long road of social neutralism. And, in doing so, it first checked the political opposition by means of a then still incomplete religious neutralism and, secondly, countered any religious differences by means of a universal religious symbolism. This is why the Grand Lodge so easily thwarted the populist attempt of the Duke of Wharton to politicize it, just as it later succeeded in avoiding involvement in the similarly populist anti-Catholic rebellion of Lord George Gordon in 1780.

The establishment in 1725 of the principle of "general charity", and of a fund "for the relief of distress'd Brethren" [p. 178] under Dalkeith was a very significant step in the formation of the whole Masonic Institution as we see it now. From the outset, charity was intended to be not only voluntary but absolutely anonymous, as it remains to this day. What, however, seems to be so typical of Masons even at that time was the way in which the concept of Masonic charity was formulated: ". . . in order to promote the charitable disposition of Free-Masons . . . each Lodge may make a certain collection, according to ability . . . lodged in the hands of a Treasurer . . ." etc. [*idem*]. Thus the foundation was laid and, what is no less important, the future financial structure of the Institution – based on the division and separation of the funds intended for Masonic Institutional purposes from those earmarked for individual human needs – was established.[47]

After Dalkeith, there followed for a while an uninterrupted line of aristocrats as Grand Masters, together with the development of rather grandiose external (that is, outside the walls of a Lodge) ceremonies, and the gradual spread, despite some setbacks, of Lodges within and outside the country. Several events, in particular, should be noted. The first is the restoration of the office of Steward, who was responsible for the preparation of Feasts. Stewards later constituted their own Lodge under Grand Master Lord Coleraine in 1728. The second is the warranting of the first Spanish Lodge in Madrid by the same Grand Master. And the third is the establishment of several Provincial Grand Lodges,[48] Lodges which were entitled by the Grand Lodge of England to warrant newly constituted particular Lodges in foreign countries and in the colonies, the first of which was in Bengal. It is by means of these colonial Lodges that a third link was established in the communication between the Colonies and the Metropolis (the first two being personal and administrative links) which was entirely free from the elements of personal necessity of the first and from the official duty of the second. And that link provided a great deal of amusement for Masons both at home and abroad, as can be clearly seen in the Minutes of the Grand Lodge, assembled in ample Form at The Devil, a public house in Temple Bar, on 13 December 1733:

. . . Brother Thomas Edwards, Esq. . . . acquainted the Grand Lodge, that our Brother Capt. Ralph Farwinter, Provincial Grand Master of East India, had sent from his Lodge at Bengal a chest of the best *arrack* for the consumption of the Grand Lodge of England, and 10 guineas for the Masons' charity . . . [p. 131].[49]

Meanwhile the reputation of Masonry in Britain as well as overseas was augmented by the initiation of the Duke of Lorraine, later the Grand Duke of Tuscany, and also, though merely nominally, the German Emperor. He was "made an Enter'd Prentice and Fellow Craft, by vertue of a deputation for a Lodge there [in the Hague] consisting of Dr Desaguliers ... etc." [p. 129]. Then, as the tale goes on, "... our said Brother Lorraine coming to England this year [1731], Grand Master Lovel formed an occasional Lodge at Sir Robert Walpole's House ... and made Brother Lorraine and Brother Thomas Pelham Duke of Newcastle Master Masons" [idem]. Here two points are of interest. The first is the sending of a deputation from the Grand Lodge to a country where at that time there was not yet a Lodge, and forming it ad hoc, so to speak (i.e., a deputation figuring as a "movable Lodge"). The second is the forming of a Lodge at home after Lord Lovel who, suffering considerably from ague and residing at that time in the house of the first Prime Minister of England, decided to "raise" both Dukes at his residence and not at The Devil, for which purpose the first registered occasional Lodge was formed; that is, a meeting with the required number of Brethren and (at least) one Master – in this case the Grand Master himself. Since that time, any Grand Master or Provincial Grand Master has enjoyed the prerogative of forming an occasional Lodge for the purpose of "making Masons".[50] What is particularly interesting to us in this episode, however, is the fact that both Dukes were made Master Masons without any particular reference to their becoming Masters of two newly-formed or previously non-existent Lodges.

This question should be treated very cautiously, for even now after at least two hundred years of Masonic historiography of which the last hundred is represented by the gigantic work of the main body of Masonic research, the Quatuor Coronati Lodge, we are somewhat uncertain about the beginning and continuation of the Third Degree, that of a Master Mason who is not necessarily the Master of a Lodge. The Master's Degree was first mentioned in about 1725, and even then it remains uncertain whether there was indeed a specific ritual of "raising" or whether it was a kind of promotion or "reward for Masonic merits ... especially for those who had passed the Chair", as Findel maintains.[51] On the other hand, even if that date is correct, there is no evidence whatsoever that the Master Degree was ever given, or "worked", by any particular Lodge before the beginning of the 1730s, and even then very rarely.[52] So the "working" of this degree as a regular practice by the Lodges really started only after Anderson's death in 1739.[53] It is in direct connection with the completion of the system of

Three Degrees that we find one other phenomenon extremely typical of Masonry: the appearance and development of specialized Lodges within the Craft.

The nomenclature of the Grand Lodge, generally the same as in any other Lodge – apart, of course, from the title of Grand Master – consisted primarily of Deputy Grand Master, two Grand Wardens, Senior and Junior, later on Secretary, and later still Grand Secretary – all of whom, from 1720, were appointed by the Grand Master, or the Master, if we speak of a particular Lodge. The Stewards or members of a Lodge responsible for preparing the Annual Feast were mentioned in the earliest records of the Grand Lodge in 1721 and they have from that time been appointed, albeit irregularly, by the Grand Wardens. The honour and privilege of this appointment implied (or was it an "antient custom"?) that they should take upon themselves, wholly or partly, the expenses involved, from which it is not difficult to infer that Stewards were usually rich, or at least richer than their fellow Brethren.[54] In 1727, under Lord Coleraine as Grand Master, the Stewards became a kind of office within the Grand Lodge, and were granted an extraordinary privilege to appoint their successors as well as the Tylers[55] and Attenders at Table. Thereafter they became not only providers and distributors of food and wine, but also social regulators of the Lodge meetings and guardians of the etiquette of the Lodges. In a very short time they became an elite group of Masonic benevolent volunteers, and "On 24 June 1735 . . . it was ordain'd that the Stewards should be constituted a Lodge of Masters . . . which shall have the privilege of sending a Deputation of 12 to every Grand Lodge" [p. 168]. This means that all past and present Stewards of the Grand Lodge (Grand Stewards) as well as being Masters of their respective Lodges and in some cases officers in another capacity of the Grand Lodge, are members of their own special Lodge, the Stewards' Lodge, with its own Master, Wardens, Stewards, etc.

An analogous phenomenon can be seen in the formation of the so-called Master Masons' Lodges, that is, Lodges which consisted solely of Masters, who were at the same time either Masters of other Lodges, previously "made" Masters in the Grand Lodge of England or a Provincial Grand Lodge, or made Masters in the Master's Lodges themselves. While it seems quite probable that the name of Master's Lodge was granted primarily to the very few Lodges which were able to confer the Third Degree, its specific use from 1733 was limited to those highly exclusive assemblies of Masters at which, as W. J. Hughan remarks, ". . . the fees for initiation being so high as to be virtually prohibitive, while for joyning Masters' Lodges the cost was merely nominal".[56]

The Stewards' Lodge and the earliest Masters' Lodges form a spontaneous and tentative start to the whole series of Masonic super-structures, which would soon outgrow the system and nomenclature of the Craft Masonry of the Grand Lodge of England and give way to the proliferation of the so-called Higher Degrees.[57] This will be dealt with later. For the moment I only want to stress that, from the early 1730s, the simple vertical hierarchy of Masonry was diversified, the term "Masonry" became much broader and far more complex than "Craft", and the very word "Mason" gradually acquired a new dimension, hardly reducible to that of a member of the Craft or Fraternity.[58] This phenomenon had far-reaching consequences. For example: an Entered Apprentice, or a Fellow Craft, while he remained at those degrees could not be anything else in the Masonic structure, for his place was hierarchically fixed both positively and negatively: in other words, he was subordinated in his Lodge to the Master or a Warden who, in their turn, were subordinated to the Officers of a Grand Lodge, whereas a Master of a Lodge could be one thing in his Lodge while holding a lesser rank in another Lodge. For instance, a Master Mason could be a Warden in his Lodge and, as such, subordinate to the Master of that Lodge and via this to a Grand Lodge. But this same Master could be the Master of a Master's Lodge, where the Master of his own ordinary Lodge was a mere member and so subordinate to him and so on *ad infinitum*. All this has assumed the form of divergent and parallel hierarchies with their different nomenclatures and, logically as well as historically, has resulted in a social separation between the Masons who played only one role and those with double, triple or greater membership in various Lodges. Later on it also resulted in a certain division and difference between Lodges whose members were members of those Lodges only, and those Lodges with far broader tendencies towards participation in the Masonic life outside a Grand Lodge.

The second consequence of this phenomenon is that from the late 1730s until now there has existed a deep ideological and sometimes religious chasm between the advocates of the Higher Degrees and the partisans of the pure and unequivocal Three Degrees Craft Masonry.[59] It is this difference that can be easily traced in all subsequent schisms, upheavals and secessions which have befallen the Fraternity in the course of the 270 years of its history.

The principle of a unique and unilinear hierarchy introduced and established by Desaguliers, Payne and their friends, and made axiomatic by Anderson, succinctly reflected in itself the pristine and elementary idealized scheme of Christian or indeed any other religious hierarchy.

This scheme appears in practically any social context as soon as a religion becomes conscious of itself. On the other hand, however, it is that very Masonic hierarchical principle which by the nature of its universalism and simplicity provided the ground for the growth, development and proliferation of a motley variety of Christian, quasi-Christian and non-Christian orders. It is the Catholic values of Freemasonry that in Anderson's *Constitutions* are so unambiguously declared in the clause concerning God and Religion, that contained the seeds of a crypto-Catholicism.[60] For, together with what A. E. Waite caustically called "an irreducible minimum" of religion there was, in fact, an equally irreducible minimum of social stratification which allowed for, or even spontaneously generated, the development of multiple and multifarious superstructures with parallel and quite independent hierarchies. Yet the very fact that all those orders have remained true to that "Masonic minimum" laid down by a dissenting teacher of the Kirk of Scotland and a Huguenot, bears witness to the immense strength and vitality of this imperative.[61] Towards the end of the 1720s, however, rumours started circulating about some irregularities in the Lodges and, particularly, about "some irregular assemblies" which were held as if they were regular Lodges in defiance of the Regulations. And it is in connection with those irregularities that Anthony Sayer, previously the first Grand Master of all English Masons, was ordered to appear before the Grand Lodge, assembled at the Devil on 13 September 1730, to be severely reprimanded for taking part in one of these irregular assemblies (or clandestine Lodges).[62] At the same time the indications of growing discontent in some Masonic Lodges are hardly accounted for by the alleged non-Christianity of the Grand Lodge and Anderson's *Constitutions*. There were, probably, not only quite a few individual Masons, but also quite a few Lodges dissatisfied with the absolute authority of the Grand Lodge, particularly in respect of "forming and constituting" new Lodges which had in theory lost all the organizational independence they had enjoyed less than a generation earlier and, in the case of the Four Old Lodges, still continued to enjoy in the 1730s.

The public at large, at the beginning of the 1730s, was already becoming aware of Masonry. There were published Constitutions, several Masonic and anti-Masonic pamphlets, some descriptions of Masonic ceremonies, "external" rituals and formulations, numerous tales of Masonic convivial habits and speeches, and even more numerous hints about their influence, contacts in high places and, particularly, their secret rituals, passwords and signs. The existence of these, however, had never been kept secret by Masons themselves, as I have already emphasized. Moreover, it is clear from the Masonic songs widely performed at that time (some of which were appended by Anderson to his *Constitutions*), that it was their secrets that were their chief pride and joy. Secrets were sung about but not their content; symbols were mentioned but not their meaning. The atmosphere was saturated with so-called information about Freemasonry, but nothing or almost nothing was known of what it really meant. And it is likely that many Masons themselves were not much more informed than non-Masons, for a crystallization of Masonic self-consciousness was still years behind the historic development of the institution itself. The appearance of Prichard's *Masonry Dissected* in 1730 represents the beginning of this crystallization.

This pamphlet, though written by an ex-Mason and blatantly anti-Masonic, marks the initial step in the long history of descriptive literature on Masonic ritualism.[63] It could hardly be denied that in his exposure of the Ritual of the three grades of the Craft he accurately describes what was actually performed in the Regular Lodges at that time, though it leaves the symbolism almost entirely unexplained and the Legend only briefly touched upon.[64] The descriptive part of the pamphlet consists entirely of a series of questions and answers which constitute what is known (in Masonic terminology) as the *Outer Ritual*. This serves as the framework for the all-important *Inner Ritual* which is the preparatory procedure for being made a Mason, and the primary process of actually *being* made one. The candidate may have already learned by heart the script reproduced by Prichard, but he will not yet fully understand what it means, nor will he know the accompanying complex sequence of actions, gestures and so forth. It is this instruction and guidance, given within the Lodge by the Master and others participating in the "making", which combines with the bare script of the Outer Ritual to transform it into a living reality of the initiation rite. So, strictly speaking, there are not two separate rituals, but a single one with two complementary aspects – one static and exoteric: a fixed written script which may be detached from its ritual context and published together with any interpretations; and one dynamic and esoteric: the ritual use of this script.

This goes some way towards explaining the initially baffling format of the dialogues which make up the Outer Ritual. The first question: "How shall I know that you *are* a Mason?" seems quite illogical to the outsider since it appears to assume that the initiate has already *become* that which he is supposed to be being made. This makes more sense if it is understood that although chronologically simultaneous with most of the Inner Ritual, the latter is ritually more significant in terms of its Mason-making powers. This entails a law of ritual division of labour. Even more light is shed when it is recognized that both the script and the fully integrated ritual are given the formula of repetitions, or re-enactments of a previous event, alluded to in the script. In the case of the *Enter'd Prentice* and the *Fellow Craft* it is their initiation as working Masons in their fictional past; and in the case of a Master Mason, it is his legendary participation in the discovery of the body of Master Builder Hiram. Two levels of reality are, in fact, in operation here: the actual present-day reality of the initiation of a non-working Mason, and the reality of his mythical past initiation as a working Mason which this present-day ritual mirrors. The Entered Apprentice and the Fellow Craft become that which they already are (Masons) in the same way that in the Master Mason' Ritual the Master becomes that which he already is (the Master Builder Hiram).

In what follows, I have summarized the essential elements of the Outer Rituals of the Three Degrees for the sake of brevity, adding some explanatory comments of my own in the right-hand column and, in square brackets, in the main text. All specific terminological words are indicated, and remarks in round brackets are theirs.

The Enter'd 'Prentice's Part

Q. How shall I know that you are a Mason?
A. By *signs* and *tokens*, and Perfect Points of my Entrance.

The questions and responses here preserve the fiction that the candidate has already been initiated as a working Mason through a previous parallel ritual, which is why he knows the dialogue by heart!

Q. What are signs?
A. All *Squares, Angles* and *Perpendiculars.*

Q. What are tokens?
A. Certain Regular and Brotherly *Gripes.*

Q. Where were you made a Mason?
A. In a *Just and Perfect Lodge.*

The fact of his being remade now as a speculative Mason underlines the conventional character of the Outer Ritual.

Q. What makes a Just and Perfect Lodge?
A. Seven or more.

Q. What makes a Lodge?
A. Five.[65]

Q. Who brought you to the Lodge?
A. An Enter'd 'Prentice.

Q. How did he bring you?

Here follows a description of the Ritual of Admission of the candidate in a working Lodge in his past as an operative Mason.

A. Neither naked nor clothed, bare-foot nor shod, deprived of all metal, and in a right moving posture (I).

This ritual consists of four elements (here numbered I–IV).

Q. How got you Admittance?
A. By three great Knocks (II).

Q. Who received you?
A. A Junior Warden . . . who carried me up to the North-East part of the Lodge, and brought me back again to the West and deliver'd me to the Senior Warden (III), who . . . shew'd me how to walk up (by three steps) to the Master (IV).

Q. What did the Master do with you?
A. He made me a Mason . . . with my bare-bended knee and Body within the *Square*, the *Compass* extended to my naked left breast, my naked right hand on the Holy Bible; there I took *the Oath of a Mason* . . . which is as follows: I thereby solemnly vow and swear in the presence of Almighty God and this Right Worshipful Assembly, that I hail and conceal, and never reveal the *Secrets* . . . that I will never *write* them, *print* them or cause them to be written . . . etc. All this under no less penalty than to *have my throat cut, my tongue taken from the roof of my mouth, my breast pluck'd from under my left shoulder.*

This is a reference to the core of the Ritual of Initiation, *the focus of the whole Inner Ritual of making a Mason.*

This serves as a reminder of the symbolic nature of secrets, secrecy and the oath as legends in themselves, since here they are being written for public consumption.

Q. What form is the Lodge?
A. A Long Square . . . from North to South . . . as high as . . . the Heavens.

This is an explanation of the Lodge as a Temple in its cosmic aspect, i.e. as the world where the Rituals are performed.

Q. Where does the Lodge stand?
A. Upon Holy Ground, or the highest Hill, or Lowest Vale of Jehosaphat, or any other secret place. It is situated . . . due East and West . . . as all Churches are . . . It is supported by three great *Pillars* . . . called Wisdom, Strength, and Beauty . . .

Q. What *covering* have you to the Lodge?
A. A clouded *Canopy* of divers colours (clouds).

This is an explanation of the macrocosmic aspect of the Lodge, i.e. as the concrete place where the Ritual is performed.

Q. What is your Lodge's *Furniture?*

A. *A Mosaic* Pavement [i.e., the floor of the Lodge], *Blazing Star* [its Centre], and *Indented Trasel* [the border round about it] . . .

Q. What is *the other furniture* of a Lodge?
A. Bible . . . to God, Compass . . . to the Master, and Square . . . to the Fellow-Craft.

Q. What are . . . the *Jewels* in the Lodge?
A. There are six Jewels. Three *Movable* (*Square* to lay down True and Right Lines, *Level* to try all horizontals, and the *Plumb Rule* to try all uprights), and three *Immovable* (Trasel Board for the Master to draw his designs upon, *Rough* Ashler for the Fellow Craft to try their Jewels upon, and the *Broach'd Thurnel* for the Enter'd 'Prentice to learn to work upon . . .)

This is an explanation of the microcosmic aspect of the Lodge – with a description of the things which are within the place where the Ritual is performed.

Q. Have you any *Lights* [i.e. the large candles placed on high candlesticks] in your Lodge?
A. . . . There are three Lights: Sun, Moon and Master Mason; sun to rule the day, moon the night, and Master-Mason the Lodge.

Q. Where stand . . . your Master, Wardens, the Senior Enter'd 'Prentice, and the Junior Prentice . . . ?
A. The Master stands in the East . . . for as the Sun rises in the East and opens the day, so the Master stands in the East (with his right hand upon his left breast being a *sign*, and the Square about his neck) to open the Lodge and to set his men at work. The Wardens stand in the West . . . for as the Sun sets in the West to close the day, so the Wardens stand in the West (with their right hand upon their left breast being a *sign*, and the Level and Plumb-Rule about their necks) to close the Lodge and dismiss the Men from Labour, paying their wages. The Senior Enter'd 'Prentice stands in the South . . . to hear and receive instructions and welcome

This deals with the symbolic topography of the Lodge.

strange Brothers. The Junior Enter'd 'Prentice stands in the North to keep off all *Cowans*[66] and Eaves-droppers . . . And if . . . a Cowan (or Listener) is catch'd . . . he is to be plac'd under the eaves of the Houses (in rainy Weather) till the Water runs in at his Shoulders and out at his shoes.

Q. What are the *Secrets* of a Mason?
A. Signs, Tokens and many *Words.* Those Secrets I keep under my left breast . . . the *Key* to those Secrets I keep . . . *in a Bone Box* that neither opens nor shuts but with *Ivory keys* . . . That Key . . . hangs by a *Tow-Line* . . . and is made of . . . no metal at all. The key is but a Tongue of good report . . . the Bone Box is the teeth, and the Tow-Line is the roof of the mouth.

Secrets are classified here on the basis of their form and the mechanism of their concealing or revealing.

Q. How many Principles are there in Masonry?
A. Four: *Point* (which is the Centre round which the Master cannot err), *Line* (which is length without breadth), *Superficies* (length and breadth), and *solid* (which comprehends the whole).

The ensuing dialogue reveals what the principles (= signs) refer to, and the parts of the body to which they correspond.

Q. How many *Principle-signs?*
A. Four: *Guttural* the throat, *Pectoral* the breast, *Manual* the hands, *Pedestal* the Feet.

Q. What do you learn by being a *Gentleman-Mason?*
A. Secrecy, Morality and Good fellowship.

Q. What do you learn by being an *Operative-Mason?*
A. Hue, Square, Mould-stone, lay a Level and raise a Perpendicular.

Q. How was your Master clothed today?
A. In a Yellow Jacket (the Compasses), and Blue Pair of Breeches (the Steel Points).

Q. How do you serve your Master?
A. With *Chalk* (Freedom), *Charcoal* (Fervency), and *Earthly Pan* (Zeal).

83

Q. Give me the *Enter'd 'Prentice's Sign.*
A. Extending the four fingers of the right hand and drawing of them cross his throat, is the *Sign*, and demands a *Token*. (A Token is by joyning the Ball of the thumb of the right hand upon the first knuckle of the fore-finger of the Brother's right hand that demands a *Word*.)

Finally, there is a description of the one Sign, one Token, and two Words particular to the Enter'd 'Prentice.

Q. Give me the Words.
A. I'll letter it with you.
[At this point they proceed to spell out the names, first of BOAZ, then of JACHIN, two Pillars of Solomon's Porch . . .].

The Fellow-Craft's Part

Q. Are you a Fellow-Craft?
A. I am.

Q. Why was you made a Fellow-Craft?
A. For the sake of the letter G. [i.e., Geometry.]

Q. Did you ever work?
A. Yes, in the Buildings of the Temple.

Q. Where did you receive your wages?
A. In the Middle Chamber.

Q. How came you to the Middle Chamber?
A. Through the Porch.

Q. When you came through the Porch, what did you see?
A. The Great Pillars . . . J. B. [i.e. Jachin and Boaz . . . etc.]

As in the previous case the Outer Ritual begins after the Inner Ritual has already been completed. The whole symbolism of the Ritual is centred on the Temple of Solomon or, more precisely, on the Lodge which represents the Temple. Two Great Pillars in the Porch, Jachin (on the right of the entrance) and Boaz (on the left), represent the divine Wisdom that has not yet been acquired by the candidate, though their names had already been given to him in the first part as mere Words.

Q. When you came to the door of the Middle Chamber, who did you see?
A. A Warden.

Q. What did he demand of you?
A. Three things: the *Sign* [i.e. placing the right hand on the left breast], *the Token* (i.e. by joyning your right hand to the person that demands it, and squeezing him with the ball of your thumb on the first knuckle of the Middle Finger), and the *Word* (i.e. Jachin).

Q. When you came into the middle (of the Chamber), what did you see?
A. The resemblance of the Letter G.

Q. Who doth that *G.* denote?
A. One that is greater than you ... the Grand Architect and Contriver of the Universe, or He that was taken up to the top of the Pinnacle of the Holy Temple.

G. here is a visual symbol of God in the Temple (i.e. Lodge), the full meaning of which the candidate does not yet know, though he knows whom it denotes.

Q. Can you repeat the letter G.?
A. I'll do my endeavour (he repeats).

Q. I'll change your Name from Friend, and henceforth call you Brother.

The Master's Part

Q. Are you a Master Mason?
A. I am; try me, prove me, disprove me if you can.

Q. Where were you pass'd Master?
A. In a Perfect Lodge of Masters.

This is an explanation of the emblematic inventory of Masonic Mastership. The Master recalls his previous degrees by Words corresponding to those degrees.

Q. What makes a Perfect Lodge of Masters?
A. Three.[67]

Q. How came you to be pass'd Master?
A. By the help of God, the Square and my own industry.

Q. How were you pass'd Master?
A. From the Square to the Compass.[68]

Q. An Enter'd 'Prentice I presume you have been ...
A. Jachin and Boaz I have been. A Master-Mason I was made most rare, with *Diamond, Ashler* and the *Square.*

Q. If a Master-Mason you would be, you must rightly understand the *Rule of Three.*[69] And M.B. [i.e. *Machbenah*] shall make you free ...
A. Good Masonry I understand; the Keys of all Lodges are all at my command.

Q. You are a heroic fellow; from whence came you?
A. From the East.

Q. Where are you a-going?
A. To the West . . . to seek for that which was lost and is now found . . . the Master-Mason's Word.

In order to become a Master in the legendary past, as now, one must obtain the Word.

Q. How was it lost?
A. By three great knocks, or the death of our Master Hiram . . . In the building of *Solomon's* Temple he was Master-Mason, and at high 12 at noon, when the men were gone to refresh themselves . . . he came to survey the Works, and when he was enter'd into the Temple, there were three ruffians suppos'd to be three Fellow-Crafts; planted themselves at the Three Entrances of the Temple, and when he came out, one demanded the Master's Word of him, and he reply'd he did not receive it in such a manner, but time and . . . patience would bring him to it; He, not satisfied with the answer, gave him a blow, which made him reel; he went to the other Gate, where being accosted in the same manner and making the same reply, he received a greater blow, and at the third his Quietus . . . The ruffians killed him . . . with a *Setting Maul, Setting Tool,* and *Setting Beadle* . . . Then they carried him out at the West Door . . . and hid him under some rubbish till high 12 again. Then, at night, whilst the men were at rest . . . they carried him up to the brow of the hill, where they made a decent grave and buried him . . .

To every Mason now who has not yet become a Master, this Word is lost as Hiram's original Word was lost on his death. Hiram was the only Master in the Lodge (i.e. the Temple) who knew it.

So, instead of becoming Masters they killed the Master, for they did not know that he was the Word. And so the Word was lost.

This was the first burial. The West was the side of the dead in Western Semitic tradition.

This was the second burial.

Q. When was he found?
A. Fifteen days afterwards. Fifteen loving Brothers, by order of King Solomon, went out of the West Door of the Temple, and divided themselves from right to left within call of each other; and they agreed that if they did not find the Word on him or about him the first word [uttered by a Brother on finding the body] should be the Master's Word; one of the Brothers being more weary than the others, sat down . . . and taking hold of a shrub, which came easily up,

They started their search for the Master's word while searching for his body.

The weary one was nearer to the dead than the others.

and perceiving the ground being broken, he hail'd his Brethren, and pursuing their search they found him ... buried in a grave ... 6 foot East 6 West, and 6 perpendicular and his covering was green Moss and turf ... and they said *Muscus Domus Dei* GRATIA, which is "Thanks be to God, our Master got a Mossy House". So they covered him closely ... and placed a sprig of *Cassia* at the head of his grave, and went and acquainted King Solomon and King Solomon order'd him to be taken up and decently buried, and that 15 Fellow Crafts with white gloves and aprons should attend his funeral (which ought amongst Masons to be perform'd to this day).

When they found him the first word uttered was MACHBENAH *– which may or may not coincide with the original Word of Hiram.*

Cassia (or acacia) meaning "innocent" was his emblematic name.

This was the third burial.

Q. How was Hiram raised?
A. As all other Masons are, when they receive the Master's Word, i.e. by the *Five Points of Fellowship*: Hand to hand; Foot to foot; Cheek to cheek; Knee to knee; and Hand in Back. (That is, when Hiram was taken up, they took him by the fore-fingers. And the skin came off, which is called *the Slip*; the spreading the right hand and placing the middle finger to the wrist, clasping the fore-finger and the fourth to the sides of the wrist, is called the *Gripe*, and the *Sign* is placing the thumb of the right hand to the left breast, extending the fingers.)

These are names of the five stages of the Ritual. Its climax is an enactment of the "raising" of Hiram from the place of his second burial.

Q. What's a Master-Mason nam'd?
A. Cassia is my name, and from a Just and Perfect Lodge I came.

Q. Where was Hiram inter'd?
A. In the Sanctum Sanctorum ... he was brought in at the West-Door of the Temple ...

Q. Give me the Master's Word.
A. (Supported by the Five Points of Fellowship the Candidate whispers "MACHBENAH" into the Master's ear, which signifies: *The Builder is smitten*.)[70]

Again the conferment of the Master's Word is a duplication of the uttering of the first word by one of the fifteen Fellow Crafts – there were no Master Masons apart from Hiram at that time.

A few remarks on the Ritual as described in Prichard's pamphlet
Masonry Dissected.

Most non-Masonic historians have either stressed the extremely eclectic
and contrived character of the Masonic Rituals, or simply denied that the
Old Testament references have any real connection with Christianity. As
for Masonic historians, the majority somewhat contradictorily regard
the rituals of Freemasonry as on the one hand unique, and certainly
not derived from any pre-Gospel Christian roots, and on the other as
having nonetheless a common origin with other Near Eastern and Egyptian hermetic traditions.

My approach to this question is quite different, for I am absolutely
sure that if something works as a ritual, a ritual it is, irrespective of how
many different separate rituals or entire ritual traditions might have
been used in the process of its spontaneous development or, often
enough, its conscious and deliberate creation. Each and every ritual
may be regarded from at least two points of view. The first is the position
of the observer who sees it in its functional totality, when the only thing
that matters is how and for what purpose it exists and is used. Whether
it was introduced five minutes or five millennia ago, or whether it is
homogeneous or heterogeneous in its origins and composition is irrelevant in this case, for this position sees any ritual holistically as an *ethos*.
In other words, it exists *sui generis* and represents a unity of action,
however complex the components might be. The second point of view
is of a scholar who not only knows about an immense variety of rituals,
past and present, which are elements of the world's religions, but also,
and probably first of all, sees in that variety several universal and elementary paradigms or invariants to which this whole diversity can be reduced
as variants or versions. Moreover, this approach presupposes that what
we call a ritual is always complex and has its own history, being syn-
chronically structural and diachronically subject to change and
transformation.

As an ethos, the Master Mason's Ritual is a ritual of obtaining the
Word through contact with the dead, in this case through an initiate
enacting the procedure of raising the dead body of Hiram (for only
Hiram both knew and *was* the Word), even though the Word he knew,
and he himself, was lost on his death. The Fellow Crafts who found
the body of Hiram obtained a Word which became, in the context of the
Ritual, *the* Word, and obtained it spontaneously through physical contact
with his corpse. The exact meaning of the word is, therefore, quite
irrelevant (it varies from "the builder is smitten" in Prichard's text to

"it stinks" in a recently found Masonic MS), because the word itself is absolute, is a symbolic word that denotes the one-ness of the Word and its dead Possessor.[71] The necromantic character of the Ritual is as obvious as is the Gnostic character of the Word. The latter is not a magical word; it does not, in itself, transform one thing into another, nor does it give one the power to become another, nor even does it give one the right to be or become a Master, but it is Gnostical in the sense that it concentrates in itself that knowledge which may or may not be understood by someone who has it, or may be understood by him in one way or another, but without which he simply cannot know anything (including himself as a Master). Words, in Gnosticism, figure, amongst other things, as the means of self-recognition. This unity of the Ritual and the Word derives from the Hiramic Legend itself, in the fact of the simultaneousness of the raising of Hiram's body and the uttering of the Word. So the only power conferred by the Word obtained in this way is the Gnostical power of actually *being* Hiram and thereby attaining knowledge of oneself and who one is.

From the point of view of an analytical observer, the picture of the ritual is quite different. The murder of Hiram and his first burial is perceived diachronically, or historically, as an instance of the archetypal and, in comparative mythology, almost ubiquitous ritual of human sacrifice performed at the foundation of a temple. Of particular interest here is the combination of two versions of this rite, both of which were very widely spread in the ancient Near Eastern and Mediterranean regions: the sacrifice of an innocent child and of a master builder, or architect, who represent the *Knower* (see Chapter 12). The search for the Word is directed towards the West, the direction of death and the land of the dead, which has its own Near Eastern and Mediterranean mythological origins. The topography of the Lodge as the Temple is West-oriented. The reversed character of the Ritual can be seen in the exhumation and reinterment of the corpse, due to which the Ritual actually became necromantic. The whole process of reversal can be conjecturally presented in the following way:

1. In the sacrifice of the child or the builder, the killing was ritually necessary and positive – it was intended for the public good. In the Masonic case the murder of Master Builder Hiram was ritually necessary and negative – it was perpetrated with selfish intention, although the outcome was good.
2. In the ancient archetypal ritual, the victim's body is put into the foundations never to be exhumed. In the Masonic Ritual it is

interred to the West of the building, to be exhumed in fifteen days.

3. In some other mythologies (ancient Indian, Medieval Jewish and Siberian Shamanist, for example), the Word is used by those who have obtained it to manipulate the corpse and exploit its power. In the Masonic Ritual the Word has no magical function and does not confer any power over the dead.

The notion of the Word came into Masonic ritual from a Gnostic, or Cabalistic tradition, and as such had had nothing to do, directly, with human sacrifice. Moreover, from the very beginning of the official Masonic tradition it has remained a kind of essential riddle, about which a Mason was condemned to speculate indefinitely – was it or was it not the original Word of Hiram? But at the time of the composition of the Ritual's text, its three chief elements – human sacrifice, exhumation and reinterment, and the Gnostical concept of the Word – had, of course, long since ceased to be in ritual use either separately or together. They did not even form the content of a myth associated with any living ritual in any culture of which the creators might have been aware. Their combination in a Masonic context is an extraordinary phenomenon, for nowhere else in recent times can such a "new" ritual be found, however ancient its roots.

The ritual to which Prichard's catechism refers – no matter whether it was taken from the actual practice of the then existing speculative Lodges, or from a MS of some working Lodge – does indeed seem to be confined entirely to the macrocosm of a Lodge. And if we take this ritual as a unity, as one ethos, no parallels or similarities with any other rituals taken from other religions would enable us to draw any conclusions about its own religious context or origin, for, as such, it has none. In order to connect the Ritual with a given religion we would have to leave its macrocosmic space and step outside the Lodge where it is performed. Then we may go back in time, following the Hiramic Legend which is directly, though by no means fully and in detail, associated with the Old Testament. Or we may consider the synchronic existence of the religious elements within the space of the Lodge, but without making any specific connection with the Ritual, taking, for example, the Christian Bible that serves as the prerequisite for any activity in a Lodge, or even the use of the term "the Great Architect of the Universe", God Almighty, who, while retaining his biblical associations, does not have any specific religious meaning. All these things are combined within the Ritual but do not affect its religious neutrality, for the Ritual has a mystical meaning of its own – contact with the dead body for obtaining the dead man's Word.[72]

The whole Hiramic Legend is not enacted in the Outer Ritual; the first part, the story of how Hiram came to die, remains in its spoken (or written) form, and the ritual action, as we have seen, starts with the search for the Lost Word – that is, for the lost body of the Master – continues with the discovery of the corpse, and culminates in its raising and the recovery of the Word.[73]

The critical parts of Prichard's Pamphlet are in sharp contrast with the quite serious exposition of the Ritual. After the author's ironic Dedication to the "Rt Worshipful and Honourable Fraternity", and a parody on the "Legendary History of the Craft", he directly accuses the Society of "imposition and fraudulence": ". . . But if after the Admission into the Secrets of Masonry, any new Brother should dislike their proceedings and reflect upon himself for being so easily cajoled out of his money . . ." etc. In the Author's Vindication, he warns the reader: "I was induced to publish this mighty Secret for the publick Good, at the Request of several Masons . . . and it will, I hope . . . have its desired effect in preventing so many credulous persons being drawn into so pernicious a society." There is, however, one phrase in the Vindication which, even if it was intended to be a joke, reveals the author's understanding of the Masonic situation in the late 1720s, if not his talent for premonition. He says: ". . . the old fabrick (of Masonry) being so ruinous, that, unless repair'd by some occult Mystery, will soon be annihilated" [p. 30]. Did he, indeed, foresee the appearance and rise of the Christian and mystical orders in Masonry? That we cannot know, but his references to these several dissident Masons may well be accounted for by the growing dissatisfaction, of both a religious and an ideological character, among the Masons living "within the Bills of Mortality".[74]

Prichard's Pamphlet proves that by the late 1720s, or even earlier, a special Masonic language was already partly formed; not the archaic or artificially archaised language of the purported Old Manuscripts but the everyday speech of the beginning of the eighteenth century adapted to the task of Masonic self-description. He seems to have reproduced in writing what was actually orally performed and which could hardly have been directly inherited or borrowed from the oral performance of the older Lodges of working Masons. This Masonic language, however, was at that time still incomplete, for while it possessed the linguistic ambiguity of figurative speech, it was not yet embedded in a fully developed religious situation. It is not enough simply to have the symbolic or emblematic meanings which generate ambiguity; it is not

91

enough to have, as can be seen in the "Prentice's Part", "Light", which is also "Candle", which is also "Master Mason", etc. The language must be part of a context that is also ambiguous because a religious situation within Masonry, in order to become the object of Masonic awareness, should not only be able to describe itself in terms of a symbolic language whose words are multivalent, but should also become symbolic itself. It should be polarized to such an extent that each of its elements taken separately as well as together admit at least two different meanings. The description of the Ritual made by Prichard provided Masonry with only one pole of that symbolic duality: the dry scheme of the Ritual with its "irreducible minimum" of ethical meaning. The external and ideological description of this aspect had already been made by Anderson's *Constitutions* of 1723. The other aspect, which one may call "mystical symbolism", had to wait for another decade or two for its description. The success of the Pamphlet exceeded all possible expectations. Within a couple of months several thousand copies were sold (there were rumours that most of them were bought by Masons). As an unintended side effect it enabled Masons to speak freely of the Ritual, which had hitherto lacked a fixed written form, and the Pamphlet has since that time served as the pattern and model for all subsequent anti-Masonic expositions as well as a number of pro-Masonic ones.

Notes

1 All references are made to the edition: *The New Book of Constitutions of the Antient and Honourable Fraternity of free and Accepted Masons* . . . For the Use of the Lodges, by James Anderson, D.D., London, 1738 (*Anderson's Constitutions*, 1738). The references to pages of this edition will be given in square brackets. As for the *Constitutions* of 1723, all references are made to the pages of the facsimile edition: *The Constitution Book of 1723*, with an Introduction by L. Vibert, London, 1923 [*Anderson's Constitutions*, 1723 (1923)]. One other edition of the latter is: *The Constitution Book of 1723*, ed. by the Revd F. A. Woodford in *Kennings Masonic Archaeological Library*, Vol. I, London, 1878 [*Anderson's Constitutions*, 1723 (1878)].

2 W. Preston, 1804 (1777), p. 209. Anderson uses the technical terms introduced (partly, perhaps, by himself) much later. So for instance, "in due Form" meant "in the absence of the Grand Master" – but whether or not there was a Grand Master at that time remains unclear.

3 *Idem*, p. 210.

4 G. Oliver, 1855, p. 6. Also see *The Constitution of Free-Masonry, or Ahiman Rezon* . . . revised, corrected, and improved with additions from the original of the late Lawrence Dermott, Esq. by Thomas Harper, London, 1801 (*Ahiman Rezon*, 1801), pp. xxx–xxxi.

5 R. F. Gould, 1903, p. 283; Findel, 1865, pp. 135–38.

6 See in Hughan, 1909, p. 40; *Ahiman Rezon*, 1801, p. xxxi.

7 However, Dermott is referring to the first two meetings of the Grand Lodge mentioned above. The first records were made only in 1722, and the real substitution, or invention, or who knows (we should not be prejudiced), the truth too, could have been written no earlier than in the first edition of Anderson's *Constitutions*, in 1723. As to what Dermott calls "recollection", this will be dealt with later.

8 I deliberately use the word "culture" here, for the very *character* of the symbolism of Masonry is that of culture, not of nature, life or consciousness, though it may refer to any or all of them. By culture I mean our perception of the social, ethical and aesthetic values that we have inherited.

9 It is interesting to note here that no Lodge of working Masons has ever been incorporated by Act of Parliament as all the Guilds were. The London Company of Freemasons, which incorporated, was never a Lodge. Further, we will see how the attempts of the Grand Lodge to achieve incorporation fell through.

10 Important documentary evidence of this lies in the *Diary of Elias Ashmole* published in 1717. See p. 157 note 5.

11 "... In the early days when Grand Lodge had no headquarters of its own, and no full-time officials ... we doubt if there were as yet any brethren who could be described as *unofficial leaders* of the Fraternity." D. Knoop and G. P. Jones, *The Genesis of Freemasonry*, Manchester, 1947, p. 176.

12 Even Dr Anderson himself, one may suppose, during all his life would hardly have attended more than, say, twenty Masonic meetings of any kind, including seven or eight Grand Lodges.

13 According to Waite (1925, p. 2), the word "Gothic", as it was used in Anderson's *Constitutions* of 1738, meant "... antiquated, uncouth and hence in need of revision".

14 A. E. Waite, 1925, p. 25

15 Though, as L. Vibert remarks, "Anderson seems to have been constitutionally incapable of copying even his own text correctly" [*Anderson's Constitutions*, 1723 (1923), pp. xl–xli.

16 "Yet tell me please, doesn't history itself begin only when something or somebody is mentioned at least twice," said Dr Valdemar Lovin. "What I mean" he continued, "is that, in order to become history, something said or seen by one person should be referred to by another as the person who said this or did that; and then, finally, there must be a third person to comment on what has been said or written by the second about the first." (That he was the last Russian Mason to be initiated before the revolution, he told me at our second meeting in 1967. Even now I cannot tell who was the first Russian Mason, though there was an old Masonic legend that Peter the Great was initiated into Masonry in Deptford during his first visit to England in 1698 or, at any rate, in 1718. See A. N. Pypin, *A History of Russian Masonry*, Petrograd, 1916, pp. 88, 498, 550.). Isn't there something far more mysterious in the *transition* from the "non-historical" to the "historical" than in the enigma of a sheer legend?

17 J. G. Findel, 1869, p. 144. The number of Lodges existing in London at that time was probably sixteen or seventeen.

18 A. E. Waite, pp. 1. 277–8; E.M.P., p. 196.

19 A. E. Waite, pp. 1. 277–8; E.M.P., p. 196.

20 W. Preston, 1804, p. 223. "It is unlikely that he became a Mason . . . prior to 1721." See in Albert F. Calvert, *The Grand Lodge of England*, London, 1917, p. 33.

21 J. G. Findel, 1869, p. 145; W. Preston, 1804, pp. 222–3; F. L. Pick and G. Norman Knight, 1983 (1954), p. 75. This communication (i.e., meeting) was the first in Masonic history where Brothers were "entertained by the *lectures* on Masonic subjects".

22 Its full title is: *The Old Constitutions* belonging to the Ancient and Honourable Society of Free and Accepted Masons, taken from a manuscript wrote above Five Hundred Years Since; Printed and sold by J. Roberts, London, 1772. See in A. E. Waite, 1925, pp. 7–8.

23 Which, according to Waite (*idem*, p. 7), "is not less than incredible". L. Vibert writes in his introduction to *Anderson's Constitutions*, 1723 (1923): ". . . Ever since Sept., 1721, it had been known that Anderson was at work on a new history of the Order . . . and it is easy to understand that the admirers of the *Traditional History*, as it stood in the *Old* Charges, would be likely to take alarm at such *modernizings*. This may be the Genesis of the Roberts Pamphlet . . ." (p. L).

24 *Idem*, pp. 7; 8–9. Are we not, indeed, at the beginning of the first Masonic controversy which, though not yet revealed to those outside the Society, became recognized (and shaped) by some of its members? The two parties, however, had not yet identified one another as inimical.

25 What follows is a slightly abbreviated text of *The Old Constitutions*, as published in E.M.P., pp. 75–83.

26 "It is said that the name *Noachidae* was applied by the ancient Hebrews to members of other nations who practised the great principles of religion and morality without accepting Jewish doctrine and ceremony . . . The three Great Articles of Noah are abstinence from blood, the prohibition of murder, and the recognition of the civil authority." E. L. Hawkins, *A Concise Cyclopaedia of Freemasonry*, London, 1908 (E. L. Hawkins, 1908), pp. 164–5.

27 How serious these claims were, and how serious was their critique, can be seen in a lot of contemporary and previously published sources, and about that I shall talk further on. One thing, however, ought to be emphasized here: almost from the very beginning of the Masonic historical tradition the confusion between historicity of a fact and historicity of a legend has overlapped the confusion between historicity of the content of a Manuscript and historicity of a manuscript itself. Dr R. Plot writes in 1686 in his *Natural History of Staffordshire* (E.M.P. pp. 31–4) about the History and Charges of Freemasons: ". . . here I found persons of the most eminent quality, that did not disdain to be of this Fellowship. Nor indeed need they, were it of that *Antiquity* and *honor*, that is pretended in a large *parchment volume* they have amongst them, containing the *History* and *Rules* of the craft of masonry. . . . One of their Articles . . . is that if any man appear though altogether unknown that can shew any of secret (Masonic) *signes* to a *Fellow* of the Society, whom they otherwise call an *accepted mason*, he is obliged presently to assist him . . . or to find some work for him . . . And many suchlike (*Articles*) that are *commonly known*; but some others they have (to which they are *sworn* after their fascion) that none know but themselves, which I have reason to suspect are much worse than these, *perhaps as bad as this history of the craft itself; than which there is nothing I ever met with, more false or incoherent*."

28 This, by the way, is one of the recurrent themes of old Masonic mysticism, though at the time when the book itself was written Freemasonry had not yet reached France. For example, when Count St Germain was asked in the 1770s if he had ever been a Freemason, he claimed that "it was likely enough, but it would be long ago, and he had forgotten". See in A. E. Waite, 1925, p. 297.

29 E.M.P., pp. 43–45.

30 R. F. Gould, 1903, p. 286. Gould ignores here the chronologically prior *Old Constitutions* which pipped Anderson's to the post in 1722.

31 *Idem*, p. 289. "Lodge No. 4 (originally ... at the Rummer and Grapes, and subsequently at The Horn Tavern, Westminster) was undoubtedly the aristocratic Lodge in 1723, when the Duke of Richmond was its Master." D. Knoop and G. P. Jones, 1947, p. 198. Some elements of the aristocracy were notably progressive at that time.

32 W. Preston, 1804, p. 223; A. Calvert, 1917, pp. 61–2.

33 L. Vibert is very sceptical of Anderson's account of this event. He writes in his introduction to *Anderson's Constitutions 1723* (1923): "... the first recorded Minute of G.L. ... placed on record that at the Festival of June, 1723, Anderson officiated for Mr William Hawkins, the Grand Warden. So also the contemporary press notices shew us that Wharton was elected in the ordinary course, indeed one account says unanimously, by G.L. on 25th June, 1722 ... but in the Constitutions of 1738 ... Anderson put forward an entirely different version ..."

34 "Wharton had thrown in his lot with the lower class of Masons ..." H. Sadler, *Masonic Facts and Fictions*, London, 1887, p. 25.

35 A. Calvert, 1917, p. 69. A. E. Waite (1925, p. 117) writes that the Duke "might only tend to ... disgrace any cause that he espoused."

36 He was the subject of a satiric poem by Alexander Pope and, "most probably, the original of Lovelace in Richardson's *Clarissa*, and in any case proved an unsatisfactory Freemason." F. L. Pick and G. Norman Knight, 1983, p. 75.

37 A. Calvert, 1917, p. 64.

38 *Cowan*: one who does the work of a Mason but has not been apprenticed in the trade according to an earlier definition (see note 66) [1598].

39 Anderson's cosmopolitanism and his Masonic universalism certainly could not be seen as reflecting the situation in London or in England, at that time, let alone the situation in the Masonic Lodges. He strove hard to shape the concrete Masonic material to hand to his (and some other Masons') historical idea.

40 "My Lord, ... I need not tell your Grace what pains our learned Author has taken in compiling and digesting this Book from the Old Records ..." *Anderson's Constitutions 1723* (1923), p. 1.

41 But even those were re-worked in a new context. *Idem*, p. xlviii. Further, Anderson himself writes: "... the *author* of this book has compared them [i.e. Payne's Regulations] with, and reduc'd them to the ancient *Records* and immemorial usages of the Fraternity, and digested them into this new method ..." (p. 58). Later on he remonstrated with the Grand Lodge that *his* book had been republished without his name and permission, forgetting that he had not named himself as author in the first edition.

42 All the references in brackets are made to *Anderson's Constitutions of 1723* (1923).

43 Though, of course, for Anderson, the 1717 founding of the Grand Lodge

was not *ex nihilo* but simply a restitution of the tradition of Grand Lodges which had fallen into destitution.

44 *sclaters*: charlatans.

45 *Early Masonic Pamphlets*, p. 110.

46 *Idem*, pp. 111–25.

47 "Charity, individual in its final effect," said Scott D., a Mason from Oxford, "but uniform as a tendency and habit within a Lodge, though arising from very different individual motivations (including those of self-interest and social convention), has become a stable attitude."

48 The Provincial Grand Lodges were, at that time, of three different kinds. The first comprised the Provincial Grand Lodges in Great Britain such as, for instance, P.G.L. of North Wales, granted at the Devil Tavern by William O'Brien, Earl of Inchiquin, G.M. on 24 June 1727. The second included the Provincial Grand Lodges in the Colonies such as, for example, P.G.L.s in Bengal or New Jersey, granted in 1730 at the "above said Devil Tavern" by the Duke of Norfolk G.M. The third embraced the Provincial Grand Lodges in independent non-English-speaking countries such as Holland or Portugal. As regards some of the Grand Lodges of the last category it remains uncertain whether they were meant for inhabitants of those countries or mostly for Englishmen who lived there temporarily or permanently. So in the case of the Provincial Grand Lodge of Russia, granted by Lord Lovel in 1731, with Capt. John Phillips as its first Grand Master, it could hardly be imagined that – in addition to the few dozen English and Dutch merchants, diplomats and doctors – it could have had more than three or four, so far anonymous, Russian members. The second Grand Master was General James Keith (1696–1758). See A. N. Pypin, 1916, pp. 88–90, 498.

49 In 1733 under the Grand Mastership of Lord Lovel "it was decided (at the same Devil) that the Committee of Charity shall have a power to give five pounds as *casual charity* to a poor Brother, but no more, till the Grand Lodge assemble" [p. 181].

50 The notion of "occasional" overlaps that of "Emergency Lodge", which, particularly in America, were convened by Grand Masters for initiation of the candidates. See in E. L. Hawkins, 1908, p. 147.

51 J. G. Findel, 1869, pp. 150–1.

52 "After 1725 all Lodges were empowered to make Masters at their discretion ... but the great majority of them either could not or did not ..." (could not simply because they were unable to raise a quorum). R. F. Gould, 1903, pp. 315–6.

53 "... Practically the Lodges before 1733 ... were not eligible to work the Third Degree ...". W. J. Hughan, 1909 (1884), p. 52.

54 "... Lady Day 1721 ... then the Grand Wardens were order'd, as usual, to prepare the Feast and to take some Stewards to their assistance ... and our Brother Josiah Villeneau, upholder ... generously undertook the whole himself ..." [*Anderson's Constitutions* 1738, p. 112.] But in 1725, "... No Stewards were appointed ... and the Duke of Richmond desired our Brother John Heidegger to prepare the Feast in the best manner." [p. 119] An earlier regulation (of 28 April 1724) "... ordain'd that at the Feast the Stewards shall open no wine till dinner be laid on the tables ... and that after eight o'clock ... they shall not be obliged to furnish any wine or other liquors ..." [p. 167]. Also W. Preston, 1804, p. 228.

55 A Tyler is an officer who "covers" the Lodge from the intrusion of *cowans.* E. L. Hawkins, 1908, p. 237.

56 W. J. Hughan, 1909 (1884), p. 54; R. F. Gould, 1903, p. 302.

57 That is, the degrees of various Masonic orders which are outside the jurisdiction of any Grand Lodge of the Craft, and into which only Masters of the Craft can be accepted.

58 ". . . The office of Steward, which was a very expensive one, became by this means associated with *favouritism,* in which rank and wealth had the preference in total opposition to the liberal and equalizing Spirit of Masonry. The Grand Lodge first introduced . . . that axiom, so abundantly practised in the Higher Degrees, that the more largely a brother contributed, the greater his weight in the Lodge." J. G. Findel, 1869, p. 156.

59 Among Masonic historians the most prominent apologist of the Higher Degrees is A. E. Waite, their arch-enemy is J. G. Findel, while W. J. Hughan preserves a precarious neutrality on the subject.

60 "When Christ is sent forth by the door it may happen that He returns at the back, and when there is no room for Him in the inn He comes to birth in the stable." A. E. Waite, 1925, p. 14.

61 Waite failed to understand that only pure Protestants could have insisted upon that which became the starting point in the history and the point of departure for all its subsequent modifications.

62 W. J. Hughan, 1909, p. 62.

63 *Masonry Dissected:* being a Universal and Genuine Description of all its Branches from the original to the present Time, as it is deliver'd in the Constituted Regular Lodges both in City and Country . . . to which is added, the Author's Vindication of himself. The third edition. By Samuel Prichard, late member of a Constituted Lodge. London, 1730. (S. Prichard, 1730). See also *Masonic Reprints* . . . With notes by John T. Thorp, XII ("Masonry Dissected"), Leicester, 1929 (J. T. Thorp, 1929).

64 N. Blackerby, Deputy Grand Master, called the pamphlet, "a foolish thing not to be regarded" [W. J. Hughan, 1909 (1884)]. However, A. E. Waite (1925, p. 118) remarks: "There is very little doubt that in however broad a sense it represented actual procedure . . . though prevailing insincerity pretends to regard all *printed* Craft Rituals as spurious."

65 "Seven are 1 Master, 2 Wardens, 2 Fellow-Crafts and 2 Enter'd 'Prentices. Five are 1 Master, 2 Wardens, 1 Fellow-Craft, and 1 Enter'd 'Prentice." [*Idem,* p. 10]. I do not know whether it would be possible to deduce from this that the Wardens also had the Degree of Master.

66 Thorp comments: "Prichard had no knowledge of the origin and meaning of this word, but confuses it with 'listener'. A cowan was one who endeavoured to pass himself off as a Mason, although he had not been regularly apprenticed to the trade. In speculative Masonry, he is one who attempts to obtain the secrets of the Order in an underhand or surreptitious manner." J. T. Thorp, 1929, p. 47.

67 i.e. three *Masters.*

68 "i.e. from the working tool of the Fellow-Craft to the Compasses of the Master", J. T. Thorp, 1929, p. 50.

69 "Probably the rule of 3, 4 and 5 in the formation of a perfect square", *idem.*

70 J. T. Thorp comments (1929, p. 26): "A word familiar to all present day Master Masons."

71 These meanings would seem to rule out its being the very word Hiram had had when he was alive – unless it was a foretaste of his own death and raising.

72 It would be very interesting to compare that very first exposition of the Master Mason's Ritual by Prichard with the latest and fullest recently by Dewar. The latter is a typical montage remade into a detailed and well-documented script, absolutely factual but unaccompanied by any awareness, religious or otherwise. See J. Dewar, *The Unlocked Secret*, London, 1966, pp. 126–75.

73 ". . . As there is no definite knowledge of the ritual . . . of a Masonic Lodge of the period, it is quite impossible to say how far this . . . 'exposure' is genuine. It is quite possible that it represents, in some measure, the early eighteenth-century 'work', but the present-day Brother will readily discover how far, and in what respects, it differs from the beautiful religious ceremony of the present day." J. T. Thorp, Vol. XII, 1929, p. 45. The use of the word "religious" here is very significant, because it implies that at Prichard's time the Ritual had not yet become religious, i.e. that it was separated from religion in its content and character.

74 Prichard gives the List of Regular Lodges at the end of the Pamphlet, which shows his considerable and intimate knowledge of the Masonic situation at that time.

CHAPTER 5

Anderson's Constitutions Revised 1738

. . . untrammelled by any laws of evidence
R. F. Gould of W. Preston

Then in our songs be Justice done
To those who have enrich'd the Art,
From Jabal down to Burlington,
And let each Brother bear a Part.
The Fellow-Crafts Song

Ironically enough, in the same way that Roberts's *Old Constitutions* of 1722 had been of positive help to Anderson's work, which it had intended to sabotage, Prichard's *Masonry Dissected* turned out to be, objectively speaking, a great boon to Masonry in general and to Anderson in particular. For Samuel Prichard did for Anderson what Anderson could never have done for himself: he brought about the essential task of producing his revised *Constitutions* of 1738. *Masonry Dissected* had brought into the open what had previously only been hinted at, and forced Anderson to abandon his reticence and be more explicit on some crucial points, though not the details of the rituals.

In the meantime, while the Brethren in and around Westminster and "within the Bills of Mortality" went on revelling and toasting, Dr Anderson appeared before the Grand Lodge ". . . in ample Form at the above said Devil . . . 31 March 1735 . . . and was order'd to insert in the new edition [of his *Constitutions*] . . . the Patrons of Antient Masonry . . . from the *beginning of time* . . . with the Grand Masters and Wardens, *antient and modern* . . ." [p. 133]. In other words, he was asked to add to his *Constitutions* of 1723 the history of the *Grand Lodge* from 1688 to 1717, and from 1717 "to this day". Almost three years later, during the Grand Mastership of Lord Darnley, ". . . the Grand Lodge at the same Devil, 25 January 1738 . . . approv'd of this *New* Book of Constitutions, and order'd the author Bro. Anderson to print the same . . ." [p. 138]. This brief reference to the development of his text, the role and importance of which for the actual history of English or any other Masonry it would hardly be possible to overstate, not only shows the determination of the Grand Lodge to have the task commenced years earlier by Anderson completed, but provides some evidence that the position of his "noble and learned" friends, such as Dr Desaguliers, Major Hadden, Mr De Noyer and Mr Vraden, was still extremely strong. It was these gentlemen who "... On 5th November, 1737 ... held an *occasional* Lodge at the Palace of Kew ... and made his Royal Highness Frederick, Prince of Wales ... an Enter'd Apprentice ... and Fellow-Craft ..." and later made him a Master Mason in the same Lodge. [p. 137]. The official status of Masonry was not only higher than ever before but, far more importantly, Masonry under the Grand Lodge of England actually turned into that very thing which Anderson and his anonymous predecessors had invented: the legend had become a reality.[1] Royal patronage became an essential part of Masonry and an element of its historical self-awareness. So it is no wonder that the good Doctor dedicated his *Constitutions* of 1738 to "The most high, Puissant and ... Illustrious Prince Frederick Lewis, Prince of Wales" [p. iii].

Now let us turn to those points in the New Book of Constitutions on which it differs from the old and, particularly, to those where the crystallization of Masonic historical self-consciousness can be most clearly seen.[2]

1) The author's "Address to the Reader" is an outright apologia of Secrecy. Secrecy is normal and necessary because "Most regular societies have had and will have their own *secrets*; and to be sure, the Free-Masons always had theirs, which they never divulged in *Manuscript*; and therefore cannot be expected in *print*: only an expert Brother, by the true Light, can readily find many useful *hints* in almost every page of this Book, which *Cowans*, and others not initiated, cannot discern [p. ix] ... But the History here chiefly concerns Masonry, without meddling with other transactions, more than what only serves to connect the History of Masonry, the strict subject of this Book. *It is good to know what not to say!* Candid Reader, farewell!" [p.x].

Moreover, what is so strongly intimated here is that not only the very idea of secrecy, but also that secrecy itself, understood as a "closed, non-written text", is opposed to an open, or written text – a Masonic history, for instance, or an anti-Masonic exposé, such as Prichard's.

2) The "pre-historical" part starts from the beginning with Adam who, though he certainly knew some geometry (for he was formed himself according to its laws), was not yet a Mason in the specific sense of the term. This specific sense can be reduced, in Anderson's description, to two primary elements, both of them connected with Masonic esoterism.

The first is "... the Masons' Faculty and universal Practice of conversing without speaking, and of knowing each other by Signs and Tokens ... which became necessary because of confusion of dialects..." [p. 6]. This point is also made concrete in the idea of "the *oral tradition* (of Masons) which was darkened by the blending of nations" [p. 10]. So, as a result of that Biblical confusion of languages (the Tower of Babel) an esoteric language came into being without which no perpetuation of Masonry would be possible. The second is the Lodge as the only form of existence of Masons, which, as we have already seen in Prichard's exposition, has an esotericism of its own. So we read that it was King Solomon who first "... partition'd the Fellow-Crafts into certain Lodges with a Master and Warden in each ... and every Brother was duly taught *secrecy*" [p. 93]. And then we move on to the central point of the Lodge's esotericism "... but their [the Brothers'] joy was soon interrupted by the *sudden* death of their dear Master, *Hiram Abif,* whom they decently interr'd in the Lodge near the Temple, according to an ancient usage ... But leaving what must not, and indeed cannot be committed to writing..." [p. 14]. So, Anderson makes his point very clearly here. He refers, as it were in passing, to the Hiramic legend, without making any mention of its ritual meaning, and still emphasizes that there is much else which cannot be disclosed except within the Lodge.

The Post-Solomon era is characterized by the appearance of the custom of Acception which, according to Anderson, has a history of at least two thousand years behind it:[3]

... Many of Solomon's Masons before he died began to travel very far abroad, and carry'd with them ... the *Secrets of the Fraternity* ... and the Old Constitutions affirm, that one call'd Vinus ... brought the refined knowledge of the Science and the Art into Germany and Gaul. [p. 16]. In many Places ... they obtain'd special privileges; and because they taught their *liberal* Art only to the *Freeborn,* they were *call'd Free Masons;* constituting Lodges in the places where they built stately *Piles,* by the encouragement of the Great and Wealthy, who soon requested to be *accepted as* members of the Lodge and Brothers of the Craft; till by merit those *Free* and *Accepted Masons* came to be *Masters* and *Wardens.* Nay Kings and Potentates became Grand Masters, each in his own Dominion, in imitation of ... Solomon, whose memory, as a Mason, has been duly worshipp'd and will be, till Architecture shall be consumed by the *General Conflagration...*" [p. 17].

A particularly interesting feature of Anderson's "prehistorical" narration is his re-evaluation of some historical personages, regardless of the received historical opinion of those figures, since the only thing that matters is how they behaved by Masonic standards. As a result of this revision, Alexander the Great was demoted and Herod became a hero. "... But tho' from ambition Alexander ... order'd to found Alexandria ... yet he is not reckon'd a Mason because at the instigation of a drunken whore, in his revels, he burnt the rich and splendid Persepolis, a city of palaces in the best style, *which no true Mason would do, was he ever so drunk!*" [p. 28]. Whereas Herod "... but for all his great faults became the greatest builder of his day, the Patron or Grand Master of many Lodges ... with his two Wardens, Hillel and Shamai, two learned Rabbins ..." [p. 40]. The "Masonization" of history continues in a similar vein arriving eventually at the origins of British Masonry:

History fails to tell us, how long Europeans in the North and West had lost their original skill brought from Shinar before the Roman conquest; but leaving our Brother Masons of other Nations to *deduce* their history in their own manner, we shall carry on *our deduction* in the Britannic Isles. [p. 55]

And then, as if he wanted to illustrate his deduction, he writes: "... Caesar reached London 55 BC ... but pursued not his conquest, because of his design to be the Grand Master of the Roman Republic"(!)[4]

3) The Part of the Masonic history covering the period between the Revolution of 1688 and the formation of the Grand Lodge of England in 1717, omitted in the *Constitutions* of 1723, is as short as it is unconvincing, even to some of his contemporaries. The author excuses himself for being so brief by referring to the lack of records "... which were lost before and ... at the Revolution, and many of 'em were too hastily burnt in our time from a fear of making discoveries: So that we have not so ample an account as could be wish'd of the Grand Lodge, etc." [p. 105]. But just before dealing with that post-Revolution period he quotes the famous extract from the *Diary of Elias Ashmole* which provides serious evidence of the contention that a few Lodges at least of non-working Masons were indeed in existence (if not yet in vogue) by the second half of the seventeenth century:[5]

On the 10 March, 1682, I received a Summons to appear next day at a Lodge in Masons-Hill, London, when we admitted into fellowship of Free Masons Sir William Wilson, Capt. Richard Burthwide, and furthermore, I was the *Senior Fellow*, it being 35 years since I was admitted; and with me were Mr Thomas Wise (Master of the London Company of Masons) and eight more old Free Masons. We all dined at the Half-Moon Tavern in Cheapside, a noble dinner, prepared at the charge of the new accepted Masons [p. 104].

About the period itself, however, not very much is said, which is all the more surprising as Dr Anderson and his old friends had a part in it.

All more or less essential information, corroborated by other sources or not, concerning Masonry in the period 1688–1717 can be easily summarized chronologically in the following passages.

. . . *Particular Lodges* were not so frequent and mostly *occasional*. . . Thus Sir Robert Clayton got an *occasional* Lodge of his *Brother Masters* to meet at St Thomas's Hospital, Southwark 1653 . . . [p. 106] . . . Beside that and the *old* Lodge of St Paul's, there was another in Piccadilly over against St James's Church, one near Westminster Abbey, another near Covent Garden, one in Holborn, one on Tower Hill, and some more that *assembled statedly*. The King (William I) was privately made a Freemason, approved of their choice of *Wren* as Grand Master, and encourag'd him in rearing St Paul's . . . and the great new part of Hampton Court in the *Augustan Stile*. This year our most noble Brother *Charles Lennox* Duke of Richmond and Lennox . . . was chosen Grand Master. Wren was his D., and father and son Strongs Grand Wardens . . . in *1697–8* . . . [p. 107].

. . . Yet still in the South the Lodges were more and more disus'd . . . Some few years after *1708* . . . Wren neglected the office of Grand Master, yet the *Old Lodge* near St Paul's and a few more continued their stated meetings till . . . Queen Ann died on 1 Aug. 1714 [p. 108].

Then, continues Anderson,

King George I enter'd London . . . on 20 September 1714 and . . . after Rebellion was over in 1716, the few Lodges in London finding themselves neglected by Sir Christopher Wren, thought fit to cement themselves under a Grand Master . . . [p. 109]

So we return again to what we started with – the formation of the Grand Lodge of England and its history up to the publication of the *Constitutions* of 1738 for, whether we believe him entirely or not, Anderson was the sole Chronicler of the period and we have been obliged to follow him in our description of the course of events until he completed his *magnum opus* and died.

4) The *Constitutions* of 1738 does not differ essentially in its religious

aspect from the previous edition, but there are some curious points, suggesting that either a few more concessions to Christianity had been made by the author, or that the emphasis on religion in general had become stronger. Sometimes he did it in a way that would seem rather clumsy to those at either end of the political spectrum of the Church of England today, but it should be borne in mind that in the 1730s Church life, as well as religious opinion in general, was no less politically polarized than it is now. The following points in the *Constitutions* of 1738 are of interest in the context of religion.

a) In the famous Charge no.1 "Concerning God and Religion", coming after the no less famous exhortation that "A Mason is obliged by his tenure to observe the Moral Law . . ." he adds, "as a true *Noachida* . . . for they all agree in the three Great Articles of Noah . . ." [pp. 43–4]. This is entirely consonant with the clause in Chapter IV of the "prehistorical" part which states that ". . . we leave every Brother to *Liberty of Consciousness*, but strictly charge him . . . to maintain the cement of the Lodge and the three Articles of Noah . . ." [p. 23]. Why did Anderson introduce Noah at this point, as if his own stand on religion were not vague and complicated enough? It was probably because, as a theologian, he wanted to substantiate his controversial thesis about the "Religion in which all men agree" by referring to Noah who, while not yet a Jew, was nonetheless a Chosen One for his righteousness. To Anderson, Noah represents the ideal "good man" and, as such, the embodiment of Masonic ethics. All true Masons should emulate him in their moral lives. The idea of Masonic religious universalism creeps into other passages. It is unclear to what extent, if any, Anderson was aware of his own "natural theology", but being a dissenting teacher he would have believed in the existence of Religion in general, apart from any specific ritual, analogous to his representation of Noah as "a good man and true", not bound by the laws of any specific religious morality.

b) The references to Christianity, though not very numerous, are nevertheless significant. In the first Charge, he draws a parallel between a Lodge and a Church. In comparing the two he stresses that just as the word "Lodge" means both a group of persons and the place of their meeting, "Church is expressive both of the *Congregation* and the *Place of Worship* . . ." [p. 144]. (Anderson's own Church, of course, while embracing both worshippers and place of worship, admitted no ritual.)

c) An instance of Christian–Masonic syncretism can be seen in the passages where Christianity and Freemasonry are combined so that the religious terminology appears as heterogeneous but, at the same time, cemented within a new and specifically Masonic context. As in the Constitutions of 1723, God is the Great and Almighty Architect of the Universe, that very God in whose religion all men agree, who "... created all things very good and according to *Geometry*..." [p. 1]. He might still be thought of as the God of a Universalist religion of Freemasonry. But when we proceed with Anderson through Genesis, and read about Methuselah's "... peculiar family [that] preserved *the good old Religion of the promised Messiah* pure and also Royal Art [of Masonry] till the flood..." [p. 4], the syncretism becomes quite inescapable. This combining of Masonry and Christianity culminates in the one overt reference to the New Testament, which even the admirers of Anderson's book could hardly fail to regard as heretical: "... The Word was made Flesh, or the Lord Jesus Christ Immanuel was born, the Great Architect or *Grand Master of the Christian Church*..." [p. 41]. This exceptional religious parallelism takes on an elegiac note, when he concludes the Book with the Words: "May this good work of charity abound, as one of the happy effects of the Love and Friendship of *true* Masons, till Time and Architecture shall be no more!" [p. 184].

The Charge on God and Religion which has always provoked controversy outside Freemasonry, represented within it neither a blunder, nor a premeditated challenge – practically nobody in the Grand Lodge, either in 1723 or 1738 found it at all objectionable or even worthy of debate. At that time, and among those who surrounded Anderson, the Universalist principles of the Charge were considered quite natural and acceptable. And, even if there were a difference of opinion on that count within the Grand Lodge, it remained unreflected in its Minutes. It would be incorrect to think of Dr Anderson, Dissenter though he was, as a particularly controversial or subversive figure. L. Vibert gives an account of his funeral published in the *London Daily Post* (May, 1739) "... Last night was interr'd in Bunhill Fields the corpse of Dr Anderson, a Dissenting Teacher, in a very remarkable deep grave. His Pall was supported by five Dissenting Teachers, and the Rev. Dr Desaguliers; it was follow'd by about a dozen of Free-Masons, who encircled the grave; and after Dr Earle had harangued on the uncertainty of life, etc., *without one word of the deceased*, the Brethren, in a most solemn dismal posture, lifted up their hands, sigh'd, and struck their aprons three times in Honour of the deceased."[6]

By the time of Anderson's death, the epoch whose chief endeavour had been the foundation of Freemasonry was over and the new task of spreading it far and wide already begun. Anderson taught the founding fathers who they were, through the fixing of their past, both in the history of the Grand Lodge and the pre-history, tracing the roots of Masonry back to the beginning of time. Thus, if the founding fathers shaped the Grand Lodge, he shaped their historical consciousness by presenting it to them as *their* history. But his greatest achievement was to establish a difference between merely sitting "at the above said *Devil*", drinking claret and port and sitting at "the same *Devil*", drinking the same claret and port, but at a Masonic dinner (". . . after the Lodge closed"). It was he who emphasized that the words and expressions spoken at any occasion other than at a Lodge were different from the same words and expressions used in a Lodge. And, most importantly, it was he who distinguished a person's religion, of whatever kind, from that "in which all men agree", in all probability without realizing that this would inevitably, and sooner rather than later, become the special religion of Freemasons, whether they wanted it or not.[7]

SOME ADDITIONAL REMARKS

As I have already said, I am not a historian. Nor, least of all, am I a person whom the early Masonic historiographers would have called an antiquary. The only propensity I share with those who convivially conversed with Dr Anderson and George Payne[8] is that particular *leisureliness* without which their strange enterprise would have never survived even the first decade of its existence. For when one lives hastily the most one can achieve is mere living, whereas Masonic leisurely living was meant to be both a history and a way of life at one and the same time. Or, more exactly, after Anderson and Desaguliers had dealt with the past of the Craft, it became clear that they could not prevent it from dominating their own present. Since then, British Masons, however rationally minded or sceptical of the legend, have not been able to escape it and have been doomed to live a double life.

At its foundation, speculative Freemasonry was an entertaining adventure, a congenial diversion, the scope and dimensions of which were never anticipated by those who initiated it. The start of its grand phase, at the end of the 1830s, can be seen now as a coincidence of three factors, namely:

1. The unexpectedly rapid growth, spread and proliferation of Masonic Lodges;
2. The corresponding increase in scale of the inner development and elaboration of Masonic rituals, rules and customs;[9]
3. The tendency to explain these first two factors retrospectively, in the constant endeavours by Masonry to revise and keep pace

with its own history, at that time still not even covering the life of one generation (1717–38).[10]

But to return once more to Dr Anderson, if he had invented everything by himself, what a supernatural energy he would have needed to produce such a formidable corpus of texts. However, one should not be tempted to allow his ability and perseverance alone to account for it. Other more objective factors were also at work. Foremost among them is that it is through British (Scottish and Irish included) Freemasonry, that the seventeenth century was able to manifest itself in the eighteenth. The memory of the seventeenth century was perpetuated in the eighteenth by Freemasonry more than by any other social or cultural phenomenon at that time. In those troubled times, only something which was at one and the same time unserious and untrivial could survive. Being a contemporary of Emmanuel Swedenborg, Dr Anderson consciously wanted a continuation of the past, while Swedenborg's struggle was "to extricate ourselves alive", spiritually, from the present, i.e. the eighteenth century. Both men were nostalgic, conservative, and directed towards the past. And it is not surprising that it was one of the Scottish Freemasons, James Boswell, who invented the new and utterly conservative genre of immediate biography in his description of the life of Dr Samuel Johnson.

Lack of imagination has characterized almost all anti-Masonic historiographical critique and prevented it from realizing that not only did Masons invent their own historical Legend but, more importantly, they have, unofficially, untiringly continued to invent and reinvent it long after the efforts of Dr Anderson. This is because the Legend is not a lie about themselves, nor just the vehicle of their self-perception but the means of their ideal self-perpetuation.[11]

So, as far as it can be established, much of the legendary history of Freemasons contained in the Masonic Constitutions and in the manuscripts published after 1722 does belong, in its essentials at any rate, to the tradition and lore of English, Scottish and, possibly, also Irish working Masons.

It is conceivable, though it cannot be proved, that some parts or elements of that Legend had been used in or manifested by the rituals of initiation in the Lodges of working Masons, prior to their accepting non-working members. It is almost certain that those parts of the history hinted at by Anderson but "not to be written" were of ritualistic character, or spoken during the ritual in his own time, and a possibility still remains that these had always existed as exclusively oral and in the oral tradition of the working Masons.

One may presume that all working Masons to whose Charges Anderson refers, as well as practically all those who were "accepted" into working Lodges during the seventeenth century, were Christian as individuals, in the same way that the working Masons were Masons as individuals. This is unambiguous in the manuscripts; Christianity was their faith as Masonry was their profession. My contention as regards Masonic or any other ritual is that the ritual is always far more deeply ingrained in its own religious situation than the beliefs underpinning it, or the ideas in the light of which it might be explained or interpreted; for the ritual, even a deliberately "invented" one, always precedes the fact of its being reflected upon by its users, or the fact of their self-awareness by means of which they relate themselves to it.[12]

The three focal points of the then dominant Protestantism – Faith, Salvation through good works and Predestination – prepared the ground for the introduction of the Ritual which not only seemed to be neutral with respect to Protestantism (undoubtedly Anderson's intention), but was also able to neutralize any specific Christian context. This might or might not have been anticipated by Anderson, but the danger was almost immediately recognized by the Vatican and Masonry was interdicted.[13]

A SHORT CONVERSATION ABOUT ANDERSON THAT TOOK PLACE IN OXFORD IN 1986

I (A.P.) I can see you don't like him, do you?
JC, a member of Quatuor Coronati Lodge No, I don't. Had he not been born English Masonry would have been much better off. Without him no split into Moderns and Antients would have ever occurred, would it, John?
John, a very learned Mason, though not a member of QCL I don't know, I have read some of his stuff and heard about him at some of the lectures at my Lodge, and as far as I can judge he was far too primitive and elementary in his approach to Masonic history even by the standards of historical credulity of his own time.
JC Not just that. I think that even by the moral standards of his time he was not an honest person, for all his activity was motivated by sheer self-interest and nothing else. He wanted to become a Grand Master, that's it . . .
I But he stood no chance at all after the second Grand Mastership of George Payne, when the tradition of electing Grand Masters only from the Nobility was established. And, in my opinion, he himself was a party to establishing this tradition. Yet wouldn't you

think that his was a more ideological task to define the historical principle rather than do research in history as we understand it?

John Of course it was, for to define the historical principle one has to be a theologian and not a historian.

JC Exactly, and that task was hopelessly muddled by Anderson, for he was a typical *dissenter* . . .

I . . . instead of being a typical decent Anglican priest, yes?

JC Well, I suppose that a typical decent Anglican priest of that age would have done the same in Anderson's place, namely, to present Masonry to Masons, as well as to the world outside the Lodges, as a Society which had no religion of its own and never would have. Because, in fact, not only has Masonry never been a religion but it was not and is not a *religious* society. But Anderson wilfully and obstinately presented the religious aspect of Masonry in such an ambiguous way as to generate the maximum of misunderstanding in Masons themselves, and to give ample opportunity of distortion to their enemies. [I have personally disagreed with this viewpoint earlier.] Not to mention all the inexactitude and tediousness of his presentation. And I think it is your essential mistake that in writing this book you have so slavishly and stubbornly followed him.

John As dissenters he and Desaguliers were never able to understand the value and significance of our Ritual – all that they cared about were opinions and external form.

Chris W. (a young Mason and student of Masonry) Anderson was a man of mixture and confusion: in order to present things as he wanted them to be presented he had to construe some notions and concepts which would have, at least temporarily, satisfied those on whom he depended in achieving his task. But Masonry, as I see it now, does not need any real history. It should be quite content with the Legend, and the Legend was formed without Anderson, and mostly after him.

The last opinion is of particular interest for it represents an intellectual strain in modern Freemasonry that seeks to deprive Anderson of any significance in the shaping of their institution. It is inaccurate in fact; Anderson was crucial in forming the Legend and very little was officially added to it in the post-Anderson era. This view brings us back to the question of whether any factual history of Freemasonry prior to the formation of the Grand Lodge of England is of any value to Freemasonry as an esoteric teaching, as an even more esoteric ritual, and as a complex of symbols the understanding of which is also esoteric according to the laws of Masonic secrecy.

Nevertheless, in the opinion of many Freemasons past and present, the *idea* of the historical antiquity and uninterrupted continuity of the Institution represents a fundamental element, and Anderson's position, particularly his emphasis on the importance of the founding of the Grand Lodge as a new improved institutional form for speculative and mystical Masonry, undermines this idea. This tension is highlighted by Chalmers Paton who, a century later, claimed to be an exponent of the "true and real ancient Masonic history". In the middle of the nineteenth century he wrote:

I have a strong desire to see the honour of our Order maintained . . . and I believe nothing can be more contrary to it than the supposition that Freemasonry is of recent origin . . . and we must feel ourselves constrained either to acknowledge that Dr Desaguliers, Dr Anderson, and their coadjutors, were honest men doing a work which they believed to be good, or to set them down as a set of the most consummate rascals that ever imposed upon mankind, and yet there is no motive for their imposture. To maintain the honour . . . of Freemasonry, and at the same time to . . . support the 1717 theory of its origin . . . is ridiculous.[14]

He finishes with a direct accusation: ". . . this 1717 theory ascribes to men of the highest character invention of a system of mere imposture . . ."[15]

John Fellows, a close contemporary of Paton, was the first to produce a mythological presentation of Anderson's Masonic exposition of the mythical history of mankind. In Anderson's historical account, as well as in practically all other known Masonic histories (including those on which the learned Doctor based his own), history starts with civilization, equated with Masonry, which goes back to Cain. His exposition stops short of Man in his natural, "precivilizational" state as represented by Adam who, although he knew Geometry, was not a Mason. In comparing Anderson's history with the ancient myth related in a fragment of Sanchoniato, the Phoenician (translated by Philo Byblius, and preserved by Eusebius), Fellows remarks that "the commencement of the former bears a strong resemblance to the latter, but instead however of permitting the first inhabitants of the world to gain knowledge gradually by the aid of experience, Anderson makes them finished artizans from the beginning."[16] More interestingly, Fellows then makes the theological observation that all inventions and discoveries of the ancient world can be reduced to the exoteric invention of the principal arts necessary for use in civil life, and the esoteric discovery of monotheism and belief in the existence of the soul after death in a state of reward or punishment. According to Anderson, both are given to man by God from the start.[17] Moreover, Fellows believes that the Ritual of Masonic initiation reflects, and even enacts in its initial parts, that "precivilizational" and "pre-monotheistic" stage in the history of mankind, and presents it as preinitiatory darkness. For, as we see in both Masonic rituals and the ancient mysteries referred to by Fellows, the Ritual, being esoteric by definition, tends to appropriate the exoteric mythologized history which is preserved in an open, non-secret, oral tradition.[18] Fellows concludes by exonerating Anderson and explaining his position: "This was necessary for his purpose, which was to show the original establishment of the Freemason Society,"[19] because – and this was evident to both Anderson and Fellows – the history of the Brotherhood could not be based on the principle of any organic or natural evolution. This is because the cornerstone of the Masonic idea of history is essentially creational. The history of the Craft is the gradual manifestation of God's great design, created in completeness and perfection from the beginning, but only gradually revealed to mankind in stages through a series of epochs.

Notes

1 In August 1738, Frederic the Great "was initiated in a Lodge in Brunswick".

2 In the Preface "this our newly printed Book is recommended as the *only* Book of Constitutions, disclaiming all other books . . ." (p. xi).

3 Besides being extremely comic, particularly from the pen of a Doctor of Divinity, these passages show us not so much an historical naïveté as a very strong tendency to neutralize all ethical and religious oppositions apart from Masonic ones. [In 1953 F. L. Pick and E. N. Knight counted among "our noble Bretheren Dr J. I. Guillotin", the inventor of the guillotine (p. 331).]

4 And a little further on we will learn that ". . . Masonry (in England) was extinguished; nor have we any vestige of it unless we reckon that of Stonehenge and allow, with some, that Ambrosius, King of the Britons rais'd that famous monument . . . by the art of Merlin . . . Others think it an old Keltic temple . . . and some have counted it a Danish Monument. But the great Inigo Jones, and his kinsman Mr John Webb, have learnedly prov'd it to be a Roman temple . . ." [p. 60]. However, even at such a blissfully dilettantic time as that of Jones, that brilliant self-confessed dilettante, John Aubrey, could not help remarking that: ". . . having compared Mr Jones' Scheme with the monument itself, I found he had not dealt fairly . . ." J. Aubrey, *Brief Lives*, ed. by O. L. Dick, Great Britain, 1982 (1949), p. 31.

5 E.M.P., 1945, pp. 40–2. The history of commentary on this passage is almost as long as that of the Grand Lodge of England (Ashmole's *Diary* was published in

1717). There are, still, some strong reasons to suppose that as early as the middle of the seventeenth century there were both the London Company of (Working) Masons and the Lodges of non-working (i.e. "accepted") Masons existing side by side. At the same time, it is clearly seen from this very passage that neither Ashmole nor other "old Masons" were Master Masons, and that the term Master was applied to Masters of the Company (as in the case of Mr Wise). See A. E. Waite, 1925, pp. 26–8; W. J. Hughan, 1909, pp. 30–1; J. G. Findel, 1869, p. 130; R. F. Gould, 1903, pp. 185–7.

6 *Idem*, p. x. Vibert concludes his Introduction, saying ". . . Today we value the Doctor's labours much less highly, but the *Constitutions* of 1723 is nevertheless one of the most important records of the Craft" [p. lii].

7 I know that A. E. Waite would never have agreed with me, nor would his followers in the field of the Masonry of the Higher Degrees. His in other respects excellent book (*Emblematic Masonry*, 1925) could have revolutionized the whole Masonic historical self-awareness had he been more aware of his own *historical subjectivity* (which he himself calls the Christian point of view). His hypothesis can be presented, very schematically, in the following way:

a) The so-called "Old Charges" of the real working Masons of the fifteenth (?) to seventeenth centuries were all Christian and Trinitarian, and remained so even after the Operative Lodges began to admit ("accept") non-working Masons.

b) Anderson, while using some of those Charges, produced an absolutely "de-Christianized" and "Deistic" version, thereby entirely separating the "philosophy" of the Craft from the pristinely Christian background of the authors and users of the Charges. In all this Waite sees the pernicious influence either of Scottish Presbyterianism, or French Huguenotism, or both.

c) He admits that Desaguliers and Anderson might have been "true Christians without any 'Deistic' tinge", but insists that theirs was a determination to have Freemasonry divorced from any concrete religion and from Christianity in the first place. And, quite naturally, they first of all distanced their Masonry from their own religion.

8 I entirely agree with Gould that the Founding Fathers who actually invented "modern" Masonry at the beginning of the eighteenth century and those who invented its history were two quite different sets of people.

9 When the game grew so enormously in size it needed a considerable adaptation of its rules.

10 Strictly speaking, there is no Masonic historical point of view on human history in general; the Masonic historian on the whole is not interested in a non-Masonic history. Unlike Hegelianism, Marxism and Psychoanalysis, Masonry has no general philosophy of history – only a historiography of self-description.

11 You can dismiss a history as a legend or regard a legend as a history, but you cannot dismiss a legend as merely a legend: a legend is itself a historical fact. What really matters is that moment of Masonic self-awareness which induced them to think of themselves as continuers of the Legend of time past, as perpetuators of that legendary past and guardians of its pledge.

12 So, however vague were its historical antecedents, contemporary Masonry starts figuring in Anderson's *Constitutions* of 1723 as a kind of movement ("Lodge-

ism" one may call it) whose main feature which distinguished it from all other (particularly "secret") organizations, consisted in that it did not oblige its members to behave, speak or think in any particular way outside the Lodge.

13 By a Papal Bull in 1738.

14 Chalmers Izett Paton, *The Origin of Freemasonry, or the 1717 Theory Exploded*, London, 1871 (C. I. Paton, 1871), p. VI.

15 *Idem*, p. 3.

16 J. Fellows, 1860, p. 121–2.

17 *Idem*, p. 119.

18 *Idem*, p. 120. But about this below, in the chapters on the Ritual.

19 *Idem*, p. 122. To this he adds, a little further (p. 123): "This history of Dr Anderson is the only authority that Masonry can produce to substantiate the extraordinary antiquity which it claims."

CHAPTER 6

Three Speeches, One Sermon and Some Early Masonic Philosophizing

The four texts I refer to in this chapter, all of which were written by very prominent Masons – one of them a no less prominent clergyman – appeared within the space of just over a decade (1726–37), and mark the beginning of what can be called Masonic philosophizing though, of course, their authors did not regard themselves as philosophers or even theologians. They pondered, however, over Masonry as a whole, as an already existing ethical, social, and psychological phenomenon which possessed its own function and meaning with respect to its members on the one hand, and with respect to the rest of society on the other. This, in turn, implies that to those four authors (though I do not doubt that there were very many other Masons thinking and speaking along the same lines, who did not record or publish their thoughts) Masonry began to acquire a dimension beyond its inner composition – its rituals, legends, regulations, etc. Masonry started to become for them a subject of speculation, and however trivial some of their thoughts might have been, they are still of immense interest to us, for they reveal clearly how ideas hitherto prevalent in British society, and to a lesser extent on the Continent, were blended with new and specifically Masonic ideas.

Francis Drake,[1] a historian and the Junior Grand-Warden of the Grand Lodge at York, delivered a speech on St John's Day, 27 December 1726. In his Dedication to the printed version of his speech he defines the difference between Masons and non-Masons: "Since I mean it entirely for the good of my Brethren, I am no ways in pain what the *rest of the world* shall think of it; because we all know none but a Mason can thoroughly understand it. It is hard, we have but a negative to all the invectives daily bestowed upon us ... and yet ... silence is the best way of answering those angry sophisters ..."[2] After having separated Masonry and himself from the rest of society, Drake – and in this he is far from being alone among early Masonic writers – praises that very society in exalted tones: "Human society, gentlemen, taken in general terms, is one of the greatest blessings of life. For this end speech and language was given to us, which does so sublimely distinguish us above the rest of the works of creation . . . Society has harmony in the very sound of the word . . .'', and so on, in similar vein.

Before dealing at length, as was usual in such speeches, with the history of mankind, he returns once again to Masonry (''our Most Antient and Honourable Society'') calling it ''one of the Noblest Superstructures that Wit can invent and Rhetoric adoren''. Almost all the phrases used by him are but clichés of that period, yet it is in such clichés that one can detect the spontaneous expression of an idea which had always been there in the background – the idea of a lasting compromise between religion and society or between, say, the tabernacle and the club. Mankind is distinguished from the rest of Creation by having society (the Building) as its form which is, in itself, good but unenlightened; Masonry (the Superstructure of the Building) is distinguished from the rest of society by possessing the knowledge of its architecture. Masonry knows the allegory of Creation as architecture knows building, and as God knows His creation. God, here, figures only twice: as the Great Architect of the Universe at the time of the Creation, and as the Supreme Grand Master of Celestial Grand Lodge at the time of the establishing on earth of the ''prehistoric'' Masonry.[3] Religion in general, as Masons then understood it, belongs to the world outside Masonry, that is to their own society or to any society, which are either divided from one another by their respective religions, or torn apart internally by competing faiths. Thus, if we stick to that Masonic picture, Masonry is opposed to the rest of a given society, as a superstructure marked by its religious unity is opposed to the whole of the building marked by its religious diversity.

A speech made by Edward Oakley, an architect and the Master of the Lodge at Carmarthen, highlights the elite *religious status* of Masons, describing them as if they not only represented the supreme force among all the world's religions but also enjoyed a special and highly privileged relationship with God.[4]

I am glad . . . to rejoice with you . . . inasmuch as it hath pleased the Almighty One, Eternal, Unalterable God, to send out His Light and His Truth and His vivifying Spirit, whereby the Brotherhood begins to revive again in this our Isle, and Princes seek to be of this Sacred Society, which has been from the beginning, and always shall be; the Gates of Hell shall never prevail against it, but it shall continue while the sun and moon endure, until the general consummation of all things; for since God, my Dearest Brethren, is for us, who can be against us?

This strongly Protestantic passage leaves no place for any Deistic interpretation. The Superior Being of Masonry is here, unambiguously and unquestionably, the God of Abraham, Isaac and the Prophets, and Masons are presented as Chosen Ones among Christians. Their Masonic chosenness is here directly opposed to that of Old Israel at the end of the following paragraph:

Ye are living stones, built up into a spiritual house, who believe and rely on the chief *Lapis Angularis* [cornerstone], which the refractory and disobedient Builders disallow'd; you are called from Darkness to Light; you are a Chosen Generation, a Royal Priesthood.

Masons, in Oakley's speech, are exalted over non-Masons as the craft of architecture over all other crafts, and as the English over all other nations ("we are in a nation that may justly claim, at this time, a precedence to all nations, by encouraging and carrying on the most beautiful fabrics"). This is so in virtue of their place in the allegorical system of Masonry, which includes in itself the Holy Writ and, therefore, by implication, the whole of Christianity. Unlike Drake, who regarded Masonry as absolutely the best society, Oakley still regards the Royal Society (of which he was a Fellow) as the model ("that Learned Body . . . who are worthy of our imitation"). The link between the Masonic Society and the Royal Society is by no means tenuous. Like Freemasonry, the latter originated from a very small circle of enthusiasts (the Philosophical Clubbe in Oxford), and once established in London, used to assemble at the Bull's Head Tavern in Cheapside.

This motif of Masonic Chosenness can be seen in a passage from the sermon given by the Revd Ebenezer Erskine before the Synod of Perth on 10 October 1732. The passage comments on Psalm 118 v.22, ("The stone which the builders refused, the same is become the headstone of the corner"): "Masons know one another, they have certain signs and words by which they are capable of distinguishing a man of their own art and business from others; so skilful builders in the House of God are capable by a spiritual discerning to know who are fit to be admitted to the work of the Temple."

Masonic philosophizing about Masonry began in England as spontaneously as had the institution itself some half a century earlier. From the very start, the Masonic attitude to society, including the State, was positive, and its attitude towards religion, including the Church of England, either positive or neutral. French Masonry, however, after having been received from England in the late 1720s consciously developed an anti-State and anti-Catholic ideology – a stand which could not help but be reflected in its negative attitude to religion in general.[5]

Andrew Michael Ramsay (or the "Chevalier de Ramsay", 1696–1743) appears on the fringe of the epoch and seems to be very much a fringe figure himself. For whatever he did, wrote, or spoke about, his position was always somewhere in between: between Catholicism and Deism,[6] between Scotland and England and, in the first place of course, between England and France, where he spent most of his life. Being a faithful Jacobite (he was knighted by the Pretender), and a "true and good" Mason at the same time, made him extremely sensitive to and apprehensive of the atmosphere that surrounded the Order in Paris. But his reaction to the Masonic situation was – due to his absolute frankness and a simplicity bordering on naïveté – wholly inappropriate. His famous speech (printed later under the title of *Discourse Pronounced at the Reception of Freemasons by Mr de R., Grand Orator of the Order*), though pronounced in impeccable French (he was a friend and pupil of Fénélon) remained incorrigibly English in tone and character. This oration immediately attracted the attention of the Church, the police, and the public at large. Fearing that it might be misinterpreted, Ramsay immediately sent it to the First Minister of the Crown, and to his powerful and influential *protecteur* Archbishop Fleuris. In his accompanying letters he stressed that the main "aim of the Order was to improve nations by the love of vertue and fine arts".[7] In appealing to the noble feelings and sense of justice in the heart of the First Minister he, a free man living in an unfree country, behaved as foolishly as did Rousseau, an unfree man visiting a free country (England), when the latter demanded that his friend David Hume suppress a London newspaper which had published an article derogatory to the Frenchman. And it is not impossible that it was Ramsay's Oration and his subsequent letters that triggered, if not directly caused, the prohibition of all Masonic gatherings in France in April of the same year (1738?). For how could he, being a Mason, a Scot, and a man of real and extensive learning, understand that what the Church and State in France were really afraid of was not just one more assembly of noblemen amusing themselves, but their growing tendency towards enlightening others?

In his oration Ramsay made three epoch-making claims. The first places the origin of Masonic Ritual "at the time of the last Crusades" and associates them with the Knights of St John of Jerusalem, the Knights Templar and the esoteric traditions of other medieval Christian Orders. The second asserts that after the suppression of the Templars in the beginning of the fourteenth century and the decline of the other

Orders, their esoteric traditions were originally grafted onto, or found shelter among, some Scottish Masonic Lodges, eg. the Mother Lodge of Kilwinning.[8] And the third maintains that those Scottish Traditions (or Orders), which are Christian by definition, though not specifically Catholic (due to their pre-Reformation origin) were still continuing in Scottish Masonry, and that he himself represented them in France as well as England.

Ramsay knew perfectly well that, being what he was, a Christian mystic and spiritual adventurer, he could never have converted a single French gentleman to the type of Masonry provided by the revived Grand Lodge of England. At the same time, he was equally aware – and this is evident in his oration – that the ethical Universalism (and, as such, neutrality towards any concrete religion, Catholicism included) of British Masonry still remained absolutely necessary, particularly because this neutrality was consonant with the spirit of the French Enlightenment, at that time not yet overtly anti-Catholic. Thus, his religious programme was focused on making Masonry less Old Testament in character, less rationalistic, and far more continental (that is, chaotic and imaginative) in its style and symbols – although it is persistently referred to as Scottish by his followers. The proliferation and spread of his Scottish Degrees was very rapid, not only in Europe,[9] but also, only a little later, in England, where it inspired the proliferation and spread of the parallel systems of the so-called "Higher Degrees" sanctioned by the Grand Lodge of England. The way in which Ramsay invented his Degrees was, in practice, quite close to the way in which his vehement critics from the Grand Lodge invented theirs. And his Utopian idea of "human spiritual unity" has had a lasting effect on the formation and development of the Scottish Order, another striking example of Masonic religious syncretism.

Notes

1 Dr Francis Drake was initiated in 1725, and in 1761 he was elected the Grand Master of the Grand Lodge of all England at York. He was a member of the Royal Society and a very learned antiquary.

2 E.M.P., 1945, pp. 197–207.

3 See above, Anderson's *Constitutions* of 1738, p. 41, where Jesus Christ is the Grand Master of the Christian Church.

4 *Idem*, p. 214.

5 In a strange way the contradictions between the French and English Masonic philosophies echo contradictions, personal as well as theoretical, between David Hume and Jean Jacques Rousseau.

6 ". . . He detested Calvin; and Spinoza may be said to have suffered for seeming

to share determinism ..." G. D. Henderson, *Chevalier Ramsay*, Aberdeen, 1952, p. 235.

7 *Idem*, p. 168. "My dearest Friend," said one of his Jacobite associates. "You cannot cheat both the Church and Police, you have to choose." But the thing was that he cheated nobody, not even himself, for he sincerely hoped that it would be possible to combine Masonry and Catholicism within French society, and Masonic Rites and Catholic Liturgy within the Society of Freemasons.

8 W. Lee Ker, *Mother Lodge, Kilwinning*, London, 1896, p. 149; R. F. Gould, pp. 274–8.

9 "The Paris [Regular] Lodge was increasingly unable to control this luxuriant growth and consequent erosion of its authority." Chr. McIntosh. *The Rosy Cross Unveiled*, Wellingborough, 1980, p. 84.

CHAPTER 7

Spread, Lull and Turmoil – 1739–1813

Ancients versus Moderns, the Royal Arch and the Founding of the Rival Grand Lodges

No person may be persuaded to become a Mason. It is correct to say that he must not be persuaded at all.
A. E. Waite, *A New Encyclopaedia of Freemasonry* Vol. I.

By 1739 the primary impulse to create was spent and the offical version fixed. However, Masons almost immediately started subjecting to critical analysis what had been invented by their predecessors and began reassessing, revising and rewriting, and adding a plethora of secondary detail to it. Anderson's History, by the mere fact of its inclusion in the *Constitutions* of 1738, had become not only official but canonical. To revise it meant altering the whole framework of Masonic ideology which, itself, can be considered as a fixing of Masons' historical consciousness as it existed in the beginning of the eighteenth century. The co-existence of the Masonic Constitutions with Masonic history, which was never particularly comfortable, very soon became so precarious that, after the reunification of Antients and Moderns in 1813, the United Grand Lodge decided at last to stop incorporating a historical element into the Constitutions. Thus the great divorce was achieved, and Masonic history became constitutionally independent.

After Anderson's death, with the History canonized, the Ritual established, and the organizational structure at least roughly worked out, the geographical spread of Masonry continued unimpeded on such a scale and with such speed that one may only wonder how the Grand Lodge of England could at that time have still remained "a movable entity", with an inventory not exceeding a dozen items, and an annual budget of not more than a couple of hundred pounds. Through the network of Provincial Grand Lodges, the Grand Lodge of England, though meeting only quarterly, continued to warrant lodges throughout the then civilized world in hundreds and, very soon, thousands. The Lodges were formed not only, as before, in pubs and taverns in this country, but among regiments, in forts, castles of grand and petty potentates, in the private homes and manor houses of English, Scottish and Irish gentry, as well as in the Colonies, in the salons of Continental courtiers and Encyclopaedists[1] and even in prisons.

Back in London, however, under the Grand Mastership of Lord Raymond (1739), the Lodges were experiencing a lull, even a decline, which might be accounted for by the too rapid expansion of Masonry elsewhere.[2] The initial impulse which resulted in the formation of the Grand Lodge, the structurization of its Ritual, and the invention of its History, became attenuated and less intense but by no means extinguished, and it only needed new blood and the candidates of the next generation to come in and give it fresh impetus. This new impetus was not primarily about *association*, though the idea of Grand Lodge was that of association and the Institution as its form. What underlay it was that powerful tendency to symbolization and self-symbolization, which was felt strongly at that time by so many people both in Britain and on the Continent, and which assumed its form and expression in the Institution of the Craft. On this subject William Preston, who was soon to become "the second Anderson", writes: "irregularities continued to prevail".[3] But what irregularities? As far as one can judge now, most of them were directly or indirectly, in one way or the other, connected with the Ritual, and with religion, symbolism and prayer. "The energies unleashed by the coming to the surface of human history of the first *openly symbolical* union of men of all creeds",[4] initially embodied in the quintessentially British form of the Masonry of the Grand Lodge of England, soon found themselves constrained by that form and broke free without seeking for new modes of realization. To put it more concisely: more than a quarter of all the early English Lodges (about seventy, and at least half of them in London) ceased to exist in the 1740s, and many of the survivors became more and more alienated from the Grand Lodge. They either became more autonomous and independent as regards their ritual and inner transactions, or seceded altogether from its jurisdiction. Finally, in certain Lodges, particularly in some of the *Old* ones in London, there started to arise disagreements and controversies of a specifically religious nature,[5] contravening the express prohibition on such controversies.

In about 1739, rumoured accusations that Masonry was in danger of becoming dominated by Jews or excessively Judaist in character, or both, began to circulate in London. Similarly, it was suggested that Masonry on the Continent was becoming perverted by the inclusion of Cabbalistic symbols and ideas incompatible with the letter and spirit of pure and genuine Masonry.[6]

But in fact Jews did not join English Masonry in any significant number, nor were they persuaded to join it. And even if there was an assimilatory tendency in British Jewry at that time, it was undoubtedly negligible in comparison with what was happening among German Jews.

It was the spirit and atmosphere of a free-thinking, non-dogmatic, and non-theological religious discussion (and not that of religious controversy, so strictly forbidden in the *Constitutions* of 1723 and 1738) that attracted Jews to the Lodge. The atmosphere had already become so saturated with biblical and Judaic images, situations and allusions, that a Jew with religious interests could not fail to feel free to discuss his own religion within the Masonic context.

Generally speaking, to understand the religious aspect of British Free-masonry, and with some reservations Freemasonry in general, one has to realize that Masonry, taken both in its origins and in its present state, provides a possibility of freethinking within religion, conceived in the broadest sense – not necessarily within the Church of England or even within Christianity. That is why Masonry appeared so dangerous to the Vatican, which issued the first Papal Bull against it in 1737, and declared it the only historical religious movement "not forgiven" even during the progressive era of John XXIII in the 1960s. And that is why, even now, there are still some attempts on the part of certain Anglican clergy to forbid Masonry within the Church of England. They feel that the Church of England has already become too permissive and that to tolerate Masonry is simply going too far. But tolerate it it did for 217 years, and only the Anglican Church's disastrous lack of both self-consciousness and self-reflection has prevented it from understanding the simplest fact – that Masonry in England has been and still is a phenomenon not only English, but Anglican too. Within the Lodge, however, Anglicans did not oppose themselves to the dissenters and it goes without saying that the admission of Jews was, for the most part, not a subject of discussion, let alone controversy.

In the 1740s, there was quite a small number of Israelites (as they were often called) among London Masons, but exactly when they started being admitted remains uncertain. Dr G. Oliver explains the initial Jewish situation in the Order in a way which clearly reveals his own strictly Masonic position of tolerance and Freethinking: "We heard at that time that certain Jews were implicated in the *unauthorized innovations* of our *continental* Brethren . . . and it was the *first notice* we ever received of the descendants of Abraham being admitted to a participation in our *Christian* privileges. From this success in procuring initiation into the *surreptitious* Masonry of the Continent, the English Jews soon became successful candidates for admission into our *symbolical* order; for it was justly contended that, as Jews were not excluded from attending Christian Churches, it would be *impolite* and *uncharitable* to close a *Christian Lodge* against them. From that period they have been received into Masonry as members of a *Universal Order*, whose principles, like those of Christian religion, are destined to cover the earth as the waters cover the sea.''[7] This passage, however historically dubious and dogmatically inconsistent,[8] is, in my opinion, a most remarkable specimen of Masonic freethinking rhetoric. Even allowing for the fact that, writing in the middle of the nineteenth century, he sometimes rather tastelessly imitates the style and language of Dr Thomas Manningham, one of the most prominent Masons and Past Grand Steward in the 1740s, this passage reveals if not a historical truth, at least the turns and moves of Oliver's Masonic historical consciousness.[9] According to Oliver: (1) Jews appear on the scene of English Masonry due to their association with the spurious and corrupted Masonry on the Continent; (2) For which (contradictory) reason they are soon successfully admitted to the true and genuine English Masonry, which is, by Oliver's definition, Christian *par excellence*; (3) Because it is Christian, it admits Jews as does the Christian Church itself; (4) That Masonry is as universal an Order as Christianity a religion, which is why such a particular and sectarian religion as Judaism might be accommodated to Masonry.[10]

The most important thing here is that Jews, in so far as they were noticed as such, were admitted to English (and to almost any other) Masonry naturally, not ideologically; as naturally as Masons themselves were rejected by the Vatican. For at the time when the notorious Papal Bull was issued (1737), the learned prelates of the Roman Curia knew virtually nothing about Masonry, not even the famous clause on God and Religion in Anderson's Constitutions. They simply acted on its reputation for dangerous Freethinking.[11] And if some of the first Jews in London Lodges regarded the symbolism and ritual of Masonry as essentially Jewish, this meant that it was seen by them on the one hand as emphatically non-Catholic, and on the other, as the fulfilment of the pledge and promise of universal biblically-based tolerance. In the early period of Masonic history the very fact of Jewish presence and participation, however numerically small, can be considered as extremely significant historically for both Masonry and Jewry. For, on the one hand, the Masonic connection with Jewry and Judaism has resulted in the enduring stigma and universally held notion of a Judaeo-Masonic Conspiracy; and on the other it has offered a powerful alternative to assimilation through Christianization.

Hostility to Masonry within the hierarchy of the Catholic Church was exacerbated by the acceptance of Jews into the Lodges in England and on the Continent but, true to form, the English Brethren did not pay much attention to the Catholic reaction against Masonry.[12] The position of Jews within Masonry is summed up by the fact that they have never formed a single exclusively Jewish Lodge in England, whereas some other non-English peoples residing in England, mainly German and Dutch, developed, at least for periods of time, their own ethnically based Lodges or Daughter-Lodges.

The main reason for a Jew to belong to a Lodge was so as to be a Jew in a non-Jewish religious situation, and to be included within the universalist and cosmopolitan context of the Lodge, even if this should formally acknowledge itself as Christian and English. As early as the 1750s the Masonic Jews became quite well known, particularly in the Old Lodges in London, for their eloquence on religious topics and their fortitude, not to speak of intransigence, in the amicable disputes with such veterans of the Masonic art of Oratory as Dr Manningham, Dr Clare, and poor Dr Dodd. In the strangest way, and quite spontaneously, without being remotely aware of it, English Masonry at that time succeeded in neutralizing Judaism within the Lodge,[13] but at the cost of neutralizing Christianity as well, as A. E. Waite and a few other critics of the de-Christianization of Masonry have complained. The Order did manage, however, to find some other means of preserving Christianity within its scope and of preserving itself within the scope of Christianity.[14]

Two precautionary measures were taken by the Grand Lodge of England. One was to limit the scale of religious discussions within the Lodge, the other to restrict the level of Masonic activity in London outside the Lodge.[15] In 1741, under the Grand Mastership of James, Earl of Morton, Martin Clare assiduously revised all previous lectures and established a new official and obligatory standard or pattern of lectures on religion, ritual and symbolism.[16] In that same year all forms of publicity, including street processions, theatrical benefits, recitations and so forth, were strictly forbidden, indefinitely. A series of limiting decisions by the Grand Lodge began, including the resurrection of one old but hitherto never implemented rule that no Mason could be a member of more than one Lodge – an attempt at halting the decrease in the number of Lodges in London. Almost all Masonic historians speak of the atmosphere of discord and decline within the Craft, and of the cloud of suspicion and disaffection surrounding it in the 1740s and 50s, but not many, it seems, seriously tried to discover the cause of this, though the period is very poorly documented. A letter written in 1743 by Horace Walpole (who was mentioned in Anderson's *Constitutions* of 1738) quoted by John Hamill, states, "The Free Masons are in so low a repute now ... that nothing but a persecution could bring them into vogue here again."[17] Nevertheless, however exhaustive the Masonic expansion of the 1730s might have been, the main reason for the subsequent hiatus in England at that time was the lack of new Masonic ideas or, more likely, their reformulation. When the "Great Schism" came about, and the first illegitimate child of Masonic law-giving, the treatise *Ahiman Rezon*, saw the light in 1756, it becomes evident, in retrospect, that the only real difference between the *Constitutions* of Dr Anderson and that of the schismatics lay not in the essence, but in the shape of Masonic teaching.

When the rival Grand Lodge of the *Antient* Masons appeared in the early 1750s, its advantage was to be found in the individual characters of its founders and leaders – the *Irish* character, according to Henry Sadler and all who have followed him from the 1890s to this day.[18] The Antient Grand Lodge was established probably as early as 1751, but its existence did not come to the notice of the Grand Lodge of England till 1753, when the first Antient Grand Master, Robert Turner, was elected. Even then there was no official reaction on the part of the Craft. Nor is this surprising, for we may suppose that somewhere in London, the second largest city in Europe at that time, some Masons met in a pub or tavern and simply decided to form their own Grand Lodge. So we may suppose that the second Grand Lodge became known to the first at the moment it wished to make itself known, and not as just another Grand Lodge but as the only true and "old" Grand Lodge *in London*.[19] At any rate, it decided to call itself the true Grand Lodge because it claimed to be older than the Grand Lodge of England. This institution, according to the Antients, was not entitled even to its thirty-five years. Lacking the minimum of five Lodges required "by an antient custom", it had never been properly formed.[20] At the beginning, there was nothing about essential principles but only about chronological priority, and chronological priority of *whom* and not of *what*. The first real challenge to the orthodox representation of Masonic ideas arose with the appearance on the scene of Lawrence Dermott, who became the Grand Secretary of the Antients in 1752.

Lawrence Dermott, a travelling printer, artist, and later a fairly prosperous London wine merchant, was a Masonic luminary of a special kind – he was practically the only true ideological reshaper of Masonry. And if, indeed, there were a number of Irish Masons in London who could not, or did not want to take their places in the English Grand Lodge, then Dermott was a man who was seeking for a vacant site to *restore* something that had never existed in the first place. In describing Dermott as ideological I use the definition of ideology as the teaching or set of ideas of whatever character, content or principles, belonging to a group of people (class, sect, nation, etc.) which is in one way or another consciously opposed to some other group with its own set of ideas, principles, etc. While each and every already formulated idea or principle may become an ideology, there are and always have been very many that have not actually (i.e. historically) done so. Masonic ideas were not and are not ideological as such, but when the "anti-Lodge" arose, its builders' task became purely ideological, for they immediately began to use Masonic ideas centrifugally within the context of their opposition to another body, the Grand Lodge of England.[21] So, Dermott started by selecting for remodelling such ideas from Masonry as he could use thereafter as ideological points of controversy with the Grand Lodge of England.

The first question Dermott asks in his book, *Ahiman Rezon*, is historical: it is about the claim to the term "Antient". The term is used, he says, because the Antients' history is truly mystical, in the sense that it is the history of mysteries and not of external events artificially Masonized. He writes in the second edition of his own Constitutions (1766) about the historical section of Anderson's 1738 edition: "I have my doubts whether such histories [as those of the origins of Masonry from Adam, or Cain, etc.] are of any use in the secret mysteries of the Craft." Then he comments specifically on Anderson's additional chapter: ". . . My intention being only to expose ridiculous innovations, and fabulous accounts of grandmasters, whose Masonical authority never existed."[22] He ridicules Anderson's history not so much as a falsification, but rather as something hopelessly trivial – the uninventive play of leisurely amateurs – when compared with the mysterious and secret real Masonic history. He dismisses, with crushing sarcasm, the historic founding of the Grand Lodge of England, thus:

About the year 1717, some joyous companions (Bro. Tho. Grinsell, a man of great veracity . . . informed his Lodge No. 3, in London, in 1753), the eight persons whose names were Desaguliers, Gofton, King, Calvert, Lumley, Madden, De Noyer, and Vraden, were the geniuses to whom the world is indebted for the memorable invention of Modern Masonry.[23]

So for the first time in its very brief history, the Masonry of the Grand Lodge of England was styled "Modern" and, by implication, non-genuine and non-universal. Because – and here the ideological character of Dermott's message becomes quite obvious – there can be only *one* true Masonry and *one* proper Grand Lodge.[24]

Now we come to the second point: the universality of Dermott's new "Antient" Masonry. Using a series of rhetorical questions he attempts to convince the reader: "Whether Free-masonry, as practised in antient Lodges is universal? – Yes. Whether what is called Antient Masonry is universal? – Yes. Whether what is called Modern Masonry is universal? – No."[25] And, of course, in declaiming all this he conveniently ignores the fact that it is he who branded the Masons of the Grand Lodge of England "Modern", and that the name was never applied to them by themselves or, until then, by anybody else. He writes: "Several eminent Craftsmen residing in Scotland, Ireland, America, and other places . . . have greatly importuned me to give them some account of what is called Modern Masonry in London . . . I had the like curiosity myself in 1748, when I was first introduced into that Society."[26] So he first sought admission into a "Modern" Lodge in order to satisfy his curiosity about the structure and discipline of Masonry as an organization, soon coming to the conclusion that it was neither sufficiently ancient, nor truly universal, and that his task was not to improve this deficient organization but to produce a new type of institution altogether which better exemplified these qualities. What exactly he meant by universal is not easy to determine. More democratic? Less authoritarian? Less elitist? He does not elaborate.[27]

The first idea calling for ideological reshaping concerned "God and Religion". On this point he is both flexible and determined. After repeating the beginning of the celebrated formulation of Anderson's – "A Mason is obliged by his tenure to believe firmly in true worship of the eternal God" – he goes on to change the rest – both in words and emphasis: ". . . as well as in all those sacred records which *the dignitaries and fathers of the Church* have compiled and published for the use of all good men."[28] So, Anderson's "Religion in which all men agree", is firmly replaced by the Christian Church with its worship, liturgy, and corpus of canonical texts. But a little further on he again joins Anderson in Charge I: "A Mason is obliged by his tenure to observe the moral law as a true Noachida . . ."[29] He then goes on to follow Anderson almost word for word. Like his predecessor, he is an open partisan of secrecy, for a really mystical (i.e. founded on mysteries) society is secret both by definition and by the will of God, and Masonry is the embodiment of secrecy understood as a universal spiritual quality:

. . . God himself is well pleased with secrecy. And although, for man's

good, the Lord has been pleased to reveal some things, yet it is impossible at any time to change or alter his determination; in regard whereof
the reverend wise men of ancient times, evermore affected to perform
their intentions secretly.[30]

In *Ahiman Rezon*, Masonry is presented to Masons as the Secret Christian Society fit for "all good men", and, of course, it is due to its
universalism that some men "bad and wicked" should, necessarily, find
themselves in it too. This is his simple apology which, it is worth noting,
is again of a markedly Christian character:

. . . As the number of good and wise Free-masons always exceeded that
of the foolish and wicked, it would be as absurd to condemn the whole
for the part, as it would be in the Jews, to condemn Shem and
Japhet for the curse brought upon Ham; or the Christians to condemn
the eleven apostles, because Judas turned traitor . . .[31]

Freemasonry is good and necessary as the only Institution which is
Christian and universal at the same time; "Therefore" – he writes – "I
humbly presume it will of consequence be granted, that the welfare and
good of mankind was the cause or motive of so grand an institution as
Free-masonry."[32] Thus, with regard to religion, the Antients, seizing on
the vagueness of Anderson's formulation and turning it to their advantage, were able to set up an unequivocally Christian Institution in compe-
tition with the less overtly Christian Grand Lodge.

Such was the ideological position of the Antients *v.* Moderns as it is
set out in the second edition of *Ahiman Rezon* (1766) and, one may
suppose, as it had existed between the time when the book was written,
in 1755, and the time of its second edition. But it might well be that
at the beginning of their historical existence the Antients possessed only
a most superficial knowledge of their opponents, and the "Moderns" no
knowledge at all of the challengers.[33] The real cause of the formation
of the Antients is still hard to determine. Was it, indeed, their dissatisfaction and disagreement with the policy and principles of the Prime
Grand Lodge in the late 1730s, or was their appearance on the scene
of Masonic history merely, or mainly, spontaneous, and marked by an
almost total ignorance of the "Moderns"? Of the Masonic historians of
Freemasonry, H. Sadler and R. F. Gould adhere to the first point of
view, while G. J. Findel and J. Hamill tend towards the second.[34] The
almost immediate success of the Antients – they were very soon recognized by the Grand Lodges of Ireland and Scotland and also (a little
later) by the *Grand Lodge of all England at York*,[35] and started warranting

dozens of Lodges at home, in the army, and abroad – might be accounted for by the Masonry's *objective* need to become more diverse and multifarious in its ideas as well as in its organizational structure.

In *Ahiman Rezon* (1766) Lawrence Dermott played his trump-card: for the first time in Masonic history he offered to Masons a Higher Degree called the *Royal Arch*, not as an addition to the three degrees Craft, nor as its alternative, but as its very essence.[36] He begins by stating that the Mason-ness of the Grand Lodge of England is not true Mason-ness because its Master Masons could not be admitted into a Royal Arch Lodge, and by asking whether it is "possible to initiate or introduce a Modern Mason into the Royal Arch Lodge? – No."[37] And it is not in the Ritual of the Craft Degrees but in the Royal Arch Ritual that the mystical core of all Masonry, including the Craft, can be found. The following passage from *Ahiman Rezon*, Christian and at the same time Gnostic, excellently demonstrates the tendency in Masonry to appropriate and re-activate some earlier mystical material of seventeenth- and, possibly, sixteenth-century Europe.

A Prayer repeated in the Royal Arch Lodge at Jerusalem: Thou hast loved us, O Lord our God, with eternal love; Thou hast spared us with great and exceeding patience, our Father and our King, for thy great Name's sake, and for our fathers' sake who trusted in thee, to whom thou didst teach the statutes of life . . . so be Thou merciful unto us, O our Father . . . and cause our hearts to cleave to thy law, and unite them in the love and fear of thy *Name* . . . Because we have trusted in thy *Holy, Great, Mighty,* and *Terrible* N A M E, *we will rejoice and be glad in Thy salvation, and in Thy mercies, O Lord our God; and the multitude of thy mercies shall not forsake us for ever; Selah. And now make haste and bring upon us a blessing . . . ; and Thou, our King, has caused us to cleave to thy great* N A M E *. . . ; blessed art Thou, O Lord God, who has chosen Thy people Israel in love.*[38]

It is clear that, putting aside all formal and ideological differences between the Antients and the Moderns as expressed in *Ahiman Rezon*, it is the Royal Arch that from the very beginning of the former figured as their only positive complex of ideas, constituting what can be considered as their transcendental philosophical basis.[39] The name of this degree owes its origin to one of the central myths of ancient Egypt: ". . . the imaginary arch made in the heavens by the course of King Osiris, the Sun, from the vernal to the autumnal equinox. The signs through which he passes in forming this semicircle, including those of the equinox, being seven, the number of grades or steps required to be taken by the Mason to entitle him to the honours of this degree."[40]

The idea underlying this degree with respect to the Three Degrees Craft is that of the twofold division of Masons: on the one hand we have Entered Apprentices, Fellow Crafts, and Master Masons who are still in "a state of profound ignorance of the sublime secret which is disclosed in this chapter";[41] on the other hand we have those Master Masons (only Master Masons are eligible for Royal Arch initiation) who have already obtained admission to that "sublime secret" and become Companions of the Order or Chapter consisting of nine Officers, the three of whom constitute "the grand council, and one denominated captain of the host".[42]

But what is all this about? As far as an uninitiated person could imagine, and particularly after having read "A Prayer", quoted above, it is about religion in general, and *natural* religion in particular. The dual character of the whole of Masonry reflects the two phases of the history, individual as well as global, of the whole of religion. Freemasonry is deemed to be a place where people who are still in a state of natural religion, pagan or otherwise – marked by their belief in a supernatural Supreme Being – are introduced into the way towards absolute monotheism. But the secret of this can be found only through the "superstructure" of the Royal Arch. The whole edifice is again thoroughly symbolic: the Candidate symbolizes the state of natural religion-cum-primary ignorance; the Master Mason symbolizes the potentiality of consummation of the state of Monotheism; Monotheism is symbolized by Osiris who is the *Logos* or *Word*, as the Master Mason in the Ritual already described *is* the lost word of Hiram; and, finally, Osiris is symbolized by Hiram.

In the Royal Arch more than anywhere else Freemasonry came to reflect upon itself as a step in the mystical ascension, through various phases of initiation, into the highest symbolism. The scheme and character of this reflection seems to be very Gnostical (in a general, and not merely Christian sense), but it reveals one other feature, deeply ingrained in Craft Masonry: its religious relativism. Religious relativism in a phenomenology of religion can be approximately described as what happens when a religion, by means of self-reflection, self-awareness, and self-description, establishes its own place with respect to some other religion as well as to religion in general. This has the inevitable consequence that the religion in question loses its absolute status, and, furthermore, that any other religion which happens to be related to the first also becomes relative. A recently published letter from Sir Ralph Verney to *The Times* demonstrates this phenomenon on quite a simple level of spontaneously expressed religious opinion:

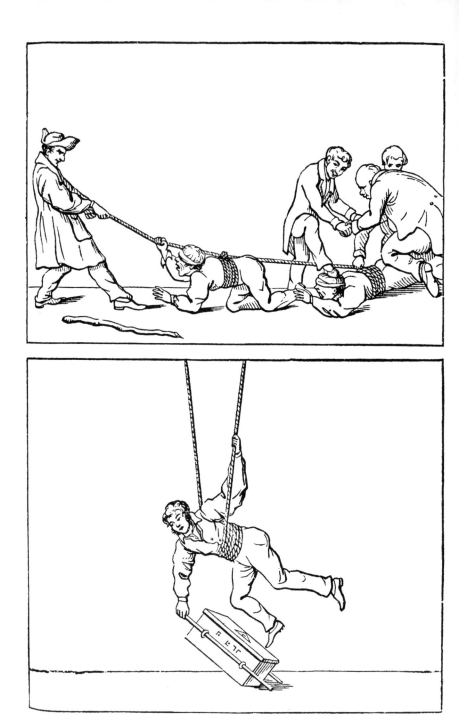

The Candidates passing under the Living Arch *and* The Descent of a Companion into the Vault of the Nine Arches.

... I have been a Freemason for the whole of my adult life and also a regular communicant of the Anglican Church. I have been privileged to consecrate more than 20 new chapters of Royal Arch Masonry ... and, as patron of five Anglican livings, to present to the Bishop for induction almost as many Anglican priests. Each of these duties has complemented the other and the prayer of King Solomon is equally relevant to both – "Hear thou in Heaven thy dwelling place and when thou hearest forgive" ... I cannot help noticing that my 20 chapters have contributed more to the happiness of Society than some of my incumbents ... Surely Synod should encourage the Holy Spirit to work through both.[43]

The main point of Verney's letter – of which he himself seems to have been unaware, since it had become part and parcel of his religious consciousness before he formed the first of his twenty Royal Arch Chapters – is that very religious relativism so typical of the Higher Degrees Masonry: that almost inbred conviction that one's own religion is, or might be, a combination of the conventional and mainstream (the Anglican Church, for example) with a rampant mystical symbolism. And the relation between these two is determined by one's own choice or God's will, or both.[44] But, however humanistic and downbeat Verney's tone, it remains an unquestionable fact that not only was the Royal Arch more Christian than Masonry *in toto*, but more mystical, and definitely more Trinitarian.[45]

The early history of the Royal Arch, if it has one, is more obscure even than that of the Antients. G. J. Findel, who disliked this rite, attributes its invention to the Chevalier de Ramsay, creator of the Scottish Degrees, who introduced it in France somewhere between 1738 and 1741. From there it was brought to England (or Ireland) around 1743.[46] While referring to it as the "French" Royal Arch, Ramsay claimed it was in fact a revival of an off-shoot of the traditional Royal Arch of the Scots. Since there is no evidence that such a tradition actually existed in Scotland at that time, he may have meant that in Masonry there was (and always had been) a mystical Quest, the remembrance or intuition of which he had taken upon himself to shape in the form of his Royal Arch.[47] Here, as in many other things Masonic, we have a constant tension between history, whether real or imagined, and non-temporal mysticism, between dated or datable events and an ahistorical memory or recollection of that which is intuited as being always there, since time immemorial.[48]

The Quest here is a process, but timeless; a course, but tangential;

an axiom, but one subject to too many conditions to be directly realized. The classical binary opposition of the European Protestant religious consciousness, natural *versus* divinely inspired, has assumed in the Royal Arch the very peculiar form of an almost indefinitely repeated symbolic formula: "A" symbolizes "B", but "B" symbolizes "C" and then "A" symbolizes "C", and so on. The Master Mason's awareness of mortality cannot be absolute but it represents the highest point that human nature can reach without Divine Inspiration or Revelation (as does the "Augustan Stile" in architecture, according to Anderson). But, as I have already mentioned, the buck doesn't stop here: *this* symbolic situation, taken as a whole, symbolizes in turn the Master Mason's mystical potential to pass from a partial awareness of mortality to that of perfect regeneration "in the Mansions of Bliss and in the Presence of the Great *I AM.*"[49] And it was Lawrence Dermott, who I am sure nobody would have suspected of inventing the Royal Arch, who by incorporating it into his supposedly more democratic Antient Masonry actually made the now "Four Degrees" Society far more elitist than what remained under the aegis of the Grand Lodge of England.

A Candidate for the Royal Arch is regarded as being in a state of darkness, but his darkness is quite different from the darkness of an Entered Apprentice, for he has already passed through the "dark night of the soul" towards the Light in the Ritual of Master Mason's Raising. Here we deal with quite another kind of symbolism centred on one's own "material and psychical organism" and connected with a certain type of contemplative interiorization of symbols not dissimilar to some yogic practices.[50] The central point in the Ceremony of Initiation is the separation of the Candidate's "material shell" from the egg-yolk of his personal consciousness: his movement across the chequered floor to the centre of the Lodge is, first of all, a test in humility and obedience completed in three stages symbolizing three approximations to the spiritual essence. And, if in the previous attainment of the Master Mason's Degrees the Master Mason's Light was achieved by his own effort and endeavour, together with his repossession of the Master Mason's Word, the impulse is now issued from the Highest and Primal Light. This Light is one with the Divine Word, and finds its reception in, or becomes self-conscious within the "efficient physiological organism ... of the illumined candidate", which "is the equivalent of *Beatific Vision* of Christian theology, and of Samadhi [the state of highest concentration]" in Buddhism.[51]

This attainment of the Light is objective, because it is the Light that appears from above within the candidate, but at the same time it is subjective as the only real content of the initiatory rite of the Royal Arch; and it is this double character of the Ritual that reflects its absolutely symbolic nature and essence. Symbol is always dual; one and another taken together, or two in one: image and thought, idea and thing, body and consciousness. In comparison with the symbolism of the Royal Arch, which is nearer to revelation, the symbolism of the Three Degrees Craft remains on the level of allegory. And it is an allegorical enactment of quite another version of the traditional Masonic history with which the Candidate is confronted after he has already completed the first part of the Royal Arch Ceremony.[52] In Royal Arch terminology the three sojourners, who represent the three aspects of man "wayfaring upon a plan of impermanence" – "passive negative un-consciousness", "active positive consciousness", and the "connecting, co-ordinating principle" – describe "their release from the captivity in Babylon, their return to Jerusalem", and their rediscovery of the Ancient Lore. This triadic structure is manifested in the constitution of the Chapter (i.e. Lodge) of the Royal Arch, the Three Degrees of which are: *Haggai* (passive individual Spirit), *Joshua* (active individual Spirit), and *Zerubbabel* (the resolving spiritual principle).[53]

A. E. Waite, who is probably one of the very few philosophers within Freemasonry, thinks that it is in the Royal Arch that Freemasonry left the domain of allegory and historical legend, and stepped into the realm of a pure symbolism of spirit, a realm where the inhabitants are no longer simply enacting historical drama, but really are back in the past itself. In the Three Degrees Craft the history, however conventionally presented and symbolically used, may still be thought of and imagined as historical, whereas in the Ritual of the Royal Arch it is ousted from the world of images and acquires a metaphysical reality – in other words it becomes a symbol of the Divine Absolute.[54] The cohabitation of Craft with the Royal Arch is itself symbolic, and sometimes it seems to me that when Dermott included the latter in the former he may have meant them to be, or to become, one, but in reality their combination only stresses their heterogeneity. For, as Waite quite aptly sums it up, ". . . the Third Degree is – historically speaking – a story without an end, while . . . the English Royal Arch is a prologomenon to another story, which is not to be found in Masonry".[55]

What follows is an abbreviated description of the initiatory ceremony of the Royal Arch according to Fellows.[56]

The Officers and Companions of the Chapter being stationed, the High Priest says: "Companions, I am about to open a chapter of Royal Arch Masons, and will thank you for your attention and assistance. If there is any person present who is not a Royal Arch Mason, he is requested to retire. Companion Captain of the host, the first care of congregated Masons?"

Captain: "To see the tabernacle duly guarded."

High Priest: "Attend to that part of your duty."

The Captain of the host stations the guard at the outside of the door, gives him his orders . . . He then reports that the chapter is duly guarded, by a Companion of this Degree at the outer avenue, with a drawn sword in his hand. The High Priest then gives two raps with his gavel, and asks the following questions: "Captain of the host, are you a Royal Arch Mason?" – "I am, that I am." "How shall I know you to be a Royal Arch Mason?" – "By three times three." He thus proceeds, as in the other Degrees, to demand the stations and duties of the Officers of the Chapter; which are as follows:

The Captain of the host is stationed at the right hand of the Grand Council to receive their orders and see them duly executed.

The station of the principal sojourner is at the left hand of the Grand Council to bring the blind by a way they know not, "to lead them in paths they have not known, to make darkness light before them, and crooked things straight."

The duties of the two last mentioned Officers in the ancient mysteries appertain to one character, Mercury, who was the messenger of the Gods, and the conductor of souls to the other world through the dark regions below.

The Royal Arch, like the other great mysteries, contains a scenic representation of a journey from this world to the next. In the way are four guarded passes, called *vails*, emblematic of the equinoxes and solstices, allegorically denominated gates of heaven, through which lies the sun's course.

Three of the Officers, stationed at these passes, are called Grand Masters of the first, second, and third *vail*, who require certain tokens and passwords of the candidates on their admission through them. The fourth officer is styled Royal Arch Captain. He is stationed at the inner *vail*, or entrance of the *sanctum sanctorum*, to guard the same, and see that none pass but such as are duly qualified, and have the proper passwords and signet of truth. The colours of their respective banners are: blue, purple, red, and white, which have the same astrological reference as the robes of the Grand Council.[57] The white banner is emblematic of that purity of heart, and rectitude of conduct which is essential to obtain admission into the divine *sanctum sanctorum* above.

In the duty assigned to the Royal Arch Captain there is an allusion to the "severe and incorruptible boatman, Charon", who was prohibited from transporting souls across the lake or river Acheron to the Elysian fields, the heaven of the ancients, without the signet of the judges, who were appointed to examine the characters of the deceased, and to grant or withhold their permission accordingly.

Nine Companions must be present at the opening of the Royal Arch Chapter. Neither more nor fewer than three are permitted to take this Degree at the same time. The candidates are prepared by tying a blindfold round their heads and coiling a rope seven times round the body of each, which unites them together, with three feet of slack rope between them.

Thus prepared, they are led into the Royal Arch Chapter which they are told is dedicated to enlightening those who are in darkness, and illuminating the Way, the Truth, and the Life.

On entering the Chapter they pass under what is called a Living Arch, which is formed by a number of Companions arranging themselves on both sides of the door, each joining hands with the one opposite. The Conductor leads them through and admonishes them: "Stoop low, brothers; remember that he that humbleth himself shall be exalted; stoop low, brothers, stoop low; we are about to enter the Arch." This is raised up for him, but lowered when the candidates come under it. They seldom pass the first pair of hands without being obliged to support themselves on their hands and knees. Their progress may well be imagined to be very slow; for, notwithstanding their humble condition, they are under the necessity of sustaining on their backs nearly the whole weight of the Living Arch above. The Conductor, to encourage them, calls out occasionally: "Stoop low, brothers, stoop low!" If they go too slowly to suit the Companions it is not unusual for them to be prodded with a sharp point to goad them on. After they have endured this humiliating exercise for as long as the Companions think fit they emerge from under the Living Arch.

Having got through the Arch, the candidates are conducted once round the Chapter and directed to kneel at the altar to receive the obligation. The Principal Sojourner then addresses them thus: "Brethren, as you advance in Masonry your obligation becomes more binding. You are now kneeling at the altar for the seventh time, and about to take a solemn oath or obligation. If you are willing to proceed say after me:

"I, A.B., of my own free will and accord, in presence of Almighty God, and this chapter of Royal Arch Masons, erected to God, and dedicated to Zerubbabel, do hereby, etc."

The *Signs* and *Stars* which form this *semicircle*, being *seven*, represent the number of grades or steps required to be taken by the Mason to entitle him to the honours of this Degree.

The Star below is the Morning Star . . . whose rising brings peace and salvation.

The Coat of Arms represents the soul's evolution.

Lion – the passionate wild-beast stage.

Ox – the stage when one, though sensuous and animal, is able to be docile and disciplined for service.

Man – the stage of human rationality.

Eagle – the stage of upward-soaring spirituality.

The Coffin represents the Soul.

The Sprig of Acacia – the germ of a new and regenerated life of the Soul.

The Chest is the Chest of the Ark.

The Snake represents Secret Wisdom.

The Two Suns are vernal and autumnal equinoxes.

Cornucopia is the emblem of completeness of the created world.

G is the emblem of God as the centre of the created universe – where *The Compasses* are an emblem of one's right spiritual direction within the worldly sphere.

The Chequered Floor is the plan of impermanence upon which man wayfares.

At the conclusion of the oath, the candidates kiss the book seven times.

The candidates are now conducted once round the Chapter and directed to kneel while the Sojourner reads a prayer.

After the prayer, the Principal Sojourner says: "Companions, arise, and follow me."

He conducts them once round the Chapter during which time he reads from Exodus, 3, 1–6:

Now Moses kept the flock of Jethro, his father-in-law, the priest of Midian; and he led the flock to the back side of the desert, and came to the mountain of God, even Horeb. And the angel of the Lord appeared unto him in a flame of fire, out of the midst of the bush; and he looked, and behold the bush burned with fire, and the bush was not consumed.

By the time this reading is ended the candidates have arrived in front of a representation of the burning bush, placed in a corner of the chapter, and the Principal Sojourner then directs them to halt, and lifts up the blindfold.

A Companion who performs this part of the action steps behind the burning bush and calls out vehemently, "Moses! Moses!!" The Principal Sojourner answers for the candidates, "Here am I."

The Companion behind the bush exclaims still more vehemently, "Draw not nigh hither; put off thy shoes from thy feet, for the place where thou standest is holy ground. [Their shoes are now taken off.] I am the God of thy fathers, the God of Abraham, the God of Isaac, and the God of Jacob."

The Principal Sojourner then says to the candidates, "Arise and follow me," and leads them three times round the Chapter, during which time he reads from 2 Chron. 35, 11–20.

[Then] . . . after the words, "and brake down the wall of Jerusalem", the companions . . . make a tremendous noise, by firing pistols, clashing swords, overturning chairs, rolling cannon balls across the floor, etc. to astonish and terrify the candidates.

In the meantime, the candidates are thrown down, bound and dragged out into the preparation room, and the door is closed. On being brought again into the Chapter, they pass under the Living Arch. This is formed on one side of the hall or Chapter; on the other side is what is called the rugged road, which is generally made of blocks of wood, old chairs, benches, etc. The conductor consoles the candidates by observing: "This is the way many great and good men have travelled before you; never deeming it derogatory to their dignity to level themselves with the fraternity. I have often travelled this road from Babylon to Jerusalem, and generally find it rough and rugged. However, I think I never saw it much smoother than it is at the present time."

By this time, the candidates have stumbled over the rugged road, and arrived again at the entrance of the Living Arch. The conductor says: "Companions, there is a very difficult and dangerous pass ahead, which lies directly in our way. Before we attempt to pass it, we must kneel down and pray."

Sundry prayers and passages of scripture are recited before the rugged path is completed. There are clauses in one of them which make it appear that the prayer in question was originally addressed to the sun, when in the lower hemisphere, imploring his return to the upper regions, as follows:

Hear my prayer, O Lord! Give ear to my supplications; for the enemy hath persecuted my soul; he hath made me to dwell in darkness. Therefore is my spirit overwhelmed within me; my heart within me is desolate. Hear me speedily, O Lord! my spirit faileth: hide not thy face from me, lest I be like unto them that go down into the pit. Cause me to hear thy loving kindness in the morning; for in thee do I trust. Bring my soul out of trouble. And of thy mercy cut off my enemies; for I am thy servant.

The most appropriate prayer as regards the mysteries of Masonry is, perhaps, the one recorded by Dermott, which is used in the Lodge of Jewish Freemasons in Israel.

O Lord, excellent art Thou in Thy truth, and there is nothing great in comparison to thee; for thine is the praise, from all the works of Thy hands, for evermore.

Enlighten us, we beseech thee, in the true knowledge of masonry; by the sorrows of Adam, thy first-made man; by the blood of Abel, the holy one; by the righteousness of Seth, in whom thou art well pleased; and by thy covenant with Noah, in whose architecture thou wast pleased to save the seed of thy beloved; number us not among those that know not thy statutes, nor the divine mysteries of the secret Cabala.

But grant, we beseech thee, that the ruler of this lodge may be endued with knowledge and wisdom, to instruct us and explain his secret mysteries, as our holy brother Moses did, in his lodge, to Aaron, to Eleazar, and Ithamar, the sons of Aaron, and the seventy elders of Israel.

And grant that we may understand, learn, and keep all the statutes and commandments of the Lord, and this holy mystery, pure and undefiled unto our lives' end. Amen, Lord.

The candidates, after having passed the four vails, by giving the signs and passwords appropriate to each, are admitted into the presence of the Grand Council, by means of a signet, being a triangular piece of metal with the word *Zer-ubba-bel* engraved upon it.

Finally, the Grand Council, being satisfied as to the intentions of the candidates, directs them to repair to the north-west corner of the ruins of the old temple, and commence removing the rubbish to lay the foundation of the new, for it was in the north-west that the Deity began his operations in the erection of the world. While thus engaged, they discover a secret vault, containing the key stone of the Arch, which had already been placed there during the preceding Degree. On the second descent of one of the candidates he discovers a small box or chest standing on a pedestal, curiously wrought and overlaid with gold: he involuntarily finds his hand raised to guard his eyes from the intense light and heat reflected from it. This proves to be the Ark containing the lost Word, Logos or sun, which accounts for the intense light and heat reflected from it. It contains also, the book of the law – Aaron's rod – a pot of manna, and a key to the ineffable characters of this Degree.

The following questions and answers occur in what are called lectures, after the ceremonies of initiation are passed:

After receiving the obligation, what was said to you? – We were told that we were now obligated and received as Royal Arch Masons, but as this Degree was infinitely more important than any of the preceding, it was necessary for us to pass through many trials, and to travel in rough and rugged ways, to prove our fidelity before we could be entrusted with the more important secrets of this Degree. We were further told that, though we could not discover the path we were to travel, we were under the direction of a faithful guide, who would bring the blind by a way they know not, and lead them in paths they had not known; who would make darkness light before them, and crooked things straight; who would do these things, and not forsake them. [See Isaiah. 42 v.16.] Follow your leader and fear no danger. Let your advance be by seven solemn steps, and at each step you must halt and make obeisance, with the awe and reverence suited to this grand and solemn occasion, for every step brings you nearer to the sacred name of God.

What further was said to you? – The High Priest read the following passage [Exodus 6.v.2,3]: And God spake unto Moses, and said unto him: I am the Lord, and I appeared unto Abraham, unto Isaac, and unto Jacob, by the name of God almighty, but by my name Jehovah was I not known to them.

He then informed us that the name of Deity, the divine Logos, or Word, to which reference is had in John [1, v.1–5] "in the beginning was the Word [Logos], and the Word was with God, and the Word was God; the same was in the beginning with God; all things were made by him, and without him was not any thing made that was made; in him was life, and the life was the light of men: and the light shineth in darkness, and the darkness comprehended it not'', was anciently written only in these sacred characters [they are shown to the candidates], and thus preserved from one generation to another. This was the true Masonic Word, which was lost at the death of Hiram and was restored at the building of the temple, in the manner we had at that time assisted to represent.

Here the whole mystery of Masonry is unveiled by a candid confession of what the Masons had so long been in search of, the lost Logos. Logos is the same as Osiris, the sun, considered as the Demiurge, the maker of the world, under the direction of the Supreme Being.

But to return to the lecture; it is stated by the candidates that the High Priest placed crowns upon their heads, and told them they were now invested with all the important secrets of this Degree, crowned and received as worthy Companions and Royal Arch Masons.

As this crowning is the closing ceremony of initiations into the Ancient mysteries, so is its imitation in the Royal Arch included in the last act of the drama.

The following address (copied from *Webb's Freemason's Monitor*) is delivered to the newly initiated Companion:

Worthy Companion, by the consent and assistance of the members of this Chapter, you are now exalted to the sublime and honourable degree of a Royal Arch Mason. Having attained this degree, you have arrived at the summit and perfection of ancient Masonry, and are consequently entitled to a full explanation of the mysteries of the Order.

The rites and mysteries developed in this Degree have been handed down through a chosen few, unchanged by time, and uncontrolled by prejudice; and we expect and trust they will be regarded by you with the same veneration, and transmitted with the same scrupulous purity to your successors.

No one can reflect on the ceremonies of gaining admission into this place, without being forcibly struck with the important lessons which they teach.

Here we are necessarily led to contemplate with gratitude and admiration the sacred source from whence all earthly comforts flow; here we find additional inducements to continue steadfast and immovable in the discharge of our respective duties; and here we are bound ... to promote each other's welfare, and correct each other's failings, by advice, admonition, and reproof.

The most interesting thing about this ritual is that it fully reveals the awareness of its makers or performers of the extremely complex, not merely syncretic character of the religious situation which it manifests.[58] Moreover, it also reveals their attempt to understand all the elements of this Ritual as conscious representations of different religions, or the different stages in one religion, which only the ignorant think of as many. And even more than that: it is in this ritual and through this ritual that the Trinitarian idea can be seen as universal and not only Christian – the stumbling block for all theological critique of the Royal Arch. The notion of natural religion cannot be avoided, however, for it was used in the explanations of the Ritual by Royal Arch Companions themselves.

So, starting with the centre and focus, the Lost Word, it is clear that it is no longer the lost identity of the Master Mason, but the lost Logos. It is neither the real name of Master Hiram, nor the Word that is Jesus Christ, but that which preceded not only the Creation of the world by God but also the awareness of that God by the world. In other words, the Word of St John "is the same as Osiris, the Sun, considered as the Demiurge, the maker of the world under the direction of the Supreme Being", which means that primary state of natural religion which preceded the time when the God of Abraham, Isaac and Jacob was worshipped as the second stage of the world. The first stage of the world represents the first stage of religious consciousness, and if a religion wants to be not only universal, i.e. ubiquitous in space (as that of Anderson's *Constitutions* "in which all men agree"), but also eternal, then we have to admit together with the Royal Arch Companions that it is God as Sun or Osiris (not as Supreme Being) who was the Demiurge and Word long before we arrived at the third stage of religious consciousness, manifested in Jesus Christ and St John.

But who, then, is the Supreme Being in this passage? Can he be identified with the God of Abraham, Isaac and Jacob as he frequently is in conventional Masonry?

We are given to understand that he is above the level of the God of any concrete religion but, at the same time, within it. For, as one Royal Arch Mason tried to explain to me, he is not the God of Christianity, nor of the Jews, nor the Superior Being of the Masons, but that Eternal Deity, ineffable and inconceivable, whose religion includes in itself Christianity as its highest humanly achievable stage, but is not, itself, Christian.[59]

The only conclusion I can come to on this subject is that the Royal Arch worked out and manifested in its ritual a syncretic, highly composite and non-theological religion into which the whole history of religious consciousness (and not of Architecture or of humankind) has been incorporated and condensed into a kind of three-stage evolution. And it is in respect to this evolution that a new hierarchy of Deities is established, a hierarchy that finds no Masonic symbolism of its own in this ritual. For the symbolism of the Ritual here is that of the ascension of the candidate to the level of the "Ancient Mysteries", mysteries which are neither specifically Masonic, nor Jewish, i.e. biblical, nor even Christian.[60] The establishing of such a super-religious hierarchy is, itself, a phenomenon too widely spread and known to be worthy of special mention here. Yet, what is really remarkable in the Royal Arch is the absolute genuineness and straightforwardness of its presentation, particularly when we came to the sacred texts in the Ritual. The Ritual mentions three of them:

1. The Holy Bible (mainly the Old Testament);
2. The secret Cabala, which is related to the Holy Bible as super-religion is related to religion; and
3. The signs or glyphs of the mysteries of the Royal Arch,[61] which are related to any Masonic texts (Constitutions, etc.) as a super-Masonry is related to Masonry.

The very fact that the Royal Arch not only introduced and established the triple scheme of natural (eternal, pagan) plus biblical, plus Christian religion, but *consciously* superimposed on it its own extremely eclectic mysticism, should preclude anyone from calling it a natural religion, or even a kind of Gnosticism, though some gnostic elements are undoubtedly there. For what we are dealing with here is not a theology, but rather a very strange specimen of religious philosophy, if and when any Companion takes the trouble to trace this philosophy to his Royal Arch experience.[62]

In fact, although it is officially recognized as the basis and foundation of the Antient Masonry, it is hard to find any reason for thinking that the Royal Arch is more congenial to the Antients than to the Moderns. The impulse to reshaping was, perhaps, equally strong in both, and the "Irish" discipline in the former, if Irish it was, proved to be by no means weaker than that of the Grand Lodge of England. Nevertheless, from the middle of the 1750s, Royal Arch Masonry began its victorious course through the Lodges of both the rival Grand Lodges, at home as well as abroad, and it is not by chance that such a luminary of the Moderns as Thomas Dunckerley was "exalted" to Companionship of the Royal Arch in 1754, not to mention the fact that in the Colonies the first Chapter was formed at least one year earlier (in Fredericksburg,

Virginia).[63] Generally speaking, however, it is safe to assume that its historical beginnings as a form of Masonry may be assigned to the mid-1740s.

The tendency to transcend history and historical symbolism in Freemasonry is as old as Freemasonry itself, and the fact that this was first achieved by the Royal Arch can hardly be accounted for by anything but the inner logic of the development of the Craft in England.

"A real, or 'historiographical', history cannot preserve the *memory* of the things eternal and ahistorical", said Robbo, my informant.

You can't write a history of God, can you? Nor can you write a history of those whose search for God includes in itself, and depends on, their exemption from history. But an ordinary Mason cannot help seeking for a *historical* reality behind the fictional history of Freemasonry, or, if he is a modern person, he would brush off all "old" Masonic history as a mere fiction (even when it is not) rather than accept the fiction as an expression of the eternal core of Masonry, and Masonry itself as an expression of some other, absolutely "meta-historical" truth.[64]

And poor Hiram, too, was ousted from the centre of Masonic symbolism to the periphery of a preparatory stage for what the Royal Arch Companions deemed to be the deeper symbolic reality of Freemasonry.[65]

There was (and still is, I am sure) something irresistible about the Royal Arch with its secondary Masonic character, its exotic ritual, and its practically untraceable historical origins. The surmise that Ramsay entirely invented it seems to me untenable, for it is likely that something of the sort must have existed which played a part in the mystical life of the seventeenth century and had been lying dormant since then, waiting for its time to rise to the surface of Masonic life in the "remodernizing" mission of the Antients.

It is paradoxical that it is the Antients, thirty-five years younger than those whom they styled "Moderns", who introduced and developed the archaic Royal Arch into what may be perceived from the outside as a phenomenon of flagrant religious modernism.[66] When Wilmshurst spoke of the Ritual of Initiation in that Order as a kind of *yoga* or *samadhi*, his was not an anachronistic reference to practices which were unknown in this country at the time of the development of Royal Arch, for it is that very strong modernistic tendency in the Antient Masonry, and particularly in the Royal Arch, which calls for such an analogy. The Royal Arch may indeed by compared to a form of yoga and its Ritual evokes direct associations with the practice of yogic inner visualization called *bhavana* in Buddhist meditation. One of the central and distinctive features of any religious modernism is its spontaneous tendency to orient itself to, or to borrow from, the religious world of the day *before* yesterday. If the seventeenth century was yesterday for the Three Degrees Craft, for the Antients, more than a generation further on, it had already become the day before that. And what they took from it was quite different from that which was taken by their "Modern" predecessors. While the latter amply drew from the Protestant tradition of the seventeenth century, the former reactivated the ancient Gnostic and hermetic tendencies which during that time lingered on in some peripheral mystical movements.

The destiny of the Grand Lodge at York seems to be, from the very beginning, connected with the Royal Arch. The famous passage from F. Dassigny,[67] where he states that in York "an assembly of Master Masons is held under the title of Royal Arch Masons, who, as their qualifications . . . are superior to others . . . receive a larger pay than working Masons", invites a metaphorical rather than literal explanation. Namely, that some time *before* it was written, there existed in York in the 1730s a variety of *speculative* Freemasons called the Royal Arch Masons who were as superior to other Freemasons as the latter were to working, or operative Masons. The Grand Lodge at York existed, more or less certainly, as the Grand Lodge of speculative Masons, at the very beginning of the eighteenth century, and declared itself the Grand Lodge of All England in 1725 (as distinct from the 1717 Grand Lodge of England). However, it became, almost immediately, virtually invisible for some thirty-six years, in the sense that there is no direct documentary evidence of its activities. At the time of its reappearance in the 1760s, it had already had several Royal Arch Chapters under its aegis. Organized into a central body of the Grand Chapter, it was probably the first institution of such a kind in England (the Supreme Grand Chapter in Scotland was formed considerably later).

Now, it is very difficult to say to what extent, if any, the Grand Lodge at York was connected with the Antients at a time prior to the early 1760s,[68] but there is no doubt that after that time their connections became very strong. The re-emergence of the *Grand Lodge of All England*, the third rival Grand Lodge, at York, in 1761[69] found the Antients flourishing and going from strength to strength. It is about that time (1761 or 1762) that the normal Three Degrees Ritual of the Antients was established and an additional Degree of "Past Master" introduced, meaning mainly those Master Masons who did not hold the Chair – those who had never been Masters of a Lodge;[70] and, finally, when in 1771, or 1772,[71] John, the Third Duke of Athol, became Grand Master of the Antients, their social status became practically equal to that enjoyed by the Moderns.

The period in the history of the Grand Lodge of England (now called "Modern" or "Prime") between the rise of the Antients and Royal Arch Masonry and the Grand Mastership of the Duke of Beaufort in the 1760s was marked, among other events, by the appearance on the scene of two really outstanding Masonic characters – William Preston and Thomas Dunckerley. The first, with whom we have already become acquainted in the course of our introduction into early Masonic history, was a natural "anti-Dermott". A Journeyman printer (Dermott was a Journeyman painter), he started in an Antient Lodge and then, around 1764, changed to a Modern one (while Dermott started in a Modern and changed to an Antient). He was endowed with a brilliant memory and a strong determination to create a Masonic historiography – not yet a history, for the latter, as I have already explained, requires the element of historical critique lacking, for example, in Anderson. Preston manifests in himself the second stage in Masonic "historicity", that of historiography, but he was not able to detach himself critically from the course of history, or, rather, from the course of Masonic events of the eighteenth century. Real history began much later with Findel and, probably in its most proper sense, with R. F. Gould. For they, particularly Gould, not only looked at the beginning (Anderson) through the "middle" (Preston), but made both of them objects of historical analysis and commentary. While Preston took for granted what Dermott rejected point blank – Anderson's conception of Masonic history – both remained partisans of their respective Masonries.[72] Preston's main work, *Illustrations*, serves as a perfect example of absolute historiographical rigidity, where the ethical, non-historical, principles of the Craft were quite consistently (and more often than not in flagrant contradiction of historical reality) used as a method of his own historical description.[73] His task was to fix the time of the still very young Masonic history, and he himself was, speaking metaphorically, the "time" of Freemasonry, for, while being its chronologist he was also an active participant and described himself – his own acts, speeches and works – as a part, and a very important one, of the course of Masonic history.

If William Preston was the "time" of Masonry, Thomas Dunckerley (1724–95) was its "space". The penniless son of a poor widow, and an illegitimate scion of George II (then Prince of Wales), he entered the navy at the age of eleven or twelve as a cabin boy, later rising to gunner's mate and gunner. Despite this low rank he became the close friend of a number of admirals and generals. Poorly educated, but nonetheless a man of extensive learning and real theological erudition, he embodies the geographical Masonic expansion of the eighteenth century. He had a positive mania for collecting Masonic Lodges, and during his forty-two years as a Mason (he was initiated in 1754) he held nine Provincial Grand Masterships, warranted at least eighty Lodges while Grand Master, and formed or was a Master in at least sixty Lodges in this country, its colonies and dependencies. He was a person who fell in love with Masonry as the only place in the world where he could "freely exercise his moral principles, put to practice his religious ideas and find the people fit and able to share them". And, however Utopian and unrealistic it might sound, he was absolutely sure that with the spread of Freemasonry the whole world might become such a place. Absolutely cosmopolitan in his convictions, he nevertheless remained throughout his life a fully committed Christian and devout member of the Church of England.[74]

Dunckerley was very different from Anderson and Payne on the one hand, and Dr Manningham, Dr Dodd and Martin Clare on the other, for he represents that puritanical streak in Freemasonry which hitherto had remained latent and unarticulated, and which only waited for the appearance of the right person to exemplify it.

He introduced into one of his Lodges (No. 108, previously No. 254 which he had moved from His Majesty's man-of-war *Vanguard* to the Queen of Bohemia's Head public house . . .) Rule No. 14: "Nor shall any *profane, immodest, political* or *religious* Discourses, or Wagers, or any *eating, drinking,* or *smoking* be permitted in the Lodge".[75] And this austere tendency, so alien to the habits and customs of the Grand Lodge of old, became, mainly due to his influence, more and more pervasive in the years to come.[76] Though he was almost a contemporary of Preston's (who calls him "that Masonic luminary")[77] his Masonic philosophy was much less centripetal and "institution-oriented" than that of his younger admirer. To him Masonry was a kind of dynamic spiritual force which, though it needed a material, organizational "frame" to hold it together, should not be restricted by this form.

All his life he suffered from poverty (while giving a lot of money to the Brethren in need), but oddly enough the Grand Lodge itself – in spite of the aristocratic background of its Grand Masters and Patrons – was very poor too. In 1762 "£264 . . . was the whole of its funded property . . . and almost its entire possessions, for with the exception of two books of records, a sword, and *possibly* a Bible . . . it had neither furniture, nor jewels, nor habitation".[78] And when around 1766 some Masons wanted to raise money to buy furniture for the Grand Lodge, their initiative was not supported even by the officers of the Grand Lodge.[79] But there was much more than puritanical zeal in his un-tiring Lodge-forming, particularly considering that there was not supposed to be any proselytizing in Freemasonry. How did he get round this ban on overt recruiting?

One interesting thing in the life of Thomas Dunckerley, as we know it from H. Sadler's work and his own letters, is that he gives away very little of the personal philosophy underlying his Masonic activity though his religious orientation is apparent. He repeats the standard Masonic position unenlivened by any individuality or idiosyncrasy. Perhaps estab-lishing Lodges, participating in them, promoting them and preserving them was an aim in itself. Moreover, no echo of living speech or conver-sation can be found among the hundreds of pages of his letters. All is dry, formal and conventional. It is hard to imagine how he attracted people to the idea of forming a Lodge, but attract them he did in large numbers. Dunckerley's contribution was to emphasize the ubiquity of Freemasonry, its omnipresence. This complements the previous tend-ency, which concentrated on its extreme antiquity. The method of ensuring Masonic expansion through space – all over the then known world – was very simple: in their letters and speeches, and particularly their private conversations, Masons constantly referred to Freemasonry and the Grand Lodge as something extremely important, influ-ential, and interesting, ignoring the fact that its importance, influence and interest resided chiefly in these very letters, speeches and conversa-tions, both with each other and with people outside the Lodges. That potent British tradition of conversing, whose appeal lay more in the art of conversation itself than in the subject matter, became the main work-ing method of Masonic expansion. Conversation became their chief weapon of conversion; the ubiquity of Masonry was largely a self-fulfilling prophecy.

This does not mean that Dunckerley was not concerned with the economy of the Lodges, and particularly those under his direct or indirect administration. He desired that their work should be more serious, or, in the religious terminology of the period, more Quietist than Predestinarian.[80] His letters and notes about his own Lodge record, sometimes drily, an atmosphere still less than austere. "At the meeting of 5 January 1769, the Brethren present were unanimously of opinion that the company would be better entertained with a few promiscuous songs ... than by any lecture."[81] Freemasonry was, to Dunckerley, the natural state of the Ideal Man; the highest possible human condition which reflects the highest state ever historically achieved before the time of a "Better Dispensation" (that is, Christianity), and which is symbolized by the Temple of King Solomon. There could be no problem, therefore, about the compatibility or incompatibility of Freemasonry with Christianity, for the former is a science related to the plan of creation devised by the God worshipped in the latter. He writes in his celebrated Oration (3 August 1792): "Freemasonry is a *speculative* science (if I may use the term) issuing from that important *practical* science, Geometry, the laws of which were observed in the *creation*, and still are manifest in the *regulation* of the world."[82] This science has, however, one other side to it: Man, being made aware of the general unity, one-plane-ness of Creation by means of symbols, is given a form of uniquely human unity: ". . . the implements of operative Masonry were made symbols of moral duties; and from the nature and interpretation of those symbols, handed by tradition down to us, we learn that the purport of them was . . . to associate all good men under the banners of *voluntary* order and vertue".[83]

Does all this mean that these "moral duties", "symbols" and "traditions" are, in Dunckerley's opinion, non-Christian? The answer must be yes, for to him the very idea of speculative Masonry is that of human universality, of human nature itself. So speculative Masonry stands in respect to operative as universal to particular, in the same way as universal Natural Religion stands in respect to the particular Christian Church.[84] As a religious thinker equally alien to both popular extremes of the time – Predestinarianism *versus* Deistic free choice, salvation by "good works" *versus* salvation "by Faith alone" – he stuck to a "Christian–Masonic" picture of the world, at the basis of which lies, again, the idea of a natural order of all things created, natural man included. "Natural", that is, primarily designed, was the notion which neutralized all conceivable oppositions and contradictions of human life, resulting in his idea of a kind of natural equality, represented by the *Level* – one of the central symbols of Masonic morality.[85] It is the equality of actors playing on the same stage. The simile of theatre is very important, for it alludes to a kind of "relativism" reigning over all things natural and created. When he says, "that we are equally born to act our parts on this great theatre of life", and then adds, "art and accident vary our chances . . . but, taking life altogether . . . we shall find a more equal distribution of good and evil than is commonly imagined",[86] he expresses that idea deeply ingrained in the British that it is the quality of performance that really matters, for the initial material is the same for all.[87]

According to William Preston, it is due to the joint efforts of Dunckerley and the Duke of Beaufort that the Craft started flourishing again in the late 1760s in London as well as proliferating in the provinces and abroad. In 1768 the Duke of Beaufort started to plan the construction of the first permanent Masonic Hall. The foundation stone was laid by Lord Petre on 14 May 1775, and the hall (in Great Queen Street) was completed in May 1776. Thus, the Grand Lodge of England ceased to be an event or a meeting only and became permanently fixed in space.[88] This example was very soon followed by quite a few provincial Grand Lodges, and a little later, even by some private Lodges too. However, "The most remarkable occurrence during the administration of the Duke of Beaufort was the plan of an Incorporation of the Society by Royal Charter".[89] Preston gives a rather sober description of what befell this plan:

In 1771 a bill [of incorporation] was brought into Parliament by the Hon. Charles Dillon, the Deputy Grand Master, but ... on the second reading of the bill, it having been opposed by Mr Onslow, at the desire of several brethren who had petitioned the house against it, Mr Dillon moved to postpone the consideration of it *sine die*; and thus the design of an Incorporation fell to the ground.[90]

That the issue was, or very soon became, extremely controversial, can be judged by Lawrence Dermott's account of it which is in sharp contrast to that of Preston:

That the Modern Masons petitioned parliament to grant them a charter of incorporation, in order to give them *the power and pleasure* of punishing every Free-mason in England who did not pay quarterage to them ... The Wisdom of parliament treated the petition with just contempt and ... the honourable speaker of the House of Commons said: 'That if the petition was granted, he made no doubt the chimney-sweepers would soon apply for a charter'. It is remarkable that the said petition was presented on (fool's day) the first of April, 1770.[91]

Six years later a counter-attack was launched by the Moderns and a law was established by the Grand Lodge on 10 April 1777 "that the persons who assemble in London and elsewhere, *in the character* of Masons, calling themselves *Ancient* ... and said to be under the patronage of the Duke of Athol, are not to be acknowledged or countenanced ..."[92] The introduction of new, and far more rigid, rules of registration, the regularization and standardization of *Quarterly Communications* and, finally, the enactment of another law, "that no person be initiated into Masonry for less sum than two guineas",[93] completes the strengthening of the stabilizing principle in the Masonic organization. No wonder that some Masons were becoming more apprehensive, if not suspicious, of the changes in the traditional setup, perhaps even of Preston himself. This now quite visible fixation of Masonry and Masons in space was by no means a reform, least of all a revolution; what happened in the 1770s seems to have been, rather, a shift in emphasis produced by those at the top, who were less connected than others with the official beginning of the Craft, not to speak of its origins in the seventeenth century.

The first genuinely internal conflict was not long in coming. Two incidents which caused it, or were used as pretexts for causing it, are described by Preston in the following way:

> ...in 1779 ... an unfortunate dispute having arisen among the members of the Lodge of Antiquity [No. 2, previously the first among the four Old Lodges], on account of some proceedings of its members on the festival of St John's ... the complaint was introduced into the Grand Lodge which determined it ... to be a *violation* of the general regulations respecting *public processions*, and various opinions being formed, several brethren were highly disgusted ...[94]

> Another circumstance ... the Lodge of Antiquity having expelled three of its members for misbehaviour, the Grand Lodge interfered, and, without proper investigation, ordered them to be re-instated ... Then the privileges of the Lodge of Antiquity *acting by immemorial constitution* began to be set up, in opposition, to *supposed uncontrollable authority* of the Grand Lodge established "by themselves" in 1717; and in the investigation of this point, the original cause of dispute was totally forgotten ... Then the Lodge of Antiquity ... notified its separation from the Grand Lodge ... and avowed an alliance with the Grand Lodge of all England held at the city of York; ...[95]

This, Preston concludes, produced a *schism* (largely of his own making) which subsisted for the space of ten years.[96] Such was Masonry's first constitutional crisis which resulted in the founding of *four* more Grand Lodges in England in 1779.[97] What, however, is particularly interesting is that the reasons adduced by Preston for that separation go far beyond the original case, for while accepting in principle the resolution of the Committee of Charity of the Grand Lodge (February, 1779), "that every private Lodge derives its authority from the Grand Lodge, and that no authority but the Grand Lodge can ... take away that power," he stresses that this resolution, "... could not apply to a Lodge which derived its authority from *another channel*, long before the establishment of the Grand Lodge.''[98] Of course Preston himself was quite a hard nut to crack and from his description of the conflict it clearly emerges that he supported the idea of Masonry as meeting and not as institution. He was, in his Masonic Philosophy, more Antient than the Antients themselves, when he wrote:

... At the end of the last and beginning of the present century, the fraternity ... had a *discretionary power* to meet *as Masons* ... the fraternity were under no restriction [imposed by the Grand Lodge] ... The antient charges were the only standard for the regulation of conduct ... and the authority of Grand Master never extended beyond the bounds of a general meeting.[99]

Here he far outdid the Antients in his emphasis on the decentraliz-ation of Masonry. Moreover, he was the only person at that time who dared, though without explicitly denying the validity of Anderson's *Con-stitutions*, to proclaim the Ancient Charges of Working Operative Masons (without naming them, of course) as the only textual *authority* in English Masonry.

A difference in philosophy is what all this was about, although Masons themselves would never have used the word in describing their differ-ences. Preston's philosophy can be reduced to an elementary idea: complete separateness coupled with absolute cosmopolitanism; or, more specifically, a hierarchical structure of the whole of humankind, where Freemasonry figures as the level at which everyone belonging to it auto-matically loses any other distinctions determined by his own *historic* (ethnic, cultural, etc.) background. And it is differences in respect of *how to be conscious* of one's own Masonic position that were at the heart of practically all Masonic internecine disputes and quarrels. Probably nowhere else was that philosophy more often and more variously dis-cussed (usually in the disguise of "morality") in the second half of the eighteenth century than in the Lodge of Antiquity. As Dr Dodd put it (or as G. Oliver has him say): ". . . this is an institution whose members are *segregated from the rest of the world* [the first point] by obligations, customs, and laws of particular [i.e. Masonic] nature, yet retain their *independence of character* [the second point] by a perfect freedom of thought and action . . ."[100] And then adds to it that, "though Masonic morality is more particularly applied to the genius of Christianity, than to any other religion, it is, in reality, neither exclusively Jewish nor Christian, but cosmopolite . . ."[101] It is that very individual independence of character, or individual freedom, which constitutes here the basis of Masonic cosmopolitanism but – and this must be emphasized – to exercise it within the Lodge a Mason must, ideally, give up his personal history and acquire the history of Masonry. It appears that the Lodge of Antiquity applied the principle of independence of character first and foremost to their Lodge, and not to themselves as individuals.[102]

If the Antients desired independent "historical" evidence, the Lodge of Antiquity desired no more than an independent position under the Grand Lodge, a position guaranteed by its own historical privileges. It seems that this Lodge was as freethinking and "intellectual" as Lodge No. 4 was aristocratic, which is probably why, as early as the 1760s, we see its members debating theology, ethics and even the Jewish question, though solely in a Masonic context.[103] The temporary schism was the last conflict within Masonry in the eighteenth century. In 1790 the Lodge of Antiquity was accepted back into the bosom of the Grand Lodge, with Preston jubilant and harmony in the Fraternity in London restored.[104] The Grand Lodge of all England at York became totally extinct about 1792, and the so-called "fifth Grand Lodge" three or four years earlier. The luminaries of Masonry were also dying out – Dr Dodd was hanged for forgery in 1777, Dr Manningham died in 1789, Dermott in 1791, and finally, Dunckerley in 1795.[105] Preston outlived them all, as a faithful chronicler of the Craft, to witness and register its vicissitudes and triumphs, as well as his own Masonic integrity, finally succumbing in 1818.

The second half of the eighteenth century saw the emergence and development of Masonic problems of quite another nature and character, some of them connected, though in a totally different way, with the central ambiguity of Masonry – that is, how to exercise its cosmopolitanism and the absolute *Masonic* freedom of its members in situations external to Masonry itself. The American Revolution was the first event of this kind. There have been no indications that the war (which amounted to a war of almost the whole Western world against England) seriously affected the bonds of friendship between the British Masons and their American counterparts. At least twenty signatories of the Declaration of 1776, including George Washington, were Freemasons, most of whom belonged to the Grand Lodges previously warranted as provincial by the Grand Lodge of England. It seems that quite a few of the prominent American Masons of that time identified the ideals of the American Revolution with the moral principles of Freemasonry.[106] Yet far more important is the fact that the English Masons of the 1770s and 1780s were also perfectly capable of separating the American Revolution from American Masonry.[107]

The participation of the French Masons in the French Revolution of 1789 presented English Masonry with a far more serious problem, particularly in view of the fact that the Prince of Wales was elected Grand Master on 24 November 1790. As a result, English Freemasonry as an institution acquired a higher status than ever before, the status of "anomalous exclusiveness", which it enjoys to this day. However, numerous attacks on French Masonry for its alleged role in the Revolution (though grossly exaggerated) could not and did not leave English Masonry unaffected. The following passage from Preston illustrates very clearly how apprehensive he was of all possible consequences of the association of English Masonry with the French Revolution:

The French revolution, which in extent and importance of effect, is the most momentous event that has happened since the religious revolutions in Europe at the beginning of the sixteenth century, having misfortunately given rise . . . to many unhappy dissentions . . . it became necessary to counteract the measures of those mistaken individuals who were endeavouring to sow the seeds of anarchy, and poison the minds of the people.[108]

Some later passages in the text reveal that the "unhappy dissentions" and "mistaken individuals" referred to here are by no means French, but English and even, probably, some of them English and Masonic. This, however, was not an outright condemnation of the Revolution as such, but rather an attempt to establish a kind of historical balance; Preston wanted to show the liberal face of Masonry, and to figure, in his own history, as an enlightened and unprejudiced chronicler. But there was more to it than that. Like Dunckerley, Preston, for all his Masonic rigour and purism, believed in the "Masonic enigma" and the special mission of the Craft in the age to come. He therefore not only wanted Masonry to come to grips with any problems that might threaten its official position or its reputation, but to relate Masonry positively, in one way or the other, to the important events of his time. You could not simply reject the French Revolution out of mindless patriotism, or even on account of its own follies. Instead, a Mason should stay away from the epicentre of the political storm caused by it, so that his position could be regarded as that of "loyal observation", so to speak. For Preston was a typical loyal observer of history, belonging himself to that thin layer of English Freemasonry sandwiched between its unthinking bottom and uncaring top, the layer which represented Masonic self-awareness.[109]

When, in July 1799, the Unlawful Societies Act was passed, the clauses about Masonry specified its being "in great measure directed to charitable purposes..."[110] And later, in 1799, Freemasonry was exempted from this Act of Parliament altogether.

It is, probably, this new stand of English Freemasonry in its relation to contemporary events ("take notice, but don't get involved") coupled with a considerable strengthening of its status within, and in relation to, the State, that allowed it to treat with a formidable sense of superiority the flood of anti-Masonic literature that appeared during the first decade of the Prince of Wales's Grand Mastership (1790–1813). The following passage from the address to the Grand Lodge of the Earl of Moira, the Acting Grand Master, on 3 June 1800, can be seen as a clear instance of that superiority:

Certain modern publications have been holding forth to the world the Society of Masons as a league against constituted authorities; an imputation the more secure, because *the known institutions of our fellowship make it certain*[111] *that no answer can be published.* It is not to be disputed that in countries where *impolitic* prohibitions restrict the communication of sentiment, *the action of the human mind* may, among other means of baffling the control, have resorted to *the artifice of borrowing the denomination of Freemasons,* to cover meetings for seditious purposes...[112]

The Earl of Moira, like Preston, did not dissociate himself entirely from the accusations of the enemies of Freemasonry, and he boldly states that the cause of "borrowing of denomination", though reprehensible, lies nevertheless in "impolitic prohibitions" which he contrasts with the free activity of the human mind enshrined in Freemasonry.

At the beginning of the nineteenth century, the spread of Freemasonry at home and abroad, no more than slightly hampered by the Napoleonic Wars and Continental Blockade, continued with increasing speed. The number of Lodges, both Modern and Antient, in England and Wales exceeded 2000, not to speak of Scotland and particularly Ireland, where Masonry became, even among the Catholics, a common feature of ordinary life.[113]

The first steps toward a rapprochement of the two remaining rival Grand Lodges were taken in the early 1790s. The process, though very slow and impeded by pride, suspicion and animosity, resulted at last in the final reunification of the Antients and Moderns, and the formation of the United Grand Lodge of England in 1813.[114] Augustus Frederick, Duke of Sussex, was elected its first Grand Master, and held this position for thirty years.

One final historical remark:

At the reunion of the two Grand Lodges in 1813, each side had to pay its own price for the unity of English Masonry. The Antients withdrew (formally, at least) all their accusations concerning the "unreality" of the Moderns and the "un-constitutionality" of their Grand Lodge and, particularly, of their forming and constituting new Lodges at home and abroad. The Moderns formally acknowledged the Royal Arch as an inalienable part of the structure of English Masonry (which was not much of a concession, for they themselves had begun to work and practise that Degree long before the reunification, though as a separate Order). The second concession of the Moderns, if that was what it was, is that the new United Grand Lodge dropped the history of Masonry, prehistorical as well as historical, legendary and mythical. Anderson's effort simply ceased to be a part of their *Book of Constitutions*, but continued to be the subject and preoccupation of historians, official and unofficial, Masonic and non-Masonic up to the present day.

Notes

1 A group of celebrated French intellectuals of the Enlightenment including Diderot, Grimm, D'Alambert, etc.

2 This is the opinion of J. Hamill (1986, p. 45), with which I agree, but only as regards Masonry as *institution* (and it is mainly the institutional aspect that interests Hamill).

3 William Preston, 1804, p. 242.

4 From the MSS of Stanislaus Poborovsky, a Polish Mason living in France and England during the 1940s and 1950s. This, of course, is an example of a purely objective etic approach, for Masons did not express themselves in such a fashion in the eighteenth century.

5 "Some disagreeable altercations arose in the Society . . . A number of dissatisfied brethren having separated themselves from the regular lodges, held meetings in different places for the purpose of initiating persons into Masonry, contrary to the Laws of the Grand Lodge . . ." W. Preston, 1804, p. 241.

6 "Rumours now arose, whence originating no one could discover, that Freemasonry was exclusively a Jewish Institution . . ." G. Oliver, 1855, p. 76.

7 G. Oliver, 1855, pp. 75-6.

8 There is no evidence for his assertion that Jews first joined some of the less than strictly authorized French and German Lodges and then sought admission to Lodges in Britain; while no unbaptized Jews would have been admitted to the sacraments anyone could attend a Christian church, including Jews.

9 Henry Sadler writes of Oliver's book: ". . . this is a most interesting book, but one in which truth and fiction are so cleverly blended as to render it extremely difficult to distinguish one from the other." H. Sadler, *Thomas Dunckerley, His Life, Labours and Letters*, London, 1891 (H. Sadler, 1891), p. 13.

10 G. Oliver, 1855, pp. 75-8.

11 To a learned Orthodox Jew the idea of the Great Architect of the Universe

would seem *theologically* no less bizarre than it would to a Catholic theologian.

12 "... At this time ... rumours were widespread in the Metropolitan Lodges, that the Order was subject to great persecutions in Switzerland, Germany, Italy, France, and Holland; and that edicts and decrees were thundered against it in all those countries ..." J. Oliver, 1855, pp. 60–1. But the Masons themselves at that time seem to have been far more amused and excited by these rumours than alarmed.

13 Count S. Poborovsky writes: "Masonry has contributed a great deal to the process of *secularization* of Jews in Europe, and secularized Jewry has contributed a great deal more to the secularization of European Christian civilization" (MSS, Addendum 12). He is right historically, for had Masonry appeared 150 years later, it would have never succeeded in the way that it did, for when it actually appeared, it was not meant to be religious, it simply was religious. This could happen only within a religious civilization, while within a non-religious one it is not enough for a phenomenon just to *be* religious, it should be *meant* to be so. Karl Marx (1818–83), a German political economist and historical essayist, was only partly right when he said that a German Jew could gain full access to German and European culture only at the price of being baptized. He would have done much better had he said that a European Jew living at the beginning or the middle of the nineteenth century (and at that time he was still Judaic by definition) had to make a choice between two *religions* in the first place, and not between the "culture" of the Ghetto and the "culture" of Tübingen or Oxford.

14 "We are of the oldest Catholic religion", insisted G. Oliver (1855, p. 67).

15 *Idem*, p. 62; J. G. Findel, 1869, p. 168; W. Preston, 1804, p. 247.

16 For before that "... each Master of a Lodge had been left to his own discretion [as regards the *form* of prayer]", G. Oliver, 1855, p. 86.

17 J. Hamill, 1986, p. 46.

18 "The substance of my theory [concerning the origin of the Antients] ... is that the Brethren who formed it ... were not English Masons ... but chiefly members of the Irish Lodges ... and the Great Majority of them were undoubtedly Irish to the backbone. I tell you, Brethren, ... that no matter what their nationality may have been, you have reason to be proud of your *Masonic* ancestors." Henry Sadler, *A Short History of the Robert Burns Lodge No. 25*. An address delivered ... on 7 February 1898 [H. Sadler, 1910 (1898)], p. 3.

19 From this follows logically, not historically, for there is no historical evidence whatsoever, that there were at that time some Lodges in London which did not recognize the authority of the Grand Lodge of England but probably, in a very vague and ideal way, recognized the authority of some other Grand Lodge – the Grand Lodge of York, for instance, which was at that time in hibernation. But why those "schismatic" Masons should necessarily have been Irish I cannot tell. The only thing which is evident is that they had never belonged to the Grand Lodge of England, so the terms "schism" or "split" seem to be quite inappropriate.

20 *Ahiman Rezon* (1801), pp. iv, v, xxi, etc.

21 Even in Karl Marx's case his theoretically deduced idea of the "class society" actually became ideological in his own sense, in the sense of "class struggle", only secondarily. Though, of course, he always insisted on the ideological character and nature of almost all ideas (not that he knew them all, though he thought he did), precisely because he saw them in opposition to another already established set of ideas.

157

22 *Ahiman Rezon*, 1801, pp. ii, iv. Dermott, speaking of Masonic mysteries, seems to be closer to the etic approach to Masonic symbolism and Ritual.

23 *Idem*, p. xxxi.

24 Thus here as well as anywhere else, an ideology tends to identify itself with the general historical tendency, which presupposes a monistic approach to its own (i.e. ideology's) history as well as to that of the whole of mankind. No matter that all this is a flagrant contradiction of the historical fact that the Grand Lodge of England was formed thirty-five years before the Grand Lodge of the Antients.

25 *Idem*, p. xxv.

26 *Idem*, p. xxiv.

27 "Possibly because of its members' social background (the original itinerant Irish members . . . who soon departed from London . . . and were replaced by English artisans, tradesmen, and minor professionals) the Antients were a much more democratic organization." J. Hamill, 1986, pp. 50–1.

28 *Ahiman Rezon*, 1801, p. 17.

29 *Idem*, pp. 29–30.

30 *Idem*, p. 2.

31 *Idem*, p. xxi.

32 *Idem*, p. 13.

33 H. Sadler writes: "I am fully convinced that at the earliest period of their existence (as he puts it in 1748–9) . . . the leaders of rival Grand Lodges knew very little of each other's origin and antecedents . . . and neither Dermott nor Preston was even superficially acquainted with the history of English Freemasonry between *1717 and 1751* . . ." See in R. F. Gould, 1903, p. 339.

34 ". . . The new sect, which under the name of Ancient Masons caused so much trouble, did not arise till a later period, and has been erroneously associated with events of an earlier date . . ." G. J. Findel, 1869, p. 159. R. F. Gould calls them "real schismatics . . . whose success was largely due to the energy and ability of Dermott". R. F. Gould, 1903, p. 342.

35 The historic capital of Freemasonry in England. *Idem*, p. 344.

36 ". . . in 1755 the war-cry of the dissentients – "Universal Masonry and Equality of all Brethren in the Lodge" – was exciting to revolt, and pointing to the Royal Arch Degree in the background as the reward." G. J. Findel, 1869, p. 174. Dermott writes (*Ahiman Rezon*, 1801, p. 57): ". . . that part of Masonry commonly called the Royal Arch . . . I firmly believe to be the root, heart, and marrow of Masonry . . ."

37 *Idem*, p. xxxvii.

38 *Idem*, pp. 55–6. The following quotations give an idea of the attitudes to the Royal Arch: "The pure Masonry in England," says Bezzant, "consists of the three Degrees and no more: the Entered Apprentice, the Fellow Craft and the Master Mason *including the Supreme Order of the Holy Royal Arch.*" Reg. Bezzant, *A Story of an "Antient" Lodge*, Cardiff, 1917, p. 20. "I do not know what 'Masonry in general' is, and I do not think that it exists at all," says Gordon Goreff, a lawyer from Chicago, "to me Masonry is *a quest*, not an Institution, and the *first step* in this quest is the Royal Arch."

39 The word "transcendental" I am using here in the non-technical sense of non-empirical, and conceivable only by pure reasoning.

40 J. Fellows, 1866, pp. 297–8.

41 *Idem*, p. 297. All people seeking admission to Freemasonry, even devout

Monotheists – Christians, Jews and Muslims – are in a symbolic state of ignorance which is to be dispelled by the various Rituals. Even the Archbishop of Canterbury could only claim to possess natural religion. This neatly returns the charge of being in a state of religious naturality to those outside Masonry.

42 *Idem*, p. 298.

43 *The Times*, 11 July 1987, Letters. But isn't it absolutely consonant with the previous Archbishop Runcie's recent statement on homosexuality that, "while it was sinful, some such relationships contributed to human good?" The London *Evening Standard*, 22 October 1987, p. 7.

44 Robbo says: "When a syncretic religion becomes aware of its syncretism it very soon changes into a kind of religious relativism."

45 "... the Royal Arch, howsoever edited in later interests, remains now that which it was from the very beginning, militantly Trinitarian in doctrine." A. E. Waite, 1925, p. 12.

46 E. L. Hawkins, 1908, pp. 25–7.

47 "Ramsay calls the French Royal Arch the *ne plus ultra* of Masonry, but ... in truth this degree ... having but little genius in it, and still less good taste, was fabricated from a confused medley of passages from ... the Old Testament, from history and fable ..." G. J. Findel, 1861, p. 183. A. E. Waite, by contrast, calls it "... a body of Theosophical Doctrine ... offering a wide vista through ways of Divine Life ..." A. E. Waite, 1925, p. 72. What a drastic polarization of opinion amongst learned Masons themselves!

48 "Here is the Quest which is behind the Quest of Masonry," says Waite, and after making a quite substantial reservation ("... though the Royal Arch has forgotten the act of Quest ..."), concludes rather pessimistically: "But I might seem to speak in an unknown tongue for too many in the Masonic Circles if I dwelt on the Science of this Sacred Mystery." A. E. Waite, 1925, p. 90.

49 *Idem*, p. 91. An old friend of mine, Frederick Reger, who is a Mason of Swedish Rite and who was, between 1934 and 1939, a pupil or companion of G. I. Gurdjieff, told me that the latter knew the system of Royal Arch in all detail and that his idea of "I AM" was very close to, if not borrowed from, that system. Gurdjieff called it "the empirical limit of any transcendental religious consciousness". It was also intimated by Frederick that Gurdjieff regarded Freemasonry (and particularly the Royal Arch) as historically the last, and the only surviving, form of the relatively unsystematic mysticism of the seventeenth century. Once he said to Frederick (in Russian, the translation is mine): "Look at Royal Arch, go through all that stuff, and you may remain as idiotic as you were before. But mind you – isn't it entirely up to you to remain or not to remain idiotic after having passed through heaps of symbols and ideas which have pretty well nothing to do with your present day's civilization and religion? Or you may, though pretty stupid of you it would be, make that stuff your own religion. But you cannot make a religion, for it is already there! You cannot even un-make it for the same reason. Old Freemasonry is one of the opportunities, stored up for you by the seventeenth century, to shape you as a religious person."

50 W. L. Wilmshurst, 1932, pp. 150–3.

51 *Idem*, pp. 154–5.

52 *Idem*, pp. 157–8. The symbolism in the Royal Arch is referred to as the symbolism of consciousness, i.e. as that which is already fixed in the Candidate's

mentality and directed towards his mentality, not towards anything external to it.

53 Or, following the scheme of the Orthodox Eastern Christianity, "the body of body", "the body of soul", and "the body of spirit".

54 A. E. Waite, 1925, pp. 92–4. So, what he says further might be understood (once again!) in the sense that what the Three Degrees Craft (even including the Degree of Master Mason) is about is ethics, natural religion, and a natural theology, while what the Ritual of Royal Arch is about is theosophy and *philosophia perennis*.

55 *Idem*, p. 97.

56 J. Fellows (S.A.) pp. 299–313.

57 Which will be given in detail below.

58 For a syncretic religion can be very simple in its own way and comprise, say, two elementary rituals belonging to two different religions. As, for instance, in some of the local cults of Central Asia, where a simple shamanist ritual is combined with a no less simple recitation of a Buddhist mantra.

59 That Mason (a vicar) did not want to be mentioned even by his initials. He added that this is not a theological conjecture but a mystical intuition and the basis of his personal religiousness (not his religion).

60 That is why A. E. Waite is right (in his own way, of course) when he refers, in this connection, to St Paul's "Stewards of the mysteries of God" (Cav. II, 3), who were *before* Christ and, probably, before the Bible itself.

61 John D., a Royal Arch Mason from Cambridge says: "In the Royal Arch Ritual you either understand nothing, absolutely nothing of what you are doing, or you understand almost all. Such is the nature of that religious [he did not say 'Christian'] experiment."

62 J. Hamill, 1986, p. 101. A. E. Waite (1925, p. 61) did not make up his mind about the differences ("in origin, lessons and legend") between the "two" Royal Arches.

63 Though we do not know if it was properly formed. See Ch. 8, pp. 168–9.

64 A. Robbo, *Unpublished Papers*, the Masonic Part, pp. 4–5.

65 Out of forty-two *ordinary* Masons whom I asked whether or not they believed that there is something in Masonry which is deeper (or higher) than a "simple association", only four (!) answered positively. Eight answers were vague and thirty negative.

66 The main feature of Modernism is the conscious revival of some historically prior cultural features in order to graft them onto some present-day phenomena.

67 W. J. Hughan, 1909, pp. 74–80. Another version is also possible, though hardly probable, that there were much earlier, at the time of the working Masons' Lodges, some special Lodges with the second part of the Master Mason's Degree, i.e. with something like the Royal Arch Degree. The same author quotes from Dr Chetwood Crawley, that the earliest known ceremony of the Royal Arch took place in Dublin, in 1743 (*idem*, p. 95). He also mentions the Stirling Rock Chapter as the first documented Royal Arch Chapter in Scotland. So that we may suppose that York served as the place of the prehistory of the Royal Arch in general.

68 *Idem*, pp. 121–3.

69 At that time their Grand Master was Lord Aberdour, under whom the Grand Lodge began to warrant the Lodges at home and abroad. R. F. Gould, 1903, p. 344.

70 This Degree later became accepted by the Moderns. As for the "normal"

ritual of the Antients, it seems to be very difficult to establish in which way it differed from the Masonic Ritual claimed to have been established in the late 1730s. For there have been some indications that in 1738 or 1739 some radical changes in the Ritual were made, which provoked dissatisfaction and discord amongst the Fraternity.

71 J. G. Findel, 1869, p. 174.

72 "Preston, however, was by a long way the greater romancer of the two . . . a Masonic visionary who – *untrammelled by any laws of evidence* – wrote a vast amount of enthusiastic rubbish." R. F. Gould, 1903, p. 338.

73 He became a victim himself of that very rigidity when, a dozen years later, he, together with his colleagues in the Lodge of Antiquity, was expelled from Masonry. Apart from being a historiographer he was the first systematizer of Masonic tests (questions), and reformer of Masonic Lectures. G. Oliver, 1855, p. 114.

74 "Though conversant in science and philosophical research, he was of too vertuous and vigorous a frame of mind, and too well-grounded in his religious and moral principles ever to suffer philosophy to lead him to infidelity." H. Sadler, 1891, p. 18. Dunckerley said in 1757 at Plymouth: "The Sacred Writings confirm what I assert the sublime part of our ancient mystery being there to be found nor any Christian Brother be a perfect Mason that does not make the Word of God his study . . ." J. Whymper, 1888, p. 218.

75 H. Sadler, 1891, p. 75.

76 "[This time] witnessed the almost total abandonment of the happy-go-lucky principle which had hitherto marked the proceedings of the executive department of the Grand Lodge." *Idem*, p. 2.

77 W. Preston, 1804, p. 263. "Dunckerley . . . a name which will endure as long as Masonry shall endure." G. Oliver, 1855, p. 113.

78 In what a sharp contrast with that passage is the following news item published 110 years later: "From the *Police Gazette*, Friday, 6 December 1872: This is a *corrected* description of Masonic Jewels stolen: . . . 1st a royal arch jewel, medium size . . . ; 2nd Knight Templar gold cross; . . . 3rd Knight of Malta silver gilt cross . . . ; 4th Knight of Constantinople, crescent of opal on bloodstone . . . ; 5th Rose Croix (18th Degree) red enamel Cross . . . ; 6th Knight of East and West occasional (17th degree) ornament . . . ; 7th Knight of Rome (Sovereign degree) crown above a cross . . . ; Also stolen, three scarf pins, one set with pearls, one dead gold, and one with pearl in centre . . . ; a large gold locket . . . ., etc."

79 J. G. Findel, 1869, pp. 178–9.

80 Quietism in the late seventeenth century was opposed to Predestinarianism in emphasizing a contemplative approach entailing the passive acceptance of God's will rather than an active approach focusing on "works".

81 H. Sadler, 1891, p. 76. Then follow the minutes of the same Lodge: ". . . On the 20th of March, 1772 . . . the Right Worshipful Master proposed several alterations in the Bylaws, one being, 'that every Mason appointed an Officer of this Lodge, pay a *Bottle of Claret* instead of Port' (Old Port was then 2s. 6d., Claret 5s.)". *Idem*, p. 77.

82 *Idem*, p. 154.

83 *Idem*, p. 155.

84 "The name of Freemason ought not then to be taken in a literal gross and material sense, as if we were simple workmen on stone and marbles. We do not

consecrate our talents and our riches to the construction of external temples, but enlighten, edify, and protect the living temples of the Most High." From a lecture on the Design of Masonry . . . by J. Codrington . . . in 1770. In G. Oliver, *The Golden Remains of the Early Masonic Writers*, Vol. I, London, 1847, p. 214.

85 A. E. Waite (1925) blames Craft Masonry of the eighteenth century for its being, unlike real or operative Masonry, non-Christian, or even un-Christian. But he did not understand that being or not being Christian depended, in the case of British Masons at least, on whether or not the principle of admission to Masonry was based on individual selection. Operative Masonry (as well as Christianity) practised non-individual admission of its members, i.e. anyone who was a stonemason could join, and was Christian. While the "new" Craft was, from the very start, individual and, therefore, not necessarily Christian. However, Dunckerley's was a very tricky and difficult case, for his was a situation in which, all his puritanical rectitude considered, there existed a perpetual tension between plain Anglicanism and far from plain mysticism. One century later J. Whymper wrote: "Thomas Dunckerley removed, supposedly, the true word of the Master Mason from the Third to the Royal Arch Degree . . . He did not write much, yet his influence on the *esoteric teaching of the eighteenth century* was without parallel." J. Whymper, 1888, p. 217.

86 H. Sadler, 1891, pp. 155, 156.

87 It is no wonder that it is in England, the most theatrical country in the world, that the words "I value several actors in the grand drama of life simply as they act parts," were said. And said they were, by a member of the most theatrical company in the world, Robert Burns.

88 This event could not help changing the whole financial structure of Masonry, for hitherto the fees were not regular and the money paid and collected was used more for food, drink and Masonic charities than for any kind of immovable property.

89 W. Preston, 1804, pp. 264–5.

90 *Idem*, p. 267; this was the *third* reading of the bill.

91 *Ahiman Rezon*, 1801, p. XIII-XIV. John Hamill's summary of the case tends to smooth over the *ideological* differences in the controversy by stating that there was a considerable opposition to the bill on the part of the Moderns too: ". . . what was quickly grasped by the Antients . . . was that Incorporation would enable the Grand Lodge to have recourse to the Courts over anyone claiming to practise Freemasonry outside the control of an Incorporated Grand Lodge . . . So intense, however, was the feeling of the Craft *against* the Bill . . .", etc. J. Hamill, 1986, p. 47.

92 W. Preston, 1804, p. 274.

93 *Idem*, p. 275.

94 *Idem*, pp. 276–7.

95 *Idem*, pp. 277–8. J. Hamill (1986, p. 52) presents these two incidents as one.

96 W. Preston, 1804, pp. 278–9.

97 Not to speak of the fifth, and very short-lived, Grand Lodge of England, which ceased to exist in the late 1780s. J. Hamill, 1986, pp. 52–3.

98 W. Preston, 1804, p. 279.

99 *Idem*, pp. 280–1.

100 G. Oliver, 1855, p. 149.

101 "The Jews without Jewish history" – as A. Robbo calls them, "the Jews the other way around, that is what Freemasons are."

102 G. Oliver, 1855, p. 169.

103 The things which were said at those debates, if one may believe G. Oliver, are quite astonishing even from the point of view of a present-day Mason of average intellectual capacity. I will give two examples. Preston said ". . . if any Brother shall rest contented with a knowledge of the few . . . signs and tokens by which we are distinguished as a *body of men set apart* from the rest of mankind for the purpose of . . . charity . . . his reward will be *carnal* instead of *intellectual.*" G. Oliver, 1855, p. 193. Dr Dodd said: "Freemasonry is an *appendage to a universal religion, of which* [the religions] of the Patriarchs and Jews were only *types* and *symbols . . .*" (*Idem*, p. 173). Yet even if these quotations are mendacious, the very fact that Oliver faked them, reflects the same tendency in his own Masonic consciousness.

104 ". . . I rejoice in the opportunity which the proceedings of the grand Feast in 1790 have afforded in promoting harmony, by restoring to the privileges of the Society all the brethren of the Lodge of Antiquity . . . falsely accused and expelled in 1779." W. Preston, 1804, p. 282. And he concludes further, saying that, "among those . . . reinstated, the *Author of this treaty* had the honour to be included." *Idem*, p. 314.

105 ". . . And coupled with his liberality, which never suffered a needy brother to apply in vain, his pecuniary difficulties ceased only with his life." G. Oliver, 1855, p. 137.

106 As, some thirteen years later, some of them identified the ideals of the French Revolution of 1789 with those of Freemasonry. Not to speak, of course, of many French Freemasons who quite definitely regarded the first stage of French Revolution as an application of some Masonic principles to politics.

107 W. Preston comments (1804, p. 323): "The Society of Freemasons in America continued to flourish under the auspices of General Washington, who continued his patronage to the lodges till his death. . ."

108 *Idem*, p. 317. Preston never wrote anything like that about the American Revolution, for the Revolution had still remained a kind of "home affair".

109 Such a layer, I am sure, has never existed in any other Masonry in the world, and without it the phenomenon of its global spread of the eighteenth century would never have taken place.

110 W. Preston, 1804, p. 346.

111 Not any more: the craven urge to justify has replaced the lofty indifference of those times.

112 W. Preston, 1804, p. 344.

113 ". . . The roll of Irish Lodges probably reached its highest figure about 1797, when scarcely a village in the kingdom was without its 'Masonic Assembly' . . ." R. F. Gould, 1903, p. 353.

114 I think that a very powerful factor in the reunion was a growing involvement of both Moderns and Antients in the Higher Degrees, particularly the Royal Arch, Knights Templar, and Mark Masons.

CHAPTER 8

American Freemasonry

A Tale to Tell

The discussion of Freemasonry in the United States within a short chapter combines all the difficulty of getting a quart into a pint pot with the representation of the treasures of Aladdin's cave within the resources of a provincial pantomime.
Bro. Fred Pick[1]

There are some men who claim they are "self-made". They are in error . . .
Bro. A. Roberts[2]

It is not easy to present American Freemasonry as a historically independent phenomenon. Nor would it be any easier to assert that the Americans simply took over where the British left off, since by the time the first Lodges in New England had been warranted and formed, British Freemasonry was itself no more than fifteen years old, and still in the throes of formation. So, American Freemasonry is neither "self-made", nor a mere carbon copy; there is much in its character and style which is far from typically British. Although by no means as self-sufficient or idiosyncratic as French Masonry, the American version exhibits many features that would have been almost unrecognizable to a British Mason of the eighteenth century.

The American Craft differs not only from that of the Motherland of all Lodges, but also from all other daughter Masonries. It remains a fact, however, that American Freemasonry was at first essentially British not only in its source, language, and historical antecedents, but also, for two generations, in its actual membership.[3] However trivial, this fact brought about three consequences of enormous importance for the future of the Fraternity in the United States.

The first is that soon after the American Revolution, Freemasonry, by virtue of being English, came to be seen by the greater part of America's population as "foreign" and on a par with other "foreign" interests, quite regardless of the fact that many of the fathers of the American Revolution (including some signatories of the Declaration of Independence) were Freemasons.[4] Furthermore, when the new

Federalist ideology came to the fore in the 1790s, it opposed itself, as champion of nationalism, to the cosmopolitanism of Freemasonry.[5]

The second is that Freemasonry came to be considered as markedly anti-egalitarian, disregarding the incontrovertible historical fact that the fathers of the American Revolution borrowed the principles of French prerevolutionary egalitarianism, which had been worked out by luminaries of the French Enlightenment, most of them Freemasons.

And the third consequence is that while being historically connected with a laissez faire Anglicanism, American Freemasonry soon found itself in a paradoxical *religious* situation. Unlike Masonry, much American religious practice combined a strict puritan ideology with a highly refined rationalistic Deism. And both Deism and Puritanism, in their different ways, were hostile to ritualism, whether it be the "barbaric" ceremonies of the Native Americans or the subtleties of the Eucharist. Against this background not only was Masonic Ritual seen as the apotheosis of pagan superstition, but the Freemasons' own blend of Deism, rationalism, and Natural religion was also totally rejected.[6] American anti-Masonic populism reached its peak at the beginning of the nineteenth century and, curiously, though demotic in its origins, this anti-Masonic populism almost immediately found its expression in the speeches and writings of some of the *crème de la crème* of American society.

In a typical but far too general description, Lynn Dumeril, an American author, defines American Freemasonry as ". . . a white, male, primarily native, Protestant society".[7] Leaving to one side for the moment its "whiteness" and "maleness" we come to its American nativity and Protestantism as two salient historical points which complement and explain one another.

British Freemasonry, offspring of an already mature civilization, showed, from its inception, a sublime indifference to its Britishness, whereas to American Freemasonry, a child of the American Revolution and merely a grandchild of that mature civilization, its nativity was a problem of national self-consciousness. English, Scottish, and Irish Lodges welcomed Jews, Germans and foreigners in the eighteenth century, in accordance with Freemasonry's innate cosmopolitanism and the spirit of its rapid international spread. But American Freemasonry, being on the margins of this expansion, began almost from the start to develop its national and communal *American* identity which, at that time, meant "non-British" by definition. Yet, it is also clear from their writings that those who were founders of both American Masonry and the American Revolution could not help feeling that it was that particular British individualism, embodied in Freemasonry, which represented the strongest guarantee of the newly-formed American individualism and free-thinking and that it was therefore their urgent task to divorce Free-masonry from the issue of nationhood. I do not think that Allen Roberts exaggerates greatly when he writes that, "Masonic historians often won-dered whether there would have been a nation called 'The United States' if . . . the rulers in Great Britain had followed the practice of the Grand Lodge of England.'"[8]

By the time the American Revolution began there were already between eighty and one hundred Lodges in existence, and most of the British – by birth or initiation – champions of American Masonry, such as Daniel Coxe, Benjamin Franklin, Henry Price, and Robert Tomlinson, were dead or very old. The split in the active part of the American population into patriots and loyalists could not help but affect the unity of the Fraternity very badly. Much worse, however, was the damage caused by the ensuing split into Federalists and Republicans (1791),[9] for that is where the idea of American nativity was coined as an essential, if not central, element of the new political ideology and it is here that we are confronted with a rather bewildering paradox that was to have a lasting effect on the destiny of American Masonry. For, while the Federalists as a political party were as British-oriented as early American Masonry, they were incipiently anti-Masonic and became, in the first years of the nineteenth century, patently and aggressively so. Their idea of American nativeness clashed with Masonic cosmopolitanism far more than with Masonic Britishness. The Jeffersonian Republicans, on the other hand, though incipiently anti-British, were far more sympathetic to Freemasonry as an institution both democratic in its spirit and decentralized (unlike its English ancestor), the very existence of which was a living manifestation of the *social* (though not political) ideals of the Republicans. When the second generation of Federalists branded Freemasons "non-native", "alien", "foreign", "subversive", and "anti-Christian", they did not know that in doing so they brought doom on their own heads, for the principle of "nativity", however useful or necessary to the nationalism of a very young culture, soon became stretched to the point where it was transformed into a political and ideological obstacle to that rapidly developing culture's self-realization. And when the pace of growth slackened, American Masonry underwent a radical change and became so "native" that its old Federalist enemies and Jeffersonian sympathizers alike would have been left amazed.

The Protestantism of American Freemasonry poses a far more diffi-cult problem for, as a term of religious self-awareness, it acquired within the American context a very different meaning from that of eighteenth-century England. As we have already seen, both Thomas Jefferson and John Adams regarded any ritual as anti-Protestant, pagan, religiously perverse and ethically pernicious (which somehow did not inhibit Jefferson's Masonic activities). Theirs was a Protestantism of an entirely rejectionist strain. Thus, describing American Freemasonry as Protestant is not strictly correct. Although its members were, for the most part, Protestant, Freemasonry in America has remained, both dogmatically and ideologically, unacceptable to very many *native* Protestant churches, organizations, and movements old and new alike. That which remained merely a sporadic and disorganized anti-Masonic critique in eighteenth-century England was a well orchestrated political and ideological *opposition* to Masonry in nineteenth-century America, an opposition so strong and organized that it eventually became the Anti-Masonic Party. And, interestingly enough, the Anti-Masonic Party reached its apotheosis in the 1830s, having the staunch Protestant John Quincy Adams as its leader, and a refined Deist Protestantism as its ideological platform, a platform that both John Adams (John Quincy's father) and his political adversary Thomas Jefferson would willingly have joined.

Protestantism was overwhelmingly the normal historical and religious background of the members of the American Fraternity, and did not yield to the specific Masonic religion of the Great Architect to the extent that it did in eighteenth-century England; but it remained a more overt and acknowledged feature of the religious life of the Lodge. What is more, irrespective of the actual religious beliefs and practice of its members, American Masonry tended to present itself to society in general as an institution Protestant by definition, while attempting at the same time to convey that it was more truly religious than any church. When Lynn Dumeril writes[10] that "although [American] Masonry mirrored the religious and moralistic content of American society's concerns and values, Masons took pains to distinguish between the internal *sacred world* of Masonry, and the external world of the 'profanes'", she is right only to the extent to which the nature and content of the Masonic religion was redefined by American Masons themselves.

Having surprisingly successfully survived the crisis brought about by the American Revolution in the period 1773–83, an attempt to accuse Freemasons of conspiracy in 1798–9,[11] an outburst of anti-Masonic emotion during the war with Britain in 1812–14, and general popular disapproval echoed in some influential quarters, by the mid-1820s American Masonry had become the most numerous non-denominational organization in the United States and undoubtedly the most powerful in New England. Here we come across a notion which, in both anti-Masonic and Masonic contexts, takes some explaining. For while, in the British and Continental (mainly French) anti-Masonic contexts of the end of the eighteenth century, the Craft was perceived as a negative and internationally centralized power of religious and political subversion, in the context of the young American Republic it acquired the opposing negative dimension – parochialness.

It was inevitable that in very many places Freemasons exercised their influence, as often as not directly, in matters concerning local, county, and state politics, and even the process of law, while not associating themselves (at least formally and openly) with any of the existing political parties or groupings. By the time American professionals and, a little later, businessmen became conscious of their social and cultural position as different from that of all other strata and classes of the American population, they discovered Freemasonry as the best possible form available for their social and cultural self-identification. It is this discovery that transformed American Freemasonry into an active social force, a force which British Freemasonry never acquired. This may go some of the way in explaining why British anti-Masons believe that Freemasonry's supposed power resides in something nebulous, sinister or even ridiculous,[12] while Americans tend to measure the value of their religions and institutions by their impact on the community.[13]

This decentralization of Masonic authority in America has, in practice, worked remarkably well. The political and economic influence of Masons – as a group united by commonly shared rules, however vaguely defined – has always been restricted to a given locality: the larger the community the more diluted the influence. Furthermore, the organizational structure of American Masonry has, from the very beginning, been based upon this principle.

This results in a paradoxical situation, where initial ideological premises flagrantly contradict the manner of their practical application. The initial ideological premise in this case was the principle of absolute centralization inherent in English Freemasonry which warranted the Provincial Grand Lodges in the Colonies, but warranted them as *Provincial*.[14] This might be compared, however superficial the comparison may be, with some *political* ideological principles implicit in the ideas of Commonwealth and the British Empire: the Masonic principle of "authority by delegation" is, in this sense, analogous to that of "limited local autonomy" in the Colonies.

However, when following the British example, the Provincial Grand

Lodge of Pennsylvania attempted, in 1779, to make George Washington the *General* Grand Master of the Colonies – in order to establish another system of centralized, Masonic authority – the appointment was resolutely opposed by Massachusetts for the reason that all American Grand Lodges were established by the Grand Lodge of England as Provincial, and no central authority as regards America had ever been authorized by the British parent.[15] So, the principle of division of power prevailed over that of centralization as if in anticipation of the ensuing split between Federalists and Republicans in 1791 and the defeat of the former following the 1812–14 war with Britain.

Compared with the British prehistory, the prehistory of American Masonry is rather sketchy. According to American Masonic histories there are three important figures in the early American Craft: Lord Alexander, Jonathan Belcher, and Daniel Coxe. The first, a Scottish Mason, said to have been initiated in the Lodge of Edinburgh in 1634 and who allegedly introduced the Three Degrees Craft into Rhode Island in 1658, was rather a legendary figure. The second, who became a Freemason (somewhere in London) in about 1704 and Governor of Massachusetts in 1730, did not leave any traces of Masonic activities connected with the Lodges in the Colonies.[16] The only proof of the Masonic existence of the third, Daniel Coxe, is the copies of his Deputations ". . . to be Provincial Grand Master of the Provinces of New York, New Jersey and Pennsylvania" in 1730, and (more gloriously) ". . . to be the Provincial Grand Master of North America" in 1731. History begins in earnest, however poorly documented, with Henry Price, 1697–1772.[17]

Born in London and settled in America in 1723, Price represents the classical British type of the generation of the first Grand Lodge of England that dominated the early period of expansion. For at that time it was still Britishness that made Freemasonry "one for all".[18] He held office as Provincial Grand Master for New England at various times from 1733 to 1768; established a private St John's Lodge at Boston; warranted or supported the establishment of dozens of Lodges in other provinces; and helped introduce and disseminate Anderson's *Constitutions* throughout the Eastern side of the continent and in the West Indies. The first American reprint of the *Constitutions* was produced by Benjamin Franklin (1706–90), a grandfather of the American Revolution and Grand Master of Pennsylvania (1734). Franklin still represents a type of cosmopolitan Mason, freethinker and Francophile wholly alien to the localism and provincialism that prevailed in the later years of American Masonry,[19] being far less an orthodox Protestant, far more Deist, and probably far less religious than his junior Masonic contemporaries who served as the concrete power-base of the American Revolution. Franklin's pure Masonic idealism was only a part of its ideological luggage.

On the eve of the Revolution, there were between ninety and 110 Lodges with between 1350 and 1500 members in the thirteen Colonies.[20] This numerical insignificance is offset by the influential position of a number of leading Masons. As well as the sixteen signatories of the Declaration of Independence, thirty members of the first Constitutional Assembly were also members of the Craft.

American Masonry, it should be emphasized, unlike the Grand Lodge of England, was not, in the main, an urban phenomenon. At the beginning of its decentralized, atomic existence, it continued to be based on small towns, townships, and provincial settlements. There, unlike its English counterpart, Masonry often functioned as a kind of duplicate of the local communities. This is where another curious difference between parent and child becomes apparent: British Freemasonry is, to its members, an idea to live by far more than an institution, however important the latter might be, whereas to American Masons Masonry is first and foremost an institution. This difference, as I understand it, may be accounted for by the fact that the British prototype reflected the predominantly urban conditions of its origin and early expansion, while its American offspring has been mainly a small-town or rural phenomenon.

When we read of "Masonic domination" in up-state New York of the 1820s, we should remember that the place was a semi-rural area of small towns where the local community was the main, if not the only, form of social life. Freemasonry there was a parallel society functioning in symbiosis with the host but without adding to it anything by way of ideas. It was not Masonic ideas that brought together Benjamin Franklin and George Washington in the context of the American Revolution. To George Washington, land surveyor, talented amateur soldier and country gentleman of distinction, Masonry was no more than one other network of local power and influence, whereas to Benjamin Franklin, a generation older than Washington, Masonry was an integral part of the aristocracy of the spirit, in the sense of the European and primarily French Enlightenment, to which Washington was entirely alien. If it is plausible to state – though not without reservation – that Freemasonry implied or reflected in itself a set of ideas shared by both Franklin and Voltaire when they met in France, it did nothing of the kind when Franklin and Washington met in Massachusetts or anywhere else in

America. The split between loyalists (to the Crown) and patriots at the beginning of the War of Independence remained purely political. However much it affected American Masonic unity, it did not affect the inner structures of the Craft, for the latter had ceased to be a place for ideas, a traditional repository of Freethinking as in France, or of Deist cosmopolitanism as in England. It was this fragmented and localized character that made it virtually impossible to forge from it one power, political or otherwise. The temporary impasse caused by the American Revolution in 1776,[21] and the ensuing isolation of American Masonry, exacerbated the process of differentiation which would have taken place anyway. When, in the 1790s, the rift ended, communication between Mother and Daughter Masonries was restored and America became flooded with English Masonic literature, it was too late: American Free-masonry had already established itself as different from English Freemasonry in style, spirit and practice. The process was completed by the second crisis, the 1812–1814 hostilities with Britain, when com-munications were severed again at a time when the nourishing stock of old European Masonic ideas was a spent force and the old guard had all died. The presidency of James Monroe (1758–1831), himself a Freemason of the third generation, was in this connection symbolic: his famous isolationist Doctrine (1823) appears to reflect the growing isolationism of American Masonry.[22]

The Anglo–American war over, and traditional political Federalism on the wane, American Masonry reached the crucial year of its history – 1826 – with the number of its lodges more than trebled (to at least 320) and its membership (over 20,000) increased tenfold since the year of Revolution.

In 1826 the episode known as the "Morgan Affair" had disastrous repercussions for Masonry in North-eastern America. William Morgan was born in 1779, joined the Craft at some time in the 1810s, and at the beginning of 1826 wrote and then published, with the help of "one Miller, a journalist", *Morgan's Illustrations*, a typically hostile exposé of Masonry by a disillusioned Brother. This genre was as widespread in North America in the nineteenth century as it was in England in the eighteenth century, and Morgan's exposition would have hardly been regarded as anything out of the ordinary, had it not appeared in an area – up-state New York – where both local Masonic influence and anti-Masonic feelings were very strong. According to the official Masonic version, "some ineffective attempts were made to procure his silence; he was then removed [accounts vary as to whether he went willingly or not] to Fort Niagara. The rest is silence, but a rumour of his murder gave rise to an anti-Masonic movement."[23] The resulting wave of protest and indignation practically suppressed Masonry in New York if not in the whole of New England, particularly after the attempts of the judiciary to bring the culprits to justice proved ineffective and another exposé, *The Light on Masonry*, by an ex-Masonic Protestant Minister, Bernard, was published.[24] Robbins does not exaggerate when he writes about the calamitous effect of the "Morgan Affair" on Masonry:

After the "Morgan Affair" . . . there ensued one of those outbursts of hysterical indignation known to all peoples at varying periods . . . Certain religious denominations were so swept away with the torrent that, having made the fantastic discovery that the Craft was not only "accommodated to the prejudices of the Jews" but adoptive of "Orders of Knighthood of Popery", excluded Masons from . . . Holy Communion . . . They were rejected as jurors, prevented from occupying even the lowliest official positions, and assembled mothers by solemn resolution forbade their daughters to keep them company . . . De Witt Clinton was forced . . . to withdraw from both his Governorship and Grand Mastership of New York . . . The Anti-Masonic Party polled close on 350,000 votes . . . in the Presidential election of 1832 . . . Hundreds of Lodges ceased to exist . . .[25]

The short-lived Anti-Masonic Party numbered among its active membership a presidential candidate, two state governors, and a great many judges and members of the Federal and State legislatures. The anti-Masonic campaign revealed itself with particular strength in the position taken by the churches, especially at opposite ends of the religious spectrum – the Catholic Church and most radically Puritan denominations – where suspicion of Masonry had been fermenting since the end of the eighteenth century. To this aspect, however, the Masonic apologists have remained blind, continuing to attribute the consequences of the Morgan Affair to prejudice, ignorance, and hostile political interests only. One of the most important Masonic authors in America, Fort Newton, writes naïvely:

How strange, then, that Masonry should have been made the victim of the most bitter and baseless persecution . . . An anti-Masonic political party was formed, fed on frenzy, and the land was stirred from end to end. Even such a man as John Quincy Adams, of great credulity and strong prejudice, was drawn into the fray, and in a series of letters flayed Masonry as an enemy of society, . . . forgetting that Washington, Franklin, Marshall, and Warren were members of the order . . .

. . . and verily, it was a mean while – Weed, Seward, Th. Stevens, and others of their ilk, rode into power on the strength of it, as they had planned to do, defeating Henry Clay for President, because he was a Mason – and incidentally, electing Andrew Jackson, another Mason.[26]

The "Morgan Affair" precipitated a flood of anti-Masonic books, pamphlets, brochures, and articles beyond any other "external" event in the history of Freemasonry, starting with Bernard's exposition and John Quincy Adams's letters, and finishing with the remotest reverberations of anti-Masonic propaganda in the aftermath of the Dreyfus Affair at the beginning of the twentieth century. (Some parallels with the latter are indeed striking.) No explanation of the historical and ideological character of this reaction appears to have been made. I venture to offer a tentative one here.

Having been, in its British origins, a typically *urban* sub-culture, Freemasonry in America found itself at the beginning of the nineteenth century in a state of wide regional diffusion, in which its primary character had been irretrievably lost, while the process of adaptation to new socio-cultural and political conditions was still at an early stage. If British Masonry, as a phenomenon, was first and foremost a kind of "abstraction" from culture, American Masonry was primarily an *organization*, a social institution whose function was partly to reinforce an as yet incomplete culture, which would inevitably develop in a parallel way to other social institutions. The fact that it appeared to set itself up as a secret alternative society made it a sinister force in the eyes both of those who wanted to see the United States as a thoroughly unified and centralized body (John Quincy Adams) and those who saw in this social parallelism a direct threat to American democracy on the State and local level. So an anonymous correspondent complains to Adams: "the citizen cannot exercise his constitutional rights without being a member of this conspiratorial society"; and Adams himself adds, "A more perfect agent for the devising and execution of conspiracies against church or state could scarcely have been conceived".[27] Here the Populist and the Statist converge in their natural suspicion of diversity and exception, a suspicion which had taken half a century to ripen and mature since Alexander Hamilton and George Washington had been both Statists and Masons.

Now, in the 1820s, in the aftermath of the Morgan Affair, a situation arose which, in retrospect, threatened the very existence of American

Masonry, for the latter, widely though thinly spread, rapidly became almost entirely divorced from its cultural roots. The anti-Masonic legislation, attempted at both local and central level, failed in the face of Jeffersonian resistance, though Jefferson himself died in 1826. It is interesting, in this connection, to note that the heart of the Jeffersonian Constitution allowed for constitutional changes, though much less for constitutional mechanisms to make them, a result of which was that both anti-Masonic and anti-slavery legislations failed. The Masons, as well as slave-owners, might have abused human beings or even the "system" (as Adams and his friends stressed), but they did not threaten the Constitution.[28]

The traditional British Masonic prohibition on politics (as well as on religion) in the Lodge was founded on a kind of religious idealism – from which American Masonry had retained the "religious" while dropping the idealism. The ageing Jefferson knew all too well that Franklin's impetus for idealism had been spent and that nothing could be more degenerate than an alliance of populist ignorance with the ideology of the Statists, his old Federalist enemies. When the provincial liberalism of the eighteenth century had died out altogether with the Masons of the third generation, the anti-Masonic opposition was left to do battle with social diversity. And on that score they had no chance of winning, for the rapidly growing cities of the north-east, New York in the first place, were breeding their own urban culture and city-liberalism, and very soon became invincible, Masonry or no Masonry. It was for the first time in history, however, that Freemasonry, while not actually prohibited, had to contend with a very strong *political* opposition and a broad *public* discontent which were assuming their democratic organizational forms.[29]

This placed a check on growth for the time being. For twenty-five years, from 1826 to 1850, Freemasonry was hardly able to maintain its membership on a level with the demographic growth of the nation, so that in 1850 there were about 66,000 Masons in the United States, more or less equally distributed between the Northern and Southern states (statistics remain very vague on this point); but by the beginning of the 1850s "Morganiana" was almost forgotten, and during the following decade membership more than trebled.

Before dealing with the tragic events of the Civil War, let us touch briefly upon a strange and curious episode which probably divided Masons in the United States more seriously than the American Revolution or the Civil War itself. This episode represented, on the one hand, a direct reflection of the *inner* tendencies of Freemasonry in Great

Britain between the 1770s and 1810s, while on the other, it was a belated reaction to the threat of a split between Southern and Northern Masons.

On 24 June 1860 Rob Morris, a past Grand Master of Kentucky, started the movement of "conservators" whose chief aims were:

> 1. A common ritual, "one to all American Symbolic Masonry", which will serve as the basis for:
> 2. An absolute uniformity of all Lodges;
> 3. The absolute secrecy of all that takes place inside a Lodge;
> 4. The "key" or "code", one for all Lodges, in which all "the esoteric as well as exoteric work" would be written down and read solely by those who could understand and use it.[30] [Here we definitely see "the writing", and not "the speech", as the main means of Masonic communication.][31]
> 5. The absolute authority of the head of organization of the Conservators, the Chief Conservator, in all matters concerning Ritual, Discipline, and Membership;
> 6. The absolute exclusion of all Lodges and individual members who refused to adopt the System of the Conservators.[32]

The movement, which aroused "unkindly feelings . . . sharper between those for and against Morris than they were between the Masons of the North and South (during the Civil War),"[33] was indeed the last attempt to de-secularize American Masonry and to prevent its subsequent adaptation to the conditions of the end of the nineteenth century. Robert Morris, a maverick, poet, and founder of the Order of the Eastern Star, was not able to play the role of an American Lawrence Dermott for the same reason that John Quincy Adams could not play the role of his father John Adams. America was in the process of radically changing its cultural patterns: the ideological monopoly of ethical Protestantism was to be checked, and the process of secularization started its march through the agglomeration of denominations. The War only accelerated the process. Morris's idea, had he succeeded, would have made out of Masonry a gigantic fundamentalist sect, but he failed, leaving the dignitaries of American Masonry quaking at the mention of his name until the end of the century. From now on it is only on the level of individuals that Masonic de-secularizing tendencies would find their expression, and not on the level of state jurisdictions, let alone de-centralized American Masonry as a whole.

While this purely internal Masonic affair aroused opposing passions for a time, its policy of unity remained steadfast throughout the potentially far more divisive Civil War. "While in the Civil War churches were severed and states seceding, the Order remained unbroken," says Fort Newton.[34] And indeed it was. After the election of Abraham Lincoln (who defeated three Freemasons: S. A. Douglas, J. C. Breckinridge, and John Bell) and just before the secession of South Carolina, John Dove, from the Grand Lodge of Virginia, wrote:

... it may be that we happened to be instrumental in allaying the angry tumult of popular frenzy. Let, then, the three hundred thousand patriotic Masons, good and true, of the United States, unite in fervent prayer to our Heavenly Grand Master, that he may ... will that this bitter cup of tribulation pass.[35]

In the aftermath of South Carolina's secession, Henry M. Phillips, the Grand Master of Pennsylvania, declared on 26 December 1860 that: "To our brethren throughout the nation we make an affectionate and a Masonic appeal to practice *out of the Lodge* those principles of forbearance, generosity, conciliation, charity and brotherly love they are taught *within it*."[36] It may be argued that this is merely the toothless rhetoric of impotent pacifism; nevertheless, at the beginning of the First World War no Socialist party or Church who professed pacifist ideals in time of peace dared to proclaim openly anything of the sort when war came. What the American Masons exhibited was not a kind of qualified pacifism which would have meant involvement in politics, but unqualified reconciliation which was, to them, a simple ethical position. But it may be argued that the line between politics and ethics is too fine here, particularly if we take into account the *moral* aspect of the Civil War and the moral stance of the North. The Masonic position during the War was far from easy, however. Let us take, as an example of the difficulties it faced, the appeal made by the Grand Lodge of Tennessee (South) to the Grand Lodge of New York (the most abolitionist North) in 1861, imploring the latter to exercise all its influence "to stay hostilities destined to continue for four years". New York, however, could not oblige, for "no appropriate action could be suggested without discussing *political* questions ... which is clearly outside the province of Freemasonry." But the plea made by Tennessee that, "if all efforts fail ... we beseech the Brethren ... to remember that a fallen foe is still a brother" was unconditionally accepted and followed, in practice, by North and South alike.[37]

The Grand Lodge of New York must have experienced some uneasiness over its equivocal response, but it had to take into account that although the majority of American Masons were "for compromise, not for war,"[38] a considerable number of New York Masons would have identified their Masonic character with abolitionism in general and the cause of the North. And the Masons of the South cannot have been insensitive to the fact that slavery as an institution ran counter to the Masonic ideals of universal love and the equality of all men before God. This may explain why the Masons of the Confederacy were more ardent and consistent than their Northern brothers in striving for compromise, although there is no documentary evidence to support this conjecture. It may also explain why American Masonic historians, such as Allen Roberts, Ray Denslow and Fort Newton, endeavoured to present the idea of compromise as part and parcel of Masonic ideology in general, rather than a pragmatic solution to an awkward political dilemma.

It is in the context of the Civil War that American Masons tended to speak and behave as if they were a "third force", operating alongside the two official opposing powers.[39] Unlike the French Masons, who used to identify themselves first with the larger trends of the Enlightenment and anti-clericalism, then with anti-clericalism and political liberalism, and finally with the radical left, and unlike the British Masons who have never identified themselves with any political party, American Masons were trying to work out their own political position. However hard they endeavoured to represent this position as "non-political", it remained political not only in the eyes of non-Masonic members of both warring camps, but also in the perception of the populace as a whole, particularly in the North, as the following tale shows:

In the fall of 1862, with the War entering its second stage, rumour spread that it was the Masons who were the real cause of the draft both in the North and South. It started in Port Washington, Wisconsin, on the first day of the draft, 10 November 1862. A mob ransacked Osakkee Lodge No. 17, and destroyed the premises, then attacked the court-house and the house of the draft commissioner (a Mason), smashing the furniture, destroying the clothing and pouring jellies, jams and preserves out on the street.

This incident, in itself trivial, served as the precursor of the greatest riot in American history, which took place on 13 July 1863 in New York City. Opposition to the draft and hatred for Masons "widened into a race riot: Negroes were hunted down and murdered on the streets . . . the property of the State administration destroyed . . ."[40] It was a typical pogrom. Masons were singled out as being identified with the adminis-tration – the establishment – at the same time as being seen as alien to the people. Blacks were, of course, a more obvious target of fear and hatred and, as is so often the case, the destructive energy of the pogromers was directed not just at one group but at two (or more).[41] Masons bore the brunt of populist reaction because popular psychology associated them with the warmongers, despite the fact that Masonry had been the only force which had spoken out against it and had tried, using the influence of the Lodges containing both Northerners and Southerners, to prevent it. But the real cause of popular hatred of Masons – as so often of Jews too – was that very alienness and their deliberately neutral position, which separated them from the populace.

During that fratricidal war the Masons on both sides showed numerous examples of compassion, generosity and nobility of spirit towards one another.[42] It could not be claimed that Masons made the Civil War gentler, but theirs was the only organization in America that was wholly conscious of the War as evil in a strict religious sense. There was an outburst of Masonic religiosity, feeling perhaps unparalleled in its history in America. Masons seriously believed in their own, uniquely religious mission of reconciliation as opposed to the opportunist, or partisan stand of practically all the Christian denominations. This found its expression particularly in the practice of Masonic funerals during the hostilities.[43]

The following story illustrates a degree of Masonic religious awareness which, for all its anachronisms, would be inconceivable in the present-day atmosphere permeated by impotent humanism and militant pacifism:

The captain of the USS gunboat *Albatross* firing into the towns along the banks of the Mississippi, John E. Hart, a Mason, had been gravely ill, and being in a delirium . . . shot himself in his cabin. An officer of his, Th. B. Dubois, also a Mason . . . went ashore under a flag of truce, and met two persons living near the shore of the river, who happened to be Masons too, and requested them to assist him in a Masonic funeral. The Senior Warden of the local Lodge, William W. Leake, an officer in the Confederate Army . . . when informed of the request said: "as a soldier I consider it a duty to permit the burial of a deceased member of the army or navy of any government, even if, as in the present instance, there is war between that government and my own. As a Mason, I know it to be my duty to accord Masonic burial to the remains of a Brother Mason, without taking into account the nature of his relationship in the outer world."[44]

This episode is a classical example of the Masonic philosophy of discrimination. For indeed, "as a soldier" and "as a Mason" are very different.[45] Being a soldier is a civic duty which, once it has become a duty, cannot be breached by a Mason, while being a Mason is a purely individual choice which entails a certain type of religious awareness which discriminates between Mason and non-Mason within a single Mason; that is, between one's Mason-ness and one's "relationship in the outer world". Masonry, in the words of our Confederate officer, is *inner, par excellence*, while the division into Federals and Confederates cannot be anything but *outer*. Masonry's conduct in the Civil War more than lived up to the principle of not bringing inside the Lodge any outer, or civic, distinctions or permitting them to cause fraternal conflict. This earned it a rise in popularity after the War, among people better informed about the actual behaviour of Masons during hostilities, and an immense increase in membership.[46] And it is that general appeal which, at the close of the century, transformed Masonry in America from being perceived as a sinister "alien" force to an exemplar of social respectability, almost converting it into a kind of middle-class mass organization, for which it would have to pay, when the time came, by becoming increasingly dull, serious and socially responsible.

However, the war was not yet over and the decisive battle of Gettysburg saw how,

... by a singular coincidence, Generals Hancock and Armisted, old friends and both Masons, were destined to meet ... not as comrades, but as opponents ... Armisted was struck by a ball. As he fell, he called out "Jan a widow's son!" [a Masonic parole of recognition] and asked, "Where is General Hancock?" The latter, who was wounded about the same time, ordered General Bingham, a Mason too, to take care of his poor Confederate friend and former comrade in arms ...[47]

After the fiercest battle in the history of America, "there was a Lodge meeting in Gettysburg, and victorious 'Yanks' and defeated 'Johnny Rebs' met and mingled as friends under the Square and Compass".[48]

This tale, however fragmentary and one-sided, might suggest that American Masonry, particularly on the Confederate side, was connected with American religious romanticism of the second half of the nineteenth century. Roberts refers proudly to the famous Confederate General, Lew Wallace, a Mason who wrote the best-selling novel, *Ben Hur*, giving fictional expression to some Masonic ideas.[49] In fact, the whole line of American romanticism from Edgar Allen Poe through Nathaniel Hawthorne to H. P. Lovecraft was permeated with and inspired by Masonic symbols, associations, and reminiscences.

The period from the end of the Civil War to the beginning of the

First World War was for American Freemasonry the happiest half-century of its history. The growing prestige of the Institution, both in its "blue" (i.e. Three Degrees) and Higher Degrees versions, the building of Masonic temples, hospitals and libraries, the proliferation of Masonic charities and, of course, the rapid urbanization of Masonry which followed the gigantic growth of the American economy and the demographic shift of people to the cities, made it one of the most decisive forms of American social life. For, socially Freemasonry was neither political, nor did it represent specific economic interests, nor, least of all, was it a purely cultural phenomenon. As R. Babham, a strange and little-known Masonic writer, put it, "our Institution is too abstract and universal, in its Deist creed, to be Christian, and too religious to be cultural" (the latter qualification could never apply to British Masonry). The central argument of Lynn Dumeril's most recent book on American Masonry is that Masonry's main social function, at that time, was to provide "a retreat from the materialistic, competitive, and *immoral* world of late nineteenth-century America".[50] This was indeed so, but to provide such a retreat Masonry would have to define, however vaguely, its stand as regards that immoral world. Here we come across the first Masonic attempts to do battle against the excesses of capitalism. In the light of the rather cool reception given by American Masons to the Great Prohibition (1920–33), it is interesting to learn that "By 1897, 22 Grand Lodges (out of 48) had passed laws forbidding Lodges from accepting petitions [i.e. applications for membership] from men engaged in the saloon business."[51]

The American Masons at the turn of the century were apprehensive about the equivocality of the situation. That some money is "less moral", or "more immoral", is evident. But isn't it also evident that money earned in the "outer world" by means moral or immoral is, or at least might be considered as being, outside the competence of the Lodge to judge, and so beyond the scope of Masonic morality? It is here that the clash between the principles of morality and equality, or, speaking in terms of Masonic symbolism, between Square and Compass, becomes inevitable. This brings us back to the old Masonic problem of an absolute equality *within* the Lodge in contrast to the inevitable inequality outside it – people (Masons included) outside the Lodge vary as much in their social and economic status as their means of obtaining money varies in its moral acceptability. The twenty-sixth President of the United States and Brother Theodore Roosevelt (1858–1919) tried to resolve this conflict by means of typically Masonic social theories. He wrote in 1898: "I enjoy going to some little Lodge, where I meet the plain, hard-working people on a footing of *genuine equality* . . . It is the *equality of moral men.*"[52]

Unfortunately for American Masonry, the reverse side of the same coin remains that you cannot be consistent in basing equality on morality. For the genuine Masonic equality is conceived as absolute; as irreducible to anything else. The Proceedings of the Grand Lodge of Virginia provide a curious example of this principle:[53]

(from S. Dacota, 1903) . . . A proposed by-law of a Lodge, fixing the fees for degrees at $40, and providing that a clergyman may receive degrees for $25, is opposed to the spirit of the laws of this Grand Lodge, and was therefore disapproved by the Grand Master. Why should we lower the dignity of Ministers and their calling by putting them in the pauper class? . . . Masonry should know no special classes . . .

So, no special classes – except for the pauper class, of course. Isn't that why enlightened critics, be they John Quincy Adams or the general populace of up-state New York, accused Masonry of elitism? The contradiction between the idea and practice of Masonic equality within the Lodge and the persistent perception of the institution as elitist by the people outside the Lodge was not only inherent in the Masonic self-awareness in both America and Great Britain, but had served as a factor separating Masonry both from society as a whole, with all its divisions, and from religion, in all its diversity. The Lodge as an asylum or shelter from the trials and tribulations of society, and as a place of harmony and unanimity, could withstand the pressure of the world outside only by deliberately choosing the Scylla of social isolation over the Charybdis of absorption. But changes in American society at the beginning of the twentieth century propelled American Masonry in the opposite direction. Lynn Dumeril writes:

. . . In the late nineteenth century the increasingly national focus of economic power had shattered the relative isolation of island communities . . . The Masons then were acutely conscious of the divisiveness in their society, but by and large had chosen to retreat to the asylum of the Lodge. Masons in the 1920s were more aggressive in . . . their nativism, anti-catholicism and American homogeneity . . . and educational unity . . .[54]

Three decades of Masonic history, from 1890 to 1920, saw American Masons responding to changing conditions in the outer world and having to choose between the unbridled individualism of private enterprise and an increasingly strong climate of state intervention and regulation.

And the price they would have to pay for their choice, made first unconsciously and then consciously, gradually became apparent. One social
factor played an immensely important role and partly determined the
direction they took: during this period American Masonry was becoming
more and more socially and culturally homogeneous. Everyone knows
that some famous names – Theodore Roosevelt, Henry Ford, Harding,
Charles Lindbergh and Luther Burbank, for example – were Masons,
but it is the hundreds of thousands of anonymous businessmen, small
traders, salesmen, and above all, white-collar workers, who constituted
a majority in and shaped the atmosphere of the average American
Lodge at the beginning of the twentieth century. And it is this growing
element of homogeneity that proved so decisive in the development
of two new tendencies in American Masonry: social participation and
secularization rather than social and religious exclusiveness. When one
Masonic author said, in 1930, that "Masonry is . . . living in a past age",[55]
he was revealing himself as a typical Masonic modernist which, of course,
Harding and Theodore Roosevelt were not.

When the white-collar members of the Blue Lodges realized that they
wanted Masonry to develop a more mundane ideology, they also realized
that to do so they had to take up an idea, however banal, where the
economic and the ethical might merge and become one. This was
the concept of service, or civic duty, as opposed to the concept of profit
in the external world of business, as well as to the idea of Masonic
sacred duties within the Lodge. It was this conception that made American Masonry so appealing to certain civic clubs, such as the Rotary Club,
founded in 1905, and at the same time caused some of those clubs to
be very similar to Lodges. "The process of Rotarization of Masonry and
Masonization of civic clubs went so far that in the middle 1930s . . .
they became, in the eyes of the lower-middle-class citizen, almost the
same thing," one conservative and nostalgic Masonic writer told me.
He concluded, rather caustically, that "by the end of the 1910s, it
became almost a mass-organization, but without sufficiently articulated
social principles to become a political force in its own right". Well, of
course, service to society as embodied in one's business activity and in
the slogan "by getting richer myself I'm making the Nation richer" was
a somewhat two-edged social programme and even more dubious as a
political principle. Something more concrete and convincing was
needed, an idea that would strengthen the self-image of the average
Mason and at the same time would strengthen the image of Masonry
in the eyes of the average non-Mason.

The Wilsonian idealism of the end of the First World War had as little appeal to the Masons on the whole as it had to the Senate. It was under Warren Harding's "Masonic Presidency" (1920–22) that American Masonry began to embrace the notions of "Americanism", "American Spirit", and, in particular, the "one for all" system of American education.

The desire to promote 100 per cent Americanism, [writes Lynn Dumeril] an outgrowth of the postwar Red Scare, led Masons to a militant expression of their own cultural identity as well as to demand that Masonry . . . take a stand in the efforts to meet the problems posed by radicalism, unassimilated immigrants, and "political" catholicism. Taken together, the demands for a modern Masonry and the concern to reinforce native, old stock American ideals prompted Masons to depart from the traditional emphasis on individual morality pursued in a sacred environment in favour of becoming more involved in the profane . . . world.[56]

By adopting the cause of public education Masons were trying to adapt to the 1920s, which were to become far more different from the 1910s than the latter were from the 1890s.[57]

Here the idea of Masonry as the "third force" manifested itself again, though in a quite different way from the Civil War era; once again the Mason's main concern was to present the Masonic stand as non-political. Here, for the first time in its history Masonry shared the central political stand of its arch-enemy, populism. And it is here, in my opinion, that Lynn Dumeril's solution to the problem is incomplete and one-sided. Undoubtedly, white-collar workers wanted, on a subjective level, and not a very high one, to present their cause – Americanism and Americanization of immigrants – as national. But at the same time, what she fails to understand is that it was the growing homogeneity within the Lodge that was objectively reflected in their own utopian "populist" ideal of the homogeneity of the most heterogeneous nation in the world. Sharing populism's most prominent qualities, American Masonry, in the process of its politicization during the 1920s, was to become statist, overtly anti-Catholic, and covertly anti-Semitic.[58]

At the same time – and this is significant when we speak of that peculiar hybrid of "populist Masonry" – while becoming more and more negative, more and more "anti" anything that was perceived as alien (or superior) to the average salesman or white-collar worker, American Masonry was becoming ridden with new *inner* contradictions after abandoning its traditional isolation.[59] For how were Masons to react to a situation in which the main organized force of populism, the deeply racist Ku Klux Klan, was playing a vital role in addressing the political needs of the lower middle classes, disenchanted, embittered and impoverished by the Great Depression? In 1929, the Texas Grand Master complained "that Lodges were suffering from factionalism caused by political controversies . . . and singled out the Ku Klux Klan as a major source of discord . . ."[60] It is no secret that there were and are American Masons belonging to the Ku Klux Klan, and this, particularly in the South, endangered the unity of a Fraternity founded on the principles of tolerance and universal brotherhood. But the very phenomenon of the politicization of Freemasonry would, undoubtedly, have engendered such a threat anyway.[61] So it is quite natural that in the 1930s very many Masonic voices, from Vermont to Phoenix, were raised indignantly against a flirtation with the extreme right of the populist spectrum.[62]

It might be argued that on the central issue, a standardized and uniform system of school education, the Masons merely transferred the principle of equality from within the Lodge to the world outside it.[63] This, in turn, must have necessitated a change in Masonic rhetoric, and the rhetoric of "asylum" in the first place. For if before the First World War it had served as a refuge from a diverse and class-divided society, the post-war period saw the idea of one American nation with one American schooling system become the pivot of Masonic activities outside the Lodge and the focus of Masonic debates inside it. Not only was it extremely difficult to "promote the *cultural* unity of America" on the basis of an average sales rep or white-collar worker, but it became even more difficult to form a new image of an abstract "simple, hard-working man".[64] Even as a lasting ideal, cultural unity of any sort takes some striving for, and a lot of manoeuvring would be necessary to present it in a Masonic light. It is remarkable, perhaps, that the problem of ideological and ethical manoeuvring arises every time a self-conscious minority takes up the case of a not yet self-conscious majority and tries to present itself as a natural ally of the majority.

The racial issue had a legendary component too, a legend that has been repeated in hundreds of books on Freemasonry, from G. J. Findel to Lynn Dumeril. As the story goes: ". . . a negro named Prince Hall was initiated in a British army Lodge during the War of Independence. There is a claim that this Lodge was fully recognized by the Grand Lodge of England, and that from it a score of years later, the Prince Hall Grand Lodge . . . was legitimately evolved. This is a claim," concludes Robbins, who gives this version, "which on close and impartial examination can be dismissed on both heads; but the belief in it cannot be ignored."[65] This is a story about the founding of separate Black Lodges, and not about the practice of admission of black candidates into Blue Lodges, neither of which has been very popular in American Freemasonry.[66]

This conflict with Masonic cosmopolitanism was noted by Robbins, who complained that "When in June 1851, the past Grand Master of New York ... proudly claimed [before the United Grand Lodge of England] that 'the principles of Freemasonry know no distinction of country or ... colour ...', he, as to his own country, and speaking for the *regular* jurisdictions, *erred* in respect to colour. Although ... immediately after the Civil War ... there were warranted two Lodges of New Jersey composed of men of colour ... and on occasion West Indian *English* Masons ... are received as visitors in American Lodges ... the phenomenon, though partly hidden or wholly ignored, remains ..."[67] While the regular jurisdictions may have tried to justify their refusal to "grant legitimacy to Black Prince Hall Lodges by claiming that they had not been legally established",[68] the fact of the scarcity or total absence of black people in ordinary Lodges has nothing to do with Masonic laws or by-laws of Lodges; it is a result of racist practice, and it persists to this day.

When I asked Jonathan B., a Mason and lawyer from Texas, about this problem he agreed, on the whole, with my conclusion, and added that he would never have proposed as a candidate a black acquaintance of his, say a lawyer or a doctor. "Why not?" "Because nobody would support the candidacy, no chance." "Then what about a member of the Ku Klux Klan as a candidate, would it be possible?" I asked. After a while he said, rather pensively, "Well, yes. You see, in my Lodge you cannot ask a person whether he is a member of the Ku Klux Klan, for if the proposer knows he is, he would not propose him, yet if the proposer does not know, nobody else would raise the question."

Another Mason, a dentist from Ann Arbor, Michigan, referred to this attitude as the "racial reticence" of Masons, and proposed his own explanation. American Masonry, he said, had become very defensive and often negative in its attitudes to the outside world. This, in his opinion, began in the early 1930s when the hitherto overwhelmingly influential organization found itself ousted from the mainstream of American life. During the Civil War there were many Masons with pro-slavery convictions (he counts himself a Mason of the fourth generation) but, he emphasized, they were not anti-black, theirs was a racism inherent in their Southern background and pedigree and thus had nothing to do with their *Masonic* ideals ("ours was loyalty to the Confederacy, not hostility to negroes"). "Now we have become hostile to far too many things and ideas", was his belief.

And indeed, the end of the Great Depression, the New Deal, the growth of bureaucracy, the increasing precariousness of the international situation in the 1930s and particularly the new atmosphere which prevailed around F. D. Roosevelt and the Federal Government, found American Masonry with its modernization incomplete and its Americanism almost superfluous. As one of my learned Masonic interlocutors from Iowa remarked: "Perhaps the bargain for the modernization of American Masonry would have to be made in one way or another, but the way they made it was a bad bargain."[69] When Chicago Masons built their Temple in 1884, then the tallest building in the States, it was to them a way of expressing themselves, of revealing themselves to America. And if in doing this they expressed the pride and self-satisfaction of all those who stood behind them, a heterogeneous collection of people, classes and groups, it was still a moral and social self-expression, not yet a political involvement with all the necessarily dire consequences of the latter. By sacrificing the exclusivity which is an essential part of Masonic ideology, they forfeited far more than their traditional neutrality towards society at large; the whole glorious past of American Masonry with its investment of millions in charities, libraries, hospitals, schools and temples, became merely the past of a nation-wide patriotic organization akin to the Daughters of the American Revolution.

What was to come, however, was a wave of secularization or "de-religionization" of American Masonry, which not only caused great discord and many a split in the Lodges, but provoked a reaction from within them which eventually cancelled the process of modernization and returned the institution, though not without heavy losses, to its pre-Second World War state. For, if the politicization of American Masonry and its rejection of traditional neutralism might have been interpreted *within* a Lodge in various ways,[70] its secularization could not help but directly threaten the Lodge at its very foundations.

Yet, strangely enough, it is in the American context where, at first sight at least, Freemasonry had become so cut off from its religious roots that we see a very strong – much stronger than in British Masonry – tendency to draw the line between the "sacred" of the Lodge and the "profane" of society around it. Herein is a clue to our understanding of the character and nature of American Masonry. The more communal and socially-oriented is the church, the greater is the need to emphasize the non- and extra-denominational religious activity. In the shifting balance of American religiousness, Masonry has provided a kind of counter-weight to the growing power of the extremist Protestant movements, objectively opposing itself now to Protestant ethical fundamentalism, now to liberal Catholicism, by changing its own balance between the religious and the social.

The Masonic partisans of secularization ran a little ahead of time when they began their "crusade' against religion within the Lodge. Theirs was a mainly negative motivation, the fear of becoming outdated.[71] Unlike the Anglican critics who accused the Masonic Ritual of Gnosticism and Deism, American Deist Protestant critics, who blamed it for Paganism, criticized the Ritual as *such*, that is for its being a ritual. From their point of view a ritual of any sort was doomed to ridicule, as an "archaic form of human behaviour", and a "survival of the sacred from the remote past", quite out of place in the twentieth century. Theirs was an absolutely "extra-religious" and emphatically secularizing position, while the stand of their predecessors in the critique of Masonic ritualism was religious and purist.

The phenomenon of de-religionization, however, when applied to American Freemasonry becomes even more equivocal than in many other cases. On the one hand this process as enhanced by the progressivists in the 1920s meant a markedly centrifugal tendency of moving the focus of Masonic activity from ritual to outward life.[72] On the other hand, and it is no less important, albeit less visible, it means a drastic reappraisal of the very idea of Freemasonry inside the Lodge, a reappraisal that can be summed up in the words of [Brother] Theodore Roosevelt, speaking in 1918: "there is genuine equality . . . in a little Lodge, not false equality . . . but the equality of *moral* men."[73] Or, as a Masonic acquaintance of mine from Des Moines put it: "So behave as a Mason, but *be* whatever you like." This confession is theologically perverse and rebounds upon the speaker as a religious person, for as with any typically Protestant dilemma, while seeking to smooth the contradiction between the "inner" and the "outer" (belief and action), it only exacerbates the difference. Although Theodore Roosevelt and my acquaintance from Iowa are equally far away from the religious core of Freemasonry – the equality of those who believe in a Superior Being – they represent, however differently, a quite consistent and purely Protestant attitude, stretched to the limit. In American Freemasonry, however hard you try to play your own role on the scene of the Masonic theatre, the backdrop remains the same, with the same everlasting tension between *homo religiosus* and *homo ethicus*, between sacred ritual and civic behaviour. Time is unable to change this backdrop. And it is not at all surprising that, when a reaction against it appears, it assumes the form and character of an impoverished negative mysticism, an example of which could be seen in the following short dialogue between myself and Jim Burgh, a Mason from Iowa and a successful designer.[74] Mr Burgh was extraordinarily frank about his ideas and ideals:

A.P. Is it all serious, I mean really serious in your case?

J.B. Yes, it is very serious to *me*. I do not bother about whether or not it is serious as such, in itself, or true, or useful. All I know is that it helps *me* in my struggle against . . . emptiness.

A.P. You mean you feel your life is empty, professionally and all that?

J.B. Yes, I do feel that way, and I think I should get duly prepared for a life that will become even emptier in future. So, I reckon, something has to be done. But I would never tell my wife or even those in the Lodge that are closest to me, no! Yet, as I realize it, our rituals might enable me to be somewhat better equipped to meet it.

A.P. To meet what?

J.B. Death. The limit of emptiness. I would prefer to be confronted with the end of my days in my Lodge. To me it would be a hundred times better than to become extinct in a stinking condominium in Miami, in the company of thousands of elderly couples in shorts and bikinis – "tanned vegetables" I call them. No, I'd rather die in a gutter.

A.P. [feeling more and more in sympathy with him] Then, if I understand you correctly, you see no positive reason for being a Mason, only negative. That is, if you were not feeling the emptiness of life you would never have joined the Fellowship, yes?

J.B. Not quite. I joined it because it was respectable and fashionable, though I did not quit it because of my attempts to overcome the emptiness. But look, isn't emptiness itself negatively positive, so to speak? Emptiness will help you to prepare for that which is emptiest of all. Even if I am alone in my Lodge in believing in its symbols of death, they are there giving me comfort.[75]

Once more, in this connection, it is necessary to stress the fact that when the role of ritual declines or is dispensed with altogether, a religion (no matter whether natural or artificial) or a religious tradition (no matter whether real or invented) will inevitably develop one of two tendencies: either the tendency to mystical experience, a kind of individual or collective spiritualism, or the tendency to ethical fundamentalism. The Mason from Iowa represents the first, while Masonic Protestantism, from the 1940s to the 1980s, with its partial return to traditional Protestant ethics exemplifies the second. Both, in this sense, could be considered as a direct consequence and natural result of modernization and secularization. Once again, I want to stress that the term "secularization" here denotes "de-religionization" of religion itself in the first place, and only in the second "de-religionization" of society as a whole.[76] This is a spontaneous process of which a person becomes aware only insofar as he sees his religion or some components thereof as archaic, outdated, or reactionary, and oneself as a person with a changed religious self-awareness, that is as a Modernist. So, as a phenomenon, modernization comes first and assumes secularization as its form.

American Masonry, unlike its British ancestor, occupies an intermediate position in American society; intermediate both religiously and socially, and as a special type of organization. Lynn Dumeril gives a curious, and somewhat incomplete, picture of this position. At the end of the nineteenth century, Americans, "depending on their class and temperament ... passed evenings at clubs, brothels, saloons, or Lodges", and in the beginning of the twentieth century, "in a period of increased leisure ... the Lodge ... filled the gap between the exclusive clubs of the wealthy and the saloons of the poor".[77] More strikingly, that intermediateness was shown with respect to religion. The Lodge's specific function was to fill the gap between the concrete religiousness of some and the abstract religiousness of others, or even between the religiousness of some and the irreligiousness of others, however queer it may sound.[78] When one of the most famous American Masonic writers, Albert Pike, was asked about the "personality of God", he answered in a purely Deist way: "Dear Sir, You would have to place your trust in God, and kneel and unite in prayer to God. Whether this is a belief in a *personal* God you can judge for yourself."[79] This was written in 1882. In 1986, when I showed this passage to Bill Cavey, a Mason from New Jersey and an architect, he reacted to it quite negatively, but again expressing the same intermediateness attitude, saying that, "The God of Masonry is *the symbol of Masons' unspecific religiosity*, and need not be specified". What, in fact, all this amounts to is "being religious, but without a religion",[80] which is a position suspended as regards any religion.

When the Masonic modernization of the 1920s began, the balance between the Lodge as a "social asylum" (that is, "an asylum *from* society") and the Lodge as a "sacred asylum" – in other words that which constituted a positive religious core of the Lodge – was lost. The progressives wanted it to be socially absolutely positive, but were unable to understand that it could be made so only at the cost of the complete "de-sacralization" of the asylum of the Lodge. In the end, the cost was only partly paid because the progressives failed to complete the job. However, enough damage was done to handicap the development of American Masonry for the next half century.[81]

It is difficult to imagine a Masonry more concerned with its own history than the American. All the fifty-two jurisdictions research, describe, and fix their past and present with maniacal laboriousness. This is their contribution to the common struggle of humankind against time, a desperate attempt to put the brakes on all-consuming oblivion. (When I said at the beginning of this book that the Masonic bibliography consists of at least 64,000 entries I did not include the thousands and thousands of American proceedings.) But the craze does not stop here; hundreds of books, pamphlets and articles devoted to general theoretical, historical and symbolic questions complete the picture of this graphomaniac obsession.

The obsession, however, is not an intellectual one. As if trying to make up for the excess of social involvement – the extravagant open ceremonies, parades, and "mass initiations", and the very public conduct of their charity – the American Masons indulge in hair-splitting research into the more tedious details of Masonic history and in infinitely repetitious examinations of the whole complex of speculative pseudo-theological problems, and all in a style which would have made Preston or even Oliver yawn out of sheer boredom. It seems that a powerful intellectual impulse was spent in the process of social adaptation.

For example, the first great subject with which a recent American author begins his work on the history of Freemasonry is the "evident difference between the outlook of British Masonic students and those of the United States" discussing the term "Temperance Lodges". He says:

The use of alcohol by American Masonic Lodges seemingly was dispensed with from the very outset ... since Masonic Lodges are all dedicated to the inculcation of the highest spiritual and moral truths ... The subject of "Temperance Lodges" was discussed with Brother Edward Newton, Assistant Librarian, Freemasons' Hall, London. We soon found that the word "temperance" might connote different things to different English Lodges: ... there were numerous Lodges which toasted their Masters in champagne; there were other Lodges whose interpretation of "temperance" only permitted the serving of sherry wine with the soup course, while tabooing alcohol on every other course . . .[82]

This genius of historical insight was doubly right in his semantic conclusions. For indeed, the tradition has at least two ways of understanding the term "drinking". Many documents confirm the British Masonic inclination to authorize consumption of inebriating potations and, at the same time, the tendency to limit that consumption by the golden rule of temperance. This is illustrated by the Masonic poet, Worshipful Master, and auctioneer, Matthew Garland of Deptford (1742–1819), who wrote:

> *Fill, fill, to the brim,*
> *Freely drink and cheerly sing,*
> *Long life and luck to him,*
> *Who does the apron wear.*[83]

And further:

> *The greatest lux'ry virtue each bestow . . .*
> *To deal out comfort by the Golden Rule . . .*[84]

When, in the 1930s, American Masonry was at the peak of its popularity, prestige and respectability, membership reached a record percentage – twelve per cent of the whole male, white, adult population (3,303,000). Never before or again were they so powerful and influential in the United States.[85] The ensuing decline of Masonry cannot be accounted for by the failure of Masonic progressivists to modernize it, or even by the drastic changes in American life after the Great Depression. As I have already mentioned, something changed in the very atmosphere of the country that made Masonry peripheral, and therefore more conservative than it had been before the First World War. As one of my Masonic acquaintances, Charles M., remarked,

for the 1920s the fact that Warren G. Harding was a Mason was far more significant than that Woodrow Wilson and J. C. Coolidge were not, whereas for the 1930s–1950s the fact that Franklin D. Roosevelt and D. Eisenhower were not Masons was far more significant than that Harry Truman was.

This perceptive remark, made by a veteran Mason (he joined a Blue Lodge in 1919) reflects the changed situation of Freemasons in the States. If the vitality of a religious organization can be proved by the size of its membership, American Masonry is vital enough; it remains numerically immense in its Blue version as well as in its still expanding Higher Degrees. Its reputation, however, still depends too much on its recognition by society, and in its conscious efforts to adapt and to seek the approbation of society it has lost its originality and flair and has, in effect, sold out.

Notes

1 F. L. Pick and G. Norman Knight, 1983 (1954), p. 270.

2 Allen E. Roberts, *House Undivided*, Richmond (Virginia), 1961 (A. E. Roberts, 1961), p. xi.

3 It is believed that the first Lodge in the Colonies was founded in Philadelphia in 1730, though formally the first Lodge was St John's Lodge in Boston, warranted in 1733. William Preston Vaughn, *The Anti-Masonic Party in the United States 1826–1843*, The University Press of Kentucky, 1983 (W. P. Vaughn, 1983), p. 11. See also in F. L. Pick and G. Norman Knight, 1983 (1954), pp. 270–276. There is also a legend that "... In 1680 there came to South Carolina one John Moore, a native of England ... In a letter written by him in 1715, he mentions having '... spent a few evenings in festivity with my Masonic Brethren'." Joseph Fort Newton, *The Builders, A Story and Study of Masonry*, London, 1918 [J. F. Newton, 1918 (1914)], p. 152.

4 W. P. Vaughn, 1983, p. 13. Fort Newton writes: "... of the men who signed the Declaration, the following ... were members of the order: (1) William Hooper; (2) Benjamin Franklin; (3) Matthew Thornton; (4) William Whipple; (5) John Hancock; (6) Philip Livingston; (7) Thomas Nelson; and no doubt [10? others], if we had the Masonic records destroyed during the war. Indeed, it has been said that, with four men out of the room, the assembly could have been opened in fact as a Masonic Lodge of the Third Degree ... Not only Washington, but nearly all his generals were Masons." Joseph Fort Newton, *The Builders, A Story and Study of Masonry*, London, 1918 [J. F. Newton, 1918 (1914)], pp. 164–5.

5 This "nationalist" ideology found a clear political expression, among other things, in the Alien and Sedition Act of 1798, "the passage of which so deeply divided Federalists and Republicans, and under which Adams, while President, had briefly considered prosecuting Priestley..." Jonathan Smith, *Jordan Lectures 1988* (SOAS, University of London), part I, *On the Origin of Origins*, p. 6. Joseph Priestley, a British scientist and theologian, was "newly an immigrant" to America, and was regarded by the die-hard Federalists and Adams as an ideological interloper and "foreign free-thinker". However, it might be supposed that it was the Freemasons who, in the 1790s, represented the "softer" line in Federalism and to whom Priestley's unmitigated Deism might have had a strong appeal.

6 This problem takes some grasping, for there were a lot of merely political, and sometimes contradictory, motives and reasons behind these religious discussions. So overtly Deistic Freemasons were blamed for their "pagan" rituals, while a "pure and refined" Deist, Joseph Priestley, was condemned for having gone too far in his flagrant anti-clericalism (to which Freemasonry was totally alien in Britain) and

scientific rationalism. For both John Adams and his son John Quincy Adams were *anti-philosophical* in the first place.

7 Lynn Dumeril, *Freemasonry and American Culture 1880–1930*, Princeton, New Jersey, 1984 (L. Dumeril, 1984), p. xi.

8 A. E. Roberts, 1964, p. 5. It is no secret that the "Tea Party" in Boston Harbour in 1773 which signalled the beginning of the American Revolution was planned and prepared in the St Andrew's Lodge, Boston. p. 6.

9 The Federalists were for stronger and more centralized federal government and business interests; the Republicans favoured decentralization and the landowning classes. Alexander Hamilton was the leading Federalist, and Thomas Jefferson the leading Republican.

10 L. Dumeril, 1984, p. xiii.

11 "Investigation proved the charge spurious, however, and this finding, along with increasing pressure from the Jeffersonian press, helped to stifle the conspiracy charge by the end of 1799 ..." W. P. Vaughn, 1983, p. 14.

12 "And that is why", as one American Mason, Dr W. Lewis, aptly remarked, "while to fight against Masonry in America is very difficult, to fight against it in England is almost impossible. In the latter case you may even be ridiculed for taking seriously that which is no more than a practical joke."

13 The perception of the difference in influence between British and American Masonries assumed a very naïve and curious character in J. Q. Adams (1847, p. xxvii) who insisted that, "... in Great Britain, the endeavour of government has been to *neutralize* Freemasonry's power to harm by entering into it and by placing trustworthy members of the Royal family at its head."

14 Sir Alfred Robbins, *English-Speaking Freemasonry*, London, 1930 (A. Robbins, 1930), p. 259. The same author makes a point of stressing the difference between an authority *directly* exercised by the Grand Lodge of England, and its formal supremacy over all other Lodges and Grand Lodges under its jurisdiction. In doing so he wants to show that American Masonry faithfully followed the British example. He writes: "Even as late as 1724, the Grand Lodge of England ... had explicitly limited its *disciplinary powers* to 'any place within ten miles of London'; and this remains, two hundred years after, precisely the area of the direct exercise of Grand Lodge discipline over ordinary Lodges" (p. 241).

15 *Idem*, p. 258. A second attempt of this kind was made in Washington, on 9 March 1822, when a convention was held to found a General Grand Lodge. The third, and last, attempt was ventured by R. Morris in 1860. See A. E. Roberts, 1964, pp. 129–33. Also, A. Robbins, 1930, p. 259.

16 F. L. Pick and G. Norman Knight, 1983 (1954), p. 270–1.

17 A. Robbins, 1930, pp. 241, 242, 245.

18 The idea of Englishness as the basis of Masonic cosmopolitanism seems to be historically valid. This is particularly so in the conditions of the eighteenth century, when Latin had already ceased to be the universal language of European culture, French became the idiom of Enlightenment and anti-clericalism, and German was yet to become the language of speculative philosophy. English was made neutral by the Masonic use of it long before the authors of the Unanimous Declaration wrote in 1776 (the first line of the original): "When in the course of human events it becomes necessary for one people to dissolve the political bonds which have connected them with another ..." "People", here, were not identified by

their language, but had come to mean a "political body" (or "organism") while language (like religion) was *natural.*

19 While Commissioner (Ambassador) in France, he was present at the initiation of Voltaire at the Lodge of Seven Sisters. F. L. Pick and G. Norman Knight, 1983 (1954), p. 272. Franklin said in 1756: "On the field of battle, in the solitude of the uncultivated forests, or in the busy haunts of the crowded city, they have made men of the most hostile feelings, and most distant religions, and the most diversified conditions, rush to the aid of each other . . ." This was the beginning of American Masonic rhetoric.

20 Of a total white male adult population of about one million. That is, less than 0.5 per cent. Compare with W. P. Vaughn, 1983, p. 11. This is a considerably smaller percentage than in England at that very time (around 56,000 members).

21 Morton Deutsch, *From Whence Came You?* London, Vision Press Ltd., 1950 (M. Deutsch, 1950), p. 17.

22 Some authors account for the isolation of American Masonry by the fact that British Masonry was, in itself, far more dynamic than its American derivation. The latter showed its dynamism only by adapting externally to changing social and political conditions, while internally remaining very conservative. A. Robbins writes (1930, p. 281): ". . . The revised and simplified ritual accepted by the United Grand Lodge of England, carrying further the English practice of *symbolizing rather than spectacularizing action,* was not of a kind to appeal to a people possessed of keen dramatic instinct and eagerness to display it, and least of all at a moment of restored national peace but remaining personal enmity. As a consequence, the American Masons clung . . . to customs England had . . . finally discarded and to teachers whom the parent country had long ceased to . . . respect." This clever passage calls for serious comment. That the historical cradle of an idea usually becomes the centre of changes in this idea, while the periphery of its spread tends to fix and preserve its pristine orthodoxy is an historical truism. What is far more important here is that the young American Masonry was keenly aware that it would have to pay for the liberty of the Craft's social involvement by being internally rigid and unchanging.

23 F. L. Pick and G. Norman Knight, 1983 (1954), pp. 217–18.

24 W. P. Vaughn, 1983, p. 20. Vaughn thinks that Bernard's "was probably the single most important anti-Masonic publication because of its detailed description of the *degrees.*" (*Ibid.*) It also contains a description of the Morgan Affair.

25 A. Robbins, 1930, pp. 287–8.

26 J. F. Newton, 1918 (1914), pp. 265, 266–71.

27 J. Q. Adams, 1847, p. viii. And further (p. xv): "Freemasonry establishes a standard of merit conflicting with that established by the Christian or the social system."

28 W. P. Vaughn (1983, p. 14) aptly remarks that, "As the historian examines the hundreds of anti-Masonic books, almanacs, pamphlets, newspapers, songs, poems, and acrostics [of that period] – the 'rhetorics of protest' – he cannot help but admit that in spite of all the anti-Masonic legitimate grievances arising from the Morgan Affair and from the Masonic domination of politics and law enforcement, in one sense the crusade attacked the right of one group of citizens to exercise the constitutionally guaranteed freedom of assembly as well as the rights of speech and press."

29 The recurrent accusation of "elitism" levelled against Masons in America in the 1830s and even 1840s had no cultural, educational or even economic motivation. It was purely political (as it was in France at that time), and was provoked by fears concerning Masonry as a potential power-base of the growing Republicanism.

30 This is echoing the attitudes and convictions of some of the British Freemasons at the end of the eighteenth century. So, John Browne writes in his famous *Browne's Masonic Master-Key* (London, 1802, p. iii): "...the Author will not be surprised to hear Cavillers condemn [this publication]; while others, when possessed of the key, will think it so obtuse and difficult to make out, that they will put it aside on the first attempt; but if they were only to study the Wards and Constructions of the Locks for twenty-four hours, at different periods, they would know more of this occult Science than if they had attended Lodges for Years."

31 L. B. Englesby, the Grand Master of Vermont, reacted angrily in 1863: "To no man's sleeve should Masonic or any other faith be pinned. Our traditions are verbal – non-written – transmitted from mouth to ear, and so handed down." In: A. E. Roberts, 1964, p. 130.

32 It is an obligation of a "full Conservator" to break down every Lodge that stands in the way of the system. *Idem*, p. 131. Also see R. V. Denslow, *The Masonic Conservators*, Missouri, 1931.

33 A. E. Roberts, 1964, p. 133.

34 J. F. Newton, 1918 (1914), p. 187.

35 A. E. Roberts, 1964, p. 9. L. Dumeril (1984, p. 255) gives the number of Masons as 221,000 for 1860.

36 A. E. Roberts, 1964, p. 8.

37 A. Robbins, 1930, p. 289–90.

38 It was Senator Henry Clay of Kentucky who said that to the Mason a compromise is an ethical, and not a political stand. Also see A. E. Roberts, 1961, pp. 7, 21.

39 The expression was, probably, used for the first time in the Russian press around 1910, when Masons were religiously and politically associated with Jews. The gutter press in Kiev spoke of "the third force of Judo-Masons" meaning "Jews and Masons together".

40 A. Roberts, 1961, pp. 137–9. He gives the number of those killed as between 74 and 1200. Other sources put it between 380 and 800.

41 In Russia, in Tsaritsyn, in 1916, the then populist leader, Monk Iliodor, appealed to the people to kill Masons, Jews, and the police, for they were "sabotaging the war efforts of Russian people".

42 This is one of them: "The Federal Army in the destruction of property at Hampton Court House (May, 1863) seized the property of the Lodge and returned it safely ... under a flag of truce." A. Roberts, 1961, p. 147.

43 "When Brother Captain Wainwright fell on the deck of the USS *Harriet Lane* and other officers (all Masons) were taken prisoner by the Southerners ... the Lodge No. 6 of Calverston was called to bury the dead enemy under command of Brother Col. H. B. Debray..." *Idem*, pp. 116–17.

44 *Idem*, p. 159.

45 The only known modern Russian poet-Mason, Maximilian Voloshin, (1877–1931) during the Civil War in Crimea, saved several people from both sides (non-Masons), out of "Masonic brotherly compassion to spiritually ignorant younger brothers".

46 "In the decade from 1861 to 1870 ... the Grand Lodge membership of New York nearly tripled in number, the total of 30,835." A. Robbins, 1930, p. 291. The number of Masons reached 446,000 in 1870, i.e., 7.3 per cent of the native male and white population of the USA. L. Dumeril, 1984, p. 225.

47 A. E. Roberts, 1901, pp. 163–4.

48 A. Robbins, 1930, p. 167.

49 A. Roberts (1961, pp. 84–5) writes gleefully that Wallace "could never have foreseen that ... his book was to become a film that was to receive (on 4 April 1960) an Oscar, and that its director, W. Wyler, would also be a Mason."

50 L. Dumeril, 1984, p. 91.

51 *Idem*, p. 75. "... eager to condemn saloon keepers, Grand Lodges were less willing to condemn drinking *per se*. By 1900 only 6 jurisdictions had passed laws to that effect..." *idem*, p. 79. But, returning to the Masonic attitude to Prohibition, L. Dumeril writes that, "they tended to support it on *legalistic*, not on moral, grounds..." *idem*, pp. 167–8.

52 *Idem*, pp. 99, 101.

53 *Proceedings of the 126th Grand Annual Communications of the Most Worshipful Grand Lodge of Virginia*, Richmond, 1904, Appendix, p. CIII.

54 L. Dumeril, 1984, pp. 146–7.

55 *Idem*, p. 179. This reflects the truism that any modernism, and not only Masonic, is a form of self-awareness that manifests itself only *after* the actual changes in life had already occurred.

56 *Idem*, p. xiv.

57 *Idem*, pp. xii, xiii. Dumeril goes on to say that, "One of the dominant themes of Masonic literature of the 1920s was that Masonry should be used to cultivate good citizenship ... and American traditionalism ..." *idem*, p. 130.

58 *Idem*, p. 123. The same author writes (*idem*, p. 121): "Masons' symbolic statements of loyalty to the government are analogous to saloonkeeper legislation." I think this is not quite true, for the latter expressed, formally at least, a moral stand, whereas the first *meant* to be political.

59 *Idem*, p. 127.

60 *Idem*, p. 129.

61 A. Robbins (1930, p. 292) speaks of "the openly displayed hostility (to Masonry) of the Roman Catholic Church and the occasional outrageous attacks of the Ku Klux Klan" (Klan Masons notwithstanding), putting them side by side as the two main forces of anti-Masonic opposition.

62 It would be useful to remind the reader that American Masonry could serve as an example of the role played by national differences in the destinies of the Craft. One might even assert that American Masonry is more different from all other Masonries than these are different from one another. At the same time that Henry Ford I, a Mason, one of the most militant anti-Semites in the world, had inspired (and probably supported financially) the publication of a virulently anti-Semitic tract, *The Protocols of the Elders of Zion*, in America, the Russian Masons were openly fighting against the upsurge of anti-Jewish feeling in Russia and the Ukraine, which *The Protocols* had provoked. And Russian Masonry was anti-Catholic mainly because of the vigorously anti-Semitic stance of the Catholic clergy in the western governorships of the Empire.

63 So, if in the first half of the nineteenth century the then still

"aristocratically"-orientated American Masonry was "a prime candidate" for suspicion "that it was against 'the common man', in the beginning of the twentieth century it *consciously* attempted to become the organization of the "common man". See L. Dumeril, 1984, p. 6. This, of course, was one more case of social flirtation which cost American Masonry a great deal, and in the long run contributed to its decline.

64 *Idem*, pp. 144–5.

65 A. Robbins, 1930, p. 285.

66 There are quite a few Freemasonries where neither black membership of white Lodges nor black Lodges has ever posed any problem. In Brazil, for example, there are at least 200,000 black and Mulatto Masons, many of whom were converts to Judaism! In France, the Black Consul of Haiti, Toussaint L'Ouverture, was made a Mason in the beginning of the nineteenth century, etc.

67 A. Robbins, 1930, pp. 283–4.

68 L. Dumeril, 1984, p. 10.

69 And he added scornfully that, "by espousing the cause of American nationalism they became a moral reformist sect", which, I think, is not the case.

70 "Masons who rejected the political role of Masonry," writes L. Dumeril (1984, p. 138), "nonetheless desired to have Masonry *mould* public opinion." The remark is quite pertinent, for it is, in fact, the epitome of Masonic rhetoric as regards politics. When Masons criticized public schools they had already relinquished the British Masonic principle of absolute individualism in favour of the rhetoric of participation. But by the mid-1930s it became evident that, as L. Dumeril put it (*idem*, p. 128), "More prevalent within Masonry . . . were men unwilling to establish Masonry as an effective political force." So, the "progressives" lost and the "conservatives" won, but Masons themselves could hardly have been aware of it at the time.

71 ". . . The predicted demise of religious faith and the churches was premature. A revival of the churches in the 1980s, as well as the continued success of evangelical religion and personal faith . . . proved it. But . . . in the 1920s . . . the fortunes of organized religion . . . were undergoing an unsettling transformation." *Idem*, p. 158.

72 *Idem*, pp. 150–61.

73 *Idem*, pp. 99, 101.

74 It took place in spring 1987.

75 When a close friend of mine, a Deaconess from Oxfordshire, read this piece, she reacted very fiercely. She said: "Your American Mason did not imbibe anything from Christianity. Namely, in your heart, you have to realize that those other people in Miami are sent to you by God so that you don't feel empty. And secondly, he does not understand that death is something to *work for*, not *struggle* against, for it is your reunion with God." This is an interesting Anglican critique of Masonic "existentialism".

76 I am quite certain that Islamic Fundamentalism is a direct consequence of and reaction to twenty years of flagrant secularization in Iran and, to a lesser extent, in Egypt. The spectrum of fundamentalism, in fact, is much broader. It can be observed now in all Christian religions, in Judaism, and even in Buddhism, particularly in Sri Lanka. In its very nature it is centrifugal, never confining itself to religion but tending, in its scope and application, to influence and rule the entire society.

77 L. Dumeril, 1984, pp. 25, 30.

78 "A Kansas Mason, also a Minister . . . said: 'Freemasonry is not only a brother-hood but a church'." *Idem*, p. 31.

79 *Idem*, p. 68.

80 *Idem*, p. 48.

81 "The attempt to modernize Masonry . . . was not prosecuted consistently enough to ensure the order's vitality . . . The inability to jettison its religious components left the order unacceptably out of step in an increasingly secular world and led to a decline [in the 1930s] in popularity and prestige from which it never completely recovered . . . the significance of the attempts to modify Masonry lies in the way in which they illuminate the transformations of middle-class values . . ." *Idem*, p. xiv.

82 M. Deutsch, 1959, pp. 5–6.

83 Matthew Garland, *Masonic Effusions*NM, London, 1819, p. 72.

84 *Idem*, p. 70.

85 In 1970, their number was 3,763,000. (7.6 per cent), and in 1995 about 4,600,000 (less than six per cent).

CHAPTER 9

Masonic History and Historicism: A Summing Up

> *What I invented ... was not a fantasy at all. I was not one of the characters it contained. I was its creation, not a candidate for admission."*
>
> C. S. Lewis, *Surprised by Joy*

To return to Masonic historicism as a phenomenon of historical self-awareness. When all is said and done, Freemasons had, broadly speaking, three main objectives: in the first place to have a history of their own, distinct as it were from the history of the rest of mankind; secondly, to present their history as the only model upon which a history of the whole of mankind could be patterned, identifying, thereby, the latter with the former; and, thirdly, to present their history together with history in general, as a symbolic manifestation of divine power which is, itself, trans-historical, and which forms history rather than is formed by it. If you take the third point alone as your stand on the problem of Masonic history, its factual side becomes irrelevant since it makes no difference then whether the Masonic Lodge on the site of Solomon's Temple was historically real or simply a creation of the fertile imagination of the Masonic authors – if in both cases it is a symbol of that which is above and beyond any historical reality. The continuing preoccupation of Freemasons with their own history and with history in general can be seen as a specific tendency of their mentality, and it is their own cultural background that generated and still generates this particular kind of historical intentionality – the direction of thought towards the *theme* of history.[1]

For Freemasons, from the time of their official historical foundation in 1717 onwards, the combination of historicism and theatricality has always had a special meaning and significance. Two main factors in particular have contributed to this, in addition to the general proclivity of the British to theatre and history.

The first is that the early post-revivalist Masons were playing as it were the part of their immediate historical predecessors – the working Masons. In doing so they were fixing their *belief* in their historical connection with the latter, for no more than two generations separated the operative Lodges from the speculative. They would also have been aware of the rather theatrical and artificial character of their Institution in general,[2] since it is Freemasons themselves who called Freemasonry "symbolic" or "emblematic" in the first place, meaning by these very terms that working Masonry, with its tools, implements, devices and rules, was so used by them that it should denote something very different from the way it had naturally existed before the middle of the seventeenth century.

During the first period of the existence of the Grand Lodge, Masons were intent on establishing a kind of tradition, more or less directly connecting them with their working predecessors. On revising and restating that tradition they very often behaved, spoke and wrote as if they were acting as those predecessors, no matter whether they were real or invented. No concrete Lodge (the Lodge of Antiquity included) could claim an antiquity going back further than the first years of the eighteenth century. However, not only did the second generation of the joyful revellers at the Lodge of Antiquity (in the 1740s and 1750s) call the whole Institution "ancient", but they identified themselves through the first attested and recorded generation of Freemasons (Anderson *et alia*) with those simply alleged to have been Masons before them, from the famous, such as Christopher Wren, to their own grandfathers or great-grandfathers whose Lodges belonged to the prehistory of the Craft. So all they could do was to ask their Masonic elders, who had invented most of this prehistory of the Craft, about the only thing they did not and could not have invented – their own immediate predecessors. Without any precise information, the second generation began to speculate about what might or might not have happened to these predecessors and their mostly unnamed Lodges. It is the generation of Heseltine and Dodd who would refer to someone living at the end of the seventeenth century as being "an old Mason whom my father used to know when he was young", and produce some unsubstantiated reminiscences concerning him. This produced a kind of historical equivocality which, from the middle of the eighteenth century, became part and parcel of the atmosphere of the learned discussions in the Lodges. The young Preston, "untramelled by the laws of evidence", wished to dispel this vagueness by transforming the invention into a sort of regular historiography, and Oliver, a century later, followed in his footsteps. But the uncertainty about the historical antecedents of Masonry persisted, and remains to this day, only marginally diminished by the total exclusion, in 1813, of Masonic history from the Constitutions, and hardly affected at all by the subsequent development of a more scientific and factual approach, the pioneers of which were Findel and Gould.

The second factor is that the Ritual of Master Mason is itself a theatrical performance which establishes the connection between the Freemason and his biblical past, and with the past of the whole of mankind.[3]

The earliest Masonic writers did not scruple to imply that in antiquity, indeed from the very beginning, a clear distinction existed between working Masons and "honorary" ones, such as Moses, Solomon and a succession of benevolent kings and patrons who, one may safely assume, were not working stonemasons. Anderson claims that at some time during the fourteenth century British Masonry borrowed from "the Societies and Orders of the Warlike Knights" (probably the Knights Templar) their sacred customs and usages, and that in the reign of Edward IV (1461–83), the Masonic Institution acquired both its complete form (Lodges, Congregations or Assemblies, etc.) determined by the Royal Charges and its inner structure and nomenclature. And at the end of the fifteenth century, significantly, Anderson states that Masons were made exempt from Henry VI's Statutes for Labourers on the grounds that *theirs* was not a "confederation" of working Masons. Again there is an anachronistic assertion of a division between "operative" and "speculative", so a separation of Science and Art from Institution had already begun in British Masonry. But whether he intended, as Preston seems to have done, that "operative" and "speculative" – terms that were only in use well after the 1717 founding of the Grand Lodge – represented at that time only two tendencies or aspects of Masonry rather than two distinct organizations is unclear.

With Anderson, the picture becomes rather more confused by the end of the seventeenth century, leaving a gap no more than partly filled with opaque references to several non-Masons who were made Masons in working Lodges, as well as to the Lodges in York and Scotland which seem to have been in a state of decline at the beginning of the eighteenth century.

Writing in 1804, William Preston asserts that "Masonry may be traced from the commencement of the world," and offers his own interpretation of "operative" versus "speculative": as operative Masonry "properly applies . . . the rules of architecture", so speculative Masonry teaches us how "to govern our passions, . . . maintain secrecy, and practise charity." From the very start the latter "is so far interwoven with religion, as to lay us under the strongest obligation to pay the rational homage to the Deity."

Arriving at the seventeenth century Preston, like Anderson, describes Inigo Jones as holding the office of Grand Master from about 1604 till 1646, except for the interval between 1618 and 1636. And like

Anderson, Preston describes an uninterrupted succession of Grand Masters, all celebrated professional Architect/Masons, during the period of the recreation of the "Augustan Stile" in England, the most prominent of whom was, of course, Sir Christopher Wren, who continued till 1702.

There follows the mysterious gap already noted, between 1702 and 1717, before the description of the official beginnings of Freemasonry as we know it. According to Preston, this was introduced by some Brethren (at St Paul's Lodge) somewhere around 1716 so that, "to increase their numbers . . . the privileges of Masonry should no longer be restricted to operative Masons, but extend to men of various professions . . ." This seems to support the contention that Preston, if not Anderson, did regard the two complementary aspects of Masonry as part of the privileges thus far enjoyed only by "working" Masons. The status of the "Lodges" whose Grand Masters were Inigo Jones, Wren, etc. is left extremely vague.

However, Preston's account of the spread of Freemasonry in the 1730s unambiguously claims that no Grand Lodge (including the Grand Lodge at York) in any European country described as existing before the foundation of the Grand Lodge of England in 1717 could be said to be properly constituted, and that all then existing European Grand Lodges were either "granted by deputation" by the Grand Lodge of England or derived from those primarily originated from the last.[4]

At the same time, while commenting on the secession of the Lodge of Antiquity from the Grand Lodge of England and its subsequent reunification with the latter in 1779, Preston states categorically that ". . . the resolution that *every* private Lodge derives its authority only from the Grand Lodge of England . . . could not apply to one which derived its authority from *another channel, long before the establishment of the Grand Lodge.* . . . [For] at the end of the seventeenth and beginning of the eighteenth centuries . . . the fraternity . . . had a *discretionary* power to meet *as Masons* in certain numbers, according to their degrees, with the approbation of the master of the work where any public building was carrying on . . . and when so met, to receive into the Order brothers and fellows . . . The fraternity were under no restrictions [imposed by the Grand Lodge]. . . . [Then] the *ancient charges* were the only standard of conduct . . ."[5]

From this it follows that, although each and every Grand Lodge in the world that was in existence at the end of the eighteenth century officially originated from the Grand Lodge of England, there might have been some British Lodges and Grand Lodges to which this historical principle cannot be applied. This is because not only might they have sprung directly from some working Lodges (whereas the Grand Lodge of England was non-working *par excellence*), they could have derived their authority from some other unknown or unrecorded Lodges or Orders which had been, if not wholly speculative, then more speculatively oriented.

This, of course, would seem to anybody with a minimum of historical judgement an attempt to have it both ways. Moreover, Preston himself, having declared the principle of the priority of the Grand Lodge of England at least as regards all continental Freemasonry, could not help taking advantage of the loophole which he had created not only on behalf of the Lodge of Antiquity, but when speaking of the Higher Degrees in England. So he comments on the opening in London (on 4 January 1787) of the Grand Chapter of Harodim thus: "Though this order is of ancient date, and had been patronized in different parts of Europe, there appears not on record previous to this period . . . such an association in England."[6] This is undoubtedly a classical figure of historical evasion often since adopted by many a Masonic writer, which is not to say that it should necessarily be historically false. Since a direct way back had been so solidly blocked by that fateful date – the foundation of the Grand Lodge in 1717 – Preston actually chose the oblique route of the Higher Orders or the Lodge of Antiquity to obtain some latitude.

J. G. Findel, however, writing in Germany in 1869, attempts a more scientific analysis. From the very start he separates the timeless conception of Freemasonry from Freemasonry as a historical institution:

The idea . . . is as old as human civilization, having its source in the human heart, as language has its in the spirit. Therefore we find this idea as already existing in the remotest ages as a shadowy presentiment. Embodied in life, it acquired forms like the modern, and so we can find its traces in the *mysteries of the ancients*, in the *Roman Building Corporations* and in the *medieval Fraternity of operative Masons.*[7]

Thus, the modern form of the idea of Freemasonry ascends to these three sources which, of course, does not mean that the Institution of Freemasonry can be directly historically connected with them:

Blinded by absurd self-conceit and an eccentric desire to prove the extreme antiquity of the Institution, many have strenuously combated the idea that the Fraternity originated in the Operative Masonry; or seeing that the ancient symbolical marks and ceremonies in the Lodges bear a very strong resemblance to those of the mysteries of the ancients, have allowed themselves to be deceived and led astray . . .[8]

Following his French predecessor in Masonic history, Abbé Grandidier, Findel regards the Lodges (*Hütten*) of German Cathedral builders in the thirteenth century as more or less the first Masonic lodges in Europe. In 1459, at Ratisbon, "some twenty years after the construction of the tower of Strasbourg . . . the Masters of the individual Lodges assembled . . . and drew up the *Act of Fraternity* which established the Grand Lodge (*Haupthütte*) and Grand Master of all Germany in Strasbourg. The Emperor Maximilian confirmed this in 1498 . . . and the statutes were renewed and printed in 1563."[9] Findel attributes to this Institution the Three Degrees (Apprentices, Companions and Masters), the complex of secret ceremonies, and a special Masonic Motto ("Liberty"). According to him, these German Masons are very probably connected with the mysteries of the ancients through the medium of the Roman Architectural Collegia of the late antiquity. This connection, however, is no more than formal, for "the German stone-masons (*Steinmetzen*) have so completely . . . metamorphosed the original signification of what they, by all possible chance, can have received from . . . the Romans, that we must regard their laws and customs as something essentially new."[10] Findel claims that some amateur members (Patrons) were admitted to the German lodges from the very beginning. The turning point in the whole Masonic history is when British and German Freemasonries converge, and this he describes somewhat obscurely: "It was only when the Fraternity of *Steinmetzen* had attained to perfection, or rather was on the decline, that the *real* history of Freemasonry *according to its existing signification* commences. In 1717 the Freemasons took the authentic laws, regulations and customs of the Steinmetzen as a Model",[11] for, as he explains, "the Roman Colleges in Britain perished during the devastating invasions of Scots and Saxons, whereas the Masonic tradition at York (together with Athelstan Constitution) is a mere fiction". And, speaking of the Masonic mysteries, he insists that the English Masons "acquired them from German *Steinmetzen* . . . who borrowed them from other German corporations . . . and partly . . . from ecclesiastic and monastic rules. . . ."[12]

So, "the modern Freemasonry is the direct descendant and successor, in an unbroken line of the Operative Fraternity of Masons of the Middle Ages".[13] Or, if we turn to British Freemasonry as described by Anderson with whom Findel agrees, the first four Lodges "were Lodges of Operative and Accepted Masons . . ." and to finish with it, the whole history of Freemasonry before 1717 is in Anderson's words, "nothing more than a history of architecture".

So Findel's account begins with the German Stone-Cutters patronized by the Abbot Wilhelm von Hirshau, Count Palatine of Shenren (1080–91) who played the same role in German Masonic prehistory as King Athelstan played in the English, only instead of York we have Magdeburg, and instead of the beginning of the ninth century, the end of the eleventh century. By the middle of the thirteenth century, and still long before the appearance of the first datable statutes, "many Lodges became independent from monasteries, and were closely bound together, forming one *General Association*. . . . They had special signs of recognition and secret ceremonies, and were . . . kept together by certain Guild-laws. They practised strict morality, were upright and honest, and were good Christians." Findel stresses that in Germany "the Fraternity of Masons was most undoubtedly . . . *a still earlier product of the spirit of association*", which, together with the spirit of Gothic architecture, flourished till the middle of the fifteenth century. This date can be regarded as the end of the golden era in the history of German Masonry and the beginning of the decline of the cathedral building. That is when the first statutes appeared in 1459 together with the first, though not yet fixed, Masonic nomenclature of the Three Degrees, and the Grand Lodge of, supposedly, all German Masons established in Strasbourg Minster.[14] The Reformation dealt a mortal blow to Gothic style and church architecture in general, but ". . . when the Fraternity was on the decline, the Assemblies meant less at improving and perfecting art, than at preserving the ceremonies, and accommodating disputes within their own jurisdiction".[15]

Then comes a historically very important remark: ". . . After [the] Reformation . . . when symbols were seldomer explained . . . and ceremonies were not clearly understood and gradually lost their meaning, in many places the stone-masons were incorporated with the Masonic Guilds.[16] . . . This was, however, not exactly the case in England . . . where they kept their ceremonies so that when the present Fraternity was established, these were still in use, and indeed needed only to have a different signification attached to them."[17] Or, to put it in other words, not only did the English Freemasons somehow preserve the system of meanings previously borrowed from the German *Steinmetzen*, but also managed to survive their own Reformation and post-Reformation periods without becoming *incorporated* into any professional organization, Guildean or otherwise. For, and this is obviously a very serious conviction of Findel's, the real Freemasons had never been a corporation in any legal sense because theirs was a Fraternity with its secrets, akin to the famous, and to some notorious, German *Vehme*.[18]

The religious views of the German Masons were "entirely opposed to the prevailing corruption of the clergy, as well as to the strict orthodoxy of the Church".[19] They found their expression in the many carvings made by stone-cutters, such as the stone-carving in Nuremberg which represents a nun in the lewd embrace of a monk, or that in Strasbourg where an ass is reading Mass at the altar, or another in the cathedral of Wurzburg, where "the columns of Jachin and Boaz" are found, suggesting that the German *Steinmetzen* embodied the spirit of Reformation before the Reformation. The last regular assembly of the German Masons was held in 1563. The Thirty Years War put an end to any building of new churches. In 1681 Strasbourg was occupied by the French, and in 1731, by order of an especial Imperial Diet, all Haupthütten (Grand Lodges) were abolished. By this time, however, the first German Lodges granted by the Grand Lodge of England may have already appeared.[20]

Passing to the English, Scottish and Irish Masons, Findel says that "they were treated like all other guilds' referring to the Statutes of Edward III (1359) and the ensuing prohibition of "all Congregations, Chapters, Regulations, and Oaths". All references in the Old Charges to Masonry prior to the fourteenth century he regards as possessing no historical value whatsoever. Their value is merely instructional ("to be read aloud in the Lodge") and their meaning merely symbolical. So, when we read about the York Charter, we should place it not in AD 926 (as it places itself), but in much more recent times when the references to "Antient Masonry at York" (with King Athelstan, Edwin, etc.) served as emblems of Masonic antiquity in general. According to Findel, the reign of Edward III (1327–76) marks the beginning of the real, as opposed to instructional, history of Freemasonry in England, which, in spite of the author's often repeated conviction that "the English Freemasons and German Stone-masons were actually branches of the same Fraternity"[21] remains, in his description, isolated, left to its own prehistorical roots and legendary antecedents. The picture becomes even more obscure when Findel, repeating the English Masonic legends from Anderson and Preston, mentions the Gallic Masons coming to England under Charlemagne, without even trying to produce at least a "generalized legendary version" which could have united Germanic, French, and English Masons in a kind of "common prehistory".[22]

This, however, seems to be a very difficult task, because, while the

English so-called Gothic Charges (of whatever origin and date) contain rich legendary material, in French and German Masonic traditions legends are scarce and often preserved in oral or non-codified form. So not only did the English Masonic Legend remain divorced from the actual English Masonic history, but, *pace* Findel, it does not find any significant Continental parallels.

Findel, however, could not help feeling that the solution to the chief riddle of Masonic history, the riddle of when, where and how a medieval professional association happened to become something much more extraordinary – not altogether professional, and not exactly an organiz-ation – should be sought for in the very character of the church builders' occupation. For it apparently started, like any other trade or profession, with having its own emblems and symbols, but unlike any other trade or profession it eventually became symbolic itself. Commenting on Preston's description of the decree, under Edward III, compelling "every artist and handicraft to keep to some one profession (called 'mystery')", Findel fails to notice the fact that mystery here is the sym-bolic form that each listed profession assumed in the medieval corporative structure. It is by virtue of its own "mystery" that Free-masonry became a curious preoccupation and a strange institution, not the other way around.[23] And that is why an unprejudiced observer, when coming across such passages in Preston (amply quoted by Findel) as, "In the third year of the reign of Henry IV [1425] the Freemasons were forbidden to assemble by an Act of Parliament", should immediately ask himself: "Who on earth *were* those Freemasons against whom the said Act was directed? Were they those artisans who indeed were subject, without exemption, to the notorious Statutes of Labourers?" Findel, however, does not ask these questions, for his was an historical approach still too close to its subject to permit that necessary distancing by which the attempts of his immediate successor, Gould, were distinguished. The English Lodges of the fifteenth and sixteenth centuries possessed a certain ambiguity that even Anderson could not have disguised. For example, Findel quotes from Wyat Papworth: "We are inclined to think, that the Lodge, or whatever it may be called, were simply the staff formed to carry on the work at those Cathedrals . . . and were quite distinct from the *trade, guild,* or *company* which might have been in existence in the same towns and at the same periods."[24]

However, the end of the Gothic period and the beginning of the Reformation would have affected British Freemasonry (of whatever kind!) in a way not unlike that in Germany had it not been fortunately, if not fortuitously, superseded by the coming of the "Augustan Stile" so praised by Anderson and his successors. This can be seen, partly at least, as a reason for either the survival of the Lodges of the working Masons in England, or their transformation into, partly again, non-working ones, or both. For what can undoubtedly be observed at the beginning of the seventeenth century in England and what, quite definitely, did not exist at that time in a Germany ruined by the Thirty Years War, is that surplus of intellectual energy which, in seeking for its form, must have found it in a wide range of associations from the Royal Society to Freemasonry. Therefore, that central controversy – whether Freemasonry originated directly from the real working fraternities of stonemasons (Findel), or was connected with the latter in a merely symbolic and imitative way (Gould), as well as whether it first appeared as such in Germany or in England – seems to be quite unimportant. For some additional (and not yet historically accounted for) factor must have appeared in England in the beginning of the seventeenth century, a kind of mighty impulse which forced some people into shaping their religious, moral, and intellectual aspirations according to the "old" moulds of a fraternity of Masons.

For Findel the one thing that remains certain is that the whole profession gradually split into those with knowledge and intellectual aspirations and those with no more than elementary skill. It is no wonder that the former found themselves consequently far closer to enlightened people of the period, while the latter were ousted into the ranks of hard physical labour whence they would eventually emerge about one century later to rejoin the institution as fully-fledged members of the Lodges of Free and Accepted Masons. In a new development, the gap between more skilled and less skilled builders gradually began to close again and ". . . persons who were not operative began to be admitted as members of the Lodges, thereby infusing into them intelligence, fresh life, and vigour. This it was alone which saved the Institution from sinking into oblivion".[25] One may, of course, ask why the institution should have sunk into oblivion in the first place, and, if it had, whether this was because it had, by the end of the seventeenth century, forgotten its own meaning. If, having originated in the old German Lodges of the cathedral builders, it came into decline together with cathedral-building both in Germany and England, why then was that decline not simply halted by the revival of architecture with the "Augustan Stile" in England instead of needing a whole "revolution" with the infusion of a new, non-professional intelligence? Findel continues: ". . . Thomas Boswell Esq. of Auchinleck was chosen as Warden of St Mary's Lodge at Edinburgh in 1600 and Robert Moray, Quartermaster General of the

Scottish Army, was made a Master Mason in 1641 and Elias Ashmole was made a Mason in a Lodge at Warrington (Lancashire) on the 16th October 1646 . . . and the Earls of Cassilis and Eglington were . . . about the year 1670 received as Apprentices by the Lodge of Kilwinning and . . . were distinguished from the working Masons by the *appellation of Accepted* Masons."[26] All these facts, for which the evidence is merely circumstantial and uncorroborated by official Lodge documentation, were related by Masonic historiographers of the eighteenth century and became a commonplace in the writings of their successors in the nineteenth century, Findel included. Where he seems to be far more original than his predecessors is in his attempts to account for the fact of the Masonic revival of the eighteenth century by the change in the intellectual and spiritual atmosphere of the time. But in doing this he stresses the distinction between the ideas themselves and their practical, and especially political, application. So insisting that "there is not the slightest foundation for an assertion that the Masons in the time of Cromwell took an active part in the political events . . ."[27] at the same time he asserts that "the resolution to throw off every burdensome yoke, introduced by Bacon in philosophy and by Cromwell in politics, soon pervaded the entire generation . . . and was one of the agencies . . . which especially effected the transformation wrought in the Fraternity".[28]

Three events, though they took place outside or on the remote periphery of Freemasonry, appear to have played a very significant part in creating the atmosphere of its crystallization: Rosicrucianism, Dupuy's *History of the Condemnation of the Templars* (published in 1650 and 1685), and the spread of English and Continental *Deist* literature. As for Rosicrucianism, it will be enough to note that Findel was, probably, the first Masonic historian who tried to present Rosicrucianism as it existed before the 1760s, as a tributary of the broad European esoterist movement of which Freemasonry constituted the main current.

Findel sees the historical importance of Dupuy's work in the striking parallels between the rules of the Templars, as described by Dupuy, and those of the Freemasons. These are also to be found in the customs of the inhabitants of the New Atlantis, described by Francis Bacon at the beginning of the seventeenth century. Even more astonishing are some passages in Joh. Amos Comenius' *Opera Didactica*, which "are word for word like those in Anderson's *Constitutions*".[29] Findel accounts for these similarities by pointing out that they were the symptoms of a general change in the spiritual atmosphere which, in turn, determined the ensuing transformation of Operative Freemasonry into speculative. This

The following plates show some of the earliest visual examples of symbolism from a number of Masonic sources, dated after 1717 and the formation of the Premier Grand Lodge of England.

Frontispiece from *The Constitutions of the Freemasons*, 1723

The *Constitutions* were written by James Anderson and became the first printed constitutions of the Premier Grand Lodge of England, founded in 1717. They comprised Charges and General Regulations of the Masons and a detailed history of the art of masonry. This frontispiece is one of the earliest visual representations of symbolism used in modern Freemasonry (i.e. post 1717). Important features to note are the classical pillars, the compass and Euclid's forty-seventh proposition, placed between the two Grand Masters. Anderson believed this to be the "Foundation of all Masonry".

Frontispiece from *The Builder's Jewel*, 1746, by Batty Langley

Langley (1696-1751) published several architectural books, a number of which were manuals for the use of country builders and artisans. The frontispiece for this particular work is another early example of the visualisation of Masonic symbolism and shows several "speculative" features. For example, three classical pillars symbolising the sun, moon and Master Mason, and the qualities "W", "S", "B" – Wisdom, Strength and Beauty. The middle pillar shows a tracing-board with a chequered floor, the letter G in a star and the pillars Jachin and Boaz. The pillar on the left shows a grouping of a square, compass and bible. The pillar on the right displays the square, level and plumb-rule. These are all important tools of a Mason and are present in the Lodge.

A silver plate jewel engraved with the date "Oct. 21, 1759"

One of the main uses of jewels is to demarcate the rank and office of various members of a Lodge. They are traditionally hung from collars or chains and worn around the neck. This type of jewel usually takes the form of a working tool. For example, the Master's jewel is in the form of a square; the Senior Warden's, a level; the Junior Warden's , a plumb-rule. Regulations regarding the official wearing of such jewels is noted in the Grand Lodge minutes of 21 June, 1727. The jewels shown here and overleaf are of plate and pierced metal and depict detailed designs of Masonic symbols and emblems. They have a more decorative than functional use.

(a) *Obverse* – the jewel is engraved with the name of the owner, William Booth, and a Latin inscription "*sit lux et lux fuit*". Interesting symbols to note are the All-Seeing-Eye, the compass, the sun and moon, two pillars at the entrance to the "*sanctum sanctorum*" of Solomon's Temple, a ladder, a level and a plumb-rule.

(b) *Reverse* – this side is engraved with the Latin inscription "*amor honor et justitia*" The square, the letter G in a triangle within a star, and the square and compasses placed on the Bible are featured on this side.

A silver pierced jewel engraved with the date 1760

(a) *Obverse* – two crossed quills are shown, representing the emblem for the secretary of a lodge, possibly the position of the owner of the jewel. Euclid's forty-seventh proposition is engraved on a scroll under the moon.

(b) *Reverse* – J. White, the owner's name is engraved along the square with his Lodge number, 71.

Silver pierced jewel, *circa* 1770

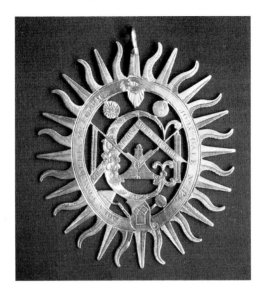

(a) *Reverse* – the name of John Gale and his Lodge number, 184, are engraved around the edge. A Latin inscription is added, "*sola concordia fratrum*". The position of the square and compass represent the Fellow Craft of the Second Degree.

(b) *Obverse* – an interesting feature of this jewel is the rays of the sun that surround the symbols. It can be noted that the position of the square and compass, with the points of the compass lying under the square, represents an Entered Apprentice of the First Degree. Working tools such as the ruler, maul and trowel are included.

English Craft Certificates

The primary use of Masonic certificates is to give proof of a Mason's membership of Freemasonry and his particular Lodge. There are two types: private Lodge certificates, which were in use at the beginning of the eighteenth century and which continued to be used to *circa* 1810; and Grand Lodge certificates, evidence of which can be seen from *circa* 1755.

(a) An example of a private Lodge certificate, dated 1808 and incorporating the name, address and age of the Freemason, the date and place of his acceptance and the date of his being made a Master Mason. It also includes the signatures of four of the officers in the Lodge. The certificate depicts an allegorical design, featuring the theological virtues, Faith, Hope and Charity. It also shows the three orders of architecture, the level, plumb-rule, square and compass.

(b) One of the oldest engraved private Lodge certificates in England. It gives the details of the Freemason and is dated 1766. It depicts the cardinal virtues, Fortitude, Prudence, Justice and Temperance, standing behind the chariot. The design also features the five orders of architecture and various tools. The sun, moon and stars, important speculative symbols, appear in the upper part.

(c) This certificate is dated 1785 and features an interesting architectural design known as "The Five Noble Orders of Architecture". It shows a classical landscape, various symbols such as the pentalpha (five-pointed star), a three-runged ladder, the square and compass, and the allegorical figures, Faith, Hope and Charity.

(d) An example of a Grand Lodge design known as the "second pillars", dated 1837. It shows three pillars in the style of the three orders of architecture, Doric, Ionic and Corinthian, two globes, common tools, the chequered floor and the rough and smooth stones. This certificate is simpler in design than the private Lodge certificates and is issued by the United Grand Lodge, which was formed in 1813.

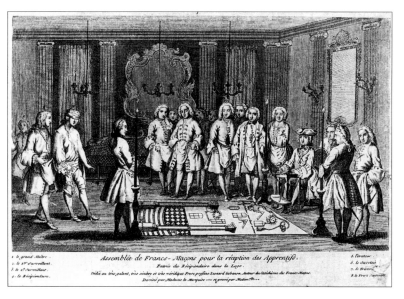

French engraving by Bernigeroth, Plate 1, 1745. "Assembly of Freemasons for the Reception of Apprentices"

The importance of this engraving is that it shows how the lessons of each degree were communicated by the Master, and how the symbols and emblems were displayed. Originally, these were drawn on the floor of the Lodge using chalk or charcoal and removed after each meeting. The use of floor-cloths, seen here, replaced this method and these were in turn developed into tracing-boards, or lodge-boards. In this engraving the candidate is blindfolded and the Master is seated wearing a hat. The members of the Lodge are shown wearing aprons. The officers are distinguishable by their jewels; for example, the Master wears a square, the Junior Warden, who is introducing the candidate, a plumb-rule, and the secretary, crossed quills. The floor-cloth displays two pillars – Jachin and Boaz, which symbolise "Forte" and "Sagresse" – Strength and Wisdom. The blazing star is featured along with the sun and moon, the chequered floor and the indented tuft.

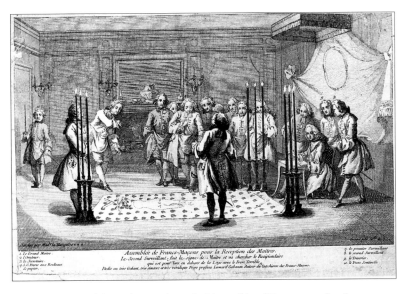

Plate 3 of the set by Bernigeroth. "Assembly of Freemasons for the Reception of the Masters"

This demonstrates the reception of Master-Masons. The Master is seated on the right and the candles, or "lights", have been tripled, two sets are in the East and one in the South-West. The design of the floor-cloth is appropriate for the Third Degree and depicts the outline of a coffin, a sprig of acacia, a skull and crossbones, and the square and compass surrounded by tears.

Lodge-Plan of the "Apprentice Fellows Lodge" from a French Exposition of the ritual entitled *Le Maçon Démasqué*, 1751

LE MAÇON DÉMASQUÉ, PLATE I

Drawing for the Apprentice-Fellow's Lodge

[*Slightly reduced: size of outer frame in the original is 14·7 × 10·6 cm.*]

(a) This has a similar function to the floor-cloths shown previously and the tracing-boards on the next page, but in this case the lodge-plans were used to accompany an "exposure" of the ritual, popular in the eighteenth century. An explanation of the drawing is provided in the Exposition.

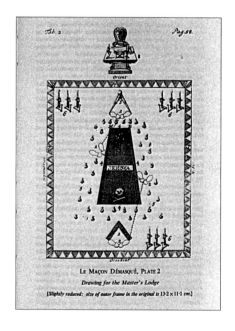

LE MAÇON DÉMASQUÉ, PLATE 2

Drawing for the Master's Lodge

[*Slightly reduced: size of outer frame in the original is 13·2 × 11·1 cm.*]

(b) This lodge-plan is for a Master's Lodge from the same Exposition, again an explanation is provided. The design is similar to the lodge-cloth shown on the previous page.

Frontispiece from two English Expositions of Masonic ritual

(a) An engraving from an Exposition entitled *Mahhabone* or *The Grand Lodge Door Open'd*, published in Liverpool in 1766. It shows a lodge-plan of a similar format to the French one shown previously. This English example, however, is more detailed, depicting symbols and emblems from the Three Degrees. At the top is the Master's chair set in the East and a Bible, square and compass laid in front on the altar. The pillars Jachin and Boaz are positioned in the West on the chequered floor at the entrance to the temple (Solomon's Temple). Other features include various tools, the sun, moon, and the square and compass set in the position indicating a Fellow Craft of the second degree.

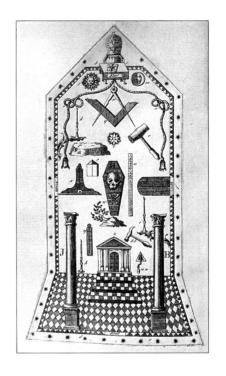

(b) This frontispiece is dated 1776 and comes from the English Exposition entitled *The Three Distinct Knocks* and is similar in style to the silver jewels shown earlier. In contrast to previous designs shown, this depicts two pillars with the celestial and terrestrial globes on top. The All-Seeing-Eye is featured and the position of the square and compass represents a Master Mason.

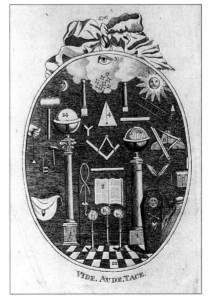

Set of Three Tracing-Boards painted by
Arthur L. Thistleton in 1836 to be used in Ivanhoe Lodge, No. 631

The use of tracing-boards or lodge-boards developed from floor-drawings and lodge-cloths and are the format the Freemasons use today. The boards are an important feature of every Masonic Lodge; each board depicts the lessons and symbols that correspond to one of the Three Degrees of English Craft Masonry. In a sense, each degree represents a stage or a step in the journey from ignorance and "darkness" to truth, knowledge and "light". The first board (a) shows various symbols and emblems relevant to the First Degree, or first stage of the Ritual. The morals and lessons that these symbolize are conveyed to the candidate by the Master of the Lodge. The second board (b) represents the Second Degree and shows the winding staircase leading up to the middle chamber of Solomon's Temple. The third board (c) bears the features relevant to the Third Degree of Master Mason and shows an outline of a coffin, skull and crossbones, symbolising death and rebirth. In the centre of the coffin is the "holy of holies", or the *sanctum sanctorum*, of the temple.

(a)

(b)

(c)

Two tracing boards from the Royal Naval Lodge, No. 59, by J. E. Godwin

The two examples shown here are Third Degree tracing-boards and are interesting for their inclusion of a body in the coffin, rather than the more common outline. It can be surmised that the body is that of the dead Hiram of the Hiramic Legend, which is central to the ritual of the Third Degree.

(a)

(b)

The following six plates are not Masonic in origin, but are examples of what may be described as Masonic symbolism. Five of the prints are dated before 1717.

(a) **The Great Hall at Syon House designed by Robert Adam in 1762**
The Great Hall shown in this photograph displays three features that can be described as Masonic. First, the chequered floor, second, the blazing star in the middle of the floor and third, the two classical pillars at the far end.

(b) **Plate V of Wenzel Jamitzer's** *Perspectiva Corporum Regularium,* **Nuremberg, 1568, by Albrecht Dürer**
This drawing includes a number of features which have already been noted on Masonic examples. For instance, the sun at the top of the picture under the star, and the crescent moon at the bottom. At each side of the moon is a collection of emblems that have been seen on the Masonic jewels and certificates, notably, the square, compass, level, ruler and plumb-line. Two cherubs are depicted holding a pair of compasses pointed at the celestial and terrestrial globes.

This emblematic brass shows a prominent sun and moon and two pillars supporting an arch. Holtgen (1986), *Aspects of the Emblem*, Reichenberger, suggests that the Corinthian column on the right represents the world and its arts, which is contrasted with the biblical pillar on the left, modelled on one of the brass pillars Jachin and Boaz that stood in front of Solomon's Temple. This and the other pictures shown here indicate that particular themes and images that the early Freemasons chose to use in their ritual were evident long before the first organised institution of Free-masonry was founded in 1717. It also demonstrates that much of the symbolism used in Freemasonry is not particularly unique, but it is the context in which the symbols are placed that imbues them with a specific significance.

(b) **An emblem from George Wither's** *A Collection of Emblemes,* 1635

The obvious Masonic feature of this engraving is the compass and also the grouping of stars in the sky.

(c) **Title-page to Sir Walter Ralegh's** *The History of the World*, **1614**
The engraving shows the All-Seeing-Eye, a globe and four pillars. The All-Seeing-Eye as a common Masonic symbol appears in England from *circa* 1730.

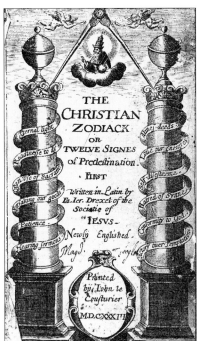

(d) **Title-page for** *The Christian Zodiack* **by Jeremias Drexel, 1633, engraved by Wenceslaus Hollar**
This depicts two classical pillars supporting a pair of globes and a compass. The importance of the pillars and compass in masonic imagery has already been noted. They are two of the most common symbols used in Craft Freemasonry.

transformation could never have been achieved without a latent period of gestation of ideas which were evidently absent in the "Old Constitutions" of the Operatives, and among which the most prominent were the concepts of English Deism. This, according to Findel, amounted to a kind of "intellectual revolution", one of the consequences of which was that Freemasonry ceased to be narrowly professional and became universal.[30]

Findel fully accepts the version of the General Assembly held on 27 December 1663, "at which Henry Germin, Earl of St Albans, was elected Grand Master . . . who appointed Chr. Wren and John Webb his Wardens" and ascribes *The Regulations* (the Harleyan MS) to its aftermath.[31] He, as do some other authors, accounts for the decline of the Lodge in York by the rebuilding of the City of London by Wren, when Masons from all over the country were engaged in the capital. This, however, did not make the situation in the Lodges of London any better. The decline seemed to have been nationwide and Freemasonry was saved from extinction only by the resolution ". . . that the priviledges of Masonry should no longer be restricted to operative Masons", which marked "the end of *ancient* Masonry" as a homogeneous institution. To this end ". . . the long contemplated separation of the Freemasons from the *Operative Guilds* was now [i.e. *circa* 1716] speedily carried into effect".[32]

In the following description of the German situation, Findel makes an important point not only as a partisan view, but also as a generalized historical observation concerning Freemasonry as a whole at that time:

The small remnants of the ancient "Bauhütten" formed partly of *Operative Masons* and partly of the *friends of Architecture* or of *Accepted Masons*, dragged on a miserable existence at the beginning of the 18th c. The Stonemasons, having completed the buildings they had to erect, were dispersed, while . . . many of the "accepted" . . . it is said, busied themselves with *Rosicrucian* philosophy, that is, with Alchemy and Theosophy, which, however, by no means prompted social intercourse.[33]

He emphasizes here the spiritual character of the Institution, leaving aside its institutional antecedents, and implies that, immediately preceding the formation of the Grand Lodge of England – with German Masonry already extinct, though her mystical ideas were very much in vogue throughout – it is English Masonry that was first to recover from the period coinciding with the end of the construction of the great cathedrals, with a renewed institutional rather than ideational impulse.[34]

With reference to the Ancient Masons, Findel raises the question of the historicity of Freemasonry in general: "... the new sect, which ... caused so much trouble, did not arise till a later period, and has been *erroneously* associated with events of an earlier date [1739]". He then sums up his critical conception: "... The *ancient* constitutions of the Masons, which had been drawn up many centuries previously, had been a binding law to all the Lodges until they were superseded ... by Anderson's Book of Constitutions.... It is impossible to ascertain whether the 'Old Lodges' had continued to meet uninterruptedly from the 13th c. up to 1712, or what had been their fate all that time."[35] So, in discussing events in the "previous" Masonic history, he refers to laws, regulations and meetings of the Lodges, and not to rituals, for these only started being introduced between 1721 and 1731. Finally, with reference to the Higher Degrees and the Royal Arch in particular, he insists that all that was "decidedly French" and utterly eclectic. He writes:

Ramsay calls the French Royal Arch the *ne plus ultra* of Masonry ... but ... in truth this degree ... having but little genius in it, and still less good taste, was fabricated from a confused medley of passages from ... the Old Testament, from history and fable, from religious dogmas and Masonic tradition.[36]

In trying to establish a direct connection between Freemasonry and English Deism, he goes much further than all the other authors before him and very many after, and not only asserts that the Deistic "... intellectual revolution ... contributed essentially to the final transformation of Freemasonry from an operative to a *universal, speculative* society ...", but quite seriously thinks that it is J. Tolland's *Pantheisticon* that might have provided the Society with the *liturgical form* for its ritual of initiation.[37] He accounts for the variations and changes in the Masonic Ritual by offering a hypothesis that, side by side with the tradition of Constitutions written in manuscript, there were "... the Catechisms [rituals] in use, which have been transmitted orally ... and had given rise to several variant readings".[38]

Before parting with Findel it is worth observing that he was the first Masonic historian to make his object of study entirely *exoteric* and – due, probably, to his very Protestant background – to present the Three Degrees Craft as the only authentic form of Freemasonry. His insistence on the historical priority of German Masonry seems to be all the more strange given that he himself was not able to provide a sufficient evidence of any strong connection existing between German and English Masonries before the beginning of the eighteenth century.

R. F. Gould begins his famous book, first published in 1903, by making a firm distinction between two aspects of Masonic history – specific and general. Under the first, Freemasonry, as it arose in the beginning of the eighteenth century, is presented to the eyes of a historian as no more than one of the very many secret societies whose shape, character and ideals were moulded after a fashion prevalent in the seventeenth century. He writes:

> . . . If, therefore, we can trace the customs of any other oath-bound societies as they existed, let us say before 1725, there is a strong probability, amounting almost to certainty, that such were in no way influenced by Freemasonry. As we pass moreover from the eighteenth to the nineteenth century, what was previously suspicion will merge into a strong probability or more. Evidence of customs now existing by no means proves that they are of very long standing. If the ceremonial of the Druses in Lebanon – that is to say, if the writers by whom we are informed, have not been misled by resemblances more or less imaginary – then I believe that these sectaries . . . adopted some practices of the Freemasons.[39]

This remarkably modernistic trend should not surprise us in Gould. He was the first Masonic historian who quite consciously saw in the Fraternity a concrete historical phenomenon, and not simply a manifestation of a universal tendency or eternal trans-historical reality. The absurdity of his diffusionist speculation about the Druzes only shows the degree of his tendency to super-modernize the history of Freemasonry.

To Gould, the general aspect of Masonic history – or, rather, prehistory – exists as no more than a conjecture and any similarity with other ancient spiritual movements is most probably a coincidence when he writes that ". . . Examples of older types of such associations may be found in the suffis of Persia", or "None of the Ancient mysteries afford a more interesting subject than those of Mithraism".[40] It is extremely unlikely that the Mithraists of old or the Sufis were of common origin with the Freemasons. At the same time he concedes that the general aspect of Masonic prehistory before 1717 may mean that Freemasonry was one of the very many secret or partly secret societies whose character was determined by factors and tendencies much older and far more general than their concrete historical manifestations. One of these tendencies was to regard architecture as symbolic of the universe and to incorporate some secret rituals of initiation into a given cosmic model.

At any rate, Gould, referring to the beginning of Masonry in Europe – in a way more or less similar to that of Findel – tries to maintain that its original character is derived from the peculiarities of the division of labour in the fourteenth to sixteenth centuries. The Guilds of the Burghers were opposed to the Guilds of the craftsmen, the masters to the workmen, the settled workforce to the journeymen, the Masons of the monasteries to the cathedral builders in towns, and so on. A certain similarity could be seen between the German *Steinmetzen* with their *Bauhütten* and Ordinances (as in Torgau, in 1462), and the English and Scottish Freemasons with their Lodges and Constitutions. The German Masonic invocation of the names of the "Father, Son, and Holy Ghost; of our Gracious Mother Mary; and of . . . the Holy Four Crowned Martyrs (*Quatuor Coronati*) . . ."[41] may be seen, particularly in its last part, as a result of some possible contacts between two Masonries, but no more than that.

Returning to Gould's treatment of facts which, even for that time – the fifteenth and sixteenth centuries – can be regarded as more or less specifically Masonic, three points ought to be mentioned. The first is the existence of individual marks and standard signs by means of which a Mason could be identified as a person belonging to the body of the *Steinmetzen* and as a member of this body in communication with its other members. So far, we know of no special ritual (akin, say, to "Hiramic") connected with those signs, although it is highly likely that their acquisition was marked by certain ceremonies. The second is about the secrets of "Mysteries" which, according to Gould, "were, without doubt, *the elaborate carving of stone, and the preparation of work and design*, in neither of which class of work was the craftsman allowed to instruct anyone".[42] The third is that "the German stone-masons received from the monastic builders a secret architectural doctrine, mystical science of numbers . . . and peculiar symbols, such as compasses, square, gavel . . . and foot-rule, which had a *moral* significance in their lodges".[43] This last assertion is meant to support Gould's conviction that the social basis of German Masonry at its inception comprised two groups of workers – monastic builders and cathedral builders; both appeared to have been either outside the Guild system or on its periphery which, itself, together with its autonomy and comparative independence from the growing power of the municipalities, predetermined the peculiar character of Masonry as an institution.

Masons, as seen through the *Three Codes* (1459, 1462, and 1563) which regulated their functions and confirmed their rights and privileges, seem to have occupied an intermediary position; they were neither

itinerant nor settled, neither townsmen nor countrymen, neither clerical nor completely secular. On the one hand this intermediateness made
German Masonry overlap but not coincide with the division of labour
in the late Middle Ages; on the other, it made German Masonry more
dependent on the socio-economic conditions and political changes
taking place on a larger scale. Together with Findel, Gould attributes
the ensuing decline of the *Steinmetzen* to the completion of the main
cathedrals, the Reformation and the Thirty Years War. The final blow
was dealt by the Imperial Decree of 1707, abolishing the supremacy of
the Head Lodge, and by the Edict of 1731 that "made illegal all Masonic
ceremonies".[44]

Gould refutes point blank the delusion "that speculative Masonry in
England and Scotland was derived from the *Steinmetzen* (as asserted by
Findel and particularly Abbé Grandidier), and leaves the subject of
German Masonry with the assertion that ". . . though there was a great
outward similarity between the usages of *Steinmetzen* and Freemasons,
no sort of connection between them was ever set up as an article of
belief until 1779".[45] The German Masons could not grow out of their
medieval type of professional mentality, and, in spite of some degree
of monastic learning ". . . the conclusion is irresistible that they . . .
never attained (unlike the English Freemasons) the level of speculative
science".[46]

The history of the French "pre-Freemasonic" Masonry, as retold by
Gould, can be summed up as follows.[47] There existed in sixteenth-
century France a strange association of journeymen, known as the *Com-*
pagnonnage, that comprised three Fellowships, namely: the Fellowship
of Solomon, which consisted of stonemasons of all religious creeds and
beliefs; the Fellowship of Maître Jacques, whose members were Catholic
stonemasons only; and the Fellowship of Maître (or Père) Soubise,
which consisted of Catholic carpenters. All of them periodically made
the Tour de France, travelling within a certain extensive area, mainly
in the south of the country, including a number of towns where they
obtained food, lodging, work, and, if the last was not available, credit.
Those towns assumed the name of *les villes du devoir*, and the journeymen
were called *les Compagnons du Devoir*. Among their original customs
mentioned by Gould the following three are particularly interesting:

1. *The funeral.* The companions stand in a circle around the grave,
the mourner kneels on one knee, a prayer is read, and, when the
coffin is lowered, "two companions step on to the four quarters
of a pair of crossed staves, each clasps the other by the right hand,

they whisper in one another's ear, remain folded for a moment in each other's arms, and retire. This is done by all present companions in turn".

2. ". . . It was customary, except among the Sons of Solomon, for Companions, on attaining the status of Master, to retire from the Companionship . . ." Gould, surprisingly, does not comment upon this custom, though he notes that it might be accounted for by the fact that in 1651 the Archbishop of Toulouse strictly forbade the practices of the companions under threat of excommunication and it still remains possible that before that date the Masters were members of all the three Fellowships. At the same time it might well be supposed that in its origin the *Compagnonnage* actually was an organization of young craftsmen by definition, and that the acception of Masters into it took place at a much later time, when the Guilds had already lost their supremacy in the towns.

3. The historical legend of the Companionship is, on the whole, very different from that of English Freemasonry.[48] According to one of their traditions, the Fellowship of Solomon was originated at Chartres, and two others at Orléans. According to the Orléans legend, the Companions of Solomon dissented from the rest of the *Compagnonnage* at the beginning of the fourteenth century, and "were taken under protection of Jacques de Molay, Grand Master of the Templars . . . who introduced mystic forms into France, Solomon and his Temple figuring in their ceremonies".

It may also be conjectured that the Solomonian Fellowship might have had some links with English Freemasonry before the formation of the Grand Lodge of England. However the historiography of the Compagnonnage is based on the materials which are of a considerably later origin than those in England, and itself "sprung into existence" only in 1839, that is at least a century after the beginning of Freemasonic historiography in England. And, what is far more important, by the time the French enterprise began, French Freemasonry had already undergone such a strong English Masonic influence that the French Masonic historiography could scarcely have remained unaffected.[49]

In attempting to trace the concrete vestiges of institutionalized Masonry in Britain, Gould starts with the three terms: Lodge, Mason, and Warden. A Lodge for stone-cutters was built at Durham in 1432. A "Warden of the Lodge of Masons at York Cathedral" is also mentioned in 1476. The first Scottish Lodge is found in the burgh of Aberdeen ("*Masownys of the luge*", 1483), followed by "*our Lady luge of Dunde*"

(1536).[50] The first mention of the London Company of Freemasons in 1376 clearly shows that at that time the term "Freemason" (*ffreemason*) was widely used. And it is not without a factual foundation that Gould insists that its meaning should be read and understood not in the sense of the French "*Mestre Mason de franche père*", but in relation to the *quality of stone, not to the status of Mason*. In other words, a Freemason is a mason who works with the "free" stones already prepared for a building work, not with the "rough" stone. And, apparently, it is in this sense that the term is used in the *York Roll* (about 1600), though its first *official* use, in the name of the London Company "is associated with the *freedom*" of that body.[51]

In his dating of the Old Masonic manuscripts, Gould is as traditional and orthodox as any Masonic historian before him. The oldest of them, the famous Regis manuscript, he dates from the first quarter of the fifteenth century; the second oldest, the Cooke manuscript from the end of the fifteenth century. With respect to both he asserts that ". . . their contents have been copied . . . from some earlier work . . ." and that "they contain *allusions* to the Assemblies . . ."[52] While admitting that there were many Masonic Lodges in the fourteenth century, Gould remains wary on the crucial subject of Assemblies, and it is here that he and Anderson part company when he suggests that ". . . although there would seem no rational foundation for the belief that the English Masons of the Middle Ages met in legal (or lawful) assemblies . . . there is evidence . . . that they were in the habit of meeting in illegal . . . assemblies for the purpose of defeating the course of legislation".[53] He writes: "The influence exercised by . . . Br. Anderson . . . has not wholly disappeared. Freemasons believe no longer in his mythical Grand Master, but they cannot abandon his equally mythical Assemblies."[54] The controversy arising from the rather muddled accounts of Freemasonry in the fourteenth century leaves open one very important question: do the notorious *Statutes of Labourers* of Edward III (1349, 1350, 1360), which outlawed all Masonic "alliances, congregations, oaths and ordinances" (including the almost legendary "exemption" on the grounds that the Lodges were non-professional or speculative at that time), really imply that the latter were *positively* legal and in force before their annulment? If they were not, the whole edifice of medieval Masonry as an institution falls to pieces. For in that case neither the above-mentioned London Company of Freemasons, nor the famous reference to "Henry de Yeveley . . . the master-mason of the Abbey of Westminster (1388–95)" and "Freemason to Edwarde the thirde" (according to a document of 1598), nor even a Statute of 1445 specifying "the wages of a *frankmason*",[55] could figure as evidence in favour of the existence of a body uniting all the Masons, legally representing them, or regulating their professional activity. The regulation of wages that followed the enactment of the Statutes – which, according to Gould, were "worse than the Black Death ... and worse than slavery to accept",[56] might have had nothing to do with the members of the London Company of Freemasons or with those employed in the building of Westminster Abbey.

The Company was merely a professional body which had no official association with any *secret* Masonic society or with the idea of an authorizing body of such a society,[57] and the Masonic Lodges continued their more or less disparate existence through the sixteenth century when, in Gould's words, ". . . Masonry had passed its meridian . . . and remained a shadow of itself ... until the end of the seventeenth century..."[58] In the meantime an entirely new custom had appeared of accepting non-professionals into Masonic Lodges, although they nevertheless remained professional in both form and function.

Commenting on the earliest properly dated record of a non-professional person being a member of a Masonic Lodge – the Minutes of the Lodge of Edinburgh 8 June 1600 mentioning the presence of James Boswell, the Laird of Auchinleck – Gould stresses that ". . . speculative or symbolic flourished side by side with operative", which, among other facts, "may be safely inferred . . . from the declaration of a Presbyterian Synod in 1562, that some ministers . . . had been Freemasons".[59] The most interesting thing, however, is that not only did non-Masons begin to be accepted, but there appeared a special category of Lodges for which the "acception" became habitual if not yet the main reason for their existence.[60]

The seventeenth century was a time of unbridled curiosity. Reading John Aubrey's *Brief Lives* (Gould refers not once to Aubrey in his book) one cannot help feeling that this curiosity was directed not only to the objects of art, the phenomena of nature and all such things as numbers, buildings, landscapes, belief systems and ideas, but, above all, to men themselves, their minds, attitudes and characters. And we might suppose, not unreasonably, that "being accepted" could have made one, in the eyes of many others, an object of particular curiosity. We may also think that at the time of uninterrupted political struggle and the most acute religious differences "acception" might have offered a kind of neutral breathing space, however narrow this might be. For at that time – and probably more than ever before – it became quite evident that politics and religion were so tightly entangled with one another that there was hardly any possibility for a person to escape from one to another. At the same time, it still seems to be highly improbable that any significant number of educated gentlemen became involved in the acception; a couple of hundred perhaps, no more than that. But this proved to be enough for Masonry to start radically changing its appearance, character and function.

One of the immediate consequences of this change was the flow of more or less first-hand information about Masonic customs and rituals provided by those accepted, which they appear not to have been warned against by their "acceptors". Moreover, sometimes it even looks as if the latter positively desired the "accepted" to spread that information to any one who might be interested. Gould quotes that famous passage from Elias Ashmole's *Diary* (March 1682) where Ashmole reveals that he was ". . . at a Noble dinner prepared at the charge of the new-accepted Masons", and that with the exception of himself and two other persons, all were members of the Masons' Company of London, and that it was thirty-five years since he had been admitted as an accepted Mason.[61] And, of course, Gould quotes amply from Dr Robert Plot's *Natural History of Staffordshire* where it is stated clearly that there was ". . . a Custom . . . of admitting *Men* into the *Society of Freemasons* . . . spread more or less all over the *Nation* . . ."[62] It appears that the Masons were aware that as a *professional body* they were in decline and began *consciously* to resolve this predicament by changing themselves into something entirely different from what they had been a century earlier, by broadening their base and appealing to a wider sphere.[63]

It seems unlikely that "accepted" or "speculative" Masonry could have sprung into existence in 1717 from the "Operative" as a Deus ex Machina quite fully formed, but independent *historical* evidence linking even Freemasonry and Architecture in Britain, let alone the other professions that became the life blood of the post-revival Lodges in the seventeenth century, is scarce.[64] Even when speaking of one of the oldest Lodges in Britain, according to Masonic tradition, the Old Lodge at York City, Gould has to admit, that though ". . . from at least 1705, it was exclusively *speculative* or *symbolical* . . . no minutes of earlier date than 1712 have been preserved".[65] And the history of Irish Masonry in the seventeenth century is equally poorly documented.

As for Scottish Masonry, Gould sees no reason to regard it as in any way different from its southern counterpart. That is why he says, "Whether, indeed, the Old Constitutions of the Freemasons fulfilled the same function in North and South Britain is indeterminable. But there is no version known which can fairly be described as of purely

Scottish origin."[66] Of course, no genealogy can be found of "Mother Lodge–Daughter Lodge" type for either Scottish or English Masonries, for the simple reason that such a mechanism for the proliferation of Lodges appeared only much later, with speculative, accepted or "adopted" Freemasonry. At the same time, and without any contradiction, Gould quite rightly asserts: "All the *operative* terms and expressions which were afterwards turned to *speculative uses* by the Freemasons of the South, namely, Master Mason, Fellow Craft, Entered Apprentice, and Cowan, are mentioned in the *Shaw Statutes*, and appear to have been in common use in Scotland from 1598 down to our own times."[67] To which he adds that, "...Two of the Lodges mentioned in those *Statutes* – of Edinburgh and Kilwinning – are in existence at this day... Several other Lodges which figure in St Clair Charters of 1601 and 1628 ... still live on, and are surrounded by a halo of antiquity, for which a parallel will be vainly sought in any other region of the globe."[68] But it is not as simple as that, for that halo of antiquity surrounding the Scottish Lodges is about tradition and not about history as such. Gould was, perhaps, the first Freemasonic historian to draw the line between tradition and historiography, and between Masonry as a *tradebody* (even though it included some non-working members, not to speak of noble patrons and protectors, such as the St Clairs) and Freemasonry as a totally different kind of association that was neither one thing nor another; neither a Guild nor a real trade-company. Thus, on the one hand, he agrees with Bain in that "...At the outset ... Freemasonry was simply an adjunct of the original association of the Craft of Masons; but gradually it became its leading feature, and the Incorporation of Masons ... became what is now known as the Aberdeen Lodge ... while in certain [other] districts where no Incorporations existed, Companies were formed..."[69] On the other hand, he has to admit that "...with the exception of the Lodge of Edinburgh, the minutes of which ... extend back to July, 1599, none of the existing Scottish Lodges is of earlier date than the seventeenth century".[70] And, again, the same historical ambiguity which he feels all the time, but is not able to overcome: "The customs of the old Scottish Lodges ... are in many instances ... survivals of usages pre-dating the era of Grand Lodges ... but the usages of the Scottish Craft, so far as they relate to the Speculative (or Symbolical) Masonry ... will only be dealt with as *known* ... in the seventeenth century."[71] So the "many nobil craftsmen of France and Flanders, and other partes" brought over by James I of Scotland in 1431, as well as the existence of an "Incorporation ... of Wrights and Masons of Edinburgh in 1475 ..."[72] would figure as that which is not known, for neither

Gould nor anyone after him has been lucky enough to discover anything historically proven about those craftsmen and their associations. And it is with reference to the sixteenth and seventeenth centuries that he states: "... the grafting of the non-professional element on the stem of the operative system ... had its commencement in Scotland ... about the period of Reformation, and ... of 49 Fellow Crafts who belonged to the Lodge of Aberdeen in 1670 ... less than a quarter were of the Masons' trade" ... "The last were known as *Dogmatics*, while the former assumed the names of *Geomatics, Gentlemen Masons, Theoretical Masons, Architect Masons*, and *Honorary Members*."[73] Moreover, Gould supposes that the tradition of the Mason's Word developed (or had existed) there before it became known in England, not to speak of the clear evidence that the first Scottish Lodge Minute Books are older than the English. We may even suppose together with Gould that the custom of acception in Scottish Masonry, if not Scottish Masonry itself, predated its adoption in the South. And it may be assumed that though at the time of the formation of the Grand Lodge of England the Scottish Lodges had been far more numerous and more deeply rooted in local tradition, it was that very event that gave the Scots a fresh impulse to unite and consolidate their Masonry. The communication between Scots and English Masonries began in 1721, fifteen years before the Scottish Freemasons elected William St Clair their first Grand Master, whereas the Irish followed the English example sooner, in 1725. Scottish Masonry, however, may have preserved more of its original and purely local features than its English counterpart, owing perhaps to a greater diversity in the customs of the various Lodges, as well as to their inherently more autonomous character and their anarchic style.[74] That is why it must have been easier for the Chevalier de Ramsay to invent his new mythology of the Higher Degrees by basing it on Scottish rather than English Freemasonry. This mythology, however, did not become a part of the "prehistory" of Scottish Freemasonry, for at the time of its invention in 1737, the latter had already been formed, following more or less the English pattern of development, and it was too late for such innovations. The Scots joined the English in their common saga, leaving the extravagances of the so-called "Scottish Rites" – with their legend of the Crusaders, the Knights of St John of Jerusalem, and the Templars – to the French. Though only temporarily, for less than a century after Ramsay's famous *Oration* we see Scottish lairds, merchants and presbyters sitting side by side with English gentry and clerics at the meetings of the "Royal Scots". However, speaking even of those "excrescences on the body of Pure and Ancient Masonry",[75] we should not lose sight of the fact that they could hardly have grown out of any other institution and against any other background, than that of the early Grand Lodge of England.

Gould's critique of the early Freemasonic historiography is sound, just, but rather flat. He writes of the *Constitutions* of 1738, that ". . . it is much to be regretted, that . . . in his [Anderson's] desire to establish the Craft to the best advantage, he should have claimed as its rulers . . . nearly every celebrity of ancient and modern times . . . from Noah to Cardinal Wolsey and Wren . . ."[76] This simply shows that Gould refuses to regard the Legend of Freemasonry as a part of its historical existence, as a historical fact in its own right, and that he does not see in the use and application of this Legend by Anderson a crucial element and stage of the actual process of Freemasonic history. In other words, he is too rationalist to understand that the borderline between fiction and fact in history is far less clear than he would like and that in the course of Freemasonic history (the present day included) fiction has very often figured as the content of a fact.[77]

The later commentators, Fred L. Pick and G. Norman Knight, came up with their own historical conception of Freemasonry in a kind of histori-cal manual for modern Masons published in 1954.[78] It can be summed up in the following propositions (numeration and paraphrasing mine):

> 1. Up to the present time no plausible theory of the origin of Freemasons has been put forward.
> 2. Freemasonry, as we know it, is of British origin, a British product, and originated among the operative Masons of Britain.
> 3. All that is not specifically British, but is incorporated into the Craft from the earliest time, i.e. shreds of ritual, folklore and some occult elements – cannot be regarded as really specific with respect to Freemasonry.
> 4. The history of Freemasonry is not so much the story of the development of a Craft Guild, culminating in such organizations as the Masons of London, as the development of a body of moral instruction communicated by means of meetings held under the seal of secrecy.[79]

On the basis of these assumptions the authors start their exposition of the *forms* which the medieval operative Masonry assumed in the process of its development, and of the *terms* in which it expressed itself to the Masons and world outside Masonry. The authors define the very notion of organization in its application to Masonry, first as a means of *inter-communication* between Masons, and only secondly as a means by which those very Masons were represented as a *body*, or *institution* within the whole system of other professional bodies or institutions (or *versus* the rest of them). They note, quite aptly, that the astonishingly large number of churches built in England during the first two hundred years after the Norman Conquest (something in the order of 5000), and the remarkable uniformity of their style and building methods could never have been achieved without the fulfilment of two conditions: first, the rapidity of movement of the Masons from one site to another and, second, the effectiveness in the exchange of information concerning the *specifications* of a building. The character of that Masonic inter-communication might have predetermined the essential feature of the first Lodges, namely, their comparative isolation from the local communities, and their independence from the Guilds and the Guild machinery.[80]

The term *Lodge*, according to the authors, might have had two original meanings, namely, (1) "the Mason's place of work, as distinct from the place where he slept and ate (according to the earliest reference of 1277)," ... and (2) "... the body of Masons working on a given site, the latter being of considerably later date" (*Shaw Statutes* of 1598, 1599).[81] Here, though in a rather different context, we return to the primary idea of the Lodge as place and meeting as it is discussed above.

As to Masonic Assemblies, the authors do not seriously believe that the existing Masonic documentary evidence confirms their existence prior to Roberts's account of 1722. This contains, as we have seen, the "Additional Orders and Constitutions ... made and agreed upon at a General Assembly ... held on the 8th December, 1663", and they consider it to be more plausible than accounts of the Great Assembly held at York in 1561.[82] And they are absolutely sure that of all the legal documents, only the Edward III Statutes provide us with specific references to Freemasons. Speaking of codifications and recodifications of the Statutes, they note that in the Act of 1563 in Queen Elizabeth's reign, the term *rough mason* is used instead of *Freemason* which, in their opinion, only shows that "by this time the latter ... had already lost its purely operative significance".[83]

Three historically indisputable phenomena are causally linked by them in ways not very different from those of Dr Anderson. These are the decline in church-building, the transformation from the Gothic to the Classical style, and the transition from operative to speculative Masonry. To these they add a sharp change in what they call "direction of labour" meaning that when labour became cheaper because of a "drastic fall in the value of money", many of the Masons became employed in the construction of the royal palaces and residences of the gentry. These, along with the building of new churches, though far fewer than during the Norman period, gradually became the task of a far more settled and less mobile workforce. In this connection it is interesting to note that the Guilds or Companies of Masons – as distinct from the old or contemporary Lodges – were permanent trade organizations strictly localized within communities and had nothing to do with journeymen of any sort. The London Company was one of them, and the fact that there had been no records of this body from 1356 to 1620 is significant, for the first records appeared specifically in connection with "acception" of non-working members. In this connection the authors assert quite categorically the existence "in ... London ... of an *inner fraternity*, known as Acception, membership of which did not necessarily follow membership of the Company", and the other way around.[84]

Thus, the little we know of the actual habits, customs, and rituals of the Masons proper came to be known almost entirely through the accepted and speculative Masons. And this is so not only in the strict historical sense – it is the speculatives who provided us with practically all the information about the pre-Grand Lodge period – but also in an epistemological sense, for it is the speculatives who developed a special interest in the Masonic past, and have continued to develop it from the middle of the seventeenth century to the present day. Stage by stage, from generation to generation they were *building up* their historical consciousness, an essential part of which was "the bridge between operative and speculative Masonry".[85] And, if one were to attempt any generalization about anything truly Masonic (as we know it now) as it existed in the seventeenth century and the beginning of the eighteenth century, one is faced with the discovery that there is well nigh nothing remaining which has not passed through the process of "building up". Even the Ritual, a *sanctum sanctorum* and the last redoubt of Free-masonic orthodoxy, "was consolidated only after the Union of 1813".[86]

So, we have come at last to the point where the history of the formation of English Freemasonry ends and, becoming thereby superfluous, was dropped from the Constitutions in 1815, very soon after the Great Reconciliation. After that, with the Ritual finally established, the Lodges renumbered anew, even the terminology corrected, recorrected and standardized, what would happen to anything that had been discarded?

The last chapter of Pick and Knight's *History of the Craft in England*, covering the period from 1813 to 1975, is of little help – to those outside the Craft, of course, not to learned Freemasons. Here we read of the regularization of the Provincial Grand Lodges, of the setting up of the Board of General Purposes, which became the most important decision-making organ within the Grand Lodge; of the new version of Constitution (1815); of the Grand Lodge Library and, of course, of the Royal Masonic Benevolent Institution. Then comes the Girls' School, Boys' School, a New Freemasons' Hall in London, and the series of Royal personages who served as Grand Masters, interspersed with a handful of mere dukes. Finally, there are the Centenaries, Bicentenaries, Memorials, Charities, and still more Charities.

The problem of the relationships between Freemasonry and religion is dealt with cursorily – just so as to cover the topic – and, as is often the case when one is hasty, the authors' attitudes to their own religion is clearly revealed. They start with a quotation from the definition, itself idiotic enough, of the Board of General Purposes, that "Masonry is neither a religion nor a substitute for religion . . . nor a competitor with religion . . . though in the sphere of human conduct it may be hoped that its teaching will be complementary to that of religion."[87] Their comment on this passage is still more idiotic: "But it both requires a man to have *some sort* of religious belief before he can be admitted . . . and expects him thereafter to go on practising his religion."[88] They pass on to the more concrete case of the relationships between Roman Catholics and Freemasonry, and to Catholic intransigence, taking not the slightest notice of the fact that Catholics *do* regard Freemasonry as some kind of a religion. Furthermore, while mentioning the case of "Brother Harry Carr . . . himself a Jew, who strove for years for a reconciliation between Church and Order . . .", they fail to see that, just as in the case of Anglican–Catholic relations, we are dealing with an immensely complex religious situation, namely, the situation where one "pure" religion (Judaism) mediates between another "pure" religion (Catholicism) and the third religion which is not "pure", but obviously syncretic. Still less are the authors able to grasp that the paradox of the situation is that the Catholic Church sees in Judaism a bona fide religion that happens now to be in error, while in Freemasonry it sees something posing as a religion – a kind of pernicious fake.[89] Since Judaism does not count as a type of Christianity, one cannot be opposed to the admission of Jews, even if they are Rabbis, into Freemasonry.[90] Whereas Roman Catholicism cannot tolerate a rival priesthood. That is why the authors conclude their uninspiring section on religion by remarking that, "The Christian rites among the additional degrees present a greater problem than the Craft Masonry, since it could be argued that some of them teach a *type of Christianity* not altogether in accordance with the principles of the Roman Catholic Church".[91]

However, the difference between Church and religion which was perfectly understood by James Anderson, a Dissenter, does not seem to be taken into account by the authors when they claim that Freemasonry in England (unlike, say, in France) has never been anticlerical. For the English Craft finds itself periodically (the present time included) in the dock not because it is anticlerical but, rather, because it is and cannot help being aclerical.[92]

Masonic history as presented in these and, practically, all other versions, is the history of Freemasonry as a *changing and developing form* rather than an organization or institution as such; a form the content of which can be reduced to five main elements:

1. Masonry as a particular institution with its various names – Masonry, Freemasonry, Institution, Society, Brotherhood, Fraternity, Craft, Fellowship, etc. – as well as its own terminology and nomenclature related to its units, groups of members and individual members – Lodge, Grand Lodge, Private Lodge, Grand Provincial Lodge, Master, Grand Master, Warden, etc. This also comprises:

a) Its inner regulations, i.e. the rules of behaviour and conduct related to the Lodge, the Grand Lodge, or Freemasonry as a whole;

b) Its own means of recognition and mutual acknowledgement which are secret and, in principle, not limited to any *one* society or country; and

c) Its outer regulations, by means of which it figures as one of many social, religious and professional organizations within a society, community, or state. These regulations are exoteric by definition.

2. Masonry as a science, profession, art, or skill.

3. Masonry as Ritual, Tradition of Ritual and esoteric knowledge of Ritual.

4. Masonry as Religious Knowledge (esoteric as well as exoteric) and Moral Instruction based on the Ritual and its symbolism.

5. Masonry as a type of social, cultural, and (eventually) political activity directed outwards – outside the Lodge, outside the Fraternity, outside a given country. This type of activity often follows patterns which can be regarded, by an external observer at least, as specifically Freemasonic and inherent to Freemasonry.

However, not infrequently we see that activity as the *reaction* of Freemasonry to society or to changes and developments in its social environment.

From Anderson to Preston the main task was to build up the pre-historical foundation for Freemasonic history, and to continue it into *their* present time: Freemasonry as a *form* was not yet fully shaped and it is the process of its *shaping* that provides the content of any historiography. With its form already completed, it became clear that from the beginning of the nineteenth century up to the present day, the history as a sequence of relevant and significant events actually stopped. And if one asks why Freemasonic *history* lost almost all its significance from that time, and then, at the turn of our century, ended almost as abruptly as it began in the beginning of the eighteenth century, the answer would be – it was meant to.

For the history of Freemasonry, as we have seen it in the previous sections and in this summary, is more than anything else a history of its formation, consolidation and spread, to which may be appended as an after-thought a history of its relations with the outside world, and a history of the opinions of its members about the outside world in its relations with them. The latter, however, really concerns Masons as individuals rather than the whole body. That is why it is so difficult to write a history of modern Freemasonry starting from the end of the last century, where Gould left off.

It seems clear, then, that the only really interesting historical theme left is the inner development of Freemasonry as a religion, and the corresponding evolution of its own religious self-consciousness. But that is just what all Masonic, as well as anti-Masonic historians are so wary of doing; they are much happier describing in minute detail the Masonic charities, the visits of the Royals to the Freemasons' Hall in London, and so forth. Even such an excellent historian as Gould was totally unable to grasp not only the specifically religious aspect of Freemasonry, but also the whole problem of the actual relationship between Free-masonry and the Churches. Nor were any of those historians who followed in his steps – from W. J. Hughan, D. Knoop, and B. E. Jones, through F. L. Pick and G. N. Knight, up to the present with John Hamill – who prefer to avoid the thorny issue altogether. Alternatively, we may say that Freemasonic religion has been relegated to the pre-historical roots of the Craft in order to avoid at any cost presenting it as one of the most essential elements in the present-day history of the Craft.

Notes

1 That the theme of history as a basic element of individual consciousness or collective ideology is a common feature of European thinking seems to be a platitude hardly worth mentioning. What, however, is really interesting, is the question of to what extent, if any, one is aware of one's history as a "real" history, and not simply as *a mode of thinking* about oneself and the world. When in the 1860s Marx came forth with his conception of the class struggle and mode of production as *the* content of the historical process, he did not mean these to be merely a manner, or even a "method" of his own historical thinking, but the two fundamentals of *objective* history itself ("I create the essence of history and give everyone his due"). To the Freemasons, the role of such a historical objectivity was attributed, probably, to biblical history. Both were, almost equally, unaware of the *intentional* and *thematic* character of their historical conceptions.

2 It is worth noting here that to the American Freemasons it was not so, because they received their Masonry as already formed and "ready to play with". That is, the work had already been done for them by the English Freemasons, and they did not need to feel that they were doing anything odd or artificial.

3 That is probably why a reaction against "mere symbolism" among Freemasons themselves has been always either Christian or in some way mystically oriented.

4 This, in turn, suggests that even though there were, or might have been, Masonic Grand Lodges or Lodges, or similar institutions, in other parts of Europe and the Near East, none of them survived by the time of the foundation of the Grand Lodge of England. And, more than that, all irregular, divergent, and even anomalous Masonic societies in Europe as well as in the whole world descend, directly or indirectly, from that one pristine source.

5 W. Preston, 1804, pp. 278–81.

6 *Idem*, p. 307.

7 J. G. Findel, 1869, p. 13.

8 *Idem*, p. 12. Here Findel establishes the framework of the historical controversy for the future Masonic historiography. One hundred and twenty years later Dyer formulated it retrospectively: "There were two main themes which emerged in the last twenty years before the centenary of Quatuor Coronati Lodge, the earlier being an increased study of William Preston Lectures . . . the other being *further resistance* to the tacitly accepted theory of a hundred years earlier, that we are all descended in some curious way from the builders of the Middle Ages . . .", Colin Dyer, *The History of the First 100 Years of the Quatuor Coronati Lodge N.2076*, London, 1986 (C. Dyer, 1986), pp. 53–4.

9 J. G. Findel, 1869, pp. 17–18.

10 *Idem*, pp. 21–3.

11 *Idem*, p. 23.

12 *Idem*, pp. 28–9.

13 *Idem*, p. 48. Which leaves unexplained the fact that all attested German Lodges after 1717 were authorized and warranted by the Grand Lodge of England. Why was this necessary if they had their own unbroken line of Lodges upon which English Freemasonry allegedly modelled itself?

14 *Idem*, p. 62–3.

15 *Idem*, p. 64.

16 Who the Stonemasons were as opposed to those belonging to "Masonic" Guilds is unclear.

17 *Idem*, p. 65. This seems to contradict his earlier assertion that in 1717 the English Freemasons took the laws, regulations, customs of the *Steinmetzen* as a model.

18 The *Vehme* was a secret society very powerful in the fourteenth and fifteenth centuries. It had its own courts of Justice, its own laws and means of executing them with respect to any person living within the territory of its secret jurisdiction.

19 *Idem*, p. 69.

20 *Idem*, pp. 71–2. See note 16.

21 *Idem*, p. 80.

22 As most historians of his time (and quite a few of ours), Findel was not able to separate the legendary character of the *content* of a text from the legend about the text itself.

23 *Idem*, p. 91.

24 *Idem*, p. 98.

25 *Idem*, p. 113.

26 *Idem*, p. 114.

27 *Idem*, p. 115.

28 *Idem*, p. 119.

29 *Idem*, pp. 124–5.

30 *Idem*, p. 127.

31 *Idem*, p. 128.

32 *Idem*, pp. 130–1. Since he has long maintained that non-operative Masons had been accepted into working Lodges, presumably sharing their privileges, he refers to the complete separation of the two types institutionalized in 1717.

33 *Idem*, p. 135.

34 *Idem*, pp. 136–9.

35 *Idem*, pp. 158–60.

36 *Idem*, p. 183.

37 *Idem*, pp. 126, 127.

38 *Idem*, p. 127.

39 R. F. Gould, 1903, p. 2–3.

40 *Idem*, pp. 3, 8.

41 *Idem*, pp. 20–1.

42 *Idem*, p. 32.

43 *Idem*, p. 34.

44 *Idem*, p. 36. That is, at the very time when the Grand Lodge of England had already begun to establish its Lodges in Germany.

45 *Idem*, p. 37.

46 *Idem*, p. 34.

47 *Idem*, pp. 45–60.

48 Although Gould remarks (*idem*, p. 48), that "... among all the fraternities there was a belief in an alleged connection of the stonemasons with Hiram, and white gloves were always worn ... by way of disclaiming the complicity of their members with regard to his death".

49 To this may be added that the declining *Compagnonnage* itself might have

been influenced by the "regular" French Freemasons whose Lodges derived from the Grand Lodge of England. Gould mentions the curious fact that when in 1803 there was the General Assembly of the whole *Compagnonnage*, one of the delegates, a *Freemason*, ". . . introduced the third (superior) order of members" (*idem*, p. 54).

50 *Idem*, p. 108.

51 *Idem*, pp. 119–22. My modest surmise is that the solution of this problem – "free man or free stone?" – should be sought not in the etymology of the word, but in the history of changes in its meaning. "Freedom" here means "Freedom of the Company" as a granted privilege (*idem*, p. 193).

52 *Idem*, pp. 129, 154. It is worth stressing again the point that these are Masonic manuscripts the authenticity of which cannot be corroborated by any independent sources. This is *not* to say however that they do not represent the truth: we simply do not know.

53 *Idem*, p. 162.

54 *Idem*, pp. 152–3.

55 *Idem*, pp. 117, 118.

56 *Idem*, p. 163.

57 Which does not mean that some or many of its members were not also members of individual Lodges. See note 64.

58 *Idem*, p. 183.

59 *Idem*, p. 184.

60 As evidence, Gould refers to two well-trodden circumstances, namely, that: "Previously to 1620 . . . certain Brethren who were members of the *Company* . . . were known to the Company as the '*Accepted Masons*'," and ". . . seven persons were received into '*Accepcon*' or . . . 'Lodge' in 1620–21, all of whom were *already* members of the Company . . ." (*idem*, pp. 184–5).

61 *Idem*, pp. 189–90.

62 *Idem*, p. 194.

63 This is my conjecture, not Gould's.

64 Plot writes: ". . . This day, May the 18th 1691 . . . is a great convention at St Paul's Church of the Fraternity of Adopted Masons, where Sir Chr. Wren is to be adopted a brother . . ." The above is from the rough copy of the J. Aubrey MS . . . and is the only contemporary evidence which tends in any way to connect Wren with the Freemasons. (*idem*, pp. 195–6.)

65 *Idem*, p. 197.

66 *Idem*, p. 262.

67 *Idem*, pp. 254–5. "The *Shaw Statutes* . . . of 1598 and 1599 . . . are *Codes of Law* signed by William Shaw, Master of King's work and General Warden of the Masons" (*Idem*, p. 253).

68 *Idem*, p. 256.

69 *Idem*, p. 252.

70 *Idem*, p. 256.

71 *Idem*, p. 261.

72 *Idem*, pp. 250–1, 252.

73 *Idem*, pp. 265–6, 267.

74 Gould writes: "there were several Lodges which never joined the Grand Lodge of Scotland . . . and there were other old Lodges which seceded . . . notably "Mother Kilwinning", and the Lodge of Edinburgh (Mary's Chapel), the cause of

the Schism being in either instance the same, namely, a jealousy of the other being at the head of the roll . . ." (*idem*, p. 276).

75 *Idem*, p. 277. Further he writes: ". . . These Scottish (or High, or St Andrew's) degrees . . . were manufactured in France . . . in contradistinction to the ceremonies actually practised by *Scottish* Masons" (*idem*, p. 320).

76 *Idem*, pp. 324–5.

77 I am not embarking on Gould's historiography of the post-Grand Lodge period of Masonic history, for it has been discussed frequently on previous pages of this book.

78 Fred L. Pick and G. Norman Knight, *The Pocket History of Freemasonry*, Revised by F. Smyth, 7th Ed., London, 1983. [F. L. Pick and G. N. Knight, 1983 (1954).]

79 *Idem*, pp. 18, 19.

80 *Idem*, pp. 19, 20.

81 *Idem*, pp. 21–2.

82 *Idem*, pp. 25, 26, 65, 66. They agree with the opinion of Anderson, that 1717 was a revival not so much of Freemasonry as of the General Assembly (p. 26).

83 *Idem*, p. 27.

84 *Idem*, pp. 43–4.

85 *Idem*, p. 53.

86 *Idem*, p. 54.

87 *Idem*, p. 132.

88 *Ibid.*

89 *Idem*, pp. 139–40.

90 All the more so since, as has already been noted, Rabbis are not priests.

91 *Idem*, p. 140.

92 *Idem*, pp. 129–31. And that is why it is an ideal place for a clergyman of any Church.

.

RITUAL AND MYTHOLOGY

CHAPTER 10

Ritual, Symbolism and Religion

A Literal Description of Ritual

Truth, whether as expressed in Masonry or otherwise, is at all times an open secret.
W. L. Wilmshurst, *The Meaning of Masonry*[1]

To me the whole ritual of Freemasonry is but a mighty reminder of that part of my own mind which is death, *and which I always forget about, being for most of my life surrounded by death, wrapped in it.*
Valdemar Lovin[2]

We have already learned a little of individual (written by Masons) and official (more or less officially recognized by them) Masonic history, including some bits of the history of Masonic ritual. We have even assumed that, as demonstrated by the examples of Doctors Anderson and Desaguliers, and the Chevalier de Ramsay, quite a few of these things might have been invented or reinvented. Now, while I am going to concentrate on the Ritual of Master Mason, the Third Degree, I should like to emphasize once again that from the point of view of phenomenology, whenever and wherever we deal with a ritual, and of whatever kind that ritual might be, the words "invention" or "to invent" are *etic*, that is, belonging to the language of the observer. Seen *emically*, from within, a ritual finds its reality in being performed, and consists of the various elements (stages, actions, speeches, sounds, instruments, accessories, etc.) of its performance. One may, and often does, invent a history or even History, which fact, if it is known, affects the claim of such a history to be taken as valid or as "real". Its status as representing historical truth is inevitably changed, though it may represent another kind of truth. But even if it is known that a ritual has been "invented" (as all rituals must have been at one time or another) this does not make it any less valid or less real; for it is the very fact (and act) of its performance that makes it a ritual. If history, real or invented, is included within the context of a ritual, it inevitably ceases to be history, for by being there, it loses its temporality and becomes a part of the atemporal enactment of ritual. It becomes infinitely repeated within a ritual and is therefore deprived of its most essential features: uniqueness, and temporal linearity.[3]

The ritual of initiation is not only the core and centre of Masonry, but it constitutes the mechanism which generates all the levels of its functional existence, as well as all levels of its understanding by Masons themselves and by those outside it as far as the latter wish to understand it.[4] What I mean by this is not only that all principal Masonic religious ideas and symbols find their place within the Ritual, but also that they are either demonstrated by the Ritual, or figure as its general or particular interpretations.

I will now give a short description of the Ritual of Master Mason as it was formed, practised and described some seventy years after the first "exposure" by Samuel Prichard, who, however hostile, I firmly believe did not misrepresent anything. The manual I have based this on is a standard Masonic handbook, "thoroughly revised by several competent and distinguished Members of the Craft",[5] all 152 pages of which are skilfully adorned on the margins with engravings of skeletons (264 in number) with an additional five engravings representing the souls of sinners in hell.[6]

Even a very superficial comparison between this manual and Prichard's Pamphlet shows that the Ritual in both of them is essentially the same, and that we are dealing with a basic Masonic ritual that must have come into being at least a decade before his sensational publication. (And this, in turn, shows how stable the ritualistic tradition of Masonry was, though I am inclined to admit that this stability can be accounted for by the fact that the main line in the development of Masonry can be seen not so much in divergence and diversification within the Three Degrees Craft, as in the growth and diversification of the Masonry of the Higher Degrees.) In the following short summary of the Ritual I will, on the whole, be following the sequence, scheme and general plan of the manual. The method will be the same as in my earlier analysis of the first two Degrees.

The text prescribes what is to be said or done at a Lodge during the ceremony. The text of the ceremony is clearly divided into two parts: (1) what is spoken and heard by Masons, usually in the form of a dialogue, and (2) what is seen and done by Masons. The latter is put in square brackets in the manual. In the text all secret words related to the Inner Ritual are either abbreviated, or replaced by dots, or both; I have supplied almost all the missing words and have indicated them. All my explanatory remarks are in italics.

235

A.1.

Now let us start with "The ceremony of opening the Lodge in the First (i.e. Entered Apprentices) Degree", which clearly demonstrates the division between "what is said" in the dialogue, and "what is done" described in brackets. The whole nomenclature of a Lodge is defined within the ceremony in the questions and answers of the officers of the Lodge.[7]

A.1.1.

[Opening starts; the Brethren are assembled, and the Worshipful Master (W.M.) gives one **knock**[8] with the **gavel** (sometimes called **Hiram**)[9], and is answered by the Senior and Junior Wardens (S.W., J.W.).]

W.M.   Brethren, assist me to open the Lodge [all rise].

Symbolically – the world is a cosmic Lodge, but more importantly, man himself is a Lodge.[10]

W.M.   [to J.W., calling him by name] What is the first care of every true Mason?
J.W.   To see that the Lodge is properly tyled. [J.W. orders the Inner guard (I.G.) to see that the Lodge is properly tyled. I.G. gives one **knock**, which is answered by the Tyler (T.) who then turns round and says to J.W. that the Lodge is properly tyled. J.W. gives three **knocks** and reports the same to the W.M. (calling him by name).]

"Tyled" means guarded against the intrusion of the profane.

W.M.   [To S.W., by name] . . . what is the next care?
S.W.   To see that none but Masons are present.
W.M.   How many principal officers are there?
J.W.   Three, namely, the W.M., S.W., and J.W.
W.M.   How many assistant officers are there?
S.W.   Three, besides the T. or Outer Guard, namely the Senior Deacon (S.D.), the Junior Deacon (J.D.), and I.G.

A.1.2.

The following passage is devoted to the description (also in questions and answers) of the places occupied by the principal and assistant officers of the Lodge in ascending order of seniority. It is abbreviated here in tabular form.

NOMENCLATURE & ABBREVIATIONS	SITUATION	FUNCTION, DUTIES
Tyler, or Outer Guard (T.)	Outside the door of the Lodge	He is armed with a drawn sword to keep off all cowans and intruders to

		Masonry, and see that the Candidates (C.) are properly prepared.
Inner Guard (I.G.)	Within the entrance of the Lodge	He admits Masons on proof, receives Candidates in due form, and obeys the commands of the J.W.
Junior Deacon (J.D.)	At the right side of the S.W.	He carries all messages and communications of the W.M. from the S.W. to the J.W.
Senior Deacon (S.D.)	At the right of the W.M.	He bears all messages and commands of the W.M. to the S.W. and awaits the return of the J.D.
Junior Warden (J.W.)	In the South	He marks the Sun at its Meridian, calls the Brethren from labour to refreshment, and from refreshment to labour.
Senior Warden (S.W.)	In the West	He marks the setting Sun, and closes the Lodge by command of the W.M.
Worshipful Master (W.M.)	In the East	. . . as the Sun rises in the East, to open and enliven the day, so is the W.M.; he opens the Lodge, and employs and instructs the Brethren in Freemasonry.[11]

A.1.3.

W.M. Brethren, the Lodge being thus duly formed, before I declare it open let us invoke the assistance of the Great Architect of the Universe on all our undertakings; may our labours thus begun in order, be conducted in peace, and closed in harmony.

Past Master (P.M.)   So mote it be.

W.M. In the name of the Great Architect of the Universe I declare the Lodge duly open for the purposes of Freemasonry in the First Degree. [He gives three **knocks**, which are repeated by the S.W., J.W., I.G., and T. . . . Then the Brethren take their seats. Now minutes of the last Lodge should be read . . . and any letters or communications. After that follows the ballot for Mr A.B., a Candidate for initiation.] [pp. 1–6][12]

A.2.
THE CEREMONY OF INITIATION

Its meaning is neither secret nor open because it depends on one's own individual understanding: ". . . it means a break-away from the old method and order of life".[13]

A.2.1.
[All being assembled and clothed . . . the W.M. opens the Lodge in the First Degree, and the Minutes of the previous Lodge are read and put for confirmation (which must at all times be done in the First Degree and no other). When the Candidate is prepared,[14] the T. gives three loud knocks, the I.G. advances to the J.W., there is an alarm. The J.W. rises, gives the **kicks**[15] and **signs**[16], and says:] "W.M., there is an alarm."

W.M.   Bro. J.W., who wants admission?
J.W.   Bro. I.G., . . . who wants admission?
[The I.G. opens the door, and asks the T., whom he has there.]
T.   [to I.G.] Mr A.B., a poor candidate is in a state of **darkness**, who has been well . . . recommended, regularly proposed and approved in open Lodge, now comes of his own free will and accord, properly prepared, humbly soliciting to be admitted to the mysteries and privileges of Freemasonry.

"Darkness" here denotes the natural ignorance of natural man. I suspect that it figures as a secret term here because it indirectly refers to another specifically Masonic Darkness, i.e. ignorance of the mysteries of Freemasonry.[17]

A.2.2.
W.M.   Then let him be admitted in due form, Bro. J.D. [The Candidate is met at the door by the I.G., who applies the point of a **poniard**[18] to his **left breast**,[19] the J.D. asks him if he feels anything, and after a reply in the affirmative, the I.G. raises his hand above his own head, to show the W.M. that he has so applied it. The J.D. then takes the right hand of the Candidate with his left, and leads him gently before the **kneeling stool**[20] near the left of the S.W.]
W.M.   [To Candidate] Mr A.B., as no person can be made a

Mason unless he is free and of mature age, I demand of you . . .
etc.

Can.   I am.

W.M.   Thus assured, I will thank you to **kneel**, while the blessing
of heaven is invoked in aid of our proceedings. [The Deacons join
their hands over the Candidate's head, holding their wands with
the other.]

A.2.3.
PRAYER

All   Vouchsafe Thine aid, Almighty Father and Supreme Governor of the Universe . . . and grant that this Candidate for
Freemasonry may so dedicate and devote his life to Thy service,
as to become a true and faithful brother . . . Endue him with a
competence of Thy Divine Wisdom, so that assisted by the secrets
of our Masonic art, he may the better be enabled to unfold the
beauties of true godliness, to the honour and glory of Thy Holy
Name.

P.M.   So mote it be.

W.M.   [To Candidate] Mr. A.B., in all cases of difficulty and
danger, in whom do you put your trust?

Can.   In God.

A.2.4.

W.M.   The Brethren from the North, East, South and West will
take notice that Mr. A.B. is about in view before them, to show
that he is properly prepared, and a fit and proper person to be
made a Mason. [The J.D. takes him by the right hand and gently
leads him up the North past the W.M., and with the Candidate's
right hand[21] strikes the J.W. three times on the **right shoulder**.][22]

J.W.   [To J.D.] Who comes here?

J.D.   Mr. A.B., etc. (as before).

[The J.W. rises, with the **sign**, takes the **right hand** of the Candidate
and says:] "Enter, free and of good report." [The J.D. takes him to
the **right** of the S.W., who passes him through the same (as before)
examination, he is then delivered to the other side of the S.W., and his
right hand placed in the S.W.'s **left**.]

W.M.   [To Can.] Do you further seriously declare on your
honour, that avoiding fear on the one hand and rashness on the
other, you will steadily persevere through the ceremony of your
initiation, and, if once admitted, will afterwards act and abide by
the ancient usages and established customs of the Order?

Can. I will.

W.M. Bro. S.W., you will direct the J.D. to instruct the Candidate to advance to the East by the proper **signs**.

[The J.D. states to the Candidate that the method of advancing from West to East is by three **irregular steps**, and after leading him to within about a yard of the W.M., he directs him to the **pedestal**, as to be enabled to **kneel** before it without any other moving of the feet.] [pp. 47–8].

East is our eternal source of Light and Life, but here we are in a state of Darkness, in the West. "Hence every Candidate . . . finds himself in the West of the Lodge . . . East represents man's spirituality".[23]

A.2.5.

W.M. [to Candidate] Mr A.B., . . . Masonry is free, and requires a perfect freedom of inclination in every Candidate for its mysteries . . . But in order to secure the great and invaluable privileges of Masonry . . . vows of fidelity are required. But let me assure you that in those vows there is nothing incompatible with your civil, moral, or religious duties. Are you, therefore, willing to take a solemn obligation, . . . to keep inviolate the secrets and mysteries of our Order? [p. 48.]

Can. I am. [p. 49.]

W.M. Then you will **kneel** on your **left knee**, place your **right foot** in the form of a **square**,[24] give me your **right hand** and I place it on this book, which is the **Volume of the Sacred Law**, whilst your **left hand** will be employed in supporting a pair of **compasses**, one **point** extended to your **naked left breast**, but so as not to hurt yourself. Repeat your several names at length, and say after me. [The W.M. and Wardens give one **knock**, the Brethren rise and place the **right hand** on the **left breast**.] [p. 40]

OBLIGATION

Can. I, A.B., in the presence of the Great Architect of the Universe, and of this worthy, worshipful, and warranted Lodge of ancient, free and accepted Masons . . . of my own free will and accord . . . promise and swear that I always shall conceal and never reveal any part or parts, etc. . . . [p. 49]

I further solemnly promise that I will not write those secrets, indite, carve, mark, engrave, etc. . . . [p. 50] . . . so that our hidden mysteries and secret arts . . . may not improperly become known . . . under no less penalty . . . than that of having my throat cut . . . etc. [pp. 50–1]

A.2.6.

W.M. What you have repeated may be considered but a sacred promise ... and I will thank you to seal it with your **lips** on the **Volume of the Sacred Law** ... Having been kept a considerable time in a state of **darkness**, what in your present situation is the pre-dominant wish of your heart?

Can. **Light.** [pp. 51–2]

"Light" here denotes the Candidate's awareness of another Light, in the East, which corresponds in its meaning to the "Light of Instruction" according to an explanation made by Thomas Dunckerley in 1792.[25]

W.M. Bro. J.D., let that blessing be restored. [The Brethren raise their hands above their heads, the W.M. utters the **words** one, two, three; at the last **word** they simultaneously bring their hands down and strike the thigh; the J.D. at this moment restores the **light**. The J.D. should gently lay his hand on the head of the Candidate to prevent him seeing any other object than the **Volume of the Sacred Law.**] Having been restored to the blessing of material **light**, let me direct your attention to three great, though emblematic, **lights** in Freemasonry: the **Volume of the Sacred Law** ... to govern our faith; the **Square** ... to regulate our actions; and the **Compasses** ... to keep us in due bounds with all mankind, particularly our Brethren in Freemasonry. [He takes the Candidate by the right hand ...] Rise, newly obligated Brother among Masons! [pp. 52–3]

"The Square is an emblem of morality ... it teaches us how to live ... with all mankind ... The Compass symbolizes 'prudence'."[26]

W.M. You are now enabled to discover the three lesser lights in Masonry[27] ... situated East, South and West ... and meant to represent the Sun, to rule the day, the Moon, to rule the night, and the Master to rule ... his Lodge. [pp. 52–3]

Bro. A.B., by your meek and candid behaviour this evening, you have escaped two great dangers, i.e. those of **stabbing** and **strangling**; ... for at your entrance into the Lodge, this **poniard** was presented to your **naked left breast**, so that had you rushed forward, you would have been accessory to your own death by **stabbing**, not the Brother who held it, as he would have remained firm, and done his best duty. There was likewise this **cable-taw** with a running noose about your **neck**,[28] which would have rendered fatal any of your attempts to retreat. But the danger which will await you to your latest hour is the penalty of your obligation, implying that as a man of honour and a Mason you would rather have **your throat cut across** should you **improperly disclose the secrets of Freemasonry**. [The Candidate is removed to the side of the W.M.'s **pedestal**.] [pp. 53–4].

    . . . Now I am permitted to inform you that there are several Degrees in Freemasonry, and peculiar **secrets** restricted to each of them. I shall now . . . entrust you with the **secrets** of this Degree, or those **marks** by which we are known to each other, and distinguished from the rest of the world . . . all **squares, levels**[29] and **perpendiculars**[30] are true and proper **signs** to know a Mason by; you are therefore to stand perfectly erect, with your feet formed in a **square**; and your body thus considered an emblem of your mind, and your feet an emblem of the rectitude of your actions. [Done.] [pp. 54–5]

    You will now take a short pace with your **left foot**, bringing the **right heel** into its **hollow**; that is, the first **regular step**[31] in Freemasonry, and it is in this position the **signs** of this Degree are communicated; they consist of a **sign, token**, and **word**; the **sign** is given by placing the **hand**, etc. It alludes to the **penalty** of your obligation, implying that as a man of honour and a Mason, you would rather, etc. The **grip** or **token** is given by a distinct **pressure** of the **thumb** on the **first joint** of the **hand**; this when properly given and received, serves to distinguish a Brother by night as well as by day; this **grip** demands a **word** highly prized amongst Masons, as the guard to their privileges . . . It must never be given at length, but always by **letters** or **syllables**; to enable you to do this I will tell you what that word is; it is **BOAZ**; as during the ceremony you will be called on for this **word**, the J.D. will dictate the answers you are to give. [The W.M. gives the **grip** and asks.] [pp. 55–6]

W.M.   What is this?

J.D.   The **grip** or **token** of an Entered Apprentice Freemason.

W.M.   What does it demand?

J.D.   A word.

W.M.   Give me that word.

J.D.   At my initiation I was taught to be cautious; I will letter or halve it with you. [p. 57]

W.M.   Pass, **BOAZ**.

[The Candidate is then conducted to the S.W., who examines him as follows:]

J.W.   [Takes Candidate by the hand to the S.W.] Bro. S.W., I present to you Bro. A.B. on this initiation.

. . . S.W.   [To Candidate] What is that?

Can.   The first **regular step** in Masonry.

S.W.   Do you bring anything else?

Can.   [Gives the **sign**.]

S.W.   The **penal sign** of an Entered Apprentice. Etc. [p. 58]

. . . S.W.   Whence this word is derived?

Can.   From the **left-hand pillar** within the **porchway** or entrance of **King Solomon's Temple**. So-named after **Boaz**, the **great-grandfather of David, a Prince and Ruler in Israel**.

S.W.   The import of the **word**?

Can.   In **strength**.[32]

S.W.   Pass, **Boaz**.

[The S.D. conducts the Candidate to **left** of S.W., and places his **right hand** in S.W.'s **left hand**.]

A.2.7.

S.W.   [Gives the **sign**] W.M., I present to you Bro. A.B., on his initiation, for some mark of your favour. [p. 59]

W.M.   Bro. S.W., I delegate you to invest our Brother with the distinguishing **badge** of a Mason.[33]

S.W.   Bro. A.B., . . . this **badge** is more ancient than the Golden Fleece, or Roman Eagle, more honourable than the Star Garter, or any other order in existence, being the **badge** of innocence, and the bond of friendship . . .

[The J.D. turns the face of the Candidate towards the W.M. who delivers to him the following:]

W.M.   . . . You are never to put on that **badge**, if there is any Brother in the Lodge . . . with whom you are at variance, or against whom you entertain animosity: in such a case . . . you will invite him to withdraw, in order amicably to settle your difference, etc. . . . Now, Bro. J.D., you will place our Brother at the North-East part of the Lodge.

[The J.D. does so, and while the Candidate is there the W.M. gives the following address:] [pp. 60–1]

A.2.8.

W.M.   Bro. A.B., at the erection of all stately and superb edifices it is customary to lay the first or foundation stone at the North-East corner of the building.[34] You being newly initiated . . . are placed at the North-East part of the Lodge figuratively to represent that

stone . . . [p. 63] . . . In a society so widely extended as Freemasonry
. . . it cannot be denied that we have many members of rank and
opulence, neither can it be concealed that amongst the thousands
who range under its banners, there are some who, from circumstances of unavoidable calamity and misfortune, are reduced to
the lowest ebb of poverty and distress. On their behalf it is our
usual custom, to awaken the feelings of every new-made Brother
by such a claim on his charity as his circumstances in life may fairly
warrant; so, whatever you feel disposed to give, deposit with the
J.D., it will be thankfully received.

[The J.D. appeals to the Candidate, who states he has been deprived
of his money, etc. The J.D. then asks if he would give were it in his
power, to which the Candidate replies "Yes". The J.D. reports the same
to the W.M.]

W.M.   I congratulate you on the honourable sentiments by which
you are actuated, likewise on the inability which in the present
instance precludes you from gratifying them . . .

[The J.D. places the Candidate in front of the W.M.]

W.M.   I now present to you the **working tools** of an Entered
Apprentice: the 24 in. **Gauge**, that represents the twenty-four hours
of the day, part to be spent in prayer to Almighty God, part in
labour and refreshment, and part to serve a friend or Brother
in time of need (that not being detrimental to ourselves or our
connections). The **Common Gavel**[35] represents the force of conscience which should keep down all vain and unbecoming thoughts
. . . so that our words and actions may ascend unpolluted to the
throne of grace. The **Chisel** points out to us the advantages of
education, by which means alone our minds become cultivated,
and we are thereby rendered fit members for regularly organized
society. [pp. 66–7]

A.2.9.

EXPLANATION OF THE FIRST TRACING BOARD[36]

W.M.   The usages and customs among Freemasons have ever
borne a near affinity to those of the ancient Egyptians. Their philosophers, unwilling to expose their mysteries to vulgar eyes, couched
their systems . . . under signs and hieroglyphical figures, which
were communicated to their chief priests or Magi alone, who were
bound by solemn oath to conceal them. The system of Pythagoras
was founded on a similar principle. Masonry, however, is not only
the most ancient but the most honourable Society that ever existed

... [p. 69], for it serves to inculcate the principles of piety and virtue ... Let me first to call your attention to the form of the Lodge. It is a regular parallelopipedon, in length from East to West, in breadth between North and South, in depth from the surface of the earth to its centre, and even as high as the heavens ... this is to show the universality of the science, and that a Mason's charity should know no bounds save those of prudence.

"... the four sides of the Lodge point to four different, yet progressive, modes of consciousness ... The 'depth' of the Lodge refers to the distance ... between the earthly ... and divine modes of mentality, and its height, the range of consciousness possible to us ... "[37]

W.M.   Our Lodge stands on holy ground because the first Lodge was consecrated on account of three grand offerings ... First, the ready compliance of Abraham with the will of God in not refusing to offer up his only son Isaac as a burnt sacrifice ... Secondly, the many pious prayers and ejaculations of King David, which actually appeased the wrath of God, and stayed a pestilence which then raged among his people, owing to his inadvertently having had them numbered. Thirdly, the many thanksgivings, oblations, ... and costly offerings which King Solomon made at the completion, consecration, and dedication of the Temple. Those three did then, and I trust ever will, render the groundwork of Freemasonry Holy. [pp. 69–71]

Our Lodge is situated due East and West, because all places of Divine worship are to be so situated; for which we assign three Masonic reasons: First, the Sun, the Glory of the Lord, rises in the East and sets in the West; Second, Learning originated in the East and thence spread to the West; Third, ... is too long to be explained here ... [pp. 71–2]

Our Lodge is supported by three great pillars ... Wisdom, Strength, and Beauty ... the Universe is the Temple of the Deity whom we serve ... [p. 72] The Three Great Pillars are emblematical of these Divine attributes; they further represent Solomon, Hiram, King of Tyre, and Hiram Abiff ... But as we have no noble orders in Architecture known by the names of Wisdom, Strength, and Beauty, we refer then to the three most celebrated, the Doric, Ionic, and Corinthian [pp. 72–3]

The covering of a Masonic Lodge is a celestial canopy of divers colours, even as in heaven. The way by which we, as Masons, hope to arrive at it is by the assistance of a ladder, in Scripture called **Jacob's Ladder** [p. 73][38]

It is composed of many staves or rounds, representing as many moral virtues, but three principal ones are Faith, Hope, and Charity: Faith in the Great Architect of the Universe, Hope in Salvation, and to be in Charity with all men. It reaches to the heavens, and rests on the **Volume of the Sacred Law**, because, by the doctrines contained in that Holy Book, we are taught to believe in the dispensations of Divine providence ... [p. 74]

... figuratively speaking, an ethereal mansion, veiled from mortal eyes by the starry firmament is emblematically depicted here by seven stars, which have an allusion to as many regularly made Masons, without which number no Lodge is perfect, neither can any candidate be legally initiated into Order.

The interior of a Lodge is composed of Ornaments (the Mosaic pavement,[39] the blazing star, and the indented or tesselated border, the skirtwork ...), Furniture (the **Volume of the Sacred Law**, the **Compass,** and the **Square**), and Jewels ... [pp. 74–6]

The Jewels ... are three movable (**Square, Level,** and **Plumb Rule**), and three immovable (the Tracing Board, the Rough Ashlar, the Perfect Ashlar). The **Square** teaches morality, and by it the Master is distinguished. The **Level** teaches equality, and by it the Senior Warden is distinguished. The **Plumb Rule** teaches justness, and by it the Junior Warden is distinguished. The Tracing Board is for the Master to lay lines and draw designs on. The Perfect Ashlar for the Fellow Craft to try and adjust his jewels on. The Rough Ashlar for the Entered Apprentice to work, mark, and indent on. [pp. 76–7]

... As the Tracing Board is for the Master ... so the **Volume of the Sacred Law** may justly be deemed to be the spiritual Tracing Board of the Great Architect of the Universe ... The Rough Ashlar ... represents the mind of man in its infant or primitive state ... The Perfect Ashlar ... represents the mind of a man in his decline of years ... [pp. 78–9]

In all ... constituted Lodges there is a point within a **circle** round which a Mason cannot err; this **circle** is bounded between North and South by two grand parallel lines, the one representing Moses, the other King Solomon; on the upper part of this **circle** rests the **Volume of the Sacred Law**, supporting Jacob's Ladder, the top of which reaches to the heavens ... [pp. 75–9] ... In going round this **circle**, we must of necessity touch on both those lines, . . . so a Mason cannot err.

The word LEWIS denotes strength, and is here depicted by certain pieces of metal dovetailed into a stone, which form a cramp, and enables an operative Mason to raise great weights. Lewis likewise denotes the son of a Mason . . . who bears the heat and burden of the day, from which his aged parents . . . ought to be exempt . . . [p. 80][40]

Pendant to the corners of the Lodge are four tassels . . . to remind us of the four cardinal virtues: Temperance, Fortitude, Prudence, and Justice . . . [pp. 80–1]

A.2.10.
CHARGE AFTER INITIATION

W.M. . . . As a Freemason, I would recommend you to . . . consider the **Volume of the Sacred Law** as . . . the unerring standard of truth and justice, to regulate your actions by the Divine precepts it contains; therein you will be taught the important duties you owe to God, your neighbour, and yourself . . . [p. 84]

As a citizen of the world, I am to enjoin you to be exemplary in the discharge of your civil duties . . . [p. 85]

. . . The three foremost Masonic virtues . . . are Secrecy, Fidelity, and Obedience [p. 86]

"Citizen of the World" means an ordinary person subject to the limitations of his (particular) society and culture; but at the same time it means an extraordinary person, a cosmopolitan Freemason.

B.1.
THE CEREMONY OF OPENING THE LODGE IN THE SECOND DEGREE

[After requesting all below the rank of a Fellow Craft (F.C.) to retire, the W.M. gives one **knock**, which is followed by the Wardens . . . etc.]

W.M. Brother J.W., are you an F.C.?

J.W. I am; try me, and prove me.

W.M. By what instrument will you be proved?

J.W. By **Square** . . . etc.

W.M. Brethren, before we open the Lodge in the Second Degree, let us supplicate the Great Geometrician of the Universe that the rays of heaven may shed their influence, to enlighten us in the paths of vertue and science.

P.M. So mote it be.

W.M.   In the name of the Great Geometrician of the Universe I declare the Lodge duly opened on the **Square**, for the instruction and improvement of Craftsmen. [pp. 7–10]

B.2.
CEREMONY OF PASSING TO THE SECOND DEGREE
B.2.1–2.

[The Lodge is open in the First Degree and the W.M. advises the Brethren and examines the Candidate; he retires to be prepared, and the Lodge is then opened in the Second Degree. When the Candidate is ready, the T. gives the **knocks** of the First Degree, the I.G. advances towards the J.W. with the **step** and **sign**, and says:] "Bro. J.W., there is a report." [the J.W. rises, gives three **knocks** and **sign**, and reports the same to the W.M.]

...I.G.   [To T.] How does the Candidate hope to obtain those privileges?

T.   By the help of God, the assistance of the **Square**, and the benefit of a **Password**.

[The I.G. demands of the Candidate the **pass, grip** and **word**, which he gives him. The I.G. closes the door, advances one pace towards the W.M., and makes the same report...]

...W.M.   ...do you, Bro. I.G., vouch that he is in possession of the **password**?

I.G.   I do, W.M.

[The Candidate is met at the door by the I.G., who applies the external angle of the **Square** to the Candidate's **breast**, and then raises it above his own head, that the W.M. may see he has so applied it. The S.D. then with his left hand takes the right hand of the Candidate, leads him gently to the left of the S.W., and directs him to advance as a Mason.]

W.M.   Let the Candidate **kneel** while the blessing of Heaven is invoked on our proceedings. [pp. 89–91]

B.2.3.
PRAYER

All.   We supplicate the continuance of Thine aid, O merciful Lord, on behalf of ourselves and him who **kneels** before Thee, may the work begun in Thy name, be continued to Thy Glory, and evermore established in us, by obedience to Thy precepts.

P.M.   So mote it be.

W.M.   Let the Candidate rise.

B.2.4.

[The S.D. takes him by the right hand, and gently leads him once round the Lodge, as follows: he directs him to salute the W.M. as a Mason, then he advances to the J.W. as such, showing the **sign** and communicating the **token** and **word**. He then salutes the S.W., and is taken to his left side.] [pp. 91–2]

> W.M.   [**Knocks**, followed by the Wardens] the Brethren will take notice that Bro. A.B. etc. . . . is about to pass in view before them, to show that he is a Candidate properly prepared to be passed to the Second Degree.

[The Candidate is again led round; he salutes the W.M. and J.W. as a Mason, and advances to the S.W. as such; he is then told by the S.D. to show the **sign** and communicate the **passgrip** and **password** he received from the W.M. previous to leaving the Lodge. The S.D. takes him to the other side of the S.W., who presents him to the W.M.]

> S.W.   [Rises, and gives the **sign of fidelity**] W.M., I present to you Bro. A.B., as a Candidate properly prepared to be passed to the Second Degree.
> W.M.   Bro. S.W., you will direct the S.D. to instruct the Candidate to advance to the East by the proper steps.

. . . [The S.D. instructs the Candidate to advance to the pedestal by **five steps**, as if ascending a **stair**; placing the **left** foot pointing to the W.M. and **right foot** to the J.W., and commencing with the **left foot**.]

B.2.5.

> W.M.   Bro. A.B., as in every case the different Degrees of Free-masonry are to be kept separate and distinct, another **Obligation** will now be required of you . . . are you willing to take it?
> Can.   I am.
> W.M.   Then will you **kneel** on your **right knee**, place your **right hand** on the **Volume of the Sacred Law**, while your **left arm** will be supported in the angle of the **Square**; repeat your several names, and say after me, etc. [pp. 92–94]

. . . [The S.D. removes the **Square**.]

B.2.6.

> W.M.   As a pledge of your fidelity . . . you will seal this solemn **Obligation** with your **lips twice** on the **Volume of the Sacred Law**. [Done.] Your progress in Masonry is marked by the position of the **Square** and **Compasses**. When you were made an E.A. both **points** were hidden; in this Degree one is disclosed, implying that

you are now midway in Freemasonry . . . [Takes him by the **right hand**.]

B.2.7.

W.M.   Rise, newly **Obligated** Fellow Craft Freemason [p. 95] . . . Now I shall proceed to entrust you with the **signs** of the Degree. Now you will advance towards me as at your initiation [which he does], now take another short **step** with your **left foot** bringing the **right** heel into its **hollow** as before; that is the second **regular step** in Freemasonry, and it is the position in which the **secrets** of this Degree are communicated. They consist, as in the First Degree, of a **sign**, **token**, and **word**, with this difference, that in this Degree the **sign** is of a threefold character: the first part . . . is called the **sign of fidelity**, and is given by etc. . . . emblematically to shield the repository of your **secrets** from the attacks of the insidious; the second part is called the **Hailing sign**, or **sign of perseverance**, and is given by etc. It took its rise at the time when **Joshua** fought the battles of the Lord in the valley of Jehoshaphat. In this position he prayed fervently to the almighty to continue the light of day, that he might complete the overthrow of his enemies. The third part is called the **penal sign**, and is given by, etc. This, you will perceive, alludes to the **penalty** of your **Obligation** . . . The **grip** or **token** is given by a distinct pressure, etc., this **grip** demands a **word**, a **word** to be given and received with the same strict caution as that in the former Degree; you are never to give it at length, but by, etc. To enable you to do this, I will tell you the **word** which is **JACHIN** [the word is spelt] . . . [pp. 96–7]

. . . W.M.   This **word** is derived from the **right hand pillar** which is in the **porchway** or entrance to **King Solomon's Temple**, so named after **JACHIN** the High Priest, who officiated at its dedication; the import of the word is "to establish", and when conjoined with that in the former Degree, "**stability**", for God said "in **strength** I will establish this mine house to stand firm for ever. Pass, **JACHIN**.

. . . J.W.   I will thank Bro. A.B. to advance to me as a Fellow Craft . . . [Candidate takes **steps** and gives **sign**. J.W. rises with the **sign**.] Have you anything to communicate?

[Candidate gives **grip**, instructed by S.D.]

J.W.   What is this? [p. 98]

S.D.   [For Candidate] the **grip** or **token** of a Fellow Craft.

J.W.   What does this **token** demand?

S.D. A **word**.

J.W. Give me that word. [Done.] etc. [p. 99]

... S.W. What is that?

S.D. The sign of Fidelity, emblematically to shield the repository of my **secrets** from attacks of the insidious.

S.W. Anything else?

S.D. [Gives the **sign**] The **Hailing Sign, or Sign of Perseverance**.

S.W. When did it take its rise? [As before, etc.] ... Anything else?

S.D. [Gives **Penal Sign**] This is the **Penal Sign** of a Fellow Craft. [As before, etc.] [pp. 100–101]

B.2.8.

S.W. By the W.M.'s command I invest you with the distinguishing **badge** of a Fellow Craft ... etc.

W.M. ... and as a Craftsman, you are expected to make the liberal arts and sciences your future study, that you may the better be enabled to discharge your duty as a Mason, and estimate the wonderful works of the Almighty. Bro. S.D., you will place Bro. A.B. at the South-East part of the Lodge.

B.2.9.

W.M. I shall content myself with observing, that as in the former Degree you had an opportunity of making yourself acquainted with the principles of moral truth and virtue, you are now expected to extend your researches into the hidden mysteries of nature and science. [The Candidate is placed by the S.D. in front of the **Pedestal**.] I now present to your notice the working tools of a Fellow Craft, which are the **Square, Level**, and **Plumb Rule** ... The **Square** teaches morality, the **Level** equality, and the **Plumb Rule** justness ... Thus, by **square** conduct, **level** steps, and upright intentions, we hope to ascend to those immortal mansions whence all goodness emanates [pp. 102–4]

The work of the Second Degree is a purely philosophical work, involving deep psychological self-analysis ... and the apprehension of abstract truths.[41]

B.2.10.

EXPLANATION OF THE SECOND TRACING BOARD

W.M. At the Building of the King Solomon's Temple, an immense number of Masons were employed. They consisted of Entered Apprentices and Fellow Crafts. The E.A. received a weekly allowance of Corn, Wine, and Oil; the F.C. were paid their wages in specie . . . in the middle chamber of the Temple; they got there by the **porchway** or entrance at the south side of the building; on entering which **porchway**, their attention was particularly struck by two great pillars, that on the left was called Boaz, which denotes "in **strength**", that on the **right Jachin**, which denotes "**to establish**" . . . for God said "In strength will I establish this mine house to stand firm for ever." The height of those pillars was 35 cubits, the circumference 12, and diameter 4; they were formed hollow, the better to serve as archives to Masonry, for therein were deposited the rolls of constitutions. They were made of molten brass . . . and the superintendent of casting was Hiram Abiff . . . They were placed at the entrance of the Temple, as a memorial to the children of Israel of the miraculous pillar of fire and cloud, which had two wonderful effects; the fire gave light to the Israelites during their escape . . . from Egypt, . . . and the cloud proved darkness to Pharaoh and his followers when they attempted to overtake them . . . after our ancient Brethren had passed those two great pillars, they arrived at the foot of the winding staircase, where their ascent was opposed by the ancient J.W., who demanded of them the **passgrip** and **password** you are already in possession of, and the **password**, I dare say you recollect, is **SHIBBOLETH**; . . . it denotes "**plenty**" and is here depicted by an ear of corn near to a **fall of water**. This word dates its origin from the time that an army of Ephraimites crossed the river Jordan in a hostile manner against Jephtha, the renowned Gileaditish general; the reason they assigned for this unfriendly visit was that they had not been called on to partake of the honours . . . and the rich spoils of the Ammonitish war, with which Jephtha and his army were laden. When Ephraimites. . . broke out into open violence . . . Jephtha . . . drew out his army, gave them battle, defeated and put them to flight, and to secure himself from a like molestation in future, he sent detachments of his army to secure the passage of the River Jordan . . . given strict orders to his guards, that if a fugitive came that way, owning himself an Ephraimite, he should be immediately slain. But if he said nay, or prevaricated, a test **word**, **Shibboleth**, which they, through a defect in aspiration, peculiar to their dialect, could not pronounce properly, but called it **Shibbolet** . . . and there fell on that day in the field of battle and on the banks of the Jordan forty and two thousand Ephraimites. **King Solomon** afterwards caused this **test word** to be adopted in a Fellow Craft Lodge to prevent any unqualified person from ascending the winding staircase, which led to the middle chamber of the Temple. After our ancient Brethren had given those convincing proofs to the J.W., he said "Pass, **Shibboleth**", and they then passed up the winding staircase, consisting of three, five, seven, or more **steps**. Three rule a Lodge (the Worshipful Master and his two Wardens); five hold a Lodge (the Worshipful Master, two Wardens, and two Fellow Crafts); seven make it perfect (the same to whom two Apprentices are added). Three are also three Grand Masters who presided at the building of the Temple: King Solomon, King of Tyre Hiram, and Hiram Abiff. Five are also five orders of Architecture. Seven also means seven years before the completion of the Temple, and seven liberal arts and sciences.

After our ancient Brethren had gained the summit of the winding staircase, they found the door of the middle chamber open, but properly tyled by the S.W., against all under their Degree; he demanded of them the **sign**, **token**, and **word** of a Fellow Craft, and then said, "Pass, **Jachin**" ... When our ancient Brethren were in the middle chamber, their attention was particularly drawn to certain Hebrew characters, which are here depicted by the letter G, which denotes God, the Great Geometrician of the Universe ... whom we ought humbly to adore. [pp. 105–12][42]

C.1.1.

The ceremony of Opening the Lodge in the Third Degree. [After requesting all below the rank of a Master Mason (M.M.) to retire. the W.M. gives one **knock**, which is followed by the Wardens (starts as before ...)]

W.M.   Brother J.W., are you a Master Mason?
J.W.   Try me, and prove me ...
W.M.   By what instruments ... will you be proved?
J.W.   The Square and Compasses.
W.M.   Brother J.W., as a M.M., whence come you?
J.W.   From the East.
W.M.   Bro. J.W., whither directing your course?
J.W.   To the West.
W.M.   Why ... have you to leave the East and go to the West?
J.W.   To seek for that which was lost, which, by your instruction, we hope to find ... the genuine secrets of a Master Mason.
W.M.   How came they lost?
J.W.   By the untimely death of our Master Hiram Abiff.
W.M.   Where do you hope to find them?

J.W.   In the centre.

W.M.   Why?

J.W.   That being a point from which a M.M. cannot err.

W.M.   Brethren, we will assist you to repair that loss, and may heaven aid our united endeavours.

P.M.   So mote it be.

W.M.   I declare the Lodge duly opened, on the Centre in the Third Degree ... [pp. 11–15]

C.1.2.

Questions which must be answered by Candidates before Raising [The Lodge being open in the Second Degree ...]

W.M.   Brethren, Bro. A.B. is this evening a Candidate to be raised to the Sublime Degree of a M.M. ... I shall proceed to put the necessary questions (concerning his previous degree, etc.).

[The S.D. places the Candidate at the left of the **pedestal** of the S.W. facing the W.M.]
   ... [The S.D. takes the Candidate by the right hand to the door, and directs him to advance and salute the W.M. as an F.C. He then retires to be prepared. Here follows the Ceremony of Raising to the Third Degree.] [pp. 37–40]

C.2.

CEREMONY OF RAISING TO THE THIRD DEGREE

[When the Candidate is ready, the T. gives the **knocks of the Second Degree**, the I.G. advances towards the J.W. with **the step** and **penal sign** of a M.M., and says: "Bro. J.W., there is a report"; the J.W. rises, gives three **knocks** with a **sign**, and reports the same to the W.M.]

C.2.1.

W.M.   [to J.W.] Bro. J.W., inquire who wants admission.

J.W.   Bro. I.G., see who seeks admission. [The I.G. opens the door, and asks the T. whom he has there.]

T.   Bro. A.B., who has been regularly initiated into Freemasonry, passed the Degree of an F.C., and has made such progress as he hopes will entitle him to be **raised** ...

I.G.   [To T.] How does he hope to obtain those privileges?

T.   By the help of God, the united aid of the **square** and **compasses**, and the benefit of a **password**.

[The I.G. demands of the Candidate the **passgrip** and **password**, which he gives him. The I.G. closes the door, advances one pace towards the W.M., and makes the same report to him.]

W.M.   Then let him be admitted in due form, Brothers Deacons.

C.2.2.

[The Candidate is met at the door by the I.G., who applies the **points** of the **compasses** to both **breasts** of the Candidate, and then raises them above his own head, to show that he has so applied them. The Deacons . . . then gently lead the Candidate to the left of the S.W., and the S.D. directs him to advance towards the W.M., first as an E.A., and then as an F.C.]

W.M.   Let the Candidate kneel, while the blessing of Heaven is invoked on our proceedings.

C.2.3.

PRAYER

W.M.   Almighty and Eternal God! Architect and ruler of the Universe, at whose creative **fiat** all things first were made, we, the frail creatures of Thy providence, humbly implore Thee to pour down on this convocation assembled in **Thy Holy Name** the continual dew of Thy blessing . . . We beseech Thee to impart Thy Grace to this Thy servant, who offers himself to partake of the mysterious secrets of a M.M. Endue him with such fortitude that in the hour of trial he fail not, but pass him safely under Thy protection through the **valley of the shadow of death**, that he may finally **arise** from the **tomb of transgression** to shine as the stars for ever and ever.

P.M.   So mote it be.

W.M.   Let the Candidate rise.

C.2.4.

[The Deacons gently lead the Candidate three times round the Lodge . . . ; the first time he salutes the W.M. as a Mason, advances to the J.W. as such, showing the sign and communicating the **token** and **word**, and salutes the S.W. as a Mason. The second time he salutes the W.M. as a F.C., advances to the S.W. as such, showing the **sign** and communicating the **token** and **word** of that Degree. He is then brought to the left of the S.W.]

W.M.   The Brethren will take notice that Bro. A.B. . . . . regularly initiated into Masonry, passed the degree of an F.C., and . . . is properly prepared to be raised to the sublime Degree of a M.M.

[In going round the third time, he salutes the W.M. and J.W. as such, showing the sign and communicating the **passgrip** and **password** he received from the W.M. previous to leaving the Lodge. He is then brought round to the left of the S.W. The S.W. rises, and, with the **penal sign**, takes the right hand of the Candidate and presents him to the W.M. as follows:]

S.W.   W.M., I present to you Bro. A.B., as a Candidate properly prepared to be raised . . . etc.

W.M.   Bro. S.W., you will direct the S.D. to instruct the Candidate to advance to the East by the proper steps . . .

[The S.D. stands opposite the W.M. and instruct the Candidate that the method of advancing from West to East is by **seven steps**, the first three as though stepping over a new-made **grave**, the other four regular; he then goes through them, and after placing the Candidate in the proper position, teaches him to do likewise.]

W.M.   Bro. A.B., . . . a most serious trial of your fortitude and fidelity, as well as a most solemn **Obligation** awaits you. Are you prepared . . . ?

Can.   I am.

W.M.   Then you will kneel on both knees, place both hands on the **Volume of the Sacred Law**, repeat your **several names** at length, and say after me:

C.2.5.

OBLIGATION

W.M.   I, A.B., in the presence of the Most High, and of this worthy, worshipful and warranted Lodge of Master Masons, duly constituted, regularly assembled, and properly dedicated, of my own free will and accord, do hereby and heaven-most solemnly and sincerely promise and swear, that I will always hide, conceal, and never reveal any or either of the secrets or mysteries of or belonging to the Degree of a Master-Mason to anyone in the world, unless it be to him or them to whom the same may justly and lawfully belong; and not even to him or them, until after due trial, strict examination, or full conviction that he or they are worthy of that confidence, or in the body of a Master Masons' Lodge, duly opened on the centre. I further solemnly pledge myself to adhere to the **principles of the Square** and **Compasses**, to answer and obey all lawful **signs** and summonses which I may receive from a Master Masons' Lodge if within the length of my **cable-tow**, and to plead no excuse save sickness or the pressing emergency of my own public or private evocations.[43] I further solemnly engage myself to maintain and uphold the **Five Points of Fellowship** in act as well as in word, that my hand given to a Master Mason shall be the sure pledge of brotherhood, that my feet shall traverse through dangers and difficulties together with his in forming a column of mutual defence and support, that the posture of my daily supplications shall remind me of his wants, and dispose my heart to succour his weakness and relieve his necessities, as far as may fairly be done without detriment to myself or connections; that my breast shall be the sacred repository of his secrets when entrusted to my care, murder, treason, felony, and all other offences contrary to the laws of God and the ordinances of the realm excepted; and, finally, I will maintain a Master Mason's honour, and carefully preserve it as my own ... So help me the Most High, and keep me steadfast in this my solemn Obligation of a Master Mason.

C.2.6.

W.M. [to Candidate] As a pledge of your fidelity, and to render this binding as a solemn Obligation so long as you shall live, you will seal it with your **lips** three times on the **Volume of the Sacred Law**. [And after the Candidate having done it] Let me once more call your attention to the position of the **Square** and **the Compasses**; when you were made an E.A. both **points** were hid, in the Second Degree one was disclosed, in this the whole is exhibited, implying that you are now at liberty to work with both these **points** in order to render the circle of your Masonic duties complete. [Takes him by both **hands**.] Rise, duly **Obligated** Master Mason.

C.2.7.

THE EXHORTATION

W.M. Bro. A.B., having taken the solemn **Obligation** of a Master Mason, you are now entitled to demand that last and greatest trial, by which means alone can you be admitted to a participation in the secrets of the Third Degree ... Your admission into Freemasonry in a state of helpless indigence, was an emblematical representation of the entrance of all men on this their mortal existence, it inculcated the ... lessons of natural equality and mutual dependence, it instructed you in the active principles of universal beneficence and charity ... but above all it taught you to bend with humility and resignation to the will of the Great Architect of the Universe, to dedicate your heart, purified from every baneful and malignant passion, fitted only for the reception of truth and wisdom, to His Glory and the Welfare of your fellow creatures. Then ... guiding your progress by the principles of moral truth, you were led in the Second Degree to contemplate the intellectual faculties, and to trace their development through the paths of Heavenly science, even to the throne of God himself. The secrets of nature and the principles of intellectual truth were then unveiled to your view. To a mind, thus modelled by virtue and science, nature, however, presents one great and useful lesson more, she prepares you, by contemplation, for the closing hour of existence ... and finally instructs you **how to die**. Such, my Brother, **is the peculiar object**[44] of the Third Degree ... it invites you to reflect on this awful subject, and teaches you ... that to the just and virtuous man death has no terrors equal to the stain of falsehood and dishonour; of this great truth the annals of Freemasonry afford a glorious example in the ... noble death of our Master, **Hiram Abiff,** who was **slain** just before the completion of **King Solomon's** Temple ... Brother Wardens! [The Wardens advance noiselessly. The S.W. stands on the left of the Candidate, the J.W. on his right.]

"Hence the Third Degree is that of mystical death, of which bodily death is taken as figurative".[45]

C.2.8.

W.M.   Fifteen Fellow Crafts, seeing that the Temple was nearly completed, and that they were not in possession of the **secrets** of the Master Mason, conspired together to obtain them by any means, and even to have recourse to violence; on the eve of carrying their conspiracy into execution, twelve of the fifteen recanted, but three of a more determined and atrocious character than the rest persisted in their impious design ... They placed themselves respectively at the East, North and South entrances of the Temple whither our Master Hiram had retired to pay his adoration to the Most high, as was his wonted custom at the hour of high twelve. His devotions being ended our Master attempted to return by the South entrance, where he was opposed by the first ruffian, who, armed with a **Plumb Rule**, demanded of our Master the secrets of his exalted Degree, threatening him with ... death; but our Master ... answered that he ... neither could nor would divulge them, but intimated that he had no doubt that patience and industry would in due time entitle the worthy Mason to a participation of them, but for his own part he would rather suffer death than betray the sacred trust reposed in him ... The ruffian aimed a violent blow at the **head** of our Master, but being startled by the firmness of his demeanour, it missed his **forehead**, but glanced with such force over his **right temple** [hence the S.W. may touch the Candidate's **right temple** with the **Plumb Rule**] as to cause him to reel and sink on his **left knee** [here the Candidate may sink on his left knee]. Recovering from this shock, our Master made for the North entrance, where he was accosted by the second ruffian, to whom he gave a similar answer and who, being armed with a **level**, smote him a violent blow on his **left temple**, which brought him to the ground on his **right knee** [here the Candidate may sink on his **right knee**]. Our Master, finding all chance of escape cut off at both those points, staggered faint and bleeding to the East entrance, where the third ruffian armed with a heavy **Maul** ... to whom he gave the same answer ... struck him a violent blow on the **forehead**, which laid him **lifeless** at his feet.

Brethren, throughout this ceremony ... our Brother has been made to represent **Hiram Abiff**, who lost his life in consequence of his unshaken fidelity ... and I hope this will make a lasting impression on his and your minds, should you ever be placed in a similar state of trial.

W.M.   Bro. J.W., endeavour to raise the representative of our Master by the Entered Apprentice's **grip** [which he does, and reports, with **penal sign.**]

J.W.   W.M., it proves a **slip**.

W.M.   Bro. S.W., try that of the Fellow Craft's [which he does, and reports, with **penal sign.**]

S.W.   W.M., it proves a **slip**.

W.M.   Brother Wardens, having both of you failed in your endeavour, there yet remains a third method, which is by taking a firm hold of the **sinews of** the hand **raising** him on the **Five Points of Fellowship**, which with your assistance I will now make trial of. [He leaves the chair from the left, and they raise the Candidate.]

... [to Candidate] It is thus, my Brother, that all Master Masons are **raised** from a figurative **death** to a reunion with the former companions of their former toils.

[The W.M. still standing, delivers the following charge, the Wardens taking their seats.]

C.2.9.

CHARGE

W.M.   Let me now beg of you to observe, that **the light of a M.M. is but darkness visible, serving only to express that gloom which**

rests on the prospects of futurity; it is that mysterious veil which the eye and human reason cannot penetrate, unless assisted by that light which is from above; yet even by this glimmering ray you may perceive that you stand on the very brink of the **grave**, into which you have just figuratively descended, and which, when this transitory life shall have passed away, will receive you into its cold bosom; let the emblems of mortality which lie around you lead you to contemplate on your inevitable destiny, and guide your reflections to that most interesting of all human studies, the knowledge of yourself. Be careful to perform your allotted task while it is yet day, continue to listen to the voice of nature, which bears witness that even in this perishable frame there resides a vital and an immortal principle, which inspires a holy confidence that **the Lord of Life** will enable us to trample the king of terrors beneath our feet, and lift our eyes to that bright morning star, whose rising brings peace and salvation to the faithful and obedient of the human race. [He takes **left** hand of Candidate, and gently moves round towards the **left**, until they occupy each other's place. Then continues.]

I cannot better reward the attention you have paid to this exhortation and charge, than by entrusting you with the **secrets** of this Degree. You will therefore advance to me as an F.C., first an E.A. [which is done by the Candidate]; now take another short step with your **left foot**, bringing the **right heel** into its hollow as before – that, my Brother, is the third regular step in Freemasonry, and is the position in which the **secrets** of the Master's Degree are communicated; they consist of **signs**, a **token**, and **words**; of the **signs**, the first and second are **casual**, and the third is **penal**. The first **casual sign** is called **the sign of horror**, and may be taken from the Fellow-Craft's **sign** (Stand to order as a Fellow Craft) by dropping, etc. etc., as if **struck** with **horror** at a **dreadful** and **afflicting sight**. The second **casual sign** is called the **sign of sympathy**, and is given by **smiting the forehead** gently with **the palm of the right hand**, etc.; the **penal sign** is given by drawing the **hand** across the **body**, etc. The **grip** or **token** is the first of the **Five Points of Fellowship** ... which are **Hand to Hand, Foot to Foot, Knee to Knee, Breast to Breast**, and **Hand over Back**, and may be thus briefly explained: with the first I greet you as a Brother; with the second I will support you in all your lawful undertakings; the third is the posture of my daily supplications that shall remind me of your wants; the fourth means that a Brother's lawful secrets when entrusted to my care I will preserve as my own; and the fifth means that I will support your character in your absence as in your presence. It is in this position ... only, that the **words** of a Master Mason are given, and then only in **a whisper**; is **M...N**, or **M...A**; both **words** having nearly a similar import. The one signifying the **death of the Brother**, the other, that the **Brother is slain**.[46]

Now you are at liberty to retire ... and on your return to the Lodge, those **casual signs**, **token**, and **words** will be further explained.

C.2.10.

[The Deacons take their wands and conduct the Candidate to the door; he gives the **penal sign** on retiring from the lodge; on his return he is taken to the left of the S.W. and directed to salute the W.M. properly.]

S.W.   W.M., I present to you Bro. A.B., on his being raised to the sublime Degree of a Master Mason, for some further mark of your favour.

W.M.   Bro. S.W., I delegate you to invest Bro. A.B. with the distinguished **badge** of a Master Mason.

C.2.11.

... [The Deacons place the Candidate before the W.M.]

W.M.   Bro. A.B. .... on your leaving the Lodge, we left off at that part of our traditional history which mentions the **death** of our Master **Hiram Abiff**; ... The Menatschim, or Prefects ... or overseers of the work, acquainted King Solomon with the utter confusion into which the absence of **Hiram Abiff** had plunged them ... King Solomon immediately ordered a general muster of the workmen throughout the various departments, when three of the same class ... were not to be found. On the same day the twelve who had originally joined the conspiracy went before the King and made a ... confession of all they knew ... Then he selected fifteen trusty Fellow-Crafts, and ordered them to go and make a diligent search after the person of our Master ... They formed themselves into three Fellow Crafts' **Lodges** and departed from the three entrances of the Temple; many days were spent in fruitless search; indeed one class returned to Jerusalem without finding him ...; but a second were more fortunate, for on the evening of a certain day ... one of the Brethren rested himself in a reclining posture, in order to assist his rising caught hold of a shrub that grew near, which, to his surprise, came easily out of the ground;

on a closer examination he found that the earth had been recently disturbed, hailed his Brethren, and with their united effort reopened the ground, and there found the body of our Master very indecently interred. They covered it again with all respect and reverence, and to distinguish the spot, stuck a sprig of **Acacia** at the head of the **grave**, and they hastened to Jerusalem to impart the afflicting intelligence to King Solomon, who ordered them immediately to return and raise the body of our Master to such a sepulchre as became then his exalted talents. At the same time the King informed them that by Hiram Abiff's untimely death the **secrets** of a Master Mason were lost, and charged them to be particularly careful in observing whatever casual **sign**, **token**, or **word** might occur amongst them, while paying this last sad office of respect to departed merit ... At the moment of reopening the ground, one of the Brethren, looking round, saw one of his companions in this situation [he gives the **sign** of **horror**] expressing his **horror** at the afflicting sight, and others, viewing the ghastly **wound**, still visible on his **forehead**, smote their own in sympathy with his sufferings. Two of the Brethren then descended the **grave**, and one of them endeavoured to raise the body by the Entered **Apprentice's grip**, which proved a **slip**; the other then tried the **Fellow Craft's grip**, which proved a **slip** also; having both failed in their attempts, a more zealous and expert Brother took a **firm hold** of the **sinews** of the **hand**, and with their assistance, raised him on the **Five Points of Fellowship**, while others ... exclaimed **M...N** or **M...A** – both words of nearly a similar import: the one "**the death of the Builder**", the other "**the Builder is smitten**". King Solomon ordered that those **casual signs**, **tokens**, and **words** should designate all Master Masons throughout the world, **until time or circumstances should restore the genuine ones**. It only remains for me to state that the third class of craftsmen ... accidentally passing the mouth of a cavern, heard sounds of lamentation and deep regret. On entering the cave ... they found three missing craftsmen who ... confessed their guilt. They were then bound and led back to Jerusalem, where King Solomon sentenced them to death ...

[Continues] Our Master was ordered to be re-interred as near the Sanctum Sanctorum as the Israelitish law would permit, there in a **grave**, from the centre, three feet East, three feet West, three feet between North and South, and five feet or more from the perpendicular. He was not buried in the Sanctum Sanctorum, because nothing common or unclean was suffered to enter there, except the High Priest once a year, and not then until after many washings and purifications against the great day of expiations of sins, for by the Israelitish law all flesh was deemed unclean. Fellow Crafts were ordered to attend the funeral, clothed in **white aprons** and **gloves**, as emblems of their innocence.

You have already been informed of the **Working Tools** with which our Master Hiram was slain: **Plumb, Level** and **heavy Maul**. The ornaments of a Master Masons' Lodge are the Porch (the entrance to the Sanctum Sanctorum), Dormer (the window that gives light to the same), and Square Pavement (for the High Priest to walk on). The High Priest's office was to burn incense . . . to the Most High, and to pray fervently that the Almighty, through His unbounded wisdom and goodness, would be pleased to bestow peace . . . on the Israelitish nation, during the ensuing year. The Coffin, Skull, and Cross-bones, being emblems of mortality allude to the untimely death of our Master Hiram. He was slain 3,000 years from the creation of the world [the foregoing may also be considered explanatory of the Third Tracing Board.]

You have already been informed of three **signs** in this Degree; the whole of them are five, corresponding to the **Five Points of Fellowship**. They are: **the sign of horror, the sign of sympathy, the penal sign, the sign of grief and distress**, and the sign of **Joy and Exultation**, likewise called the **Grand** or **Royal sign**. For your information, I will go through them, and you will please copy me [he shows the **signs**]. This is the **sign of horror**, that of **sympathy**. This is the **penal sign. The sign of grief and distress** is given by passing **the hand** over the **forehead** in this manner; it took its rise . . . when our Master was making his way from the North to the East entrance of the Temple, when his agonies were so great that the perspiration stood in large drops on his forehead, and he made use of this **sign** as a temporary relief . . . This is the **sign of Joy and Exultation**, likewise called the **Grand or Royal sign**; it took its rise . . . when the Temple was finished . . . and King Solomon and the Princes . . . went to view it . . . and were so struck with its magnificence, that . . . exclaimed, Oh Wonderful Masons! . . . On the Continent, **the sign of grief and distress** is given . . . by interlacing the fingers **and raising** the hands to the **forehead**, exclaiming, "Come to my assistance, ye children of the widow!"' (. . . for all Master Masons are Brethren to Hiram Abiff who was the son of the widow).[47] . . . The working tools of a Master Mason are **Skirret,**

Pencil, and **Compass** . . . but as we are not all operative but rather speculative or free and accepted Masons, we apply these tools to our morals. So . . . **the Skirret** points out that straight and undeviating line of conduct laid down in our pursuit of the Virtue; the **Pencil** teaches us that our words and actions are observed and recorded by the Almighty Architect . . . ; and **the Compass** reminds us of His unerring and impartial justice . . . in defining for our instruction the limits of good and evil . . . Thus the Working Tools of a Master Mason teach us to bear in mind and to act according to the laws of our divine Creator, so that when we shall be summoned from this sublunary abode, we may ascend to the Grand Lodge above, where the world's great Architect lives and reigns for ever.

End of the ceremony of raising to the Third Degree. [pp. 113–45][48]

Notes

1 W. L. Wilmshurst, *The Meaning of Masonry*, London, 1932 [W. L. Wilmshurst, 1932 (1922)], p. 9.

2 From my fifth conversation with Dr Lovin. I had the good luck to meet him after his return from the concentration camps, where he spent about twenty years, in three instalments: 1929–34, 1938–45, and 1946–54. He told me that during all that time he had not met a single Mason. Nor had he ever been asked about Masonry or Masons by any of his CK, OGPU, NKVD, or KGB interrogators.

3 In other words, history becomes a kind of myth in a ritual, where from it may emerge again as a kind of history by means of a historical reconstruction. This process is brilliantly shown in C. S. Lewis's novel, *Till We Have Faces*.

4 The word "generation" here implies at least two different procedures closely associated with one another. The first is that within the *ethos* of a ritual it is the ritual that determines the place and significance of an idea or a symbol, not the other way around. The second is that when we analyse the whole phenomenon of Masonry into "religion", "ethics", "history" and "ritual" as separate and simultaneously existing, or synchronic elements of its structure, it is again the Ritual of Masonry which determines the relation of all these elements to each other. In saying this I am aware of the similarity of my approach to ritual to some of the gnostical and neo-platonic ideas and to the conception of F. Staal. See Frits Staal, *Rules Without Meaning*, Peter Lang, New York, 1989.

5 *The Perfect Ceremonies of Craft Masonry* . . . as taught in the Union's Emulation Lodge of Improvement for Master Masons, Freemasons' Hall, London, 1874 (The Perfect Ceremonies, 1874).

6 The Worshipful Master says: "Let the *emblems* of mortality which lie around you lead you to contemplate on your inevitable destiny . . .", *idem*, p. 131.

7 I repeat: all that is done is in square brackets, and all "secret" words are bold.

Some symbological commentaries will be given in the Notes, though sometimes explanations are included in the main text.

8 *Knock* here is an emblem of his will over the Lodge. More generally speaking, a knock measures the time (and rhythm) of the ritual. A knock is not a sign, technically speaking, and this is stressed in several Masonic manuals.

9 *Gavel*: "the emblem of Master's authority and of the 3rd degree in general." Arthur Edward Waite, *A New Encyclopaedia of Freemasonry*, William Rider, London, 1921, Vol. I, p. xvii. "It is not to be confounded with a *mallet*, also employed by many masters as their emblem," pp. 110–11. It is also "one of the working tools of an Entered Apprentice . . . and a symbol of divesting our minds of all the vices and impurities, and an emblematic instrument of maintaining the order in the Lodge." Albert G. Mackey, *A Lexicon of Freemasonry*, sixth ed., London, 1873, p. 113.

10 W. L. Wilmshurst, 1932, p. 91.

11 ". . . the seven officers typify the following sevenfold parts of the human mechanism: W.M. – Spirit (Pneuma); S.W. – Soul (Psyche); J.W. – Mind (Nous); S.D. – The link between Spirit and Soul; J.D. – The link between Soul and Mind; I.G. – The inner sense–nature (astral); T. – The outer sense–nature (physical)." W. L. Wilmshurst, 1932, p. 106.

12 Though all these matters are obviously external to the Ritual, they are related to it not only by the ceremonial character of their performance, but also through their being referred to within square brackets in the manual. The reader has already noticed that so far we have had the following secret words: "knock", "to knock", "gavel", and "Hiram". Let me remind the reader that in the case of admission the decision taken by the Brethren should be unanimous – this is one other "outer" formality.

13 And "a turning away from the pursuit of the *popular* ideas . . ." W. L. Wilmshurst, 1932, pp. 10, 11.

14 The preparation of a candidate, here only referred to, constitutes the preliminary stage of the Inner (secret) Ritual.

15 *Kick*: here the word denotes a movement of the body, as distinct from gestures and signs (see above, note 8).

16 *Sign*: here a sign by gesture. The reader is advised not to seek for logical consistency in the use of such terms as "sign", "emblem", "gesture", "movement", etc., for they are used here merely technically.

17 That is, the "natural darkness" of "pre-Masonic" ignorance of the candidate.

18 *Poniard* here is an instrument of initiation and an emblem of danger ("initiatory danger").

19 *Left breast* here emblematically is the "feeling" or "understanding" of the candidate.

20 *Kneeling stool* is the emblem of obedience.

21 *Right hand* is an emblem of fidelity. A. G. Mackay, 1873, pp. 290–1.

22 *Irregular step*: a specifically Masonic step. Ritual manuals and Masonic encyclopedias and dictionaries specifically avoid its description.

23 W. L. Wilmshurst, 1932, p. 29. "In the West" means "in this world", and also "in the world of reason". North symbolizes the sense, and South "intellectual activity". *Idem*, p. 93.

24 *Square* is usually referred to as a *symbol*, i.e. not as an emblem. See in *Kenning's Masonic Cyclopaedia*, ed. by A. F. A. Woodford, London, 1878, p. 603.

25 "... It is my intention to diffuse all explanatory light, *not* strictly forbidden, respecting this ancient and mysterious Society". In: H. Saddler, *Thomas Dunckerley, His Life, Labours and Letters*, London, 1891 (H. Sadler, 1891), p. 154. Here, the "double pattern" common to mystical teachings, is quite transparent: two darknesses, two lights, everlasting duality of "exoteric/esoteric", the constant interplay of the exoteric and esoteric meanings of the same words, etc.

26 *Idem*, p. 156. Almost everything is symbolic here. The only difference between symbolic and non-symbolic things is that now, at this very moment, the first symbolize something else and the latter don't. But the next moment they do!

27 *Lesser light*, i.e. "Three candles placed in a Masonic Lodge, east, south, and west respectively." *Kenning's Masonic Cyclopaedia*, 1878, p. 419. These candles represent emblematically the Sun, the Moon, and the Master of the Lodge.

28 *Cable-taw* with a noose about your neck is a typical example of Masonic *initiatory symbolism*. A. F. A. Woodford writes: "this is a common Masonic expression, which for many reasons we do not deem it well to dilate on here." *Kenning's Masonic Cyclopaedia*, 1878, p. 91. In a later work the "definition" is even more enigmatic: "The length of a Master Mason's Cable-Tow, or the distance within which attendance at his Lodge is obligatory, is usually stated to be three miles." E. L. Hawkins, *A Concise Cyclopaedia of Freemasonry*, 1908, pp. 42–3.

29 "The Level morally teaches us ... the equality of our nature ... that we are equally born to act our parts in this great *theatre* of life". H. Sadler, 1891, p. 155.

30 A. F. A. Woodford (*Kenning's Masonic Cyclopaedia*, 1878, p. 557) simply states that "Perpendicular has also an allegorical and moral teaching in Freemasonry", while in our text it figures as a *sign of recognition*. The only thing that can be asserted with certainty, then, is that this term should be regarded as having two meanings, external and internal.

31 *Regular Step*: Note that unlike an *Irregular Step*, a Regular Step is described here, though without its symbolic meaning.

32 *Strength* is, figuratively, one of the *Supports of the Lodge*. *Kenning's Masonic Cyclopaedia*, 1878, pp. 605, 606.

33 *Badge*: Apron.

34 The exact location of the cornerstone is still a highly debatable matter. In some of the ancient urban civilizations it is the location of the cornerstone sacrifices that determines its place.

35 *Common Gavel*, according to *Kenning's Masonic Cyclopaedia*, 1878, p. 127, is the same as *Gavel* (see above, note 9).

36 *Tracing Board*: "primarily the depicting of the plan of a Lodge with all its symbols and degrees on a piece of linen which could be spread out when required and rolled up when not in use ... Then gradually the design on the floorcloth was transferred to the Tracing Board proper." E. L. Hawkins, 1908, pp. 235–6. A. F. A. Woodford summarizes it a little differently (*Kenning's Masonic Cyclopaedia*, 1878, p. 619): "it was the wooden board on which the Master Mason drew the designs for the operative Masons ... Now there are tracing Boards for the three grades of speculative Masonry, and they contain emblematical representations of the teaching and tradition of each grade."

37 W. L. Wilmshurst, 1932, pp. 93–4. This, I stress, is again an example of an individual explanation of symbolism of the Lodge.

38 *Jacob's Ladder*, referring to Jacob's vision (Genesis, XXVIII) is symbolically

interpreted by A. E. Waite (1921, Vol. I, p. 271) as a representation of "the hier-archic scale of correspondence between things above and things below; between faith in the Great Architect of the Universe and union of the soul with God at Great height . . ." According to A. F. A. Woodford (*Kenning's Masonic Cyclopaedia*, 1878, pp. 348–9), this symbol was introduced into Craft Masonry about 1776 by Th. Dunckerley who probably took it from Chevalier A. M. Ramsay's Higher Degrees. The usual formulation of its symbolic function is that "The Angels go up and down (by that Ladder's steps in vertue of a general '*bond of amity*')."

39 "The floor, or groundwork of the Lodge, a chequer-work of black and white squares, denotes the dual quality of . . . terrestrial life and . . . human nature – good and evil, positive and negative." W. L. Wilmshurst, 1932, p. 96.

40 *Lewis* as a building technical term denotes a heavy lifting device consisting of "an iron clamp inserted in a large stone, in a prepared cavity, for the purpose of attaching it to a pulley, so that it may be raised to its proper elevation or carted away." (*Kenning's Masonic Cyclopaedia*, 1878, pp. 421–2). Its general Masonic meaning is the name of the eldest son of a Mason (or Mason's widow) or a deno-tation for candidates for Masonic initiation.

41 W. L. Wilmshurst, 1932, p. 120.

42 The text of the Second Tracing Board (B.2.10) is a typical case of the explanation of a particular *ritual* within that very ritual. Furthermore, it explains the origin, function, structure, and interior of the Lodge, as well as the meaning of the signs, tokens, and words used in the Lodge in terms of several biblical plots which have no ritual significance in their primary biblical context. Within the context of Masonic ritual, however, these plots acquire a new theme – the Lodge – which means that we deal here with legend rather than with myth. I distinguish between legend and myth in the following way: a legend represents a kind of quasi-history, a concrete, if invented, connection with a specific past, through the deeds of specific individuals; a myth, by contrast, is always something essentially atemporal and universal, and, as such, transcends the activities of its protagonists.

43 This unequivocal declaration of the right of a Mason to place his public duty before his private Masonic obligation gives the lie to the claim that Masons are bound by oath first and foremost to one another at the expense of their duties as citizens. Any Mason who chooses to subordinate his "public evocations" to Masonic loyalty follows his own conscience and not the official line.

44 The *peculiar object* here is a *corpse* as a concrete manifestation of mortality.

45 W. L. Wilmshurst, 1932, p. 126. This is the limit of presenting anything as figurative of anything else. More about this in the section on Double Mythology.

46 "It is the loss of the Word, the Divine Logos, or basic root of . . . our own being. In other words, the soul of man has ceased to be God-conscious and has degenerated into the limited terrestrial consciousness of the ordinary human being." *Idem*, p. 130.

47 Son of the Widow is, therefore, another general designation of a Mason.

48 "It may be stated, however, that this ceremony alone constitutes the Masonic Initiation. The First and Second Degrees are, strictly, the preparatory stages leading up to Initiation; they are not the Initiation itself." *Idem*, p. 132.

CHAPTER 11

Ritual and Instruction

Then I realized for the first time what word-and-gesture-perfect Ritual can be brought to mean.
Brother Rudyard Kipling, *In the Interests of the Brethren*[1]

The Ritual of Freemasonry possesses its own objectivity. This simply means that all possible differences in the intentions, characters and consciousnesses of its performers notwithstanding, it remains materially the same, not only throughout its historical existence as an event repeated on numerous concrete occasions, but also as an abstract object of reflection. I may or may not know its meaning or meanings and my knowledge of it may or may not coincide with that of other persons; it may be close to or far from the objectivity of the Ritual itself, but nevertheless this knowledge of mine remains dependent not only on my cultural background but, in the first place on my intentions which give it a particular purpose. It depends, in other words, on my own states of consciousness which render it subjective and determine the character and direction of that subjectivity.[2] And it is to this subjective knowledge that the Ritual is opposed as an absolutely objective thing, the meaning of which may be known in numerous different ways, if indeed, it is known at all. This is true of all rituals proper.[3]

To understand the extent and degree of one's subjectivity as regards the Ritual we may start by addressing ourselves to the whole spectrum of general opinion about it, ranging from ". . . hundreds of thousands of men suffering the indignities of Masonic initiations . . ." and "the Master Mason's ordeal",[4] through ". . . The Masonic Ritual makes me feel (when I take part in it as a J.W.) stabler and nicer than anything else . . .",[5] to "our only link to the eternal, the Divine tradition of Spirit".[6] General opinion, however, although thematically directed by and towards the Ritual is expressed from the standpoint of, say, ethics or external theology, or simply one's personal response, but usually not from the standpoint of the Ritual itself. The last includes all its material (visual, audible, etc.) instruments and many other things, and also all expositions and interpretations, which, after having been generated by it, become *ritualized* and themselves form a special and highly technical part of the Ritual. They range from quite concrete explanations of meanings of words and elementary objects to the very complex and abstract interpretations of the meanings and purposes of the whole Ritual. So, the Ritual of Freemasonry not only does and speaks, but it also speaks of what it does and speaks. More than that, diverse elements of the ritual are at various stages interpreted differently, so that there is a hierarchy of levels of interpretation. This, in turn, necessitates the formation and development of a very precise technical language or meta-language by means of which the Ritual describes itself in words, terms, and expressions, the meanings of which very often differ from their ordinary meanings given in the dictionary, as well as those words, terms and expressions that are peculiar to Masonry and are not to be found in any ordinary dictionary.

The knowledge of what is seen, heard, spoken and done within the Ritual – of all that is described in the Manual/Chapter 10 – is itself a ritual knowledge, and as such constitutes a part of the ritual. But the epistemology of the Ritual cannot stop there for, as it has more than once been suggested by luminaries of Masonic thought, there can be another kind of knowledge which is supposed to grasp the cosmic meaning of the Ritual, and not only its macrocosmic meaning for those who actively or passively participate in it. This meaning which, according to one of them, "is left entirely unexpounded ... and unrealized by Masons",[7] and according to another is ". . . *the undeclared purpose*, which is justified by the content of the Rites",[8] seems to transcend the sphere of the Ritual. It goes beyond that which is known about the Ritual within the Ritual itself and cannot be covered by its self-description since, as another author explains, "it is not about the ends of beings, but about the End of Being".[9] This other transcendental Masonic knowledge seems to be of an eschatological nature, having as its central theme "the end of the World", and "the universal conflagration, when the Architecture and Masonry shall be no more", leaving us uncertain as to whether it is Christian in character.

The structure of the Ritual is very simple:[10] it establishes relations between its various elements in time and space and, by fixing the elements of the Ritual within its time and space, it arranges them in a hierarchical order at the top of which we find "the moment of rising of a Master Mason", which is the natural focus of the whole performance. The structure of this ritual, however, is not given to us in its real time and space, but in the chronological sequence and spatial ordering set out in the text of the Manual: it is manifested and organized in the structure of the text. Here we have the Ritual cryptically described, its elements named and explained, the explanations named and interpreted, and these interpretations very often reinterpreted, with all the "what is whats", "who is whos", and "what means whats" strictly arranged within the sequence of the text.

As I have already said, when history is included within a ritual it shrinks; it is reduced to the size of a core-event of the life of a ritual, forfeiting its temporal one-directedness and uniqueness. In a ritual it is enacted again and again as a whole, and the sequence of its stages may be changed or sometimes even reversed so that it ceases to be history and becomes something else – an allusion, a myth, or a legend – which is wrapped up in the ritual and assumes that ritual's temporal and spatial dimensions. Like a chrysalis, history lies dormant in mythical form within the cocoon of ritual, waiting to be released from it by an ethnographer, mythologist or historian who demythologizes, reconstructs, or reinvents it again as, for example, the history of a secret society, tribe, nation, culture, or the whole of humankind. This description of the position of history within ritual is, of course, entirely *etic*. Emically, however, the Masonic Ritual treats the history within itself simply as history, and not as a myth or legend, even taking into account the Masonic idea of the Hiramic Legend as an allegory of human history. So when we read at the beginning of the *Explanation of the First Tracing Board* that, "The usages and customs among Freemasons have ever borne a near affinity to those of ancient Egyptians . . .", etc.,[11] we should consider it not as fantasy, nor even as the possibility of a historical reconstruction, but as an example of an inner (within the Ritual) history which remains an important emic element in the structure of Masonic religious consciousness.

The main difference between Prichard's exposé and the manual is that in the former the Inner Ritual can only be inferred from the questions and answers, while in the latter it also appears in brackets,[12] and is subsequently given either a concrete or a general interpretation in the exhortations of the Worshipful Master and the Charges which follow the initiation.

The scheme outlined in appendix C shows the relation between the parts of the manual containing interpretations of the Ritual (I, II, III, V), and the part where the Ritual itself is described (IV).

I. *An interpretation of the Hiramic legend*: ". . . how the Master Mason's *word* was lost and (its *substitute*) found . . ." [pp. 139–40]

II. *The first interpretation of the Ritual*: "a lesson in mortality" [p. 125]

III. *The legend* of the death, burial, and raising of Hiram (as told by the W.M. to a Candidate). [pp. 126–9; 136–41]

IV. *The description of the enactment of this Legend* by a Candidate who "is laid as a corpse in the grave", and then raised (i.e. the *Inner Ritual* itself). [pp. 117–18; pp. 128–30]

V. *The second interpretation of the Ritual:* "it . . . expresses that gloom which rests on the prospects of futurity, . . . it is that mysterious veil which the eye of reason cannot penetrate unless assisted by the light from above . . . by which you may perceive that you stand on the very brink of the grave into which you have just *figuratively* descended and which will receive you again into its cold bosom . . ." [from the W.M.'s Charge, p. 131]

The arrows in this scheme clearly show that, in the space of the text of the Manual, the description of the Ritual figures as the natural centre of the text, the focus towards which all elements of its content gravitate, and as a place where they find their meaning, and only one meaning at that. This is particularly important, because we are all too accustomed to think about the relation between ritual and its interpretation in terms of whatever it might be – myth, legend, moral or scientific principles – in a way diametrically opposite to that which I am going to present now. Our habitual approach to practically any ritual is based on the assumption that a ritual, taken by itself, cannot have its own meaning and that only an explanatory text of some kind can endow a ritual with the meaning which determines for us its perceivable and comprehensible form. Following this idea, the Eucharist, for instance, would depend for its meaning on whether we accept its theological interpretation as transubstantiation (Catholic), as remembrance (Anglican), or as a mere symbol (Pentecostal). In contrast, the structure of the text of the Ritual of Raising demonstrates that all its interpretations can have concrete meaning only in as much as they are related to this very Ritual, for on their own they remain generalities and commonplaces without any concrete meaning at all. So when the Worshipful Master says that the Ritual is "a lesson in mortality" whose purpose is to illustrate mortality, it means that mortality, as a common destiny and universal predicament, acquires its real and concrete meaning in the Ritual, not the other way around. Likewise, the idea of the lost Master Mason's Word, let alone the Word itself, has no meaning outside the Ritual, for it cannot be deduced from any of Masonry's ethical or religious principles such as the principle of mortality. Yet, historically, of course, it may be that the idea of the Word as the essence of the Highest Knowledge, before it appears in Masonry, was related to or derived from some very ancient patterns of religious thought, connected with some other rituals, where it assumes a quite different meaning. The same applies to light; only *in* the Ritual and *through* the Ritual does light become that very Light of the Master Mason, which illuminates his vision of death.

Speaking of the elements of text, all its basic units, its most elementary passages, sentences and phrases wherein meaning is fixed, are organized, at first sight at least, according to the simplest possible formula:

A is B, B means C

Within the text there may be a series of these explanatory formulas yielding a number of inner or "ritualized" interpretations.[13] To make it easier to understand this formula, let us return to the four passages, which I have paraphrased below:

The three *lesser lights* in Masonry are the Sun, the Moon and the Master. This means that the Sun rules the day, the Moon rules the night, and the Master rules the Lodge (A.2.7).

The grip (or *token*) is . . . a distinct pressure of the thumb on the first joint of the hand . . . it is intended as a means to distinguish a Brother by night . . . and by day (*idem*).

The word is Boaz; it means strength (A.2.9). Your *body* is an *emblem* of your *mind,* and your *feet* an emblem of the rectitude of your actions (A.2.6).

And finally, in 'V' of the diagram, we read that the Ritual of Raising expresses the "*gloom* (of the prospect of death) – the *mysterious veil* which the eye of reason cannot penetrate unless assisted by the *light* from above . . . by which you may perceive that you stand on the very brink of the grave, into which, a moment ago, you have *figuratively* descended" . . . etc.

The last example is particularly interesting because it reveals not only the Masonic philosophy of the Ritual of Raising, but the philosophy of each and every initiatory Ritual in the world, in so far as an initiatory ritual expresses and interprets itself in a ritual text. The essence of this philosophy is that whatever we might deal with or find in a ritual is by definition related to something else, to something which is found only on a level higher than that on which a ritual is materially executed (but still *within* it, not outside it) be it physically, orally, audially, visually, etc. So, in our example, the "Light of Masonry" is but a figurative expression of the "Light from above" (Divine Light); the Candidate's "gloom" is an expression of the "Mysterious Veil"; his descent into the "grave" is figurative in relation to his real death, etc; the Master Mason's word (*M...A*) is but a substitute for what was lost and what shall not be found until the end of this period of the world, and, finally, Masonry itself is doubly emblematic: first with respect to working or operative Masonry, and secondly with regard to the higher mystical forces by means of which God rules the whole universe.

In its form and structure the text of the Masonic Manual strictly follows the almost ubiquitous general pattern of the world's ritual instructions. Recently I staged a curious, though quite elementary, experiment. I made a copy of a couple of its pages, deleted all references to Freemasonry, replaced them with *x*s, *y*s and *z*s, and showed this piece of text to several scholars, asking them (after having established that none of them had anything to do with Masonry) for their opinion on its origin and character.

The first, Professor D., an authority on Zoroastrian religion, said: "This is very similar to a late, and rather degenerate version of a certain group of Medieval Zoroastrian rituals."

The second, Dr C., a specialist in Tibetan religion and northern Buddhism, remarked: "The form is absolutely the same as that of the classical Sogshods (Buddhist Tantrist Ritual Manuals) of the seventeenth or eighteenth century. More than that, some passages even look as if they were literally translated from the Tibetan."

The third, Professor E., a renowned orientalist, returned it to me with a cynical laugh, saying: "The text from which you claim to have extracted these pages does not exist. You must have faked it since it is far too standardized and common to all religions to be genuine."[14]

When we pass from the text of the Ritual to the Ritual itself, we find ourselves within a space which is organized in a way quite different from that in which the text is organized. The space of the Ritual is presented to us as a kind of field where the Candidate Mason moves as ritually instructed by the Worshipful Master, Principal Officers, Assistant Officers and, first of all, the very text that we have already looked at. This field symbolizes the Lodge – because the Lodge symbolizes the World, as the Candidate symbolizes ignorant Man, as the Master symbolizes Knowledge, and so on. All movements of the Candidate, in his enactment of the Hiramic Legend as well as of what precedes it, are regulated by the directions of the compass, the sum of which constitutes the space of the Ritual within the Lodge. These directions signify:

1. The *Geographical*: ["Brother A.B., whence come you? – From the East. Whither directing your course? – To the West", etc.] The Candidate goes from the East to the West, and then back, from the West to the East.

2. The *Epistemological*: The Candidate moves from total ignorance to the Knowledge of the Word, or from the total darkness to the light which would enable him to "*leaven the death*".

3. The *Soteriological*: The Candidate moves through the Ritual, from profane life (in the West) to the East, then again to death (in the West), and back to a new life (through Raising) in the East.

4. The *Mystical*.[15] The Candidate moves in search of the Word which was lost in the realm of Life in the East, and can be found in the realm of Death, in the West – the Word which is what a Mason really is, not only his real Name (in the late Gnostical traditions one's real name, whether one knows it or not, is oneself).

The emphasis on mortality was, and still is, very strong, serving as the only idea that links the Inner Ritual of Master Mason with the whole complex of the Outer. When a person enters a Lodge, leaving behind *his* religion, and steps into the rarefied world of the religion of the Grand Architect of the Universe, the Great Geometrician, he already knows that the Ritual exists, and that the meaning of the Ritual, together with its symbolism, lies outside both his own religious position and the religion of the Lodge. The phenomenology of this religious situation can be described in the following way:

1. The religious position of a Mason before entering the Lodge, or outside the Lodge, is Masonically described as acknowledging a "belief in the existence of a Superior Being", a belief which, itself, is not a religion, though it might or might not be combined with his participation in one religion or another. Such a belief cannot be regarded as having anything at all to do with the Masonic religion of the Great Architect of the Universe since it is the pre-requisite of admission to Masonry. A Mason must hold it before he enters the Craft.[16] It would be better, therefore, to call it "an idealized concept", or a general opinion, or a personal conviction rather than a belief, particularly when the latter term is associated in one's vocabulary with faith and thereby with some concrete religion.

2. The ceremonial prayers and references to the Great Architect of the Universe, belonging to the Outer Ritual, represent the form of Masonic Religion in the sense in which the Lodge can be considered as the form of Masonic Ritual. They are related to the Ritual through their common symbolism (God – Grand Master of the Universe, Hiram Abiff – the Master, etc.).

3. The Death of Hiram Abiff and its re-enactment in the Ritual is connected with Masonic Religion only through the symbolism of death. That is why all analogies with the Crucifixion and Resurrection of Jesus Christ are spurious; a Master is the "raised Hiram", but Hiram himself did not resurrect, and that is why, as we are given to understand, the whole Ritual is symbolic, while the Holy Communion, by orthodox theological definition, is not. The Candidate is not meant to believe in his literal "transfiguration" into Hiram, whereas a Catholic is meant to believe in Transubstantiation. The idea of Mortality here, with its own emblems (not symbols!),[17] such as the skull and the skeleton, covers the space between the religiously *neutral* Ritual, the Ceremony, with its uniquely Masonic religious rhetoric and the definite or indefinite personal religion of a Masonic Candidate.

The substitution of the Word is of special symbolic significance here. As we have already seen in Prichard's exposition, the genuine word was lost and had to be substituted (though the text does not use this word) by the "first word spontaneously uttered by one of the Brethren after Hiram's corpse was discovered". And this substituted word, Machbenah, whatever its exact meaning might be (and there is a considerable difference of opinion on the subject among Hebrew linguists), designates the situation of the murder of Hiram and/or subsequent contact with his corpse: the situation mirrored in the Master Mason's Ritual. In the Manual, however, the word designates a Master Mason and serves as his real (though generic) name.[18] So, the name *M.* figures here as a *ritualistic* designation of *symbolic* self-discovery, as the dead body of Hiram which cannot speak is a symbolic substitute for Hiram; as the Ritual reproduces the original series of events; and as a Master Mason is no more than a substitute for the spiritual reality which is lost together with its name, and will remain so "... until time or circumstances shall restore *the genuine one*..." [p. 20]. But so far, the substituted secrets constitute the essence of Masonry, as the substituted name is what a Mason is.[19]

There are no religious principles or truths which can be described as specifically Masonic in the Master's admonitions, or in the explanations of the Ritual, though it includes the Grand Architect of the Universe. This is not to say, however, that the Ritual is not religious, or that Masonry is not a religion. Here lies the main difference between Masonry and practically all modern theosophical teachings, including Anthroposophy. For the latter are entirely *truth-oriented*; they are conscious not only of their own truths, but also of the fact that their ceremonies and symbolism are merely a means of attaining them, and it is into those truths that their members are initiated.[20] Whereas in Masonry, even when it is said about a ritual that it illustrates a truth, such as when "lying in a grave" illustrates mortality, this truth remains general, one and together with its illustration or "lesson", and invariably returns us to the Ritual itself of which it is a part.

As a complex phenomenon of religious consciousness "the God of Masonic Religion", whatever the opinions of the Committee specially appointed by the Synod of the Church of England to investigate Masonic activities within the Church, or even of the Grand Lodge of England, might be, can be reduced, etically, to three ideas:

> 1. The idea of a *Superior Being* in the existence of which a Candidate for Masonry must believe;
> 2. The idea of the *God of "Religion in which all men agree"* of Anderson's Constitutions; and
> 3. The idea of *The Great Architect of the Universe*, though being a concretization of the two, still possesses his own biblically coloured features, owing to the legendary biblical context within which he is firmly placed.[21]

Only through the last idea is the Masonic God connected with Masonic Ritual and Masonic Symbolism or, more exactly, the symbolism of the Masonic Ritual.[22]

The notion of religious symbolism is, speaking phenomenologically, a tautology. This is so not only because there is no religion without symbols as its universal representations, but first of all because there is no symbolism existing outside a religion. We may even go so far as to state that symbolism is an aspect of religion, or that both religion and symbolism are the aspects of one and the same structure of consciousness which we call now "religion", now "symbolism". And only having said this, we may try to look at symbolism as something more specific and concrete.

The word symbolism denotes the existence and use of the things which represent the whole of one's conscious universe, that is, the universe one is conscious of. I use the word "ones" in a merely conventional sense, for, although the number of such universes may, in principle at least, be as large as the number of individuals, I am nonetheless fairly convinced that in fact it is considerably smaller, for the same conscious universe may be, and actually is, inhabited by very many individuals. So, in the end, we see that the number of symbolic things representing them is not very large either. I cannot prove this, of course, but I am absolutely certain that it *is* so and cannot be otherwise due to the nature of our consciousness and of the one physical universe we inhabit. Evidence for this exists in the purely empirical fact that the same symbolic situations are repeated not only throughout human history but across the diversity of human cultures in geographical space.

And, finally, we should always bear in mind that symbols are not necessarily physical things, or visual images. They might just as well be sounds, words, or their combinations, and also far more complex things, such as plots, legends, or myths.

The very word *Masonry*, for example, the Ritual, the whole complex of ceremonial together with its words, technical terms, figures and images, taken as a single phenomenon considered in its entirety, allows for at least two interpretations, one specific and the other general. According to the first, Masonry is first of all – Masonry. That is, all the architectural terminology, imagery, and emblematics are necessarily connected with, and inherent to, the Masonic phenomenon and all its situations. From this it would follow that it is not by chance that God is the Great Architect of the Universe, or the Great Geometrician, or the Great Grand Master of the Universe: that it is not mere convention that the Universe is the Lodge, that man is a Mason, and the idea of Mortality is manifested in the Legend of the death of Hiram and embodied in the ritual of his dying and rising. More than that, the very fact that the most widely spread of all the present day's secret societies is the Society of Freemasons, and not of Free Sailors or of Free Miners, would be then seen as having its own philosophical, religious, and ethical meaning, a meaning which could never be found in any symbolic context other than the Masonic.[23] This in turn means that the terms Masonry, Mason, Building, Lodge, Architect, Master, and so forth belong not only to the primary symbolism of Freemasonry but also, and particularly from a Masonic point of view, to the universal symbolism of the whole of humankind.[24] The Lodge then would figure as the macrocosm, the only place where the laws of the spiritual cosmos can be made manifest and can be realized by a Mason who represents the microcosm through his enactment of the Ritual. Only there, within the four walls of the building in which they meet, can the "impenetrable veil" be penetrated by the beam of Masonic Light assisted by the Light from above.[25] And only through the Ritual might one obtain access to the knowledge of universal mortality, as well as the knowledge of one's own individual death, which is tantamount to one's ultimate self-knowledge. The last then would be seen as fixed by and materialized in the Master Mason's Word as its symbol, while the whole of the Ritual would be understood as a symbol of the Knowledge of Universal Mortality.

The entire history of Freemasonry, if looked at from this angle, appears (as it does in the old Charts, Anderson's Constitutions and elsewhere) as the symbolic analogue to the history of mankind, and therefore there is no need to bother with verifying facts and details, because, in a mystical, ethical or religious sense, all that has been relevant in human history has been Masonic by definition. So, if God Himself engraved the laws of Architecture on Adam's heart, it does not matter who the first Masons were, or who the first man who became aware of himself as a Mason was (Cain or Noah, Nimrod or King Solomon, Euclid or Octavian Augustus): history itself blends with symbolism and loses its factual texture,[26] for everything in history is perceived as an example of Masonry at work – Masonry here possesses an absolute character.

Another interpretation, which I call general, by contrast considers Masonry as a case, an example, or variant of some more general universal religious (or mystical) principle which, though being historically manifested now in Masonry, now in the ancient Egyptian rites, now in the Eleusinian mysteries, remains itself totally self-sufficient and unaffected by its manifestations.[27] The whole symbolic situation of the Ritual assumes its relative character in this interpretation. So from the point of view of Drake, Anderson, or even Dermott, the fact that the Word, as revealed in the Hiramic Legend and obtained by a Candidate in the Ritual, was a substitute regarded as predetermined ("So was it fated . . .") and necessary, to such a prominent Masonic theorist as A. E. Waite it remained just "an unfortunate circumstance". Waite, though unaware of it, employed an etic interpretation, when he wrote that "The death of our Master Builder (Hiram) left the Temple unfinished . . . and our *Symbolical* Masonry – in like manner – is without its coping-stone".[28] Thus, in interpreting the whole of Masonry, and not just some things in it, as symbolic we have to admit that it cannot be understood as a whole without our unearthing something that lies behind it of which it itself is a symbol. But what is this something? Is it "the Religion in which all men agree"? Or "the mystical principle of the Universe of which one cannot be aware without passing through the Ritual"? Or, finally, "the Ritual itself, the ultimate meaning of which has remained lost since the loss of the genuine Word"? To answer these questions within the limits of the second kind of interpretation, one has to accept that there must be in Masonry some objectively existing religious content, the presence of which can be understood through the Ritual, given that the latter has already been understood symbolically, whether or not Masons themselves suspect its existence.[29] Therefore, when I say that Freemasonry is a religion, and that that religion can be understood only through the symbolism of Masonic ritual, I make my judgement without recourse to any criteria of religion, religiousness or religiosity used in Christianity or any other concrete religion, Masonic included.[30] If considered from the point of view of this interpretation, the whole phenomenon of Masonry would be etically seen as *a symbol* of that religion. I fully realize that Masons themselves have used the word "symbolic" in a different way and in a sense more often than not closer to the meaning of "emblematic" or "figurative" than "symbolic". Nevertheless, even from their most concrete uses it is transparent how thoroughly permeated with symbolism the whole Masonic system is. Not only do all the main building tools serve as emblems of speculative Masonry, three of these tools serve in the Hiramic Legend as substitutes for weapons (Hiram was done to death by the Heavy Maul) in exactly the same way as that in which speculative Masonry is the substitute for the real Masonry, and as a Candidate for admission is the substitute for, or an emblem of, the primarily ignorant man.

Masonic history within this interpretation is, and quite naturally, treated as a kind of epiphenomenon of that religious symbolism to which I have already referred above. A. E. Waite writes: "To affirm Speculative Masonry, e.g. in Egypt, is to affirm our specific and conventional system of morality, illustrated by building symbols and a building myth. Still less does it enforce any thesis of antiquity to cite its existence from presumable time immemorial . . ."[31] His friend Wilmshurst goes much further. He asserts that ". . . our present system is not one coming from antiquity . . . There is no direct continuity between us and the Egyptians, or even those ancient Hebrews who built, in the reign of King Solomon, a certain Temple at Jerusalem. What is extremely ancient in Freemasonry is the spiritual doctrine concealed within the architectural phraseology; for this doctrine is an elementary form of the doctrine that has been taught in all ages, no matter in what garb it has been expressed."[32] The last opinion implies the then (early 1920s) very widely spread idea of *philosophia perennis* (perennial philosophy) rather than that of universal religion, yet the fact remains that the thoroughly symbolic character of Masonry does admit such an understanding though not very many Masons would agree with it today.[33]

Paradoxically it is because of the relentless symbolizing of all its elements that Masonry has so often been denied its religious status by both Masonic and non-Masonic writers. Historically, however, it can be accounted for by the very strong iconoclastic and anti-representational tendency in this island; a tendency much stronger than the theologies of its Churches, and much more stable than the religious indifferentism and scepticism (as alive today as they were 270 years ago) of its lay and clerical inhabitants. It is this tendency that impedes Masons from seeing the religious basis and meaning of their Ritual, for in their own cultural background religion has already been separated from symbolism, and ritual from religion – after all, the English and Scots had to pay for the religious excesses of Bloody Mary on the one hand, and of the extremist Presbyterians on the other. Throughout most of those 270 years Masons have tried to convince themselves and "the gross of the world" that theirs is not a religion, yet they still have to listen to their "progressive" opponents in the Synod of the Church of England repeating their habitual accusations of Pelagianism and Gnosticism, and, of course, above all, of trying to set up a substitute for Christianity. It is time the Grand Lodge simply gave up as a bad job either stating the obvious, that ". . . Freemasonry is not a danger to Christianity, but its very helpful companion",[34] "Masonry has no theology",[35] or claiming that "There is no Masonic God".[36] If they really believe the latter they would then have to admit that the Great Architect of the Universe is either another name for the God of Abraham, Isaac and Jacob, and the Father of Christ, or another way of referring to the "Superior Being" acknowledged by each and every individual Candidate for acceptance to the Degree of Entered Apprentice.

Practically all attempts to explain Masonic religion and philosophy have been terribly muddled on account of a very basic methodological error: they almost always confuse the "logical" aspect of its description – its being or not being a true religion, or a true Christianity or a true anything, which may be decided by an external observer using the objective criteria of his description – with its "theological" aspect – the prior assumption, when describing Masonic religion, that there is a true or untrue Christianity (Catholicism, Protestantism, etc.) or that there is something true or untrue in Christianity. The most typical question, such as "Is Freemasonry compatible with Christianity?", very often implies: "Is that puerile nonsense, or that dangerous deception, anti-Christian?" Another frequent question is: "Is Freemasonry a natural religion?" For many critics, again, its supposed naturalness sets it against the revealed religion of Christ.

I would answer this last question in the negative. As a non-Christian observer of religion, I would prefer to characterize Freemasonry as a *syncretic religion* which cannot be natural by definition, for it *knows* itself as syncretic, while a natural religion does not know itself as natural. It is obvious that the last term serves as a term of theological language not as a term of religion itself. Thus Freemasonry combines, syncretically, Christianity and some elements of Judaism and Gnosticism, with Masonic Religion.

It would be useful now to explain very briefly what I mean when I use the term syncretic religion.

I do not regard syncretism as a general category in a phenomenological description of religion. On the contrary, I am inclined to regard it as a particular case of a religious situation far less often observed than the case of religious synthesis. I call syncretic a religious situation in which the elements of two or more different religions are present, and these differences are recognized by those involved in that situation. It is that phenomenological distinction, consciously made and admitted by a person within his own religion, which distinguishes synthetic and syncretic religious situations and constitutes the primary feature of the latter. The second feature of a syncretic religious situation is the inter-changeability of these heterogeneous elements in its ritual. A third feature, which seems to be more complex, is that of ritual parallelism; that is, when we observe the difference between two or more rituals within one religion but can, at the same time, observe some parallel or analogous beliefs underlying those rituals.[37] A synthetic situation, on the other hand, presupposes features belonging to other religions co-existing within one religion, which may be identified without the adherents of that religion being aware of their heterogeneousness.

Religious syncretism in English Freemasonry can be seen in its historical perspective too, for the Lodges of working Masons that existed in the seventeenth or, perhaps, even the sixteenth century, were, though definitely Christian in character and membership, non-religious in their scope and function. They became religious only when the lost Master Mason's Word became the focus of their ritual and the central theme of their legend. For, as far as anybody knows, in no manuscript of operative Masonry can we find a single trace of the Lost Word.[38]

There has never existed what can be called a theological context in Freemasonry, since all their teaching, instead of being based on a set of primary religious postulates or ideas, is directly related to and derived from the interpretation of their symbols. Symbol is and always was primary in Masonry, starting with its very name, "Freemasonry", and ending with such a complex symbol as the "Theological Ladder".[39] In other words, if in Christianity the symbols represent the primary dogmas (such as the Holy Trinity, the Incarnation, the Redemption, etc.), in

Masonry they represent a coded progression of the Masonic universe taken in both its aspects: historical (from Adam to us) and individual (from birth to death, or from initiation into apprenticeship to the achievement of mastership). However, if we delve further, we come to the strange conclusion, already noted, that the Masonic universe is itself a symbolic notion which represents something else unspecified. It is not a particular symbol or a set of symbols that really matters here, but rather symbolism in general, understood as the inner tendency in the Masonic teaching to symbolize all the things that are significant or important.

But what is particularly interesting is that this Masonic tendency towards symbolization has strongly influenced the character and content of the whole anti-Masonic critique, and particularly the most extreme proponents of this critique. It is hardly surprising then that such a naïve and simple-minded critic of Freemasonry as the late Steven Knight could not help claiming that the "simple" Masons of the Craft really know almost nothing, nor are they able to do anything worth doing, all knowledge and power being concentrated in the Higher Degrees. But what knowledge and what power? That, even he was unable to say, let alone the members of the basic Three Degrees Craft. The extremist Russian right-winger and fanatical monarchist, Selianinoff, writing some seventy years before Knight, maintained that even the members of the Higher Degrees knew nothing and had no real power, for there was something behind even the highest levels of their hierarchy, and that something was the Elders of Zion, whose aim was to take over, rule and finally destroy the whole world through Masonry. But the imagination of Odo Wyatt, a Mormon preacher, outstripped even these lurid fantasies. He wrote in 1887: "The Craft is the instrument in the hands of the Arch Royal and Knights Templar, who are the instrument of the Israelites, who are themselves the instrument of the Devil. Only the Devil knows that." Well, in company with Odo Wyatt.

So, what we can see is a correspondingly mystical or symbolic turn in the anti-Masonic propaganda which began to emerge somewhere in the 1860s. To the arch enemy of Freemasonry John Quincy Adams, however, a rather more sophisticated man than Odo Wyatt, Steven Knight, or David Yallop, everything was perfectly simple. He wrote in the beginning of the 1830s: "This is a secret society whose secret rituals are unChristian, whose secret aims are unconstitutional . . . whose secret rules are illegal, and whose behaviour is often immoral and criminal." No mention of levels behind levels. This is straightforward in comparison with what was to come. The "spiritual" anti-Masonic critique unconsciously mirrored the symbolism of its object with symbolism of the hidden – whose dark side is the image of conspiracy, something "lying behind" which is always more powerful than the visible, audible or knowable. So, beginning with a notorious anonymous pamphlet entitled *Invisible Power*, a series of disclosures about Masonry follow one after another until we come across the international Jewish conspiracy, "The Unknown Power of Evil", or the Anti-Christ himself.

However, the most interesting point in this scheme of the "ascent of Evil" is, of course, the idea of Ignorance; the presupposition underlying which is that a symbol does not know itself but is a representation of something which does know, or at least, knows better. So, the Craft does not know that it is manipulated by the Higher Degrees. The Higher Degrees do not know that they are ruled and controlled by the two Highest Degrees (thirty-second and thirty-third), the two Highest Degrees do not know that they are being used by the Elders of Zion; and even the Elders themselves do not know that they are the means by which the Anti-Christ will come into the world. In the recent Soviet critique the Anti-Christ was substituted by the CIA; in the Cold War Western critique he is substituted by the KGB, and in the German Fascist critique of the 1930s he became redundant and the Elders of Zion figure as the apex of the hierarchy of evil.

Thus, the whole subject of the anti-Masonic "spiritual" critique can be reduced to two aspects:

1. Masonry contains a series of symbols which are used without anything but the most superficial knowledge or understanding by those who use them.[40]
2. Masonry is an ascending hierarchy, the levels of which do not know who is above them at the top of the hierarchy, but have malign power over those below.

It is therefore the character of Masonic symbolism itself, at least partly, that has determined the character of anti-Masonic critique, but no more than partly. The other essential factor is the present-day religious situation, one of the most distinctive features of which is the urge towards complete and total openness or, to put it in a more Christian way, a strong tendency towards theological clarity. This tendency, the populist nature of which leaves us in no doubt, might be summed up in the following conversation:

Peter W. (a vicar): If the Archbishop of Canterbury knows it, whatever it is, I should be able to know it too.

Larry B. (a Mason): So if my vicar knows it, then I should be able to know and understand it too!

Dr Gordon R. (a Jesuit): That's ridiculous; you're not supposed to know what your priest knows, even an Anglican, for it would be the same as saying that an Entered Apprentice in your Craft should know, if he wants to, what the Master knows.

Larry: That wouldn't matter because even if he knew what the Master knew an Apprentice wouldn't be able to understand a word of it.

Gordon R.: Ordinary people do not usually make a distinction between knowledge and understanding.

What follows is a series of discussions between several other persons, Masons and non-Masons, and myself, on the nature and character of Masonic religion or non-religion.

So far I have done my best not to interfere during my conversations, or to offer my own religious terminology and my own opinions about religion. This, among other things, means that in my questions I use the term religion only if it had already been used by Masons themselves when answering my previous questions. Ted, as usual, started the conversation.

Ted (a Master Mason and motor mechanic) Honestly speaking, I don't think I belong to any particular religion and, if I was forced to choose between them I would have chosen Buddhism rather than anything else. By the way, the only religious image I have got in my house is a wooden statue of the Buddha.

John (a Master Mason) How idiotic. First of all, Buddhism is not a religion but a philosophical teaching and, second, how can you deny belonging to a religion if you accept The Great Architect of the Universe?

Ted Religion is what I think and feel about supernatural things, and my relation to those things.

John What then is your relation to the religion of Freemasonry?

Ted When I joined the Craft I already had my own religion, and I joined the craft not to get it from them but to share it with them.

John However, in saying this, you deny to Freemasonry any truly religious role in the sense of its being one concrete religion.

Ted Christianity in Freemasonry is revealed mostly in the Higher Degrees of the Higher Degrees and to an ordinary Mason it is totally impossible to reach the degrees from thirty-first to thirty-third.

A.I. Why is this so?

Ted Because you can't be initiated unless you're invited, and your chances of being invited are practically nil. Not to mention the fact that in order to get in you have to have an almost photographic memory, or you wouldn't be able to cope with memorizing all the ritual and the terminology.

Geoffrey (an insurance broker and very learned Mason of high repute) I am of the opinion that the Higher Degrees are absolutely essential, and that the Three Degrees of the Craft may be considered as a mere filter for admission to them.

John In other words, in the first Three Degrees our Masonry is non-Christian, while the higher up we go the more Christian and therefore the more heretical we become?

Ted You can put it that way.

A.I. So since your very admission to the Craft depends on your belief in the existence of a Superior Being, you are supposed – as a minimum requirement – to be *religious*. Afterwards it is up to you to proceed or not from your general religiousness to the religion. And if religiousness means "I believe", then religion would mean "I make" and "I belong".

Although Ted doesn't practise any particular religion, he regards himself as a religious person not only because he believes in the "supernatural", but also because he sees himself as a *moral* man. As he puts it, "for me, Masonry is a very personal code of behaviour and thought". This attitude is echoed in the words of Terry, who, in the most unambiguous way, considers himself "an absolutely religious man". He is a Baptist. He said once: "My mother is a staunch Catholic, but as a boy I never liked it and I became a Baptist of my own accord when I was still in secondary school". For him "all Masonry is mainly about moral principles ..."

I will conclude by quoting two non-Masons who reject the view that Masonry constitutes a religion:

Simon V. (an academic and religious scholar from London) Theirs is not a true religious society because their aim is not a perpetuation of any religious tradition, but a pursuing of their own self-interest.

The rejection made by Judith T. (a very active Quaker, and member of CND and Greenpeace) is of a far more specifically religious character: "I do not regard them as a religious organization, or a religious people, or as having their own religion, for three reasons. Firstly, they do not have temples and their ritual is more social than religious. Secondly, they do not pray in any real way. Thirdly, they do not practise silent meditation."

I do not question the sincerity of the answers received in my interviews but sometimes I have to elucidate their meaning, and in such cases I usually ask my interviewees whether they agree with my interpretations or not. This is my interpretation of Geoffrey's views on Masonry and religion obtained in a separate interview. He subsequently checked it and agreed entirely with its form and content.

> 1. Belief in the existence of a Superior Being is, in itself, not a religion.
> 2. This common belief in the existence of a Superior Being is not part of the concrete Masonic religion.
> 3. This belief is to be regarded solely as a precondition for entrance to the Craft, the *non*-fulfilment of which makes a person totally unacceptable (I stress the negative character of my formulation). As such, it is no more and no less than a personal conviction which some Masons see as a purely ethical, and not a religious, conviction. It does give rise to some complications, however, for one's own religion may or may not be compatible with this precondition. Buddhists, for example, do not believe in a Superior Being.

A prominent Mason, Howard K., told me the following interesting story about the last three candidates he had recommended to the Craft:

John A., a teacher, wanted to be accepted and he had told Howard beforehand that he was an Anglican but that, from his point of view, the reason for his being an Anglican as well as the reason for the Church of England itself was that "it gives me and those around me a certain form. It shapes our social context, so to speak, and to me personally it simply does not exist outside that context." His candidacy was rejected for he did not believe in the objective (that is, non-contextual) existence of any entity or power of supernatural character.

Richard C. was a designer and artist who had once been a Quaker. While explaining his personal religious position, he said: "All of us humans have the Spirit or God in us. And in this I undoubtedly believe". When asked if he believed that very Spirit or God to exist as such, that is, not merely in him and in all human beings, he answered: "No, I certainly don't". He was not accepted.

S. Singh, a Sikh wine merchant, when answering the same question said: "Of course I believe in the existence of such a Being, for how otherwise could I believe in the sacredness of our Teachers and Scripts?"

The last case is particularly interesting because his own religion, Sikhism, does not include any belief formulated in that particular way. We may say that his answer reflects his own individual stand of which he might have been unaware until he was asked to define it. He was accepted.

The following is an interview with Franco M.-T., an eminent Italian historian of religion and someone who knows a great deal about the roots and origins of Masonry.

A.I. Do you think it is possible that Freemasons perform their Ritual not knowing exactly what they are doing? That is, not knowing that it may have another deeper meaning or even whether their Ritual or its performance as it stands is correct.
Franco I think it is quite possible. More than that, one may conjecture that we deal with some ancient ritual which perpetuates itself objectively through being performed by Freemasons. There is a probability that the performance of that ritual by Freemasons is then one form of the existence of this ritual.
A.I. Do you seriously think that any Masonic ritual can be regarded as logically or historically connected with the idea of the Great Architect of the Universe?
Franco As I understand it, the philosophy of the Great Architect of the Universe is simply one aspect of Masonry which has no direct relation to the ritual of initiation, which is another aspect of it.
A.I. Then, in my opinion, knowledge of the ritual would be different from knowledge of the philosophy of Masonry. I still think that what really constitutes the objective content of the Masonic tradition is former knowledge; objective in the sense that, in principle, such a knowledge does not depend on whether it is or is not understood by Masons themselves. While that which we call philosophy has no meaning without its understanding.
Franco I suspect – but this is no more than a vague surmise – that the hermetic tradition might be perpetuated in the seemingly artificial vehicle of Masonic ritual. And I think that the concept of the Great Architect of the Universe is immanentist and non-personal, and therefore it also smacks of a kind of Gnosticism.
A.I. Do you think that He, the Great Architect, sees a Mason during the ritual?
Franco No, never, for if He sees him, He must be a person.

A.I. I think that the Masonic perpetuation of ritual for ritual's sake was expressed in the unbelievably rapid spread of Masonry in the eighteenth century. Although they would not have been aware of it at the time, when they established new Lodges all over the world, this amounted to spontaneous ritual activity of an external kind, in addition to the Ritual of Initiation.

AN OBJECTION

Mark Waddle (a teacher and non-Mason) I refuse to call Freemasonry a religion, for a religion is that which, in principle at least, unites all people, while they unite an infinitesimal fraction in opposition to the rest of us.

Geoffrey We do not oppose ourselves to you. On the contrary, we are ready to accept you if you want to be accepted, and if you *can* be accepted, of course.

Mark For heaven's sake, to join the club of half-mad snobs!

Geoffrey What exactly are you complaining about? We don't complain about your attitude to us, yet you complain all the time about the *absence* of any attitude of ours to you.

Mark I am speaking of your attitude to *people*, not to *us*.

Geoffrey In doing so you have already separated yourself from the people on whose behalf you are arguing. Masons are not supposed to talk about two particular subjects – politics and religion – for the very reason that they tend to divide, not unite. They are not discussed during our formal meetings for, merely formally, they are not a part of what is going on in the Lodge or what Freemasonry is about. Nor can they be discussed at our dinners for it is forbidden by custom.[41]

FATHER COPPLESTON

When I saw the late Father Coppleston (Professor of the History of Philosophy at the University of London and a Jesuit priest) I put the usual question to him in the following way: "Do you agree with Mascalls' definition of Freemasonry as a *natural* and therefore definitely *non-Christian* religion?"

Father Coppleston I do not regard it as a religion at all and have never seen it as such. I admit that there are some religious elements in it, but we can find religious elements almost everywhere – in ethics, in philosophy, even in science, which by no means gives one reason to call them religions. Speaking specifically of this country I can't quite see the point of calling Freemasonry a religion, Christian or non-Christian. The majority of people here tend to look at it as a benevolent society whose members may be, and very often are, Christian believers. So, not only Freemasons themselves, but people in general, do not see Freemasonry as incompatible with Christianity, though I know that the other side, that is, the Catholic Church, does.

A.I. Is there any difference, then, between your opinion and the opinion of most people?

Father Coppleston No, there isn't, for now I am not speaking as a Catholic theologian. I fail to see the dilemma. Indeed, the very fact that Freemasonry is in practice so easily combined with Christianity or any other religion by believers themselves may serve as an indication that it is not in itself a religion, and the problem of whether it is Christian or non-Christian, or natural religion simply disappears.

A.I. Yes, but only given that the solution of this problem rests on Freemasons themselves in the first place, who are undecided, and on Christians in the second. I agree with you, that here we deal with a case when we have to rely on other people's religious self-awareness as a primary fact. But, having done that, I may then reverse the argument and ask them – Do you think that that kind of Christianity, which is so easily compatible with Freemasonry, is a religion, or rather the *true* religion? [In my opinion, as it will have emerged by now, two religions are combinable, though, emically speaking, one of them will inevitably claim that only *it* counts as the true religion.]

Father Coppleston Yes, there may be room for doubt, though this question requires of one a real theological competence, while now I am talking to you as a Catholic, a philosopher, and an Englishman, but not as a Catholic theologian.

[I am afraid that the word "religion" is used rather feebly by both Father Coppleston and myself as "religion in a loose Christian sense as understood by the Masons and the majority of Englishmen".]

Notes

1 From C. M. Brown, *Nigerian Ritual As Taught in Emulation Lodge of Improvement*, London, A. Lewis Ltd, 1952, p. X. Kipling was one of the very few poets in Great Britain after Robert Burns who joined the Society (I do not take into account the utterly unserious and short-lived Masonic career of Oscar Wilde). His Masonic obituary reads: "Rudyard Kipling, of Burwash, Sussex, on 17th Jan. 1936. Bro. Kipling was admitted to membership of the Correspondence Circle [of Quatuor Coronati in May 1918.]" *Ars Quatuor Coronatorum*, Vol. XLIX, 1939, p. 134.

2 All that William James (in *Variety of Religious Experience*) called "states of consciousness", and considered as basic and generative factors in each and every religious experience, can be subsumed under the heading of the "psychological" or "subjective". So, for James ritual figured as derivative from, and secondary to, the *actual* mental states of its collective or individual performers. What an appalling mistake for a great thinker! No state of mind can generate even its own *content* (religious object, myth, situation, plot), let alone a ritual, because all mental states are "empty" unless intentionally directed towards some concrete object existing apart from, or other than, those states. For instance, a state of religious ecstasis until it has focused on a particular pre-existing thing – an icon, prayer or incantation, ritual, etc.

3 ". . . the import of . . . that which lies behind the Mystery of Raising is left for those who can find it. . . . and the whole question lies open therefore to those – if any – whom it concerns, for their *individual* settlement". A. E. Waite, 1925, p. vii.

4 J. Dewar, 1982 (1966), pp. 28, 126. This is a splendid example of the highly unconscious (i.e. *objective*) subjectivity of Dewar.

5 From an interview with Robert D., a plumber.

6 From an interview with Arthur S., an Italian teacher living in England, who is S.D. in a Lodge.

7 W. L. Wilmshurst, 1932, p. 5. Unrealized in the sense that though some may acknowledge that it exists they do not know it personally.

8 A. E. Waite, 1925, p. vii. This again alludes to the "Double Truth" Mythology on which I will concentrate later.

9 A. Robbo, *The Fifth Letter to L.* (unpublished), *circa* 1979.

10 I am saying this as a person who has never seen it, but only read and thought about it, which makes my position more subjective (in the sense I have already mentioned) than that of any Mason.

11 A. E. Waite (1925, p. 24) comments: "To affirm speculative Masonry – e.g. in Egypt – is to affirm our specific and conventional system of morality, illustrated by building symbols and a building myth."

12 Leon D., an Aberdonian Mason and lawyer, told me that, ". . . the secrecy of raising is a convention, a sheer convention which we stick to as a part of the ritual itself." And only when I insisted that he should explain himself more succinctly, he added, rather condescendingly: "What I meant is that what is done is done irrespective of what you may think or feel about it. This is the meaning of secrecy." I, for my part, think that his explanation is an impeccable example of a genuine and spontaneous phenomenology: secrecy here is not related to any hidden truth lying outside or beyond the ritual. And initiation itself here is not an initiation into a

kind of Highest or Higher Knowledge, but into the knowledge of the Ritual. That is why the analogy with Gnosticism seems to me to be rather partial.

13 So-called serial interpretations may also occur outside the text where one and the same term is explained both in ritual and non-ritual meanings. As an example of serial interpretation of a term belonging to the outer ritual, let us take "Lewis" (A. 2.10.):

> a) "Lewis" is the son of a Mason. "Lewis" also means strength;
> b) Lewis is depicted here (in the Lodge) by certain pieces of metal dovetailed into a stone, which form a cramp (and enables an operative Mason to raise great weights . . .);
> c) ". . . The name 'Lewis', traditionally associated with the Craft, is a modern corruption of *Eleusis* and of other Greek and Latin names associated with Light" [W. L. Wilmshurst, 1932, p. 186].

14 The last remark is at least partly true, for textologically speaking, by deleting the Masonic references, I in effect falsified the whole text.

15 "Mystical" means no more than "about the *mystery* of the Word". But at the same time the word "mystic" was used by Masons themselves, as we see in R. Burns's "Address to Deil":

> *When Masons' mystic word and grip*
> *In storms and tempests raise you up,*
> *Some Cock or Cat your rage maun stop,*
> *And strange to tell!*
> *The youngest Brother ye wad whip*
> *Aff straucht to hell!*

16 This state of a Candidate's possessing the "mere minimum" of religiousness is described in the *Lectures* read by the Worshipful Master, or a Master, as a state of complete darkness and utter spiritual poverty. For in this state the *veil* remains impenetrable, that is, a person has not yet learnt the lesson in mortality!

17 Emblem, unlike symbol, figures here as a mere external sign or badge whose application is far more formal and dependent on the rules and habits of a particular religious organization, whereas symbol always has a universal spiritual meaning. This is not to say that one and the same *thing* cannot have both symbolic and emblematic uses, as, for instance, the skull.

18 Arthur Robbo writes: "In the Middle East and Caucasian regions the practice of giving a newly-born male child a special name which nobody (including the child itself) should know, was and still is a very widely spread custom". *Unpublished Papers*, the Masonic Part. Section on Names (quoted with the author's permission), p. 6.

19 "In any Gnostic tradition one is what one is called . . ." M. Eliade, *Briser le toit*, Paris, 1985, p. 126.

20 The idea of a religious truth includes in itself not only a religion's awareness of a distinction between truth and ritual (or ethics, or symbolism, etc.) but also a distinction between one truth and another. That is, it includes in itself the idea that the truths of "my religion" are different from those of another. And it is this distinction that the Religion of Masonry is probably not aware of. And if its religious opponents are, it remains a fact of their own religious consciousness, and not that of Freemasons.

21 The problem of legend and the legendary will be discussed in Chapter 12.

22 Both "a Superior Being" and "the God of religion in which all men agree" smack very strongly of the god of "natural religion". The last, however, is not so much the Natural religion of David Hume and Lord Herbert, as that which used to permeate the tabernacles, parlours and coffee-houses of London and Edinburgh, throughout the second half of the seventeenth and the first half of the eighteenth century. The Great Architect of the Universe was intended to refer to "the God of the Lodge" – probably an attempt to particularize the extremely vague concept of a "Masonic God".

23 After having written these words, where the professions of sailor and miner were picked by me at random, I learned to my amazement that the sailors and shipbuilders in ancient Egypt had their own very secret initiations, and that the miners in some regions of Southern Germany were, in the Medieval period, organized in secret societies with the secret passwords, tokens, etc. See also W. L. Wilmshurst, 1932, p. 25.

24 Here I would like to remind the reader that this approach is *emic* (see the last pages of Chapter 3), that is, it follows the rules and laws established by the object of investigation (i.e. not by the investigator). This approach also presupposes the uniqueness of the subject of investigation.

25 While writing about this, I cannot help drawing a curious, and perhaps spurious, analogy with Ancient Indian symbology, where the highest symbol, *Brahman*, figured at the same time as *the beam* (i.e. an element of building structure), and *beam of Light*.

26 This idea, itself very symbolic, finds its extreme expression in the book (rarely quoted) written somewhere in the mid-nineteenth century by John Fellows; *The Mysteries of Freemasonry: or an Exposition of the Religious Dogmas and Customs of the Ancient Egyptians*; showing their identity with the order of Modern Masonry, with some remarks on the Metamorphoses of Apuleus, London, W. M. Reeves . . . (here J. Fellows, 1866).

27 This interpretation can be made, strictly speaking, only when an investigator (or a Mason) places himself outside Masonry, and is concerned with and conscious of such differences and distinctions in it, which are either unobservable from within or irrelevant. This interpretation is opposed to the previous one as etic to emic. An observer of Masonic symbolism and religion should combine both these interpretations in his approach. In this connection it would be interesting to quote from C. G. Jung, who wrote in his autobiography that he modelled his coat of arms upon that of his grandfather, an ardent Mason and Grand Master whose own coat of arms was also devised by himself for his own, non-Masonic, use. Then Jung, not being a Mason, invented his with ". . . a cross, azure . . . a blue bunch of grapes in a field d'or . . . and separating these is an etoile d'or in a fess azure. The symbolism of these arms is Masonic, or Rosicrucian." C. G. Jung, *Memories, Dreams, Reflections*, London and Glasgow, 1980 (1961), p. 259.

28 A. E. Waite, 1925, p. 79.

29 Not being a Mason, I am at liberty to hypothesize on this subject knowing, at the same time, that many Masons are doing the same. The "religious content" here is by no means opposed to the Ritual or symbolism of Masonry, and figures as a mere substitute for a concrete knowledge of what could be called Masonic religion.

30 The words *to understand* and *understanding* here are used in a hermeneutic sense (see Chapter 3). My understanding of the religious objectivity in Freemasonry implies the hermeneutical rule, that to understand a thing or a phenomenon, I should become it, which is entirely impossible without suspending my objective knowledge of it. Objective here means that which at the moment of knowledge is not (and cannot be) me. That is why to meditate upon one's mind as a stone is an understanding, while to imagine one's mind as configuration of biological, biochemical and psychological functions is a kind of knowledge quite inapplicable to the study of religious phenomena.

31 A. E. Waite, 1925, p. 24.

32 W. L. Wilmshurst, 1932, p. 25. Thus, the idea of the Doctrine (or Philosophy) here goes first and constitutes the content, or essence of Masonry. This very general and relative interpretation of Masonic symbolism seems to me to be quite congenial with that of one of the most influential mystical teachers of our century, G. I. Gurdjieff (1874—1949), who used to say of his own teaching: "I do not teach you religion; I teach you how to be able to become a religious person".

33 At the same time, some other Masonic writers, particularly those who see a religion (if not *the* religion) in Masonry, tend to regard it as ritualistic by definition and, given the primacy of ritual, symbolic only by derivation. "What are emphatically called the *mysteries*, is but another name for *religion*" – says John Fellows (1866, p. III), and this equation leaves us in no doubt, naïve as it is, that to him religion is being reduced to the tradition of perpetuation of secret ritual which in the main has remained that which it was from the beginning, beyond the reach of memory. The only difference, then, between his opinion and those of Rodney Needham, Stuart Hampshire and C. G. Jung, would be that while they tried to reduce the notions of "tradition", "ritual" and "religion" to one or another set of basic elements, primary factors, or innate elementary tendencies, Fellows saw these notions as primary, basic, and elementary in themselves.

34 From a letter by M. B. S. Higham (Masonry "no substitute for religion"), *The Times*, 11 July 1987.

35 John Hamill, *The Craft*, London, 1986 (J. Hamill, 1986), p. 151.

36 *Idem*, p. 152. The book is an excellent apologetic (not to say ideological) summary of modern English Masonic historical *self-reflection*. But when Hamill states that Freemasonry lacks the three basic elements of religion, i.e. dogma or theology, liturgy, and means of salvation, he fails to understand that his *criteria* for deciding what is or is not a religion are, themselves, Christian and theological, and that what he offers the reader (both Masonic and non-Masonic) is nothing but a circular definition of religion. So, if you want to define Masonry in Christian terms, then you have to be prepared to discuss it on the terms of the Church of England. According to James C., a curate from Bristol and Chaplain of a Lodge, "An understanding of symbols plays the role of theology in Freemasonry". With this I agree.

37 The syncretic character of Masonic religion could be illustrated, if taken in a *Christian* context, by the following episode. A friend of mine, Michael Murray, a Lewis (a Freemason's son) and oriental scholar, describes just such a situation: "One of my neighbours, still a practising Mason, recently died. He was quite a high-up member in a local Lodge in West Yorkshire. The funeral was held in the parish church where there was an Anglican priest officiating, but the lessons read out seemed to be peculiar to Masons and not the norm for a Christian burial service.

There were psalms and a lot about mortality and some strange words and gestures added. There was a feeling in me of the service being hijacked by Masons." The reader is invited to compare this tale with our short description of Dr Anderson's funeral above.

38 "Allied with no external religious system itself, Masonry is yet a synthesis, a concordat, for men of various race, creed or sect, and its foundation principles, being common to them all . . . admit of no variation". W. L. Wilmshurst, 1932, p. 28. Here the author uses the word synthesis in the sense in which I have used syncretism.

39 See Jacob's ladder, Ch. 10, note 38.

40 Understanding, in the hermeneutical sense I have been using it, has a subjective and individual character.

41 Restrictions were placed on these topics by the Grand Lodge in the 1740s (see Chapter 7). Prior to this, however, theology and religious matters were hotly debated.

CHAPTER 12

A Digression on Comparative Religion, Comparative Mythology and Comparative Psychology

It is not so much the particular terms that cause the trouble, but the inherent difficulty in translating the phenomena into any terms at all.
Rodney Needham, "Percussion and Transition"[1]

I am, I confess, no more than vaguely reminiscent of the sources of my scholarly information. As for the sources of my inspiration – them I remember as clearly as I saw them when, still young, I began to drink from the fountain of knowledge.
Count S. Poborovsky[2]

According to the comparativist method, in order to compare two phenomena present before one, one must have a basis for that comparison which is always in the past by definition, for only then can one see in a present phenomenon an actualization of a past phenomenon, or a past phenomenon as the source of the two or more things which are to be compared. Thus, for example, when a scholar of comparative religion, mythology, or folklore tried, at the turn of the nineteenth century, to prove that the Masonic Ritual is a typical rite of initiation, the three main components, or stages of which are the act of dying, the passing through death, and the emerging from death, he simply meant by this that the existence of such a rite in the remotest past makes it the origin or prototype of all similar rites observed in the course of human history, up to the present time. So, what we can identify now as being one type (type in the sense of repeated pattern or configuration of elements) in many different rites derives from, and owes its typicality to, a single common historical prototype. In other words, prototype goes first, and type second.

The beginning, and particularly the middle, of the twentieth century saw that approach giving way to a kind of meta-historical theory, where history itself, including the present and, possibly, even the future, becomes a scene where the main factors at work are more or less abstract, operating quite independently of the conditions of time and place. These factors are perceived as constants of human behaviour, individual or collective consciousness or of language, and thought to be existing and working more or less spontaneously. If considered from this angle therefore, whatever we can identify as common or similar in various religious rites, no matter whether present or past, is thought to belong to one type not because of the common source or origin of those rites, but on the strength of their being various expressions or manifestations of that very type which itself is permanent and ubiquitous. So here, type goes first and prototype second.

The classical comparativist approach, however useful in establishing similarities in various religions – and the similar ways in which some religions differentiate themselves – has entirely failed to take into account the distinction between the subjective and objective aspects of religious phenomena. This distinction, which may or may not coincide with the distinction between *emic* and *etic* approaches outlined earlier, presupposes that the observer of a religion is aware that his own knowledge of that religion is one thing, and its knowledge of itself is another. And even if both are identical in their factual content, they remain different in nature and character. Let us take the example of Masonic Ritual discussed earlier to illustrate this distinction.

Many Masons themselves claim that their Ritual is very old; that it reaches back to, or can be identified with, some of the most ancient mysteries found in Egypt, the Near East and Mediterranean region, and even that these ancient rites were Masonic. But they also maintain that their ritual is not pagan, for it preceded paganism as the latter preceded Christianity; and more than that, that their Ritual continued within the pagan religions and constituted, or coincided with, the esoteric, hidden core common to all those religions – their secret monotheism. This core, together with the open monotheism of the Hebrews, persisted until the coming of Jesus Christ and the beginning of Christianity, with respect to which it figures as older than Judaism (or anything else, for that matter). This claim must be considered as an expression of the subjective aspect of the Masonic religious complex.

A partisan of the modern comparativist approach to religion, after taking into account this text of Masonic subjective self-awareness, may offer several objective interpretations. One possibility is that in the Masonic Ritual we discover the primary patterns revealed by any initiatory ritual and, for instance, that the presence in the Ritual of a symbolism coinciding with the symbolism used in ancient Egyptian rites only demonstrates that both are manifestations or modifications of the same basic patterns. They do not, therefore, descend from or ascend to one another; since they are inherent to religion, or ritual, or human behaviour, or the human mind, or the structure of the human brain,

Royal Arch Coat of Arms

and so on. According to this view, they are considered as abstract properties which can be called archetypal only since they are more easily traced
in the past than observed in the present. The most interesting thing
here, however, is that in those objectively observed abstract properties
the observer may discover a meaning which may or may not be known
by the actual performers of the ritual: meaning which may or may not
have its subjective aspect. In this connection it is instructive to turn to
some well attested cases where the performers themselves do not know,
by their own admission, the meaning of their actions. The Mayan priests,
for example, in the sixteenth century confessed quite candidly that the
meanings of many of the rituals they performed, and of some symbols
they used, had been irretrievably lost long before the coming of
the Spaniards.[3] Similarly, when I tried recently to find out what two
particular symbols in the coat of arms of the Royal Arch meant, none
of the six Royal Arch Masons whom I consulted was able to explain
them to me. If we return to the oft-rehearsed subject of Masonic secrecy
and suppose (though it would be a supposition I do not in fact share)
that it is the meanings that have been kept secret by the Masons, not
the rites or symbols (and so effectively that many Masons themselves
do not know them), then the situation would seem to be very similar
to that of the Mayan priests. John Fellows writes: "There can be no
pretext for retaining a secret, when the cause that gave it birth
no longer exists. Besides, the Masons do not profess the doctrines of

paganism, they merely repeat the ceremonies, parrot-like, without any regard to or knowledge of the original *intention*."[4] But, of course, there will always remain the possibility for a comparativist observer of the Ritual to establish, as an objective fact, that the things that Masons themselves are not aware of at all – or are aware of but not as an objective fact – are observable in other similar religious situations.

Setting aside the deliberate intention to deceive, a participant, when asked the meaning of something by an observer, may reply that he does not know, or give an explanation which from the observer's etic standpoint is objectively mistaken. The latter must, nevertheless, take these reports absolutely seriously for only from them can he deduce the emic and subjective side of a ritual.

In a Channel Four television programme the Grand Secretary of the Grand Lodge for 1987–8 replied to questions from an audience of students and young people on various aspects of Masonry. They voiced the overwhelming suspicion that there must be something really sinister about Masonic rites on account of their being kept secret, particularly since only one of the sexes participates in them (as if a sinister thing would be less sinister if performed by both men and women). The Grand Secretary tried in his most avuncular manner to persuade his critics that there was nothing really suspicious about Masonic rites, that, on the contrary, everything about them was very pleasant and good fun, and that the secrecy itself simply added a little spice to the harmless games of well-meaning, benign and charitable gentlemen. In describing this miserable episode I am not being ironical. Quite the opposite. To me the Grand Secretary's opinion of the meaning of the Masonic ritual is all-important for I see in it that very subjective aspect which I am talking about. In fact, the Grand Secretary, with the condescension of an old Siberian shaman patiently explaining to a young Methodist missionary the meaning of the Shamanist drum-beating, tried to explain to his audience only one side of the subjective attitude of the Masons to their own Ritual: the side which I have called theatrical, and which is invariably present in *all* rituals – Shamanist or priestly, theurgic or liturgic, initiatory or curative, monotheist or pagan. Which, of course, is not to say that ritualistic theatricality alone can be regarded as one of the meanings, or meaningful elements, of the Masonic or any other ritual. Far from it. For an initiatory, ritual will become meaningful only when coupled with, or complemented by, secrecy. Only when so combined do theatricality and secrecy constitute one of the meanings of a given ritual, which the performers may or may not be aware of; which may either be known by them and constitute a part of their

subjective awareness of it, or remain a purely objective element unconsciously carried within it till the end of time (in which case John Fellows
would say that the Masons repeat the Ritual like parrots, and the Mayan
priests would complain that its meaning had been lost long ago).

In terms of comparative religion, it appears that secrecy is an obligatory feature of most of the known initiatory rites, and it is definitely
connected with almost all rites where a person is initiated into the status
that enables him to perform this initiatory rite himself with the function
of priest. This intermediate position does not exist as an empty, pure
form, it has its own mythological content. It is this content that, practically everywhere and at all times – from the Hittite mythology of the
second millennium BC to the Eskimo mythology of the twentieth century AD – is connected with the dead, with the world of the dead, with
spirits of the dead or, as we see it in the Masonic Ritual, with one dead
person (Hiram) in particular. For what it is always about, in one way
or another, is the death of the Candidate and the birth of the performer.
And it is these death myths that are enacted in the initiatory rites of
the kind just mentioned, and always in the most expository or theatrical
manner. This, however, is not to suggest that such performances serve
only, or even mainly, to persuade or convince those witnessing them, the
inner audience, of the efficacy of the ritual in question. It is subjectively a
theatre for oneself in the first place, and only in the second (and quite
differently) is it made known to the outer audience of the uninitiated,
the general public interested in the case of Freemasons. The secrecy
forms an additional dimension for a ritual, confining its execution to
the very limited human space of those who know the myth and how
to enact it within physical space and astronomical time, determined by
the concrete location of the ritual (in Masonry, the Lodge) and the
length of its performance (the Master Mason Ritual lasts one and a half
to two hours).[5]

However, apart from the three dimensions of space within which the
enactment of the myth in any ritual takes place, we have – and this is
immensely important – the space and time of what is enacted, that is,
of the myth itself. In a ritual, as in the theatre, these dimensions vary
widely: the space of myth may be undetermined, or as large as the space
of its enactment, or it may be a real or imagined geographical area
(such as the Temple of Solomon and Jerusalem with its outskirts in the
Masonic Ritual of Raising), or the earth, or the sea, or the heavens, or
the whole cosmos. Likewise with time: again it may be indeterminate
or uncertain (as in the Ritual of Royal Arch), or as precise as the exact
length of the ritual (as in very many Shamanist curative rites), or it may

extend to include the entire human history, or an almost infinitely long cosmic process. But even when the time and space of performance do coincide with the time and space of myth they remain different, for they belong to two different realities and the very fact that the performer lives simultaneously in both of them produces in him, whether he is conscious of it or not, a powerful psychological effect.[6]

I call this effect psychological for the simple reason that it perceptibly changes the mentality of the performer – perceptibly in the sense that he himself is subjectively aware of these changes and able to describe them to others. When the Grand Secretary exerted himself to enlighten his uncomprehending interlocutors on Channel Four, and said how pleasant it was to perform the Ritual, he was, I am sure, perfectly sincere. For the regular, or even sporadic enactment of a myth might produce in someone who undergoes such an experience a very strong feeling of his or her own life as somewhat scenic and theatrical and as something which is, itself, in a kind of intermediary space between its own reality and that of the myth enacted.[7] And furthermore, the enactment of myth arouses a certain sensation of detachment or autonomy from the everyday reality of life.[8]

If it does not, then you are not a person for ritual, you are not an actor in the esoteric theatre, enacted for oneself, where one experiences a direct reversal of the most noticeable feature of modern theatrical art. Instead of playing other people's lives for other people (theatre imitating life, so to speak), you will be playing for yourself on the scene of your own life, acting in the play which is real only for you and not to an audience consisting of other people (life imitating theatre). But this only happens, of course, if you look at theatre and ritual from the point of view of theatre, not of ritual.

In any event, secrecy, together with theatricality as its inalienable companion, remains an essential feature of practically all transitional rituals or *rites de passage*, and the Masonic initiatory rites are no exception. This is the feature which cannot be accounted for either by the character of Masonic tradition, or by the character of Masonry as a social organization, or, least of all, by the secretive character of Masons themselves: the character of the Ritual itself. And that, ultimately, is what has made Masonry secret.

All this, of course, is not to say that secrecy (along with theatricality) is necessarily either an element of the content of the Masonic, or any other initiatory ritual, or the only phenomenon accompanying it. Moreover, phenomenologically speaking, secrecy should be regarded as an *epiphenomenon* derived from the very structure of initiatory ritual, i.e.

from its mythological content and the way this content is organized and distributed in space and time. It should be noted, however, that in some very particular cases the idea of secrecy may figure as a part of a ritual's mythological content or even – as in the Hiramic Ritual – to serve as the point of departure in the mythological plot.[9] [It is interesting to note that, as an epiphenomenon, secrecy seems to be analogous to the use of percussion in transitional rituals.][10]

Turning from the essential characteristics of the Masonic initiatory Ritual, described in previous chapters, to its mythological content, enacted by its performers, it can be seen that this content holds one remarkable element in common, in one form or another, with thousands of other rituals throughout the world: not only was Master Hiram killed, but his body was maimed before his death and mutilated after he died. This phenomenon, so abundantly observed, studied and described in the ethnographic and anthropological literature of the nineteenth and twentieth centuries from Sir James Frazer to Bronislav Malinowsky, and from Lucien Levy-Bruhl to Claude Lévi-Strauss, still – or so it seems to me – needs to be explained in at least one of its aspects: namely, that mutilation of body postmortem and death are, *mythologically*, two different phenomena.[11] It is the former that is usually enacted in the ritual, very often constituting its focus, while the latter remains, even when it figures in a myth, a far more commonplace and relatively natural event. It would not be an exaggeration to say that mutilation following violent or non-violent death is inherent to ritual, is perhaps itself inherently ritualistic, as a fact of human consciousness.[12]

In the Ritual of Freemasonry we see a clear symmetry: the maiming of Hiram's body (three blows), his death and improper burial, followed by his exhumation, the disintegration of the corpse, and its subsequent recomposition. The first is reflected or repeated in the last. In order to be properly buried in a sacred site his body had to be dismembered and put together again ("limb by limb, joint by joint"), for such is the pattern of myth, a pattern which seems to have been (all historical associations notwithstanding) contrary to, and incompatible with, the rules of the ancient Jewish religion which forms the broader context of Hiram's death, and into which the Hiramic myth was, at one time or another, deliberately inserted. So what we see here is the enactment in a ritual of a necromantic myth, all of which takes place within the framework of the most anti-necromantic religion in the world, a religion where even slightest contact with *any* dead body is, and always has been, regarded as an abominable ritual pollution.[13] And it is not too risky to suppose that the postmortem dismemberment of Hiram reflects in itself the almost ubiquitous myth of the dismemberment of a god, a myth which is a mainstay of comparative religion, and which has been observed in at least twenty cults, dead and alive, from the worship of Osiris in ancient Egypt to the cults of Kali in ancient and modern India, and from the Shamanist cults of the Indians of South America to their counterparts in northern and north-eastern Siberia.

A SCHEMATIZATION OF THE HIRAMIC RITUAL, AS DESCRIBED IN CHAPTER 10.

The Ritual clearly follows a tripartite scheme:

The maiming of Hiram's live body	*The death of Hiram*	*The decomposition or dismemberment of Hiram's dead body, and its recomposition*

This scheme is complemented by a triple sequence of burials:

The first burial ("casual")	*The second burial ("proper" though temporary)*	*The third burial ("formal", i.e. according to Jewish rules)*

In the light of a comparativist approach, the maiming of Hiram's live body, the dismembering of his corpse and its subsequent recomposition (however unintentionally, it is in fact a mutilation) appear not only as *symmetrical*, with the death of Hiram as the centre of the symmetry,[14] but also as two different and not infrequently separate rituals. As distinct performances they figure in a number of cases when the body of the performer is symbolically (and sometimes literally) mutilated, or dissected either by other participants, or by the protagonist himself, without its resulting in death or subsequent dismemberment again of the corpse. That is what we see, for instance, in the Shamanist practice of the Yakuts, where a great shaman, in the initial phase of the ritual trance, sees his body dismembered before he gets in contact with his spirit-assistant. Or, as in the curative seances of some of the Ket (a Yenisseyan tribe) shamans, where the body of the patient is dissected into many pieces each of which is washed, cleaned and then put together again.[15] But all these events, as I understand them, take place in an animist context, that is, in the context of a belief in the existence of spiritual beings (usually animals) able to influence or control the course of affairs in the material world. However phenomenologically deficient the theory of animism as a primary stage and "natural minimum" of religion might be, it still reflects the present state of our thinking about what *we* call religion.[16] At any rate, the maiming of Hiram's body can be seen as reproducing the trials of the soul either before physical death, or during the intermediary state (or stage) between physical death and the complete transformation of soul.[17] Even in such an utterly non-magical and non-ritualistic religion as early historical Buddhism, the Buddha Shakayamuni suffered greatly from a terrible and partly self-inflicted disease before he died.[18] After his death and the consummation of his body by fire, his bodily relics were picked up and distributed between the eight groups of his worshippers. The last detail presents a direct analogy to the dismemberment of the dead body of Hiram, and both follow the same mythological symmetry.

The Hiramic Ritual exhibits another general feature belonging to almost all transitional rites: everything that is experienced by the protagonists in these rites (or any myths which reflect such rites) is experienced not by him as himself in his own person, but by him as if as someone else. He becomes another in the process of the ritual. Thus, the Candidate is "tortured" as if he were Hiram, dies as Master Hiram died and, as a result, he becomes the Word and figures as Master Hiram from then on. If, however, we dare digress from that rather literal Masonic explanation, and follow the more gnostically oriented Masonic philosophers, we will see quite another manifestation of otherness in this Ritual, namely: that the Word is understood not as a Mason, but as the soul of a Mason or as the symbol of the soul. Then all that happens to the Candidate does, in fact, happen to the soul which he was not aware that he possessed before the Ritual began. Therefore it is his own soul, which is a Candidate's "other", whose transitional sufferings and passions he enacts in the Ritual. Man as a performer acting (i.e. suffering) as his soul can be found in thousands of rituals and in the plots of numerous myths, legends and fairytales. Three things are important to note.

To say that the soul acts, suffers and dies, is not a solecism, for, as can be seen in countless ethnographical and anthropological contexts, a soul is not necessarily immortal: it may have its own life and death, not to speak of the fact that in some of those contexts a person may have several souls, some of which are more mortal than others. Secondly, the soul here is not opposed to the *body* of the performer: such a simple dichotomy marks the infancy of the theory of animism as espoused by Sir Edward Tylor and, no more than partly, by Sir James Frazer. For, as is convincingly demonstrated by ancient and particularly early medieval Indian mythology, the soul may also have its own "body".[19] And, thirdly, there are certainly a number of cases in the history of religion where a person's soul is thought of either as positively mortal, or as indefinite with respect to its mortality or immortality. The soul here (as well as the supernatural a little further on) is conceived of simply as that which is secondary to, and a concrete and particular case of, the otherness manifested in any *rites de passage*.

This, in turn, presupposes a variety of ways in which the soul can exist and the uniqueness of the way in which the performer acts as that entity, due to the strict limitations imposed by the scheme of the ritual on the actions of the performer. For the notion of otherness seems to be not only phenomenologically primary in relation to that of soul, Hiram, the spirit of an ancestor, and so forth, but also far broader than these, as represented in the mythology and folklore. When, in the introduction to the Ritual, the Candidate embarks on his journey in search of the Word, he is, still, himself, not another, and his assuming the names of Boaz and Jachin (emblematized by two pillars) marks no more than his admission to the context of the Ritual, in terms of space – the Lodge as meeting place – and time – the duration of the meeting of Masons. The ritual itself as, probably, any other transitional ritual, has a very succinctly drawn dividing line that separates a candidate's still natural state, he as himself, from the transformed state of "him as another", and it is this transformation that is transitional *par excellence* and that is kept secret, or hidden, in one way or another.[20] And more than that, it can be suggested, however historically or ethnographically unprovable this may be, that, phenomenologically speaking, it is in the transitional ritual that otherness as a structure of consciousness finds its manifestation.[21]

The most interesting point, however, is that the formula *the performer acts (or suffers) as his soul*, in a transitional ritual may work the other way around; the soul, spirit, god, or any other supernatural entity, acts (or suffers) as a man, animal, tree, stone, or any other natural thing, animate or inanimate. The supernatural dies as natural. It follows that animate versus inanimate is not among the basic distinctions of a phenomenology of religion. Moreover, in a wide spectrum of myths the distinction between natural things that may be inhabited, temporarily or permanently, by the supernatural, and the supernatural as that which may inhabit the former, seems to be even more important than the distinction between "the sacred and the profane" (as formulated in the 1900s by Emile Durkheim, and in the late 1930s by Mircea Eliade). The sacred, then, can be reduced to all the things (as well as times, places, words, etc.) which are marked by the presence of the supernatural. So, in the case of the Masonic Ritual, for example "the Word" is sacred, while the soul to which the Word is symbolically related is supernatural.[22]

The second stage of the Ritual, where the Candidate becomes as if another – that is, Hiram – brings us to the second general type of ritual, the Eucharistic, where a body is broken up and distributed to the participant(s) so that they may, symbolically, become or partake of the essence of that body. The disintegration, dismemberment and subsequent recomposition of Hiram's dead body belong to this type of rite.

Contrary to the first general type, the rituals of the second are characterized by a marked centrifugal tendency; the performer's action is directed outwards rather than inwards, even in some instances outside the ritual itself. A eucharistic Ritual is, in principle, indefinite, and can be endlessly repeated. It represents a mirror-image of the transitional ritual to which, as it was pointed out earlier, it is symmetrically related. In the case of the Masonic ritual taken as a whole, as one very complex ethos, the singling out of its eucharistic phase would be by no means a simple task. Starting with the natural, though violent, death of Master Hiram (natural on account of its being related to Hiram's physical body), it is this death which serves as the axis of symmetry and main divide in the Ritual.

The very event, or fact, of Hiram's dead body, if presented as constituting one element of the ethos, clearly has a tripartite structure, consisting of three more or less different, and ritually heterogeneous, parts: the disintegration of the body through putrefaction, its dismemberment by the Masons, and its recomposition. The first stage of this necromantic complex occupies an intermediary position between the natural and the supernatural, and between the transitional and eucharistic types of rituals. On the one hand, what we have here is an entirely natural phenomenon of a decomposed corpse, a phenomenon which is equal to death in its ritually extremely polluting effect. On the other hand, and this is certainly true so as far as the Hiramic legend goes, we have here the idea of a dead body as that which may provide one with a clue to the secret of the Word, or as that from which the Word may directly or indirectly be obtained, for the corpse, though a natural and inanimate thing in itself, serves as an instrument for or repository of the supernatural. (This is an excellent example of a thing which, while not being sacred, is unambiguously supernatural.) The corpse as an instrument or repository of the supernatural is also an animist notion that is immensely widespread, from Vetala, the "Flying Corpse" of Indian Folklore, to the *ro-longs* of Tibetan folk-tales – and is considered as inhabitable or usable by the spirits of their previous possessors as well as by other spirits, or even by those still alive who know the secret of how to govern and control a corpse by means of magical words or combinations of sounds – *mantras* – uttered or written.[23]. All this, however, is provided that a corpse is not completely decomposed, but still fit enough for magical manipulation, which, of course, Hiram's corpse was not.

So, by the second phase of the Ritual we arrive at the idea and the use of a dead body, which had already undergone two significant alterations of the primary animistic scheme: the body is putrid and therefore unfit for magical purposes, and instead of using the body and controlling it by means of the Word, the performers dismember it in search of that very Word. For a ritual to have an inverse scheme is a commonplace in comparative religion, and our use of the word primary here is a mere terminological convention having, probably, no historical basis at all, but it may help us to understand the modifications in religious phenomena when these are not given to us in a historical sequence.[24] So, if the disintegration of Hiram's corpse is natural and spontaneous, though also symbolically enacted in the Ritual, its dismemberment is deliberate and intentional: the task is to find and become the Master Mason's Word, in his body. And this re-gathering of what has been dismembered gives a peculiarly Masonic turn to the Eucharistic type of ritual, reversing its usual direction and using recomposition rather than distribution to become the supernatural element.

The Eucharistic character of this phase of the Ritual becomes even more overt in the exotic modifications made in a number of the Higher Degrees where some distributive elements of the Eucharist are inserted. John Fellows writes:

In the practice existing in a *modern* degree of Masonry, denominated *Le Petit Architecte* . . . a potion [of a kind of "sacrificial cake" made up of poppy-seed and honey] . . . is given to the Candidate, which, he is told, is *a part of the heart of Hiram*, preserved ever since his assassination . . .[25]

This interpretation, of course, finds itself at variance not only with the reassembling of the body before the (second) burial of Hiram, but also with Hiram's official funeral.

In another light, the last phase of the Ritual, the recomposition of the decomposed body, symbolizes the reintegration of "fallen man", man in general, as well as the man who had lost the "Word–Soul–Self" and remained in the darkness of ignorance. Under this Neo-Gnostic interpretation, the meaning of this phase of the Ritual corresponds, on the whole, to the concept of *the eternal return*, elaborated by Mircea Eliade, according to which any death ritual can be seen as also initiatory: after his "second death" (the "first" being symbolized by the ritual of initiation proper) the protagonist returns to the pristine, sometimes pre-creational state of spiritual wholeness and wholesomeness, a state that was symbolically prefigured in the initiatory rites. "Otherness" here assumes its quasi-temporal aspect: by recomposing the body of Hiram (i.e. the Candidate), the Ritual brings the Candidate back to his golden primordial past of knowledge, happiness and innocence, the past where he becomes one with his "other" life which is more real and, at the same time, it brings the Candidate forward, towards the future which is his final, actual physical death; it prepares his body for the conventional funeral which lies outside the Masonic ritual.[26]

In writing all this I am bearing in mind that even such a seemingly simple and unquestionable binary opposition as "naturally decomposed body" versus "supernaturally resurrected body" by no means exhausts the problem even if we confine ourselves to the Masonic context. In the Rosicrucian legend, the body of Christian Rosenkreutz, the founder of the Rosicrucian Fraternity (who lived 106 years) was discovered some 120 years after his natural death still untouched by decay. This intermediate position might well suggest that what we deal with here is a kind of hibernation, quite reminiscent of the "half-death half-sleep" state which is ascribed to the King of the Grail in the twelfth-century poem by Wolfram von Eschenbach.[27]

The transition from the last phase of the Ritual proper to the conventional Jewish obsequies ordered for Hiram by Solomon reflects the ambiguity of that phase. For while the ritual core of the Hiramic legend suggests that the recomposition of the corpse is a *magical* act – an act of supernatural transformation – the context of the legend as a whole suggests that the recomposition is but a preparation of Hiram's dead body for his funeral, the Judaist character of which leaves no place for anything at all supernatural in connection with dead bodies. As we have already seen, within the instructional context of the Ritual the Candidate is told by the Worshipful Master that through his symbolic suffering and dying as Hiram, he will be duly prepared for his own real and natural death. And it is this death that is followed by an extremely sober and austere funeral rite of the sort performed upon the decease of Dr Anderson; far more sober and austere even than the Jewish funeral rites performed for Hiram. During the official explanation of the procedures of the Ritual, the strongest emphasis is put on the mortality of the Mason/Candidate, on his death as a natural phenomenon, on the subsequent decomposition of the corpse as a natural phenomenon, and on its recomposition for reburial as a merely formal act of "symbolic preparation" for his ultimate *Masonic* (no longer Jewish, as with Hiram) funeral rites.

This cannot help bringing us back to the Masonic Ritual in total as the clearest example of what I have called religious syncretism, and the investigation into how this strangest phenomenon of religious consciousness found its manifestation in the context of such a Ritual.

Let us start then from the end, from the Master Mason's real death and subsequent funeral. This ceremony in no way pertains to the Ritual of the Master Mason or to any other secret ritual of Freemasonry, though it might appear incomprehensible to any mourners who were not Masons.

The end is that very short, specifically Masonic rite which is performed after the usual Anglican, Baptist, Catholic or other service has already taken place. The Masons there are fully aware that their actions are not only the last before burial or cremation, but essentially different – different because their *non-Christian* character is self-evident, not only to any Christian present, but also to any Freemason who may be performing them. I do not know whether they would regard their reciting the Psalms and clasping hands as Judaist, or more Judaist than Christian, or at least, as neutral to both Christianity and Judaism. But I am absolutely certain that the Freemasons performing these last rites, among whom are very many Anglican priests, including some bishops, know very well that what they are doing is perfectly compatible with either Christianity or Judaism, or both. The actual Masonic funeral rite is related to a Christian (or any other) funeral rite preceding it in an analogous way to that in which the ancient Jewish funeral rite of Hiram is related to the three phases of the Masonic Ritual of initiation of Master Mason. Both ceremonies betray the markedly *syncretic* character of these three phases. As the actual Masonic funeral rite neutralizes the spiritual, soul-oriented, character of a Christian burial service, so the Judaist funeral rite in the Hiramic legend neutralizes the essential animism of the three episodes which lead up to it – mutilation of the body, decomposition, both natural and deliberate, of the dead body, and its recomposition. It does not follow from all this, of course, that Freemasons and Jews do not believe in the existence of the soul and life after death – far from it. What really follows is that both Freemasonry and Judaism, when observed within the syncretic context of the Ritual, are not obviously oriented towards the ideas of soul and life after death. And it is this syncretic context which always generates the type of self-awareness marked by *religious relativism*, without which Freemasonry simply cannot be described or understood at all.[28]

Returning, once again, to the funeral rite in the Hiramic legend, but this time looking at it in the light of religious syncretism, we will see that there is no contradiction between the Judaist concepts of naturality of death and the impurity of the corpse, and the third phase of the Ritual, the recomposition of the body. For the syncretic framework of the Ritual, the Hiramic legend itself – irrespective of when and where the legend was formed, or became the vehicle for actual or reconstructed patterns of earlier rituals – reflects in its structure and plot some ideas about other rituals which were abstracted from their actual performances long before the legend was adopted and moulded by Freemasons for their own purposes. We called this phase of the Ritual – the recomposition of Hiram's body – ambiguous, exactly because it contains an idea which would seem totally magical and animistic if looked at from the point of view of the two previous phases, and totally formal and natural if looked at from the point of view of the subsequent funeral rite. In a comparativist perspective, all known ritualistic attitudes to the dead body form a spectrum with two polar extremes: the maximal annihilation of the body, represented by classical cremation where no relics or ashes are kept, and its maximal preservation represented by the ancient Egyptian custom of mummification. The Jewish burial service may be placed somewhere in the middle, for the disintegration of the corpse is left to nature. The corpse is not a theme in Judaism.[29] Nor, as has been noted, is the soul. Judaism, through its very formal and conventional funeral, neutralizes the magic and mythology of the third phase of the Ritual which, in turn, de-mythologizes and casts the light of *monotheism* over the first two phases. Let us not forget, however, that not only are the three phases of the Ritual given to us in the, formally at least, Jewish context of the whole legend but that the whole legend is given to us within a Masonic context. And here we have the next step: it is the religion of Freemasons that neutralizes, to an extent, the absolute Jewish monotheism of the legend in the way the latter has already neutralized the animism of the Ritual.

But the syncretism of the Masonic religious situation is not exhausted by this triple context, that is, the three phases of the Ritual within the Jewish context of the legend, and that Jewish context within the Masonic context of the whole Ritual. For being itself syncretic, Freemasonry enters into a very complex relationship with Christianity without being, however, amalgamated into it. Christianity provides Freemasonry with its ideas of religious universalism but never becomes dissolved in Freemasonry, always remaining on the margins of its Ritual, occupying a peculiar intermediate position between its esoteric teaching and the exoteric individual religious consciousness (and conscience) of its members. The role of Christianity within the syncretic complex of Freemasonry can be excellently illustrated by the writings of two prominent Masonic authors of the nineteenth century, William Hughan and the Deputy Grand Master of the Punjab, Josiah Whymper. In the introduction to Whymper's book, Hughan states that ". . . the original principles of Freemasonry were based on Christian *Catholicity* . . . and they all tend in the direction of *absolute cosmopolitanism* and *religious universality* . . ."[30]

However Masonically trivial this statement might seem to be, it contains quite an interesting idea, of which its author must have been fully aware: that Christianity is, for Freemasonry, a kind of point of departure as regards religious catholicity (i.e. universality), and that the main religious aim of Freemasonry as a religion is to become even more universal than Christianity. Whymper goes further in this direction. At first he establishes for Freemasons a *degree* (!) of Christianism higher than that reached by Christians themselves, which he identifies with *theism:*

. . . A mere believer in God is not thus eligible as a Mason; if he believes in Him, and yet does not believe that He will answer prayer, the doors of M—y remain closed. This point alone brings us to *Theism as opposed to Deism*, being a Masonic requirement.[31]

Then he establishes the initial, unequivocally Christian, postulates in relation to Freemasonry, which would have done honour to an ordinary Christian gnostic living, say, in Alexandria in the third century AD, adding some reservations about the ability of members of various creeds (including Christians) to accept them:

. . . Craft Masonry, in its complete Degrees, insists on a *belief*:

    1st, In a Revelation from God to man;
    2nd, In a Resurrection;
    3rd, In the immortality of the soul;
    4th, In the Logos of St John.

We know that *these* conditions *can not* be accepted by many . . . the Buddhists reject all of them . . .
. . . We cannot assert that any known religion, except the *Christian*, *accepts all of them.* The *Parsee* belief is perhaps that which approximates closest to our requirements.[32]

And, finally, he allocates to Christianity its due part in the whole syncretic balance of Freemasonry which begins to figure as the "World Religion":

. . . At the present time it is impossible to assert that any *initial* form of religious belief affords a common point of union for even half the human race ... On the one hand the Christian Mason has stifled his feelings, he has cancelled and done away with Christian allusions, so as not to cause offence to others, and to obtain *universality*. On the other hand, the Hebrew appropriates to himself the Royal Arch degree, which the Christian has thoughtlessly turned adrift ... The Christian is distinctly the sufferer by the result. He alone has abandoned his religion, whilst the brethren of all other beliefs have asserted theirs.[33]

The last passage is immensely curious. Not only does it declare syncretism (practically identical to universalism here) as the way Freemasonry exists as a teaching and institution, but it posits it as that which underlies Freemasonry as the absolute religious principle. Absolute in the sense that it is neither historical (original) nor psychological (intentional), for it pertains to the *objectivity* of religion and thereby does not depend on one's being aware of it in one's own religious life or practice. From which, by the way, it follows that Christianity figures as just a *particular* case – *primus inter pares* – amongst all the various religious practices. It is that objective religious principle which is opposed, not only to all historical manifestations of the non-historical patterns described above, when speaking of the general features (secrecy/theatricality) and phases of the Masonic Ritual, but to those patterns themselves.

Thus, if in the composition of its ritual, the character of its symbolism, and the principles of its organizational structure Freemasonry can be studied objectively – as an object of anthropology, sociology, ethnography, or psychology of religion – in its awareness of itself as non-historical, non-psychological, and even non-religious (in the sense of a particular religion) it defies any comparativist, structuralist, or historical approach. Masons, as well as structuralists or comparativists, may or may not disagree, but what I am talking of now is a fact of Masonic *religious consciousness* exposed by a very learned and devout Brother, and as an observer of Freemasonry I am privileged to include it within the field of my observation and make it a part of my subject of investigation.

Notes

1 Rodney Needham, "Percussion and Transition", *Man*, 1967, Vol. II (R. Needham, 1967), p. 609.
2 From a personal letter of Count S. Poborovsky.

3 They may simply have been preserving their religious secrets from prying Spanish eyes!

4 J. Fellows, 1866, pp. 132–3. And he emphasizes below (*idem*, p. 148): "They [i.e. the Masons of the Three Degrees] knew not what was meant by the ceremonies; they were pleased, however, with the shows."

5 As Zinovy Zinik, a writer and theatre critic, has pointed out, the astronomical time of the performance of a play is fixed within its external limits (i.e. the beginning and the end of a play as a whole, and of each of its *parts* or *acts* taken separately), but within these limits the actors can enjoy a certain "time freedom", i.e. they can improvise with time and space as far as the external limits allow, unlike in the cinema, where time and space are fixed once and for all. It is from this intentional freedom in theatre – as Ralph Richardson suggested – that the most positive affective states of the action are derived. Ritual shares that peculiarity with theatre, being, in fact, even looser than the latter with respect to its external limits.

6 Which, according to some recent works on dreams, seems to be quite akin to the effect produced by so-called "lucid dreams".

7 This returns us again to the highly speculative notion of the three realities – empirical, metaphysical or mystical, and intermediary, i.e. experienced in ritual (or in a "lucid dream") – that can be used in a merely instrumental way for the description of religious phenomena and particularly ritual. See in Rodney Needham, *Primordial Characters*, University Press of Virginia, 1978 (R. Needham, 1978), pp. 61–8.

8 This, of course, brings us back to the problem of the effects produced by performance on the performers, a problem which is relevant to ritual. To sum it up: a ritual enables one to have another life, endowing the performer thereby, with an additional degree of personal freedom but, at the same time, severely limiting his freedom in that other life by the imposition of the ritual's own structural limits. A performer becomes on the one hand freer, for he can always choose between his ordinary life and a ritual, but once *within* a ritual, his choice is limited, for his behaviour has already become "ritualized", i.e. formalized by the rules of the play, so to speak. But all this is about the inner or psychological state of a performer; it cannot be perceived by those who perceive the play, though it can be shared by them in their own way.

9 Still, I am inclined to see this as an exception. For the fact that Hiram was brutally murdered for refusing to reveal the secret (the Word) can be accounted for by the possibility of the whole Ritual being rethought and reinterpreted post factum, in order to *explain* the secrecy. This, however, is no more than conjecture.

10 R. Needham, 1967, pp. 608–12. In fact, what he says about percussion is almost literally applicable to secrecy: ". . . this quality [of sound] is significantly associated with transition from one state to another or with mediating between one category and another such as earthly and spiritual." And further, while characterizing "numbers" and "percussion" as "symbolic" factors, he writes: ". . . They are vehicles for significance but they do not convey explicit universal meaning . . ." 1978, pp. 10–11. It would not be superfluous to note in this connection that percussion is amply used in some Masonic rituals and particularly in the Royal Arch Degree. J. Fellows, 1866, p. 302.

11 Mythological, as always in this book, does not mean non-logical or, least of all, pre-logical: it simply means "found in the context of a myth" where there does

not exist any thinkable binary opposition, such as mythological/non-mythological. Nor does the relative constancy of forms and plots of mythological texts suggest that these are more easily recognizable as myths than other forms and plots are as non-myths. Moreover, I am quite sure that the situations of our ordinary everyday life, private as well as social, are not any less uniform or repetitive than those found in the contexts of myths, legends, or fairytales. Had some not yet existing descriptive psychology ever described the former in the way the latter have been described by Aarne, Thomson, Andreev and Propp, the popular notion of the immense richness of the situations of so-called real life would have been radically changed, if not destroyed altogether.

12 Here lies an operational definition (one of very many) of mythology: consciousness may pick up some situations – its own or those of another consciousness – and call them mythic. In this sense the opposition of logical or scientific thought to mythological thinking is as historically conditioned and phenomenologically deficient as the opposition of theology to mythology, or any other such binary divisions to which our ideologies are so addicted.

13 Poor Dewar (1968) is desperate to show his abhorrence of this ritual, exhibiting a typically ancient Jewish attitude to necromancy, even when this is present in an entirely symbolic way. Modern humanists tend to react to symbols even more strongly than to reality, and rightly so!

14 That the death of Hiram, as described in the Legend, is not, itself, a ritual, is stressed by the fact that it is not followed by a ritual, though it is enacted by the Candidate as an element of the Masonic Ritual.

15 N. N. Ksenofontov, *The Yakut Tales of Shamans* (in Russian), Moscow, 1931; from the oral report on the fieldwork among Kets in the summer, 1960 (by V. N. Toporov).

16 Those following the shamanistic tradition do not, of course, refer to themselves as animists. A "classical" theory of animism was proposed by E. B. Tylor (*Primitive Culture*, London, 1873), and developed by Marett (1903, 1908); see also: W. A. Lessa and E. Z. Vogt, *Rider in Comparative Religion*, fourth ed., London, 1979, pp. 7–19; V. Ya. Propp, *The Historical Roots of the Fairytale* (in Russian), Moscow, 1947.

17 *The Tibetan Book of the Dead* is full of descriptions of the trials experienced by the dead in an intermediary state (*bardo*) between dying and death, and between death and reincarnation.

18 While referring to this episode (as described in the *Maha-Parinibbana-sutta* of the *Sutta-Pitaka* of the Pali canon), I am occupying the position not only of an external observer of the Buddhist *religion*, but also of a person aware of his exclusively etic approach to it. For, according to some *Buddhist* commentaries on the passage, the disease, though *willed* by the Buddha, was a merely physical phenomenon, had physical causes, and was, itself, the immediate material cause of the Buddha's *physical* death.

19 Ancient Indian culture certainly provided the background for the most absolute and absolutist conception of soul (or, properly speaking, self, *atman*) which was regarded as eternal, uncreated, and un-affectable by any material acts or influences. It is in the context of this conception that the idea of three bodies appeared, namely: the body of soul, the body of mind, and the body of body.

20 This divide also has its *cognitive* or epistemological side, namely: it marks a

transition from ignorance (as it is stated in the Worshipful Master's speech before and after the Ritual) to knowledge. The latter is to be understood as both the knowledge of the Word, and the Knowledge of what has hitherto been hidden, i.e. the Ritual itself.

21 It may also be asserted that *psychologically* the transitional ritual generates in the performer some mental (emotional, affective, etc.) states which would *enable* him to act or think in a way he would never be able to act or think outside those states. Only acting and thinking *as another, not as himself,* can the performer do what he does and think what he thinks in the course of the ritual. There is a wide spectrum of these states, ranging from ritually induced trances, to extasis and, in particular, the states of possession.

22 When all is said and done, we may say that "the sacred" is given to the external observer in *a phenomenon* (temple, ritual, festival, myth, etc.) which might be described as a whole (*ethos*), or as a function or cluster of functions. Whereas "the supernatural" is a purely *relational notion* in the phenomenology of religion, a notion which cannot be a term of description of the facts observed, but which can be used in an *interpretation* of those facts by the observer as well as by the observed. So, when in a commentary on a passage from the Vedas (the sacred books of the ancient Indians) we read that the "soma [a potion used in their sacrificial rituals] which we give to the Gods and drink ourselves is not the real soma", we understand that, using our descriptive language, the soma which we give and drink is sacred: it has a certain function, but there is another soma which is supernatural. Similarly, when we read in some Masonic books that the Masonic Ritual has a meaning and power that cannot be realized by its performers, for such a realization is *about* the performance itself, this meaning and power can be described as supernatural, in relation to the sacredness of the Ritual.

23 One of the later modifications of this idea having, probably, its source in the Egyptian magical practices of the Hellenistic period, can be seen in the medieval Jewish legend of the Golem.

24 Provided, of course, that we use the term primary, and other such-like terms, as *mere abstractions of our own understanding.* So "the past" of which we were talking at the beginning of the chapter is, in fact, also no more than an abstraction of our understanding of the facts of religion.

25 J. Fellows, 1866, pp. 152–3. This, according to some of the Masonic theorists, alludes to or derives from the Christian Eucharist, which may or may not be so. What *is* most essential here is that although in the context of the Ritual Hiram *is* the Word, and the Word is the Soul, as the central personage of the legend enacted in the Ritual, he remains an *ordinary mortal.* A mortal man, not being a spirit, is not supposed to know – according to his mythological context – what would happen to him after his death. In an extremely interesting commentary on one of the early Celtic mythical cycles, the brothers Rees note that the great sorcerers know *how* to transform themselves miraculously into various animal forms, but while being in those forms are not aware of themselves as sorcerers who actually started this line of transformations. So what we have here can easily be reduced to two main points. The first, that both the sorcerers and things or beings into which they are transformed are *natural* and endowed with a kind, or degree, of awareness appropriate to the physical status of the being: a man, or a leaf, or a stone, or a dragonfly, etc. The second, what counts as *supernatural,* is the transformation from one being into

another, a transformation which can be imagined as resulting from the sorcerer's conscious impulse at the time of transformation followed by non-consciousness while abiding in that other thing. See in A. Rees and B. Rees, *Celtic Heritage*, London, 1973.

26 This "outside the Ritual" character of the Masonic funeral, its non-mystical, non-transformational meaning, and an extremely rationalistic understanding of it by Masons themselves was strongly emphasized by almost all Masonic authors of the eighteenth century. "The last offices paid to the dead, are only useful as *lectures* to the living ... Fix your eyes on the last scene; view life stript of her ornaments and exposed in her *natural* manners; you will then be convinced of the futility of those empty delusions ..." W. Preston, 1804, p. 205.

27 This kind of "hibernation" is one of the most widespread *motives* of German, Celtic and Caucasian folklore.

28 The Masonic apologists of the nineteenth century were very apprehensive of the possible theological consequences of the use of the notions of "syncretism" and "relativism" (or their equivalents) in the descriptions of the Masonic rituals and beliefs. They were not able to accept the fact that their religious situation was syncretic and relativist, and always tried to present it in terms of belief alone, i.e. as monotheistic by definition and Christian by implication. One of the most typical cases of such a stand can be seen in: Chalmers Izett Paton, *Freemasonry, Its Two Great Doctrines ...*, London, 1878.

29 Here I would like to note that the whole spectrum of ideas connected with funeral rites can also be seen as having three, not two, extreme cases. The Egyptian mummification would then be opposed to the Judaist burial, as the maximum of non-natural (artificial) preservation is opposed to the maximum of natural disintegration, and to the Indian funeral pyre, as the maximum of non-natural preservation is opposed to the maximum of non-natural destruction. These three extreme cases I am inclined to regard as abstract non-historical patterns of the human religious attitude to the dead body.

30 J. Whymper, 1888, p. iv.

31 *Idem*, p. 158.

32 *Idem*, pp. 168–9.

33 *Idem*, p. 205.

CHAPTER 13

Hiramic Ritual as Legend, Plot and Theme

A Simple Comparativist Sketch

I am now passing from the study of Masonic ritual and its mythological and cultic associations, perspectives and retrospectives, to a brief investigation of the text proper, or the Masonic tale.

Hiram Abiff's death as told and thereafter enacted within the Ritual is a Masonic legend, a legend not only in the dictionary sense of an "un-authentic Story handed down by tradition and popularly believed to be historical" (*OED*), but also in the sense of actual content. Thus, a core plot may itself be mythological (that is, singled out by the mythologist as an abstract, general, or even universal pattern of events and situations, ritualistic, or symbolical, or all three together – but when it becomes an event or situation happening to a certain named person or persons, at a certain time and in a certain place, it is no longer important whether it is real or imaginary. "Core plot" here is a philological abstraction, or more exactly, a mythological *invariant*, in relation to which the plots of concrete legends would figure as *variants* or *versions*.[1] In this purely methodological sense it might be said that the actual core plot of the Masonic legend called "the Death of Hiram Abiff" could be reduced to, or historically preceded by, the *themes* (not core plots) such as "the Death of the Master Builder" and "Death on the Building Site". For theme here denotes the direction of a person's thinking when he or she is conscious of one thing in the plot as being another, or rather, when one thing is interpreted as another. In this case the plot, the Murder of Master Mason Hiram, might be interpreted as a concrete and particular version of the theme of the Death of the Master Builder, which if given to us in an actual text may figure as a plot or core plot or, in its turn, as a concrete and particular version related to the Death on the Building Site as its theme. For the more general the theme, the less likely it is to coincide, literally, with the specific plot in a given text.

This approach is, of course, very conjectural, for how are we to treat all those plots in modern European literature where the accidental, or even self-inflicted death of a Master Builder – as in Ibsen – is a part of the plot? Could we account for this plot by spontaneous influence, conscious borrowing, unconscious or subconscious projection?

How should the relationship of the Masonic legend to the description of Hiram in I Kings and II Chronicles be understood? For a start, the biblical description is a *primary* text – primary in the sense that it is the *text*, and not a plot or a theme, to which the Masonic Ritual refers as its basis, and which is invariably regarded by Freemasons as the source of the tale of Hiram within the Ritual. And it is primary as a text that is interpreted by Masons themselves not only in and during the Ritual, but also in their lectures, books and pamphlets which could be regarded as secondary (tertiary, etc.) texts in relation to the biblical account of Hiram's doings and circumstances. The biblical text would also be primary as the object of *my* interpretation, in my attempt to relate to it the Masonic legend as well as to other texts.

The extracts from I Kings and II Chronicles below are given in abbreviation.

I Kings, 6, 37. In the fourth year [of Solomon's reign] was the foundation of the house of the Lord laid in the month Zif.

38. And in the 11th year, in the month Bul . . . was the house finished . . . So was he seven years in building it.

II Chronicles, 2, 3. And Solomon sent to Huram [an alternative spelling of Hiram], the King of Tyre, saying

7. . . . Send me now therefore a man cunning to work in gold, and in silver, and in brass, and in iron . . .

11. Then Huram . . . answered in writing which he sent to Solomon [saying] . . .

13. And now I have sent a cunning man, endued with understanding, of Hiram my father's,[2]

14. The son of a woman of the daughters of Dan, and his father was a man of Tyre, skilful to work in gold, and in silver, in brass, in iron, in stone, and in timber, in purple, in blue . . . also to grave any manner of graving . . .

I Kings, 7, 13. And King Solomon sent and fetched Hiram out of Tyre.

14. He was a widow's son of the tribe of Naphtali,[3] and his father was a man of Tyre, a worker in brass: and he was filled with wisdom, and understanding, and cunning to work all works in brass. And he came to King Solomon, and wrought all his work.

15. For he cast two pillars of brass of eighteen cubits high apiece . . .

21. And he set up the pillars in the porch of the temple: and he set up the right pillar, and called the name thereof Jachin: and he set up the left pillar, and called the name thereof Boaz.

The plot here is very simple: when the House of the Lord was finished, Solomon asked the King of Tyre to send him a man skilful in all metals. Huram sent to Solomon Hiram, a wise man and cunning in all works in brass and other metals. He was a widow's son. His mother was of the daughters of Dan (and of the tribe of Naphtali), and his father was a man of Tyre and a worker in brass. Hiram cast two pillars of brass and set them up in the porch of the temple, and called the right pillar Jachin, and the left, Boaz.

The core plot of the Masonic legend of Hiram's death, in its most condensed form, might be presented as follows: the Master Mason Hiram Abiff was murdered on the building site of the almost completed Temple of Solomon by three wicked builders (apprentices?). He was put to death for not revealing to them the most secret Word of the Master Mason.

The main relation of the core plot of the legend to that of the primary biblical text (and not the other way around, for the primary text was in no way *intentionally* related to the legend) is that in both of them the main protagonist is *the same person*, but in the legend something happened to him which *did not* happen to him in the primary text (though it *might have*): first, he was not killed on the building site and was not, in fact, a master builder, and second, the actual work of building was already completed. But that is why this is a legend in relation to the primary text, for one of the defining characteristics of a legend is that its core plot is based on or derived from another (consciously or unconsciously, knowingly or unknowingly) though the theme of the original may change in the process.

The theme of the Masonic legend is the death of the Master Mason . . . and this is so objectively, just as any outsider might read or hear about it as part of the Ritual, as well as subjectively, just as the Masons themselves understand it and speak of it. But the text of the biblical passages referring to Hiram the brass-worker does not reveal to us its theme subjectively, though, of course, we may have some objective doubts about the relation between our two core plots.

First, not only was Hiram changed from a brass-worker into a master mason, the perimeter of Solomon's Temple into its previous building-site, and the religion of Yahweh into that of the Great Architect of the Universe, but, far more importantly, the porch of the Temple with its two pillars was isolated from the Temple itself, and each of the pillars assumed, in the legend and Ritual, its own religious significance.

Moreover – and this is a merely objective factor of which neither of our texts seems to be conscious – there is also an interesting separation, both in time and space, of the constructional and architectural elements of the Temple from the decorative and ornamental. For, as has been stressed by various biblical scholars and historians of architecture, the pillars themselves had no real function in the construction of the porch, serving as a mere embellishment.[4] But if this is so, would it necessarily mean that the genuine, original function of these two pillars, i.e. in the place from which Hiram came, was a merely decorative and ornamental one?[5]

And now we come to the third conjecture, namely that the two pillars cast of brass by Hiram were not only an external ornamental addition to the stone Temple, but were also in themselves part of a religion totally extraneous to that of the Temple. Pillars, in Phoenician Tyre, symbolically represented the chief city-god of Tyre (or the Lord, *Melek*)[6] in this particular case, Melkart. There are some indications at the same time, that pillars might have been phallic symbols of Melkart as the divine male principle, as opposed to divine femininity represented by the goddess Ashtart. As to why they are twinned, some scholars think it may be accounted for by the fact that in the most ancient Semitic cult of Ashtart she manifested both male and female principles.[7] This strange grafting of some elements of a quite different, alien and polytheistic religion on to the House of the Lord is emphasized by the fact that it is Hiram, and not Solomon or the High Priest, who *named* the pillars.[8] What, however, is most interesting in this situation of religious syncretism involving the Temple is that the Masonic tradition has extracted the twin pillars from the biblical context and included them in the context of Hiramic legend and Ritual as that which had belonged to the religion that existed prior to that of Solomon's Temple. And, intriguingly enough, this was done in an entirely non-conscious and objective manner, distinctly reminiscent of the manner in which Solomon himself included the pillars into the Temple complex. To penetrate into the *sanctum sanctorum* of the Temple you had to pass through the two-pillared porch, which yields the apt symbolism of passing through the portals of an old religion to gain access to the new. And, indeed, if we take into account the fact that the Phoenician cult of Melkart and the Semitic cult of Ashtart had been attested in Egyptian sources as far back as the sixteenth century BC, it would not be unsound to suppose that not only the creators (and protagonists) of the Masonic legend had been aware of it as old and their still relatively recent religion as new.

However, we ought to stress that the very words "old" and "new" are used here mythologically, not historically, even if their use be chronologically established as well. For what we are dealing with now is religion as an element of mythology, not the reverse. In this sense, the metal of Hiram's pillars represented an older religion and the stone of Solomon's Temple (during the building of which the use of metals was taboo) a newer one – in spite of work in metal representing a "newer" technological development than the age-old work in stone.[9] Simply there are two different mythologies involved: in one, underlying the historically newer monotheism of Yahweh, the older tabooing of metals in sacred buildings was presented, while in another, underlying the historically older cults of Ashtart and, probably, Melkart too, the newer metals were in sacred use.[10] For that which figures as a cult or religion with its own mythology in one context – in this case Phoenician – could objectively – that is, from the point of view of the external observer – figure as a mythology comprising a cult in another context: Jewish. But what cult and what mythology?

In answering this question we find ourselves in a rather paradoxical situation, for, in the first place, apart from the famous Temple with its twin pillars, well nigh nothing definite is known of the cult proper of Melkart in Tyre.[11] And in the second, Melkart, as he figures in his own mythology, is a *new* god with a *new* cult; his worship was considered as an innovation, if not a kind of religious upheaval. According to Josephus Flavius, the first King of Tyre (Hiram I) "tore down the old temples and erected new ones to Heracles [Melkart] and Ashtart . . ."[12] So, if we move forwards to the first half of the ninth century BC, we may conjecture that a Phoenician (or Canaanite) temple ransacked and destroyed in Jerusalem was the temple of Melkart (II Kings, 11, 18) who was called by a generic word "Baal" (Master), but there is no mention of the *name* Melkart in the Bible, nor do we find it among the names of the Kings or high priests in Tyre or any other Phoenician city.[13] That he and his cult seem to have been a religious innovation in the world of the ancient Phoenician, Canaanite and ancient Semitic religion in general is supported by the fact that he "appears in the sources *only* from the days of Hiram [the first?]".[14]

"Melkart", writes G. Herm, "is without doubt the most interesting figure in ancient oriental mythology".[15] The son of Ashtart (identified with Venus)[16] and El (identified with Kronos), he stands at the intersection of several mythological roles and functions. While always connected with the sea and seafaring – he was the first who dared to navigate in the open sea, sitting on the trunk of a tree – he is the chief enemy of the element of water (he killed Prince Sea and King River). This suggests, mythologically, his association with the elements of earth, air and fire and especially with tree (symbolically represented by columns and pillars).[17]

Melkart's second, mythological feature is that of founder of the city and the first builder. According to Eusebius, the Tyrian myths speak of him as one of the race of demi-gods who, after the creation of the world by another god or gods, invented all the things useful to man, and in particular the art of building. He landed on a small island on the Syrian shore and erected two pillars there before he built the Temple which contained his sanctuary (grave).[18] On one of the Canaanite stellas Melkart holds the battle-axe in his left hand and the *ankh* in his right.[19] This, in itself, is quite pertinent to the Semito-Masonic mythological associations for however enigmatic might be the origin, function and significance of the Phoenician (and Egyptian) symbol of the *ankh*,[20] the literal meaning of the Hebrew word (*anakh*) is "plummet". And it is in this sense that it figures in the Bible (Amos, 7, 7–8), where God appears before Amos on the wall, with the plummet in his right hand, threatening the Jews with the measuring of their sins and misdemeanours.[21]

And finally, the third feature of Melkart's mythology is that he is neither mortal nor immortal:

... dying, burnt, buried, avenged, and resurrected each year ... and yearly after burying him with ceremony on the mountain of Saphon his beloved wife Anat (to whom he made love seventy-five times per night) wreaks a bloody vengeance upon one of his many murderers. She cuts him with a sickle, winnows him with a shovel, scorches him with fire, grinds him in a mill, and then scatters his flesh over the field as food for the birds ...[22]

Melkart's violent death and the no less violent slaying and dismemberment of his murderer are followed by a funeral pyre where the element of earth is combined with that of ritual fire. Moreover, after being burnt and buried Melkart, according to a Canaanite legend, becomes God of the underworld, and he himself burns the corpses, from where he gained his other epithet, the Master of Furnace.[23]

It is this extremely complex mythological melding of the human and the divine, the living and the dying, the burners and the burnt, the builder and the navigator, the sacrificer and the sacrificial victim, that characterizes Melkart's cult. Its most prominent feature, closely connected with our theme of the Death of the Master Builder and the plot of the Masonic legend, is the abundantly attested practice of human sacrifice at building sites. The sacrificial victims were usually small first-born children whose burnt or semi-burnt remnants were deposed in urns under the foundations of buildings. This ritual, often called *Molok*, was widely practised from the beginning of the first millennium B C among Canaanites in general, but particularly in the Phoenician colonies throughout the whole Mediterranean area. Sometimes lambs were sacrificially killed side by side with male infants or used as a substitute for the latter, but first-born boys remained the most common sacrificial victims, cremated and buried under the foundations of palaces, fortresses and temples.[24]

The data of archaeology and comparative folklore clearly show that the ritual spread far beyond the Mediterranean region and its victims were not limited to first-born male infants. William Watson writes:

The excavations in sector C (at Hsiao T'un, Anyang, the Shang Dynasty, *c.* 1 2 B C) which revealed the building foundations of palaces and temples produced evidence of a vast slaughter clearly connected with the consecration and the spiritual guardianship of the buildings, much of it, one must assume, performed in a single rite. Sacrificial pits were dug around the edge of the foundations of the principal buildings. In front of the east–west building in the north the pits held cows, goats, and dogs. On the east side of the long north–south building were buried chiefly groups of headless human skeletons. Outside and either side of gateways (the position of these being inferred from alignments of the boulders serving as pillar foots) were buried kneeling men and women, the former armed with halberds and some holding shields, all facing south. Below the pisé foundations cows and goats were buried, and within the pisé, dogs, singly and in groups of five. In the space which must have formed a court enclosed by the buildings, besides men holding weapons and bronze vessels, five chariots had been buried. Four of these burials had been disturbed, but one intact pit contained the discernible remains of the chariot's complement of four horses and three armed men.[25]

It would not be too hazardous to suggest that both Phoenician and Chinese sacrifices are but two particular cases of a broader group of rituals corresponding to the broader mythological theme of Foundation Sacrifice. As a ritual and theme, Foundation Sacrifice figures in the science of comparative religion and folklore as equal in importance to Funeral Sacrifice and Ritual of Initiation.[26]

And finally, the plot of a Japanese legend of very ancient origin establishes a concrete link between the theme of Foundation Sacrifice and that of Death on the Building Site, giving us the key to an understanding of the Masonic legend in the sense of all the three themes:

Foundation Sacrifice, the Death of the Master Builder, and Death on the Building Site.

This is the plot of the legend:[27]

1. Situation. (a) Unsuccessful construction of a bridge, or a bridge repeatedly washed away by flood. (b) Repeated flooding of the river damages the bank.

2. The Adviser. A person speaks up, suggests a human sacrifice and recommends how to choose a victim, either a stranger,[28] or one wearing trousers which have a patch or a cross seam on them. The adviser himself turns out to be the one who fits these specifications. He warns a young girl (his daughter) not to speak up in the future and is sacrificed.

3. Consequence. (a) That is why in making trousers, cloth should never be joined in the middle. (b) Some years later the daughter marries, but because she never breaks her silence she is to be divorced. She is being led back to her own home by her husband, when on the way a pheasant cries and is shot by the husband, a hunter. The wife chants a poem:

The pheasant would not have been shot
If it had remained silent.
My father dug his own grave as a foundation sacrifice,
By speaking up.

The husband realizes the reason of his wife's silence and takes her back.

But how can the ritual slaughter of Phoenician boys or Chinese warriors performed at the very beginning of a building process be connected with the legend enacted in the symbolic ritual of killing the Master Mason after construction had finished?

In answering this question we arrive at five conjectures about possible sources of the Masonic legend, encompassing seven themes of the fifteen total in the chart which might have merged in its overall composition.

1. That the biblical tale of Hiram, itself mythologically neutral and containing no information of any cult other than that of Yahweh, carried in its core plot, implicitly through the figure of Hiram, the Tyrian brass-worker, and through the twin-pillars representing the Tyrian cult of Melkart, the theme of Foundation Sacrifice.

2. That the explicitly mythological core plot of Masonic legend combined in itself the elements of three other themes, to wit:

the Death (murder) of the Master Builder (for Melkart was God Builder), the Death and Resurrection of a God, and the Dismemberment of a Body – the God's or his murderer's.[29]

3. That the theme of Death on the Building Site might have come independently from some other cults and mythologies of the Mediterranean sphere, and was then included in Masonic legend by way of mythological synthesis;[30] so it might be supposed that this theme eventually merged with the four other themes of the legend at some later stage.[31]

4. That the obviously far more general and universal theme of the Dying and Resurrecting God found its reflection in the recomposition of the decomposed/dismembered body of Hiram.

5. And finally, that the theme of Burial represented by the burial of Melkart and his connection with the element of earth on the one hand, and to his role of Lord of the Underworld on the other, was echoed in the thrice-repeated burial of Hiram.

The following scheme will show, in the light of these conjectures, how the plot of the Hiramic legend might be related to the seven themes either directly or through the plot of the biblical passages which refer to Hiram (see endpapers).[32]

The scheme suggests the possibility of connections between the themes and the respective moments of the plot of the Masonic legend. Let us start with Hiram. He was intentionally taken from the biblical passages into the legend (B $\rightarrow$ A) as its main protagonist and *persona dramatis* and changed from a brass-worker [B(I)] into a builder and architect [A(I)] so as to fit in with the theme of the Death of the Master Builder [T(4)]. Although there is almost no possibility that the compilers of the Legend knew the story of Melkart, either as implicitly contained in the biblical tale (C $\rightarrow$ B $\rightarrow$ A), or directly (C $\rightarrow$ A) – objectively (unintentionally) it may have provided the content. It might also be supposed that this theme [T(4)] either directly informed the plot of Masonic legend [T(4) $\rightarrow$ A(I), (V)], or did this through some other non-biblical source or sources unknown [T(4) $\rightarrow$ X]. This might also be the case with all the other themes associated with the worship of Melkart.

The theme of the Word [T(10)] reflected in A (VII), does not figure in the cult and mythology of Melkart but plays the central role in the plot of the Masonic legends serving as the focus of action and the main motivating force both negatively, for the murderers of Hiram, and positively, for his friends and avengers. More than that, the Word here ties together all elements of the plot. It not only makes the things happen in the way they actually do happen both in the plot and in the Ritual, to Hiram and all the other people involved but, by endowing the sequence of events with their "whys" and "hows", informs the plot as a whole.

It is at this point where the two-dimensional plot formed by the theme of the Death of the Master Builder superimposed on the plot of the biblical tale of Hiram, the brass-worker, combines with the theme of the Word, acquiring a third dimension and becoming the fully fledged Masonic legend. But how does it become so? The answer follows from a simple comparison of A(II), B(II), C(II) and D(II) in the scheme.

By virtue of officiating at the ritual of Masonic initiation into the Word, the Master Mason Hiram is a priest *par excellence* [A(II)], as are Melkart by virtue of erecting the twin-pillars for his own shrine [C(II)], Hiram, the brass-worker in the Bible, by virtue of reproducing these pillars for Solomon's Temple [B(II)], and Romulus, by virtue of being the First Augur of Rome. However, while the priestly function of Romulus was divination, that of Hiram was initiation, and, more specifically, initiation into the art of building *through* the Word, or initiation into building *and* the Word together.

The Word here is not only a mythological theme but a "mythic entity", an idea that – at least in the ancient Semitic world – combined in itself two inseparable things: "naming" and "building" (we have already noted that the Semitic word *sham* means both "name" and "building"). Language assumes its ontological status: the Word by its very being makes everything be. Furthermore, the "naming" side of the Word entails the naming of actual men and turns them into the protagonists of a legendary plot, thereby building up a legend.[33]

So, we can surmise that if the theme of the Death of the Builder changed the biblical Hiram from a brass-worker into a builder, the theme of the Word not only made him the Master of the Lodge of Masons [or the priest, A(II)], but also made him the *person named Hiram*; that is, "this" Hiram, not that or any other Hiram. And we know that King Hiram's father was also Hiram (or Huram), probably that very Hiram I who at the beginning of the tenth century BC introduced the cult of Melkart as the state-cult of Tyre.

Themes (1)–(4), in their relation to the plot of Masonic legend, represent a cluster of themes all of which can be subsumed under the generic rubric of Death on the Building Site [T(4)]. But does this mean that theme coincides with, or finds its textual materialization in, a concrete plot? And the second question, then, will be: in what relation to the given concrete plot of a myth, legend or any other folklore text would stand the theme or the themes already known before asking the first question, where the plot is deduced from the theme? Indeed, without answering these questions how can we know in what relation, if any, the plot of Masonic legend would stand to the sacrifice of a dozen mounted warriors under the foundations of a palace in ancient China, or to the suicide (or was it an accident?) of Master Builder Solness in Ibsen's play of that name? [T(4) → T(15) → G]

It is one of the assumptions of a phenomenology of myth that myth may or may not be conscious of itself as related to a ritual or another myth. For those who performed the sacrifice of the first-born boys under the foundations of Phoenician buildings, or the sacrifice of the warriors under the foundations of buildings in China, were perfectly aware that what they were doing was a special building ritual [i.e., T(1) and T(2)], with or without an associated myth, whereas the Worshipful Master performing the Ritual of Master Mason in the Masonic Lodge, while being aware of it as an *initiatory ritual* (which is not listed in our scheme), would be hardly aware of the possibility of another ritual or rituals being included in it with corresponding mythological themes. Not to speak of Ibsen, who was unlikely to have been conscious of the fact that the core plot of his play might have a direct relation to the theme of the Death of the Master Builder [T(4) → G]. For, by consciously enacting the legend of Master Builder Hiram within the Masonic ritual of initiation, the candidate becomes Hiram, while not being conscious that this enactment is, itself, objectively related to a theme or themes other than those connected with or centred around the ritual of initiation, i.e. the themes T(2), T(3) and T(4). The Hiramic ritual as a whole is *performed*, while the parts of it which reflect the other rituals simply *happen*.

From this it might follow that Death on the Building Site [T(3)] can, in its relation to the Hiramic legend, be seen as a particular case of the broader theme of Foundation Sacrifice [T(1)]. The same could be said of the theme of the Death of the Builder [T(4)] in our legend and in the myths of Romulus in Rome, Melkart in Tyre, or even Solness in nineteenth-century Norway. For all these deaths occurred *after* the building in question had been completed. It is at this point that we arrive at the remarkable phenomenon of reversal of time in mythology. There are numerous cases in the world's folklore when, after the completion of the building, a builder, a founder of a city, a stranger, or any other man, woman or child are sacrificed, or conversely, simply die if the Foundation Sacrifice [T(1)] is *not* performed [T(1) → (4)]. So, instead of being consciously performed at the start of the building work the Foundation Sacrifice takes place spontaneously after the building has been completed. It would figure, then, as the pure objectivity of mythological consciousness and, when we pass, in a structure of "mythic" consciousness (in a theme, plot, tale, etc.), from the subjectivity of the conscious protagonists to the objectivity of that which simply happens, time in the myth is being reversed.

But there is far more than that in the theme of Foundation Sacrifice. In fact, as the theme of the Word explicitly informs the plot of the Masonic legend, so the theme of Foundation Sacrifice informs it implicitly and from outside the text by endowing it with an objective mythological motivation. Objective, for the obvious reason that the formal religious context of the legend remains exclusively Jewish and Monotheistic, and a Foundation Sacrifice would have been absolutely out of the question there. But someone had to die on the building site of the Temple since the foundation sacrifice had not been performed $[A(V) \leftarrow T(3) \leftarrow T(1)]$ and it could only have been Hiram, for his was the central and exceptional position of Master Builder and high priest of a secret religious order $[A(I,II) \leftarrow T(3) \leftarrow T(1)]$. And, as there is a reversal of time when, instead of marking the beginning, the Foundation Sacrifice takes place after the completion of the building works, there is also a reversal of roles: the priest who performs the ritual of initiation becomes the victim in the ritual of Foundation Sacrifice $[A(II) \leftarrow T(1)]$.[34]

It is the Japanese legend (F) that lays bare the inner, thematic structure of our Masonic legend, helping us to disentangle the complex knot of the threads of its plot. Using the most elementary method of comparative folklore, by comparing these two legends it is possible to show how some of the moments of Hiram's peregrination from life to death can easily be reduced to certain universal mythological themes: themes which have been obscured in, or almost obliterated by, the process of transformation of an archaic and obsolete ritual into the textually fixed Masonic legend which, in its turn, became the central part of a "new" and more complex ritual. The central principle of transformation of a ritual into a legend can be formulated in the following way: that which in a ritual is conscious of itself (i.e. of its aim, its motivation, the course and order of its performance, etc.), becomes unconscious of itself in a legend. In other words, that which, in a ritual, is *performed* according to certain well-known general rules and follows a certain traditionally-established general plan – general, in the sense that the ritual is repeated wherever and whenever necessary and by whomsoever is entitled to perform it -- in a legend simply *happens*, not as a part of a repeated pattern, but in a given place, at a given time, and to a given named person. So the priest or the sacrificial victim of the ritual becomes the protagonist in the legendary plot, and the conscious subjectivity of the ritual gives way to the conscious objectivity of the legend or folk-tale.

The protagonist of a legendary plot either does not know the ritual in question, or knows it only partially, and it is through its respective themes that we are able to reconnect his absent or partial knowledge with the ritual.[35] So, in the legend, Hiram did not know about the Foundation Sacrifice although he happened to be its victim. What Hiram knew was the Word which is related to a different theme and belongs to the quite different, Masonic ritual of which he was the priest. The Adviser's lack of silence about his knowledge of the Foundation Sacrifice was the cause of his death as was Hiram's silence about his knowledge of the Word. In both cases, however, we are dealing with the same ritual silence [T(11)] which becomes conscious of itself in the Masonic legend on account of its being part of a *new* ritual, and which is the other side or aspect of the knowledge of ritual. And both the knowledge of the Foundation Sacrifice in the Japanese legend and the knowledge of the Word in the Masonic one are dangerous not only in the context of their respective plots, but also as such, due to their esoteric character.

It is here that, once again, we come upon the mythological phenomenon of the ambivalence or ambiguity of knowledge. For, as has already been said, it is the knowledge of the Word [T(10)] which made Hiram the Master of the Lodge [T(10) → A(II)] and his silence about it which killed him [T(11) → A(V),(VI),(VII)]. And it is his ignorance [innocence T(12) → A(X)] of the Foundation Sacrifice that on the one hand marks his belonging to *another* ritual and, thereby, his rejection of the pagan cult of Melkart [C(XII)], but on the other hand it symbolizes that he was an *innocent victim* of this cult [a "first-born boy", a "sacrificial lamb", C(XII) → A(X)], and that the villains who murdered him played *objectively* (that is, without knowing it) the role of sacrificers in this cult.

But, of course, all that has been said of Hiram's knowledge, silence and innocence here is based only on what the Masonic legend made of him. Because if we go from our legend back to its source, in other words to Hiramic passages in the Bible, the interpretation would change quite drastically. For how on earth could Hiram the brass-worker, himself Tyrian and working on the temples of Melkart in Tyre [B(I),(II)], not know perfectly well the cult in which he had been professionally involved for so many years, serving his namesakes Hiram I and Hiram II of Tyre? The answer is as simple as it is self-evident: Hiram of the Bible is a *stranger*, a Phoenician, as he is in the Masonic legend (and Ritual) where the fact of his being a stranger was, together with his previous knowledge, removed from the surface of the text into the subtext in the process of transforming into our Masonic legend the biblical passages, which contain, in the background, the cult of Melkart.

The theme of the Sacrifice of a Stranger [T(13)] occupies a rather peculiar place in the world's folklore and mythology.[36] Master Hiram is described in the Bible as a stranger who knows how to work in metals, which was an alien knowledge to the Jews, but his being a stranger from Tyre, though quite explicit in the tale, was not thematized there. In the Masonic legend, on the other hand, Hiram is not described as a stranger, but his being a stranger is implicitly thematized because of his knowledge of the Word and its Ritual (to possess this knowledge one must always be in some way "estranged"), as the alienness of the Adviser in the Japanese legend is thematized because he knew the Foundation Sacrifice. Both are sought out because of their respective knowledge by those who do not know. But it is here that we are confronted with the very essence of the theme of the Stranger: the Stranger's knowledge is always *partial*. So, let me repeat what has already been said in a different context: Hiram knew the Word of the Masonic Ritual of initiation but not the ritual of the Foundation Sacrifice nor, what is far more important, that he was to be its sacrificial victim; whereas the Adviser knew the ritual of Foundation Sacrifice but, like Hiram, did not know that he was to be its sacrificial victim. In other words, theirs was a magical (sacred, ritualistic) knowledge, but not a self-knowledge. Why is this so? Because – and this will be a purely mythological answer – their other knowledge has already made them strangers to themselves, for theirs is the role and function of that knowledge which precludes them from knowing their own destiny – from knowing themselves. In fact, it is this peculiar "complementarity" of these two knowledges that makes a man a Stranger, and not the other way around.

We do not have a chorus, as in *Oedipus Rex*,[37] accompanying the enactment of the Hiramic legend in the Ritual of Freemasonry, but we have, instead, the words of the Worshipful Master explaining to the initiate the meaning of various stages of the performance in an everyday and quite non-mythological way. Such is the style of the late legends through which the eternal mythological themes have survived up to the present day. But even now we are able to feel the vigour and breath of the ancient myth of the Stranger under this disguise of theist rhetoric and dry Protestant didactics.

What is also particularly interesting is that combination of these two themes, the Sacrifice of the Stranger and the Word, which is a commonplace in the Gnostic texts. So we read in *The Treasure*, an early Mandaean text: "Ruha, the daemonic mother of the Planets, and the Planetary Demons ... said: 'We will kill the Stranger ... We will confound his party ... so that he may have no share in this world. The whole house shall be ours alone ...'" Then further in the same text: "Adam felt love for the Alien Man whose speech is ... estranged from the world." And, finally, in the Gnostic Gospel of Truth: "[When the Stranger appeared] the Word appeared, the Word which is in the hearts of those who pronounce it ..."[38] Not only does the Word issue from the Stranger in the Hiramic legend, it *is* the Stranger as the Word of Master Mason *is* the Master Mason. Therefore, gnostically speaking, the Stranger is to be sacrificed so that the pre-creational state may never again be reached and what has been created may not be returned to the pristine state of "pure name" and unmixed Divine Light. And that is, in fact, what the Masonic legend is about and what is enacted in the Masonic Ritual of initiation. For Hiram is murdered and the Word remains un-retrieved and lives in its barbaric substitute as a bare reminder of the loss.

And, finally, the fact that Hiram, both in the legend and the Bible, is the son of a widow [A(III), B(III)] is extremely significant; for "the son of a widow" is the most widely spread nickname for a Mason, used by working Masons themselves long before the speculatives began their victorious march in Britain at the beginning of the eighteenth century. Comparative mythology provides us with some material on the basis of which it might be suggested that this circumstance is, on the one hand, one of the distinctive features which make a person a hero of a myth, along with his quality of being strange and so forth, while on the other hand, it is intrinsically connected with the general mythological issue of knowledge. Indeed, a possible mythological conjecture is that the son of a widow is a person who does not know his father [T(14) → A(III)], whose father died when he was a small child.[39] But apart from this, sons of widows together with twins, youngest sons, orphans and bastards, constitute a contingent of possible candidates for victimhood and thereby for the role of mythological hero. The Hiram of the Masonic legend, by virtue of being both a stranger and a son of a widow, a metal-worker and a builder, a layman and a priest, embodies that multiple union of opposites which predestines him, and him alone, for the task of being the first and the last knower of the Word,[40] which was not known even by King Solomon, whom Masonic tradition makes the Grand Master of the Israelite Masons.

In summing up the main points of this highly conjectural comparativist section, the following general suggestions can be made about the sense and essence of Masonic legend in its relation to ritual:

1. That Freemasons, when they perform the Ritual of Master Mason, are subjectively conscious of it as a ritual of initiation, but are not conscious of the Foundation ritual, which happens during the enactment of the legend of the death of Hiram.

2. That this may lead one to a far broader hypothesis about mythology, namely that any myth or ritual (for they share the same *thematic* approach) can exist objectively as the plot in a text, or as a sequence of actions and events in actual human behaviour where there is no subjective awareness of them *as* myth and ritual. And in this sense, then, it is possible that very many events, actions, or individual states of consciousness can be seen as non-conscious, spontaneous enactments of a ritual or a myth.

3. That this double mythological situation – when one ritual is included in another as the objective within the subjective, or, in a more general way, when a plot or an event not conscious of itself as myth or ritual *is* a myth or ritual if looked at from the point of view of the mythologist – necessitates a third position. This position entails the existence of something (or somebody) which either is the *knowledge*, or knows that what seems to be one thing is, in fact, another, or includes another in it. In the Masonic case, it is the knowledge that what seems to be the memory of what happens spontaneously to Hiram is, in fact, the lost memory of the ritual of Foundation Sacrifice; what seems to be an ordinary murder is an act of sacrifice, a plain villain a sacrificial priest, a man murdered for a particular non-sacrificial reason a sacrificial victim. The Master Mason's Word as a theme is related both to the ritual of initiation (in the scope and motivation of the core plot of our legend) and to the whole group of the "Building Sacrifice" themes (also rituals), in the structure of the plot and in the sequence of its elements. [These themes T(1),(2),(3),(4), in their turn, enter into their own relations with each other, which constitute the "mythological space" of this second, inner ritual of Freemasonry.]

It is this threefold composition of Masonic legend – the subjectivity of the ritual of initiation, the objectivity of the ritual of the Foundation Sacrifice and the Knowledge of the Word that knows the subjective in the objective – that determines the gnostic character of Masonic philosophy and the central element of it, the conception of *double truth*, a conception from the point of view of which not only the myth or the Ritual of Freemasonry but Freemasonry in its entirety should be understood as a phenomenon which is one thing for itself and quite another to those who know its objective meaning. The following scheme reduces the core plot of the murder of Master Builder Hiram to its basic elements and relates it to several other legends sharing the same core plot (see note 32 and endpapers).

Themes

    1. Human sacrifice (Foundation Sacrifice).
    2. *** Sacrifice of the first-born boys under the foundations of a building.
    3. ** Death (or murder) on a building site.
    4. *** Death (or murder) of the builder (or founder) on the building site [?].
    5. * Death and resurrection of a sacred person (god, etc.).
    6. *** Dismemberment (or decomposition) of the dead body.
    7. *** Recomposition of the body (as a resurrection).
    8. * Burial: the grave as the entrance to underworld (with earth and fire as two main elements).
    9. *** Repeated burial [?].
    10. The Word.
    11. ** Silence (of the victim).
    12. ** Innocence (of the knowledge of the Ritual).
    13. ** The Sacrifice of Strangers.
    14. ** The person does not know (or does not recognize) his father.
    15. *** Human sacrifice as crime (murder), accidental death, or suicide.

A. *Core plot of the Masonic legend:*
    (I) Master Builder Hiram,
    (II) the Master (i.e. priest) of the Lodge,
    (III) the son of a widow, when
    (IV) the Temple was almost completed,
    (V) was murdered on the building site, because
    (VI) he did not disclose (i.e., remained silent)
    (VII) the Word to the villains.
    (VIII) His body was hidden ("buried" the first time), then found and

(IX) "reburied" (the second time) with

(X) a twig of acacia. After that

(XI) the "substitute" Word was discovered,

(XII) the body dismembered, then

(XIII) put together again and given

(XIV) a proper funeral (the third burial).

(XV) The murderers were put to death.

B. *Core plot of the biblical passages:*

(I) Hiram the brass-worker,

(II) working for the temples of Melkart in Tyre,

(III) the son of a widow,

(IV) when Solomon's Temple was completed,

(V) cast the twin-pillars at the porch.

C. *Some elements of mythology and cult of Melkart:*

(I) Melkart, the founder (builder) of Tyre,

(II) who erected the twin pillars of his shrine (as the priest?),

(III) the city-god of Tyre,

(IV) was maimed

(V) and murdered.

(VI) His wife burned his body on the funeral pyre,

(VII) buried him,

(VIII) and avenged his death by killing and dismembering the body of his murderer.

(IX) Each year he is murdered and then resurrected.

(X) After his death he becomes the king (god) of the underworld and

(XI) the "Master of Furnace".

(XII) The sacrifice of the first-born boys under the foundations of temples and fortresses was the central feature of his cult.

D. *Some moments in the core plot of the legend of Romulus and Remus:*

(I) Romulus, the founder (builder) of Rome,

(II) the first high priest, and

(III) the city-god of Rome,

(IV) murdered his twin brother Remus at the building site.[41]

(V) He was murdered,

(VI) and his body dismembered by the patricians.

E. *The foundation sacrifice of warriors in twelfth-century* BC *China.*

F. *Core plot of the Japanese legend:*

(I) A bridge is repeatedly washed away by the flooding of a river.

(II) A knowledgeable person suggests that a human sacrifice is necessary and recommends . . .

(III) a victim, possibly a stranger, and advises how to choose that victim.

(IV) The adviser turns out to be the victim.

(V) He warns his daughter not to speak out in the future.

G. *Core plot of Ibsen's* The Master Builder: Solness, the master builder, commits suicide (?) by throwing himself from the tower of his building.

Notes

1 Philological terms are italic here, when first used. "Tale" here means *how* it is actually communicated, "content" *what* is communicated, and "*legend*" refers to the literary or folk manner of its telling. Of course, it goes without saying that one concrete plot or variant can be in our interpretation related to two or more core plots as its invariants, once we have already established the *thematic* direction of our thinking on the text. It also ought to be noted here that the term "core plot" (or "plot") can be applied to the content of texts only, while the term theme, to both texts and events in general. The term "core plot" is used here in the sense approximating that of Aristotelian "plot" or "plot-structure" (*mythos*). See in: *The Poetics of Aristotle*, translation and commentary by Stephen Halliwell, Duckworth, London, pp. 11, 37, 40.

2 "Hiram my father's" refers to the fact that apparently, builder Hiram Abiff was a dependent of, or employed by, the King of Tyre's father, also Hiram.

3 The apparent contradiction between the daughters of Dan and "the tribe of Naphtali" here was resolved by J. Liver's explanation that the tribal territory of Dan lay in the district of Naphtali. H. J. Katzenstein, *The History of Tyre*, Jerusalem, 1973 (H. J. Katzenstein, 1973), p. 100.

4 A question remains here about metalwork, particularly since all the stonework was done by Jews and Phoenicians – if not mainly by the latter – together, and only work in metals by Phoenicians alone. "The men of Solomon and Hiram, the King of Tyre, worked together in the work of *construction* of the Temple". (H. J. Katzenstein, 1973, p. 101).

5 Owen Whitehouse notes [*A Dictionary of the Bible*, ed. by J. Hastings, Vol. VIII., Edinburgh, 1927 (1900), pp. 879–84] that stone pillars were used in more developed Semitic cults as symbols of divinities separated from the altar proper. The Phoenician twin pillars made of metal are, in his opinion, specific of the cult of Melkart. As for the constructional and architectural function of Boaz and Jachin, T. W. Davies [*A Dictionary of the Bible*, ed. by G. Hastings, V.I, Edinburgh, 1924 (1898), pp. 308–9] is inclined to the opinion that ". . . the pillars stood in the porch, unconnected at the top, and that the only function they served was that of ornamentation".

6 Melkart appeared in Phoenician religion in Tyre alone, and later became one of the chief deities of the Phoenician diaspora, but was never specially assigned to any other Phoenician (let alone Canaanite) city on the Eastern shore of the Mediterranean Sea. What used to be called the Pillars of Heracles (Straits of Gibraltar) had originally been called the Pillars of Melkart. See in: H. J. Katzenstein, 1973, p. 313; Gerhard Herm, *Phoenicians*, trans. by C. Hillier, London, 1975 [G. Herm,

1975 (1973)], p. 173. Also see an article of L. B. Paton in *Encyclopaedia of Religion and Ethics*, ed. by J. Hastings, Vol. IX, Edinburgh, 1917, pp. 891–2.

7 See an article of L. B. Paton in *Encyclopaedia of Religion and Ethics* ed. by J. Hastings, V. II, Edinburgh, 1909, p. 115.

8 This is a very interesting case, where a mythology, Canaanite or even generally Semitic, finds itself separated from a religion ... For the naming of the things in the Masonic Ritual is a supernatural act performed by a mortal man on God's order, just as Adam named the things of creation (Genesis 2, 19–20). Moreover, the pillars were named by a stranger whose god, Melkart, was in a way mortal too (that will be discussed further) and whose naming was as spontaneous as that of a builder in the Masonic legend who by a "slip of tongue" uttered the Word of Master Mason. Even more interesting, as I am informed by Dr Tudor Parfitt of the School of Oriental and African Studies, is that the word *shem* in Hebrew designates both "name" and "monument/building".

9 As stone might have imitated wood in the ancient building constructions so metal might have imitated stone. Herm [1975 (1973), p. 125] writes: "The two pillars of the temple of Melkart in Tyre, reproduced as Boaz and Jachin in Solomon's Temple ... might have evolved from the holy *stones* which once lay under a tree dedicated to Baal Melkart ... "

10 This mythological idea of separation of the "old" from the "new" is historically formulated by G. Herm (*idem*, pp. 90–1) as follows: "The archaeological research ... indicates that the Phoenicians, who have already built large stone houses in the Bronze Age, then developed in the Iron Age [i.e. after the arrival of the Sea Peoples] a model for public buildings.... A detail of the Temple which ... was particularly typical of Phoenician architecture – the pillars of Boaz and Jachin, which towered skywards in the outer courtyard on the left and right of the entrance – had ... no connection with any part of the Jewish liturgy, but were a part of Canaanite temples according to Herodotes ... the temple of Melkart at Tyre had two pillars of the same kind ... " A little further he adds that, "the plan of Solomon's Temple was Phoenician ... " (p. 102).

11 " ... Nothing else is known of where and how he was worshipped in Tyre itself ... " *idem*, p. 126.

12 *Idem*, p. 66. He was probably the grandfather of Solomon's contemporary, and reigned in Tyre somewhere in the beginning of the tenth century BC.

13 *Idem*, pp. 127, 181.

14 *Idem*, p. 91. This opinion is shared by C. Bonnet-Tzavellas in *Redt Tyrus; Studia Phoenica I*; ed. by E. Jubel, E. Lipinsky and B. Servais-Soyez, Leuwen, 1983 (C. Bonnet-Tzavellas, 1983), p. 196. B. Soyez calls Melkart a "young god" as opposed to such "archetypal" gods as Osiris. Brigitte Soyez, *Byblos et la fête des Adonies*, Leiden, E. J. Brill, 1977, p. 74.

15 G. Herm, 1975 (1973), p. 109; G. Conteneau, *La civilisation Phenicienne*, Paris, 1926 (G. Conteneau, 1926), p. 43.

16 Ashtart was also equalled to Aphrodite. "To Philon, [writes A. Baumgarten (*The Phoenician History of Philo of Byblos*, Leiden, E. J. Brill, 1981, pp. 180, 195)] it was usual practice to identify equivalent Phoenician and Greek gods: El = Kronos, Melkart = Heracles, etc."

17 G. Conteneau, 1926, p. 43.

18 *Idem*, p. 42; C. Bonnet-Tzavellas, 1983, p. 196. "He invented the art of

building by having succeeded, according to Phoenician myths, in constructing a hut of grasses, rushes, and seeds." G. Herm, 1975 (1973), p. 173.

19 *Idem*, p. 141.

20 "... the famous (Phoenician) 'sign of the goddess Tanit' ... is either a decorative object composed of a betyl and a solar disc divided by a horizontal arm, or a development of the Egyptian *ankh*, or something else."! Sabatino Moscati, *The World of Phoenicians*, trans. by A. Hamilton, London, Weidenfeld and Nicolson, 1968 (1965), p. 139. Also pp. 155, 159 160.

21 Dr Tudor Parfitt stresses that "plummet" was the primary meaning of this word in very many Semitic languages (Arab, *anuk*, Assyr, *Anaku*, etc.)

22 G. Herm, 1975 (1973), pp. 111–16.

23 Tal., p. 139; C. Bonnet Tzavellas, 1983, p. 197.

24 G. Conteneau (1926, pp. 137–8) attributes this "building ritual" specifically to the Canaanite cults of a special class of deities called Baals (masters) to which Melkart belonged. He refers to the excavations at Gezer where the semi-burnt bones of children were found and, particularly, to the temple of the goddess Tanit of Carthage where, under the foundation, red urns with the bones of children and lambs were laid. The lambs, however, constituted not more than fifteen per cent of the content of the urns (*idem*, p. 138). See also in: Giovanni Garbini, *J. Fenici; Storia e Religione*: Istituto Universitario Orientale, Seminarie de Studi Asiatici, Series Minor, XI, Napoli, 1980, pp. 152, 153, 187–203.

25 William Watson, *China before the Han Dynasty*, London, Thames and Hudson, 1961, p. 79.

26 Its definition being "A human being buried alive at the base of the foundation of a building or bridge (as we see it in Celtic, Welsh, Finnish, Lithuanian, Spanish, etc. folklore)." Stith Thompson, *Motif-Index of Folk-literature*, Vol. V, Bloomington-Copenhagen, 1957 (V. S. Thompson,1957), 5–261, p. 318, "Buried alive" here rather narrows the theme, but this is the definition of a *motif* (a notion adopted by the Finnish school of folklore) which in my understanding of myth, legend and ritual, either represents a part (version, concretization, etc.) of a theme, or corresponds to a core plot.

27 Quoted from: Hiroko Ikeda, *A Type and Motif, Index of Japanese Folk-Literature*, FF Communications IV 209, Academia Scientiarun Fennica, Helsinki, 1971, pp. 212–13. I am deeply thankful to my colleagues, Sarah Allen, Angus Graham and Timothy Barrett, who provided me with all necessary Chinese and Japanese information on the subject.

28 An analogous situation from medieval Armenian folklore was reported to the author by Dr Levon Abrahamian: after having failed to erect a bridge which was washed away again and again, the master builder sees a prophetic dream where he is told to sacrifice the first person he meets the next day. It happens to be his son.

29 At the end of the Masonic legend Hiram's assassins were put to death anyway. The theme of dismemberment of the God Founder of the City is, probably, reflected also in the Roman legend where Romulus, the founder of Rome and its city-god, was dismembered after his death by the Patricians.

30 Synthesis, but not syncretism. The latter is clearly seen in the combination of the Masonic Ritual with Jewish religion, e.g. Hiram prayed to Yahweh before being murdered, and was given a Jewish funeral, though he was a Tyrian.

31 This theme is succinctly reflected in Livy's tale of the death of Remus, the twin brother of Romulus and co-founder of Rome, who was killed by Romulus for "jumping contemptuously over the newly raised walls"; or according to another version, because he jumped over the furrow ploughed by Romulus, which marked the boundary of the city-wall. Livy also mentions in his tale of Romulus' death that, after the founder of Rome disappeared, suddenly, in the violent thunderstorm, "there were some who secretly hinted that he had been torn limb from limb by the Senators – a tradition to this effect, though certainly a very dim one, has filtered down to us." T. Livy, (Titus Livius), *The History of Rome*, trans. by W. M. Roberts, Vol. I, London, M. Dent and Sons Ltd, 1937, pp. 9, 20. J. G. Frazer refers to this episode in *The Golden Bough* (third ed.), V. IX (*The Scapegoat*), London, Macmillan, 1920, p. 258.

32 The arrows in the scheme (see end papers) show relations of themes to the elements of plots and moments of ritual. The interrupted arrows show possible or hypothetical relations of the elements of the cult of Melkart to the elements of Masonic legend. The dotted arrow show the *intentional* relation of Masonic legend to the Hiramic passages in the Bible. The themes related to C only are marked by single asterisks, those related to both C and A by triple asterisks, and those related to A only, by double asterisks.

33 The problem of the Word as Language and Being will be treated separately in the next section.

34 I think that T(3) and T(4) overlap with the theme of Human Sacrifice as Crime [T(15)], a very complex mythological construct which combines in itself both subjective and objective moments of *ritual* and *crime* and their mutual substitution. This, of course, presupposes that the myth is aware of the distinction between *profane norm* and *sacred crime*. See R. Gerard, *La violence et le sacré*, Paris, 1972.

35 Knowledge is not a separate theme in the world's mythology, for it underlies all other themes, serving as a general factor or a common denominator in almost every myth. It is that which happens to a protagonist of a myth or legend in connection with knowledge (or absence or lack of it) that constitutes a mythological theme.

36 V. S. Thompson, 1957, S-265, p. 320.

37 Oedipus Rex is a classic example of the type of Mythic Stranger who knows how to solve the riddle of the Sphinx (i.e., "the supernatural") but does not recognize *himself* as the son of his father and his mother. That is, mythologically, he is not aware that in killing his father he performs the ritual of Sacred Patricide and in marrying his mother, the ritual of Sacred Incest of the priest-kings of Mediterranean antiquity.

38 Hans Jonas, *The Gnostic Religion*, Boston, Beacon Press, 1966 (H. Jonas, 1966), pp. 72, 76.

39 A classical mythological parallel to this could be seen in the case of Oedipus, who did not recognize his father when he met him, and who already was "the son of a widow" when he married his mother.

40 Interestingly enough, Hiram is the only "son of a widow" personally named in the Old Testament. See: Alexander Cruden, *A Complete Concordance to the Old and New Testament.* London, 1894 (1737), p. 556.

41 It might also be held that the tale of Remus's death in Livy (see note 31)

has the same structure: that the objectivity of the missing ritual of Foundation Sacrifice was included within the ''subjective'' ritual of the Augurs, whose priests were both Romulus and Remus.

CONCLUSION

CHAPTER 14

Freemasonry: A Phenomenon of Social Abstraction

I am inclined to think that the appellation of MASON implies a member of a RELIGIOUS SECT. . .
William Hutchinson, *The Spirit of Masonry*[1]

We are afraid of words. The author of the epigraph to this section was not. Or, at least, he was not afraid of being called a member of a religious sect – an appellation which the majority of present day Freemasons would reject with some indignation and which the majority of present day anti-Masonic writers would take up with great gusto. Furthermore, the main reason for many people's being afraid of being called "a member of a religious sect" is not that they may seem ridiculous, silly, or credulous in the eyes of society, but that the fact of their belonging to "a sect" may separate them from that society, make them objectively, against or irrespective of their own intentions and motivations, isolated from it in one way or another. This becomes particularly clear in the cases of some sects and religious movements imported to Britain from other countries and rooted in other cultures, such as, for example, Hari Krishna, Nichiren Buddhism or even Jehovah's Witnesses. This, however, is unsurprising, for these sects and movements have very little or nothing to do with our civilization or our society, both from our point of view and theirs.

The author quoted in the epigraph to this section, William Hutchinson (1737–1811), was not only a prominent Freemason, but a distinguished lawyer, a serious historian, and a well-known public figure. He was not in the least worried about calling himself a member of a religious sect for at least two reasons: firstly, that he knew perfectly well that his was a sect which was his civilization's flesh and blood (even considering all hypothetical Egyptian and Chaldean antecedents); and secondly, that he thought (rightly or wrongly, it does not matter) that the fact of the isolation of Freemasonry from society as well as the character and degree of this isolation was determined by Freemasonry, not by society. His opinion, of course, was as subjective as that professed by society or by established religion. So I will try to tackle this question under a slightly different angle, different from both the Freemasonic point of view and the view of society.

Again, I will start with some rough statistics. Out of *thirty-six* books dealing with general problems of British civilization and culture published in the UK and the USA between 1958 and 1988, only *two* give a passing mention of Freemasonry; out of *seventy* books dealing with general problems of politics, political ideologies, and political ideas in Great Britain, the USA and Western Europe, and published in the UK and the USA during the same period, only *one* mentions Freemasonry. Out of two hundred monographs chosen at random, and devoted to various concrete subjects related to culture, civilization, politics, and political thinking – excluding Masonic literature – of the same regions, and published in the same countries during the same period, only in *three* are references to Freemasonry found. Finally, out of *thirty* general works devoted to religion and religious ideas in Europe and the USA, and published in the UK, Western Europe and the USA, in only *two* is Freemasonry given a very brief treatment as a separate religious phenomenon.

With an index of references less than $1/40$,[2] Freemasonry in the same samples comes far behind the Salvation Army ($1/31$), Moral Rearmament ($1/27$), the Mennonites ($1/24$), and Scientology ($1/33$). This is strange, bearing in mind that the membership of these four organizations in the UK taken together would scarcely amount to half the number of Freemasons. Even the practically non-existent Rosicrucians are mentioned more often ($1/36$). Evidently, it is only Freemasons and those who choose Freemasonry as their particular subject, rather than writing about religion in general, who write about it, and almost nobody else. This fact itself is very interesting, for it shows, albeit indirectly, that the subject of Freemasonry is treated by non-Masonic authors – mostly unconsciously, I am sure – as something apart from almost all other subjects of civilizational, social, ideological and religious character.

This is in contrast to the more than 64,000 titles of books, articles and other publications devoted exclusively to Masonry and written by, or (though far less often) specifically about, Freemasons. This all points to the considerable isolation of the very subject of Freemasonry as a civilizational and social phenomenon within a civilizational and social context, for however abstracted from social reality Freemasonry might have been, the fact of its spread, propagation and literature remains civilizational and social by definition.

Why is this so? Let us start with what is more general – civilization. While it is an exaggeration to claim, as quite a few Masonic writers have done, that Freemasonry has made a great contribution to British

343

civilization, it is absurd to ignore Freemasonry altogether, as the majority of the authors of the books on British civilization have done and continue to do. Freemasonry is a part of British civilization; more precisely it is one of the ways in which the latter understands and expresses itself. This is not to say that either British civilization, as represented by those who analyse it, ignoring Freemasonry, or Freemasonry itself is aware of this. On the contrary, neither appear to be conscious of Freemasonry's epitomizing function.

Does this mean that in the course of almost three centuries of their history the Freemasons have, somehow or other, contrived to remain separate as a subject from the rest of the cultural and civilizational topics dealt with in the written word? And if that were so, how could they have also involved in this dubious scheme those non-Masons who wrote on any relevant subject other than Freemasonry, but which, by rights, ought to include some reference to its role in British life? Having become "speculative" and having thereby separated manual work from that of mental activity, building symbolism from the building profession, ritual from religion, and behaviour in the Lodge from any other behaviour, did they not become a kind of living social abstraction of our time; a time where everything is social or sociologically explained? And is a "social abstractedness" itself a social phenomenon too?

The answer to this is that it undoubtedly is a social phenomenon, and a very interesting one at that. Having started with separating the professional symbolism from the profession of the Masonic craft, and this craft from the Craft, as a Brotherhood of those who used that symbolism for their own particular end, the British Masons, unlike the Americans, went on "abstracting" themselves from practically all other social phenomena, while, at the same time, being actively involved in these very phenomena when they were not in the Lodge.

I would venture the following explanation for this. From the beginning of the eighteenth century up to the present day, Freemasonry has been regarded as "an utterly unserious thing, although . . ." And what comes after "although" may be "harmless" or "pernicious", "amusing" or "sinister", "socially acceptable" or "subversive" and so forth. The formula "an utterly unserious thing, although . . ." has always served to maintain not only a certain balance, however precarious, between positive and negative in the outsider's opinion of Freemasonry, but first and foremost, a balance between the perception of it as both unserious and serious. For indeed, if you are yourself a serious person, you cannot treat something subversive as unserious in its political consequences. Similarly, being a theologian, you cannot regard the Ritual of the Craft (let alone the rituals of the Higher Degrees) as a mere joke without taking account of its quite serious theological implications, particularly when the Ritual is performed by an Anglican priest. It becomes even more interesting when the anti-Masonic invective of the clergy (such as the criticism made by the Catholic priest, the Revd. Walton Hanna) are repeated by secular or even atheist critics (such as James Dewar), whose anti-Masonic stand is, usually, merely political. In their resentment of Freemasonry, they still try to appeal to British society (of which the clergy are a part) as a whole.

Herein lies the danger of breaking the fragile balance between the contradictory attitudes towards Masonry. One very serious German Catholic lady remarked to me that "the Freemasons really do not mean anything save to themselves, but compromise the very *idea* of religion in Germany". It was a remark that clearly epitomizes just such a break, for it confuses subjective and objective criteria. What this remark really means is that "Although they are not serious, they nevertheless do great harm to German religion by their very unseriousness." This, in turn, means that, being considered unserious from her outsider's point of view, but at the same time being regarded by some as a religious organization, Freemasonry disseminates a kind of trivializing "religious unseriousness" that only contributes to the increasing materialism and agnosticism in modern Germany.

This example is instructive. For hardly anybody from outside a given religion can, when speaking of it, avoid confusion: he almost always confuses the seriousness of the attitudes of the religion in question towards the problems which *he* considers serious with the seriousness of its attitude to itself. If the modern Catholic church cannot help showing its absolute seriousness towards abortion, deprivation and poverty in the Third World, and its own New Liberation Theology in Latin America as matters of doctrine, Freemasonry as an institution cannot show *its* seriousness towards the same problems for the simple reason that they do not form part of the Masonic ideological framework. Similarly, while Judaism cannot remain dogmatically indifferent to the physical and mental state of a believer before he enters the Synagogue in the morning, and requires him to observe the ritual of purificatory ablution, Freemasonry does not care to know what a Mason did before he entered the Lodge, or what will he do after leaving it. That is why it is totally senseless to blame Freemasonry for the fact that some Masons in the police force are guilty of nepotism, or cover up for each other's wrongdoings, or that Brothers in the profession favour their own kind, or that prominent members of the Craft are sometimes to be found in brothels. All this may be true, and it may show how immoral they are as policemen, as professionals, or as husbands, but it can go no further than this. Freemasonry, by the letter and spirit of its constitution, is not concerned with private individual morality. Each member must act according to his own conscience, however much his fellow Masons may deplore the consequences (or aid and succour him for that matter). They act in this area as individuals and not as Masons. So it was inevitable that Masonry, with its institutional indifference to the problems and dilemmas of the world at large, became *abstracted* – for want of a better word – from the changing socio-cultural conditions of the world and forfeited its right to be taken seriously by it.

Furthermore, the terms "apprentice", "master" and "work" in such exhortations in the Old or Gothic Constitutions as "an apprentice should be honest with his master", or "he should not fornicate", or "he should be good at his work", became part of the symbolic apparatus, separated from their primarily ethical context. Previously, a Master Mason on a building site and a Master in a Lodge were not merely one and the same person but one and the same *thing*. But after the Lodge became abstracted from the building site and brought the latter inside it as a symbol, it could not be concerned with the real building site any more than it could with a real battlefield or general elections, although Freemasons as persons outside the Lodge may have been very much concerned with, or involved in, all these things. That is, having been abstracted from the actual profession of building, Freemasonry became abstracted from this actual builder's fornication, or dishonesty, or whatever. Far more important, however, is that in principle, at least, a fornicating builder, having entered the Lodge, becomes as abstracted from his building profession as he is from his fornication. Thus Free-masonry, being within itself very social, has managed to become and remain, in principle, divorced from the various social realities of its separate members as well as, to a degree, from the reality of society around it.

This is too simple and general to be entirely true, as sociological generalities usually are, but it is true to the extent to which society in general reacts to the social, political and religious non-involvement of Freemasonry, and react it does with an utter ambivalence: it is irritated by the non-involvement of Freemasonry, which it condemns for its unseriousness, while strongly suspecting at the same time that it *must* be maliciously or anti-socially involved: no social institution can *really* be indifferent to society. Here, a curious question might be asked: has the attitude of the outside world in regarding Freemasonry as something utterly unserious influenced Masonic self-consciousness in this respect? Evidently it has – particularly if one takes into account how accomplished the English are at doing unserious things seriously, and vice versa. But who says these are not serious things? Definitely not Freemasons themselves, for they have usually taken their activities very seriously. That, however, was reflected in their attitude to the accusations flowing from outside, and was not at all indicative of their attitude to themselves. This problem was formulated, though slightly differently, by an Italian hermeneutist, Franco Micchelini-Tocci, and my Masonic friend Geoffrey K.: the focus of Freemasonry is its Ritual, which, in contrast to the main rituals of the Catholic Church and the Church of England, is not supposed to intercede either with the course of events in the world outside Freemasonry or with the lives of Freemasons outside their Lodges. So, it is the game that matters most, not the team or the club, nor even obtaining a result that has any meaning beyond the Ritual itself. On the other hand, the results of the main Christian rituals are intended to have an effect which is not confined to the concrete physical space of the Church or even to the individual lives of its congregation. Dogmatically speaking, each Christian ritual is objectively beneficial not only to churchgoers but to the whole world.

"Social justification for any ritual is in its positive effect on the community that supports, cultivates it and preserves its tradition, or at least, its positive effect on those who perform it", says Jules Lombard, the self-styled Grand Master of one of the schismatic French Lodges, and further declares: "The true Masonic Ritual does not and cannot have that *social* effect even on the Masons themselves."

He is quite right: no social activity of any Mason could be accounted for or derived from the Ritual. Therefore it would be essentially erroneous to affirm, as so many often do, that the social behaviour of Freemasons is determined by the fact that they are Freemasons. Moreover, it could not even be said to be determined by so-called "Masonic ideals", since from the point of view of Freemasonry, one joins the Lodge precisely because one already possesses these ideals, and not because one wishes to acquire them by joining a Lodge. In other words, to become a Freemason is tantamount to performing or participating in the esoteric Ritual of Freemasonry in order to acquire the right to do this. And this right can be acquired only by being subject to a ritual which, itself, has absolutely nothing to do with anything exoteric, ideals included. This intention is diametrically opposed to the intentions of the Freemasons' most ferocious historical enemies, the Jesuits, for whom there is, in principle, no division whatsoever between esoteric and exoteric, inner and outer, individual and social, religious and political. Yet nobody would dream of accusing the Jesuits of unseriousness. It is worth remembering in this connection that the Society of Jesus was dissolved by Pope Clement XIV in 1773 precisely because the Jesuits were becoming *too* social and were adapting too actively to the changing social conditions of the world in which they proselytized. When in the following year (1774) the Marquis de Pombal, himself a good Freemason, expelled the Jesuits from Portugal and Brazil (and even exterminated some of them in the process), he did so not because of their secrecy and esotericism, nor even because of his own Masonic loyalties, but for fear of their direct political involvement and growing political influence. He was very serious too, not as a Freemason, but as a statesman. When this benevolent and liberal gentleman persecuted the Jesuits, he was scarcely aware that in doing so he was repeating almost exactly what Philip "the Fair" of France did to the Knights Templar some four hundred years earlier, and what the Jesuits themselves would undoubtedly have done to Freemasons, had they only been able, some hundred years later.

Nevertheless, to return to our problem, even in its abstractedness, Freemasonry could not help repeating some essential features common to a number of religious sects and particularly those where ritual is secret, esoteric and *a fortiori* the most fundamental component of religious activity. It is worth repeating that there often exists within certain ritualistic religions a section where ritual is everything or almost everything, and where a special religious knowledge is regarded as derived from ritual and not the other way around. Very often such sections are considered eccentric or nonsensical, even from the point of view of the religion of which they form a part; nonsensical because the ritual is performed for its own sake and not on behalf of anyone or anything else within that religion or outside it. But, as has already been stated more than once here, Freemasonry is not consistently regarded as a religion by other religions and is only judged half-heartedly or inconsistently as such by the minority of Freemasons themselves. Masonic Ritual, therefore, seen simply as it is, divorced from a religious context, appears to the former as sheer nonsense and to the latter, unsurprisingly, as pure ritual. Freemasons, when they explain their Ritual, explain it very extensively, that is, on the one hand they explain its historical origin and roots, and on the other what it means symbolically (or emblematically, following A. E. Waite) to themselves. An external observer like me tries to explain it by means of comparing it with other rituals and ritual in general, taking into account Masonic explanation as an *inner* understanding which, in a way, pertains to that very Ritual and is one with it. And in doing this an external observer cannot help feeling that not only from the point of view of the world outside the Lodge must its ritual be seen as nonsense, but that Masons themselves could not help seeing it as nonsense if they were to put themselves in the place of those from outside. That is where "Masonic unseriousness" begins, in that unavoidable ambiguity of the relation of Masons to their Ritual: the Ritual is objectively the basis of their unseriousness – although subjectively they are deadly serious about it – as well as of the whole institution. Without the Ritual Freemasonry would simply be another Rotary Club or Society of Oddfellows. With its Ritual it is comparable to Buddhist tantrism – and in this respect more religious than the Church of Scientology, Quakerism, or even the Low Church.

May I, as an outsider, venture a guess that there is something in the British character which corresponds to that Masonic ambiguity, something which is congenial with Masonic unseriousness, and probably something which, while binding the British man to social conventions, strongly impels him at the same time either to indulge himself in the complete (though usually temporary) anarchy and chaos of an entirely unconventional and often anti-social life, or to secure for himself a place in an organization, itself extremely conventional but entirely abstracted from all other conventions of society? And, indeed, does not such an extreme representative of solitary seclusion from society as Robert Louis Stevenson represent but one of its three faces, the second and third being embodied in William Blake and Oscar Wilde? The fact is not that you cannot be serious all the time, but that all the time you have in your character that streak of unseriousness which only waits for the opportunity to assume its form – be it the self-imposed isolation of a learned recluse, wild indulgence in debauchery, or the eccentric "parallel" society of Freemasons. In trying to sum up more precisely what I mean, I would have to stress, once again, that the concrete shape of Freemasonry can be accounted for by the fact that it is a religious society, but one *without* its own specifically religious message or cause. For message implies the idea of an appeal to the world outside, while cause means that there is some work to be done for the sake of the future – be it the future of Freemasonry, or the rest of human kind, or both. But Masonry, despite its rapid spread as an *organization* in the eighteenth century, has always been a phenomenon oriented centripetally and to the past, never centrifugally and to the future.

Freemasonry, as I see it here and now, is flesh and blood of the very spirit of the seventeenth century. This is particularly true of Freemasonry in Britain, a country which still feeds on the fodder of the nineteenth century and regards some leading ideas of the beginning and first half of the twentieth century as novel, or at least as intellectual extravagances. Civilizational nostalgia is a cultural pastime of the British. But this is also true of Freemasonry everywhere – this may in part explain why the Nazis hated the Freemasons almost as much as the Jews and the Gypsies, and certainly far more than any other group among the European population, Communists included. They could not help sensing that Freemasonry, apart from being avowedly cosmopolitan and trans-ethnic (as, indeed, were the Communists at that time), was irredeemably *historical*. The Nazis, in company with the Communists then (before the notorious "self-liquidation" of the Third Communist International in 1943, by Stalin's order), were utterly anti-historical in their extremely negative attitudes towards the history of European culture in all its decadence. They were also determinedly trans-historical in their ideology: trans-historical in the sense that the final aim of the National Socialist movement was to establish an "eternal order" beyond the course of history; to start the "last phase", whereby the dead weight of history would be cast off, and the New Man, freed from the inherited burden of his culture, would begin his victorious march through a universe without a past. Freemasonry and Jewry formed islands of historicity in a Europe torn apart by the Second World War and demoralized by militarist and totalitarian ideologies.

Seen in this light, the extremely anti-Masonic stance of the Communists can also be easily understood, though in a slightly different manner. Unlike the Nazis, the Marxists began to shape their ideology as historical, as the ultimate theory of history, while still allowing European culture (Christianity included) to stand, although no more than temporarily, as a relative value. More than that, Freemasonry itself, particularly in France, was utilized by the Socialists as an anti-clerical force, with the Jesuits as the chief clerical opposition. And until the mid-1920s, Communism tolerated International Freemasonry as a still somewhat progressive force, despite its Christian associations.

The change came with a reinterpretation of the Marxist philosophy of history. On the one hand Marxism essentially remained *the* method of explanation of history, at the very centre of which was the revolutionary idea of the development of means of production within the framework of the modes of production. Yet, on the other hand, there appeared the idea of a proletarian class which was destined by the objectivity of the course of history to bring that very history to its end. The working class, previously conceived of as the "grave-digger of capitalist society", became the grave-digger of history itself. This position, which was clearly more trans-historical, gained ground in the international Communist movement from 1916 to 1936, during which time Freemasonry came to be regarded as an utterly hostile element, not only because of its being a variety of bourgeois ideology (belonging, in other words, to the previous historical stage by definition), but also and foremost, by virtue of its being a stronghold of European historicity in a context where the objectively dominant tendency was anti-historical. And all the more so since Freemasonry in the 1930s was probably the only international organization which even numerically rivalled the Third Comintern. When, however, the Soviet leadership turned away from the internationalist orientation of the previous period to a kind of Russian chauvinist Communism (explicitly in 1942, implicitly as early as 1937–8), the emphasis of the anti-Masonic propaganda quite logically shifted from the bourgeois historicity of Freemasonry to bourgeois cosmopolitanism and "foreignness".

I think that nothing reveals the basic ambiguity of Freemasonry more than the shifting, though in essence unchanged, attitudes of its adversaries. Totally cosmopolitan in its ideology, it is also the quintessence of European enlightenment culture, in the form that this took in the seventeenth century. Being entirely Judaeo-Christian in its initial premises and born of the English and partly the German Reformation, it remains catholic in its universal character and spread. And finally, being undeniably British as regards its official origins, it still bears some distinctive traces of its continental, and first and foremost German, antecedents.

In the secular and mostly non-Christian civilization of today, Freemasonry plays objectively – irrespective of whether it is aware of it or not – the role of conserver and storer of cultural – more especially Christian – values.[3] Moreover, unserious and irrelevant as it may appear from the point of view of both de-religionized society and secularized religion, it constitutes a crucial factor in the impending re-religionization and re-Christianization of society. The Church of England and Catholicism, on the other hand – though in different ways – are still desperately trying to adapt themselves to the changing conditions of modern society, which itself is as doomed to degeneration and decline as was its predecessor – the European Christian world of the turn of the century. The otherwise useful maxim "better late than never" does not apply here. For a religion to adapt to the conditions of secular modernity is never a good bargain, but the Church of England has not yet learnt that lesson. There is no denying, of course, that the present situation of the Church of England is far more complex than that of British Freemasonry. The former, being a willing part and parcel of British life, insists on complicating matters by inflating its significance in direct proportion to its increasing marginality, while the latter merely stands aside. It just goes on without expending too much effort in showing what it is. Might not the Church of England have deposited some of the social neutralism and asocial individualism peculiar to it in the institution of Freemasonry so that they may be stored there until the time is ripe for them to be requested back?

Speaking historically, one may think of British Freemasonry as of a certain shape, moulded by history, for individual religious self-awareness; a shape which, once moulded, has continued to exist without any fundamental change practically since the time of the unification of both Grand Lodges, Ancient and Modern. We have already learnt that the subject of history consists of the changes in its objects, and that the shifts in Masonic religious self-awareness are perceivable only in their external manifestations, and almost exclusively in the relations of Free-masonry with the outside world. But since these indicators of inner development have been few and far between during the last two hundred years or so, one must fall back on the conception of "external" Masonic history as a series of reactions to Freemasonry by the world outside, and of Masonic counter-reactions to these. And that is why, while deliberating over the changes in modern British Freemasonry and trying to find in them some trends which could be seen as specific to our time, we would again end up at the point at which we began the introduction: the rapidly moving world versus the almost static body of symbolic builders.

The only thing then left to ask for a curious external observer would perhaps be: could that gap in the velocity of historical change between Freemasonry and the rest of the world (country, society) account for all, or most, of the so-called Masonic problems?

But the theme is drawing to its close. The main trend in present-day Masonry in Britain is that it has definitely been on the defensive since the end of the Second World War. I am inclined to think of this trend as being determined by three main factors:

1. That Freemasonry in Britain, as an institution, does not consti-tute a political, politically influential, or politically influenced group.[4] Unlike their generally more left-wing French colleagues, British Masons are more or less evenly distributed from the slightly

left of centre, through the centre, to the no more than slightly right of centre of the political spectrum. That is what has eventually made Freemasonry in this country an easy target for the radical left critique, as well as for right-wing populist accusations. 2. That due to the conditions and circumstances of its origination and spread, Freemasonry in this country has never been anti-clerical. For not only is British Freemasonry inconceivable without the inclusion of Anglican clergy, but its very functioning – particularly in the higher echelons of the Craft and in the Higher Degrees – is very clerical in character and style. From this it follows that however sharp might be the ecclesiastical critique of the Masonic involvement of the clergy, it remains, in a rather strange way, an inner or domestic business of the Church of England, or of the United Grand Lodge, or both, but it never assumes the form of a conflict between the Church and Masonry, as is the case in France. 3. And finally, that it is precisely due to their political non-involvement, social abstractedness, religious vagueness, and ideological unseriousness, that the Masons in Britain spontaneously worked out and developed an entirely informal and loose infra-structure, an infra-structure which can be conceived of as a set of unsystemized "soft" preferences, based on the following principle: that when there is a choice between two options (or candidates, if it is about jobs or contracts) of equal value, one Masonic and another non-Masonic, then a preference is given to the first. It may be dubious practice, but I do not think that there is much more to it than that, or more sinister than the "old boy" network in whatever guise it may take.

Summing up what has been said of Masonic politics and economics taken together, I conclude, together with Lynn Dumeril, that Freemasonry does not mediate between its members and the outside world.[5]

However, these three factors – political, religious and economic – determine the present-day situation of Freemasonry in the eyes of an external observer, though only in so far as he is concerned with that which seems to be changing and temporary in the reaction of the Fraternity to the changing world and vice versa. Furthermore, in the whole balance of forces and tendencies which characterize the Masonic situation, these factors are far outweighed by other factors which have characterized the institution from its very inception and will not cease to characterize it in time to come. Indeed, I would never have dared even to start writing this conglomeration of facts, ideas, considerations and speculations (of others as well as my own) if I had not felt, from the outset, that the *theme* of Freemasonry is much broader than Freemasonry itself. Because, in the final analysis, it is about the fixation of that which is most essential to British civilization and which when grafted onto other civilizations, Western and Oriental, new and old, revealed itself as essential to all of them, or as the old Count S. Poborovsky remarked, essential in its "non-essentiality".[6]

Notes

1 William Hutchinson, *The Spirit of Masonry*, London, 1987 [W. Hutchinson, 1987 (1775)], p. 21.

2 The index of references shows how many references a particular item has per unit of text, within a given period of time. Freemasonry, therefore, is mentioned once per forty-three units of text in the period 1983–5.

3 One of the typical characteristics of the Masons' preservation of civilization is that at each stage of cultural development, while preserving these stages it remains almost entirely alien to all new artistic and cultural tendencies, starting with the sentimentalism and romanticism of the end of the eighteenth century (very conservative itself), and ending up with the literature of the Victorian period.

4 For if it were a power, it would be a power without politics, or even without policy. "Freemasonry's influence is for moral, not material improvement." [M. B. S. Higham, Grand Secretary, in *The Times*, 20 September 1988, p. 13.] Even allowing for Masonic rhetoric, I am inclined to think that one cannot but accept this self-description of his as a clear instance of genuine Masonic self-awareness.

5 L. Dumeril, 1984, p. XII. That is why she calls Freemasonry an "expressive" organization, unlike a trade union or a political party, which mediate by definition and are thereby classified as "instrumental" organizations.

6 This is not a pun, for very often we do regard as "non-essential" that which, though not playing a significant role in our everyday life and language, spontaneously reveals itself as significant to all epochs and civilizations in general. That is why the application of the word "archetype" to Masonry as organization (and not only as Ritual) is quite justifiable (L. Dumeril, 1984, p. XI).

APPENDIX A

A Sociological Annexe

. . . sociological phenomena are objectively studied only to the extent that their subjective meaning is taken into account and that the people studied are potentially capable of sharing the sociological consciousness that the sociologist has of them.

David Pocock, *Social Anthropology*[1]

The notion of the *sociology of religion* – and I have all along been treating Freemasonry as a religion or, at least, as a religious phenomenon – is used in two very different senses. Firstly, it studies a religion as a part, aspect or element of a society or of a social group. The society in this case is the object of investigation, and the religion in question figures as an additional dimension in that sociological investigation, side by side with some other dimensions such as social psychology, social linguistics, social statistics and so forth. When used in the second sense, sociology of religion studies a religion taken as a primary object of investigation where "the social" would figure as that which is derivative from and modelled upon "the religious", serving very often as a function of the latter and not the other way round.

To give a simple example, let us consider, for instance, the phenomenon of unilinear vertical hierarchy in the Catholic Church in the fourteenth century. From the point of view of the sociology of religion in the first sense, it reflects the essential features of the structure of medieval European feudalism. From the point of view of the sociology of religion in the second sense, it may well be regarded as a reflection of the Catholic Christian iconographic scheme, and in part the theological conception of the hierarchy of Divine Powers within the framework of Christian monotheism.[2] In this short account I will try, in an inevitably rather over-simplified way, to combine these two sociologies of religion, adding to them, whenever possible, some elements of the third approach – a phenomenology of social perception. This may prove useful in any attempt to understand the forms which individual religious consciousness assumes when it manifests itself in its social or societal aspects.[3]

Let us take a simple problem: the social composition of Freemasonry. Few anti-Masonic male authors would have been unacceptable to, or least of all disqualified for, Freemasonry for any reason other than lack of desire on their part to join it (not to mention the fact that some of them actually were Freemasons prior to becoming anti-Masons). The class or social status of those who wrote, and still write, for or against Freemasonry is a false problem, sociology or not, for it is *writers* who write, and *profession* here is far more important than any other sociological category. And strange to say, it is one's profession (including that of "gentleman")[4] that is registered in the official Masonic membership registers for, let us not forget, the name "Freemason", though a *professional* title, symbolizes a *religious* institution just as the name "Fisherman" symbolized the early Christian Church. The profession of Mason here is the symbol of religion, not the other way round, and that is what made the late A. E. Waite so indignant; that the "emblematic Freemasonry" of Dr Anderson "usurped" the emblems of working Masonry to denote "a kind of Universal Religion", while the traditional Institute of professional Masons was unequivocally Christian. Everyone knows that to be a Christian is not a profession (even if one has none other) unless one is a priest, although this is a case that we shall consider later.

Now let us look at the chronological List of Worshipful Masters of Lodge No. 302 in the city of Bradford (1794–1944). Out of the 110 Worshipful Masters listed below there are seventy-six different recorded occupations. The number of persons involved in one occupation is put in brackets; all occupations other than trades are in italics, and trades connected, directly or indirectly, with architecture and building are marked with asterisks: 1. Bagging Manufacturers (1); 2. Innkeeper (1); 3. Bookseller (1); 4. Hat-maker (1); 5. Painter(1)*; 6. Cordwainer (3); 7. Grocer (1); 8. *Bank-clerk* (1); 9. Sty-maker (1); 10. Shopkeeper (1); 11. Woolsorter (1); 12. Joiner and *Architect* (1)*; 13. Worsted-Spinner (1); 14. *Gentleman* (2); 15. Printer (3); 16. Stone-Merchant (1)*; 17. Dyer (2); 18. Chemist (1); 19. Draper (2); 20. Merchant (9); 21. Broker (2); 22. Hatter (1); 23. Soap Manufacturer (1); 24. Builder (2)*; 25. *Architect* (3)*; 26. *Surgeon* (1); 27. Manufacturer (3); 28. Cashier (2); 29. Stationer (1); 30. Jeweller (2); 31. *Dentist* (1); 32. *Traveller* (1); 33. Engraver (2); 34. Leather Merchant (1); 35. *Solicitor* (2): 36. *Comptroller of Taxes* (1); 37. Woollen Draper (1); 38. *Borough Surveyor* (1); 39. *Commission Agent* (1); 40. Stuff Merchant (1); 41. *Clerk in Holy Orders* (3); 42. Joiner and Builder (1)*; 43. *Stockbroker* (1); 44. Tailor (1); 45. Machine-maker (1); 46. Wine Merchant (1); 47. *Journalist* (1); 48. *Surveyor* (2); 49. Cigar-Manufacturer (1); 50. *Accountant* (1); 51. *Civil Engineer* (1); 52. Plasterer (3)*; 53. *Vocalist* (1); 54. Wool Merchant

(4); 55. *Schoolmaster* (1); 56. *Chartered Accountant* (1); 57. Boot Merchant (2); 58. Boilermaker (1); 59. *Insurance Manager* (1); 60. Butcher (1); 61. Clothier (1); 62. Motor Agent (1); 63. *Commercial Traveller* (1); 64. Yarn Salesman (1); 65. Dye-ware Merchant (1); 66. Agent (1); 67. Jeweller's Agent (1); 68. *Foreign Bank Manager* (1); 69. *Electrical Engineer* (1); 70. *Chief Superintendent of Police* (1); 71. Contractor (2)*; 72. *Insurance Secretary* (1); 73. Textile Representative (1); 74. Engineer's Merchant (1); 75. Warehouse Manager (1); 76. Dry Goods Salesman (1).⁵

The picture reflects an immense proliferation of what have traditionally been called trades, and the predominance of these trades over other occupations (or "callings", as they figure in the list). Out of seventy-six callings and 110 persons practising them, we find only thirteen non-trade occupations (that of "gentleman" included) with only eighteen persons practising them. Moreover, among the latter there are only eight so-called professions proper and ten professional people. Such an abundance of trades and scarcity of professions and other occupations does not seem to be surprising, taking into consideration the economic situation and conditions of life in Bradford in the nineteenth century. However, even considering the regional differences and historical changes, such as the difference between Bradford then and Covent Garden in 1794 – not to speak of the changes which took place in both Bradford and Covent Garden between 1794 and 1944 – the fact remains that it is traders who have always constituted the social basis of Freemasonry in Great Britain. In this connection it would not be superfluous to remark that among those 110 Worshipful Masters only three were clergymen and only fourteen belonged to eight trades directly connected with building and architecture.

It is interesting to compare our historical list of the professions of the Worshipful Masters of the Mother Lodge of Bradford, continuing over a period of 250 years, with the professional composition of the membership of one quite ordinary Lodge taken at random in present-day West London (recorded in March 1987):

1. Builder (3); 2. Contractor (2); 3. Pharmacist (1); 4. Shopkeeper (3); 5. Butcher (1); 6. Travel Agent (1); 7. Salesman (3); 8. Telecom Engineer (2); 9. Light Engineer (1); 10. *Computer Programmer* (1); 11. *Civil Engineer* (1); 12. Plumber (1); 13. Newsagent (1); 14. Carpenter (1); 15. *Methodist Preacher and Voluntary Social Worker* (1); 16. Policeman (1); 17. Wine Merchant (1); 18. Fireman (1); 19. Joiner (1); 20. Garage owner (1); 21. Motor Mechanic (2); 22. *Assistant Bank Manager* (1); 23. Second-hand car dealer (1); 24. *Insurance Broker* (1); 25. Electrical

Engineer (2); 26. Grocer (2); 27. *Ex-serviceman* (1); 28. Publican (1); 29. Fishmonger (1).

Even considering that the number of Bradford Worshipful Masters is three times that of all members of this suburban London Lodge (110 to thirty-nine), and that in the first case we have the distribution of occupations over a span of 250 years while in the second we are looking at only one year, it is remarkable that the ratio of occupations to trades in the Bradford Lodge from 1794 to 1944, and in the West London Lodge in 1987, is practically the same – 1.4.

This demonstrates the considerable stability of the occupational composition over the years of English Freemasonry, and the largely trade-oriented character of it. All this, of course, is not to say that there are no Lodges that are more homogeneous professionally, or even any consisting of persons of similar occupations or of one occupation only. There are Army Lodges, and Navy Lodges. An acquaintance of mine told me that his Lodge (in Mayfair) consists of eight *doctors*, three *solicitors*, two booksellers, one *mathematician*, two architects, three *teachers*, one *writer*, two *surgeons*, and two *judges* – the proportion of professions to trades is here completely reversed. But speaking of ordinary Lodges – that is, those Lodges whose membership is mainly local and which are composed basically on the principle of neighbourhood – the variety of occupations is as great now as it was in the Mother Lodge of Bradford.[6]

Its records describe some of the occupations of the ordinary founding members of this Lodge:

It is at this stage (1794–5) that the Minutes begin to record the callings . . . and we are enabled to see that . . . they include a pattern-maker, a hatter, a cordwainer (the old style of the shoemaker . . .), a canal-waterman, an innkeeper from Wisby, an engineer and a millwright from Bowling, where iron was already being smelted and wrought, a worsted manufacturer, and a gentleman who had newly come to reside at Crossley Hall in the fields beyond Fairweather Green.[7]

Two salient factors contributed a great deal to the formation and development of the religious situation which could be, however putatively, regarded as the background of the formation of Lodges such as these, at least in England, if not in the rest of Protestant Europe. Firstly, the Reformation dealt a mortal blow to a large section of the medieval division of labour (which by no means always coincided with other divisions such as class or estate) – the *clergy*, who then and now, in non-Protestant Christianity, fall into the social category of actual or potential performers of rites or sacrificers. And according to the modern classification of sociology of religion, the rest of the Christian population, the laity, would be counted as believers. This is not an entirely valid classification, however, for "believers versus unbelievers" was not an opposition made until the beginning of the eighteenth century, or before the inception of institutional speculative Masonry. For pre-Reformation Christendom the whole meaningful cosmos consisted of believers: either the true believers who followed Christ, or those whose beliefs were deficient, or downright wrong – Jews, infidels, heathens. Unbelief as a possibility simply did not exist before the sixteenth century, taking some two centuries to become crystallized as an idea.

Protestantism abolished the division of Society into "sacrificers" and "non-sacrificers". In this connection, what the Protestant ethos is about can be reduced to "one's religious belief and one's mundane profession". This formula establishes an *inner* (that is, within the same individual) division into the religious and the non-religious, instead of dividing the whole of society into two such categories, and includes, for example, to illustrate the limit of its social concretization, a dentist who is a Baptist lay preacher in his spare time. The notions of "belief" and "believer" assumed a new and specifically religious meaning, and they became not only terms of Protestant religious self-awareness, but also terms for Protestant awareness of all other religions including Freemasonry. Nor is it surprising that for nearly three centuries they continued to remain, in one way or another, the main terms used for description of any religion by those observing it from outside, most influentially, of course, by ethnographers and social anthropologists in the nineteenth century and the beginning of the twentieth century. The idea that the basis of Christianity is the ritual was ousted by Protestant theologians and scholars alike into the realm of Catholicism, paganism, or common superstition. Protestantism lost not only the category of sacrificers as a social group, but the *idea* of an autonomous religious action, conveniently forgetting that, historically, not a single known religious belief, idea or conviction has ever emerged from any context other than that of ritual.[8]

When a newly initiated Master Mason says at the end of the Ritual "I am Hiram", we should not take it that he believes that he really is Hiram. For, in the context of this, as well as practically any other ritual, a belief or thought are neither primary nor formative in relation to ritual itself. On the contrary, it is ritual or, rather, its performance that by *its mere fact* generates the very phenomenon of "belief" or "believer". Nor, as we have already learnt from the description of the Ritual of initiation of Master Mason, could the phrase "I am Hiram" express, or be in any other way related to, the Candidate's "belief in the existence of a Superior Being". Strictly speaking, the phrase expresses nothing that is not part of the Ritual.[9]

The term religion almost inevitably involves the idea of what we would call a profession (minister, priest, lay preacher, guru, etc.) or, more generally, a vocation or calling. It means that in almost every known religion it is possible to single out a certain degree of a participant's personal involvement beyond which he or she *objectively* – from the point of view of an external observer – becomes a kind of "religious professional". From the point of view of any system of social differentiation, social stratification and specialization in terms of division of labour, religion can be described not only as an aspect of society as a whole but also as a social phenomenon in its own right, as a society within society.[10] Therefore, the category of professional specialization is applicable to it as to any other complex social phenomenon.

However, and it does not take a great deal of thinking, sociological or otherwise, to realize it, having or even expounding beliefs cannot count as a profession in the sense just described. The social anthropologist and the sociologist can make it their profession to *conceptualize* religion and that, in fact, is what each one untiringly does himself while at the same time accusing every one else of doing it. This kind of conceptualization is not the business of religion, however, since primarily what religion conceptualizes is not its ideas/beliefs, and so forth, but its specifically religious actions: its basic rituals.[11] And that is the core of what is, in some religions only, called "theology", which, of course, is a profession. Protestant theology represents then a kind of parasitic activity consisting of the reinterpretation of Catholic theology and secondarily, the reinterpretation of texts. When the Doctors of Divinity rushed into Freemasonry at the beginning of the eighteenth century, it was partly because of a lack of any opportunity for a specifically religious *professionalism* in their religion; they were driven to the secret societies to make up for the *deritualization* of their religion.[12] For it is abundantly clear that, speaking of Freemasonry as an already formed religious institution, the Third Degree of Craft Masonry symbolizes or substitutes the priesthood as it still exists in Catholicism. In Freemasonry, as we know it from the beginning of the eighteenth century, and as it has known itself from that time, the performance of the Ritual of Master Mason is priestly by definition, and each Master Mason is a sacrificer in his own right.

It can be understood from direct observation of the phenomenon of

Freemasonry – and not indirectly inferred from our own conceptualiz-ation of it – that this phenomenon has filled the social need for a priestly occupation, that category in the division of labour of which the Protestant priests as actual, and laymen as potential, sacrificers had been deprived by the Reformation.

Looked at from this angle, therefore, it was not the natural social status of Joseph Holt Buckley, Gentleman, that made him the Master of the Lodge for 1836, and it was not the social ambition of Mr Isaac Walmsley (Master of the same Lodge for the next year) to preside over Gentlemen, that united both of them in Freemasonry; it was their intention to become sacrificers that made them Freemasons. In other words, it was the need to become *professional* priests, to attain an active spiritual authority in a ritual context, that united all of them – shoe-makers, hatters, lawyers, Dissident Preachers, Anglican priests, gentle-men, and working stonemasons – under the banner of *symbolic* Masonry. Moreover, it was that very same tendency that gradually, in the process of its development and expansion, assumed a rich variety of forms and proceeded in several different directions, chiefly:

1. a reaction against professional Masonic symbolism (the war against "Emblematic Masonry");
2. the broadening of symbolism by means of including many non-Masonic symbols and endowing the Ritual with mystical meanings as well as adding to it some more mystical elements, particularly in the Higher Degrees;
3. the re-Christianization of Freemasonry.

All these directions, described in detail in the previous chapters, can be conceived of in terms of a sociology of religion as attempts to strengthen the professional function of the Master Mason, to make it more and more concrete and thereby isolate it as far as possible from any other occupation within the then prevalent system of division of labour. That is why a Dissident Preacher and a Doctor of Divinity who were not priests at all, as well as an Anglican priest, who was not suf-ficiently a priest, recovered in the Masonic Ritual their complete priestly function and, having once done so, spared no effort to isolate *this* profession as much as possible from their normal "external" religious duties. And this is mainly why so many religiously self-conscious Free-masons, and particularly many Protestant priests, have tried so desper-ately to present Freemasonry to the public at large as *non-religion*, for should they present it as a *religion*, they would have either to acknowl-edge that being a Protestant priest is no longer a truly *religious* profession since its divorce from the sacrificial function of the priesthood, or to confess to their own religious bigamy.

As it is presented now to the eyes of an external observer, Freemasonry can be seen as the illegitimate child of British Protestantism of the seventeenth century. This would undoubtedly be a sheer historical truism to a historian, and a rather dubious historical metaphor to a sociologist or an anthropologist of religion. But it is that very Protestant religious ideology or, following Max Weber, Protestant Ethic, that made out of a strongly institutionalized and often hereditary – in the sense of successive generations following the family tradition – profession, an extremely individualized "calling" with an utterly individual self-awareness. The seventy-six callings listed in the records of the Masters of the Lodge of Hope of Bradford demonstrate a very curious situation which could be described by a series of five oppositions, namely:

1. *Inside the Lodge*, the diversity of members' occupations is opposed to the *one* profession of Master Mason, the profession of sacrificer;
2. *Inside the Lodge*, a variety (in principle, at least) of individual religious beliefs is opposed to the one general Masonic belief in the existence of a Superior Being;
3. *Inside and outside the Lodge*, the Church of England with its relatively indeterminate attitude towards the relation of belief to ritual is opposed to an absolutely determined, self-sufficient, religiously autonomous ritual, independent from any specific belief, including belief in the existence of a Superior Being;
4. *Outside the Lodge*, for those who are in one way or another interested in Freemasonry, their own relation to religion (agnosticism and atheism included) is always seen by themselves as absolutely determined and therefore opposed to the indeterminacy of Masonic religion in general, and the non-relation to any other religion, in particular;
5. *Outside the Lodge*, the Institution of Freemasonry, which neutralizes the vertical *stratification* of society with its variety of different social statuses, is opposed to the external social order, however "just and fair" it may be according to the official Masonic view.

So whatever Freemasons themselves might think or say, I, as a privileged external observer,[13] cannot help seeing in each and every Master Mason a *priest*, and in all of them taken together a kind of priestly caste.[14] According to the sociology of religion, as I understand it, to be a priest means three different things, or three different aspects to which what we empirically observe as a priest can be reduced.

1) The priest as an embodiment of the practise of his religion – he is the form which it assumes in its actual and visible functioning. He is a professional who *does* religion.

In the case of Freemasonry any reflective, organizational and ideological activity of a Master Mason is possible only on account of his being, in the first place, a performer of the Ritual. His activity, when he reflects upon his physical performance and explains it to others in terms of "beliefs" and "convictions" that he and all Freemasons have espoused, is secondary.

However, to those who see him performing the Ritual, as well as to himself, he is the man who knows *Religion*, and not just the Ritual. But what kind of knowledge might this be if it is not that which is generated from reflection on the Ritual? The question is as intricate as it is interesting to the sociology of religion, and the answer would undoubtedly vary not only from one religion to another, but from one concrete situation to another within the same religion. Even if you take as an example the exemplary priest, an Indian Brahmin living in the third or fourth century A D, his is the ideal knowledge of a triple character – three knowledges in one. The first is the knowledge of all that a Brahmin has the *right to know*, that is his privilege not shared by any other group in society. He possesses this knowledge in virtue of his *status* in society, and not in virtue of his *position* within his religion. The second is the specific knowledge of the rituals he performs, which, all said and done, can be reduced to "know-how". The third is about the rites and religion as a whole, and embraces a certain necessary minimum of general information – of a mythological, soteriological, ethical, legal, historical character – which is related to his religion. The main thing about the third knowledge of the priest is that, though in each particular concrete case of his ritualistic activity it might be seen as the natural background of the ritual and the basis for its interpretation, within the framework of his religion as a whole it is always generated by the ritual and derived from it. For the ritual is the initial point of any religious discourse, and the know-how of ritual, however remote from religious speculation, has always formed for that discourse the set of postulates, which in Protestant ideology, and in post-Protestant science, assumed the name of *beliefs*.

The Master Mason is a priest who, interestingly enough, does not possess the first of these priestly knowledges, for the simple reason that he has no social status as such in his society – his professional position of priest is limited to his Lodge. His second priestly knowledge is highly specialized, for it is confined to a very small number of rituals (no more than four, excluding the Higher Degrees) which always remain the same in form and content. Moreover, speaking of Craft Masonry of the Three Degrees, it is mainly the knowledge of the Ritual of Master Mason that counts, and it is so specialized because the Ritual itself is almost entirely isolated from any system of clearly defined religious principles, beliefs or dogmatic postulations. These were left to the previous individual religious backgrounds of the Master Mason-priests. And that is why the third priestly knowledge acquires in a Master Mason such a peculiar character: it consists first and foremost in a symbolic interpretation of the Ritual, and not its interpretation in terms of beliefs or any of the other elements that make up the non-ritual background knowledge of the Indian Brahmin.[15] This can be seen as a specifically Masonic way of responding to Protestant theology without entering into conflict with it. Moreover, it could even be described as a reaction against Protestant ideology by means of neutralizing its theological core.[16]

2) The priest as invariably exercising a certain *power* within his own concrete religious setting, a power which may or may not be extended to some other situations in his religion as a whole. Here lies the difference between recognition of the priest's competence in making and knowing the religion (i.e. acknowledging his power in general), and his right to *exercise* that competence (i.e. his *actual* power) outside his own immediate religious context.

3) At the same time the priest possesses a certain social status varying from place to place, period to period, society to society and culture to culture; a status by virtue of which he may have the authority to exercise his power within his own society – those who acknowledge his spiritual authority. Catholic priests also exercise a temporal (social) power within the society of Catholics. The Master Mason, on the other hand, has no society in that sense, for while remaining in his Lodge and officiating at the Ritual, he is socially divorced from his co-believers in his own non-Masonic religion, if he has any. And Freemasonry as a priestly corporation is also entirely neutral to any other priestly corporation, such as a monastic order or any religious institution or community, for it is separated from and objectively opposed to all of them as a special and highly specialized group of priests who as priests do not possess any *social* status outside the whole body of Fraternity.

The two extreme cases of the priestly situation are firstly, when all persons belonging to a given religion are priests; and secondly, when there are no priests at all. (Freemasonry offers the possibility of exemplifying the first – in many smaller Lodges all the members are

Master Masons). The triple functioning of priest determines the exceptionally complex character of what may be termed choice *within* religion. Since the time when, in Europe at least, the priesthood ceased to be quasi-hereditary, which historically coincided with the time of the separation of all or most of the priestly functions from the main bulk of Protestant denominations, the problem of choosing what to accept and what to reject within one's religion, rather than embracing it in its totality, became a part of one's religious self-awareness.[17]

From my interviews, it appears that very few Freemasons, when still candidates, wanted to be admitted to the Craft specifically in order to become performers of the Ritual (in spite of my speculations as the unconscious intentionality which impelled them Masonry).[18] So, *subjectively* (from the point of view of Freemasons themselves), the main motivations remain non-religious or non-specifically religious. Out of forty persons from various Lodges whom I asked about their reasons for becoming Freemasons, only seven named the Ritual or an interest in it as the main motivation. For sixteen it was "to be in decent company"; for eleven it was more or less "to be able to do more good to society"; and for two it was a matter of better opportunities for promotion and so on. I asked the same group of interviewees to put in order of preference the main points of their interest in Freemasonry now – that is, after admission – and gave them five choices, namely: (1) interest in Ritual; (2) socializing with interesting people; (3) socializing with useful people; (4) sharing beliefs and ethical principles; (5) charity. Eighteen of them put (1) (the Ritual) first, ten – (2), six – (4), two – (3), and four – (5). Quite a reversal of priorities had taken place.

When I discussed the question of priesthood with six very learned Freemasons belonging to the Higher Degrees and offered them my interpretation of Master Mason as a priest, four of them agreed entirely, one said that my interpretation was valid only with respect to the Higher Degrees, and one rejected it point blank. Unsurprisingly, in contrast to the candidates for the Three Degrees Craft, the five who agreed with my interpretation, in one way or another, accounted for their joining the Higher Degrees by their acute interest in more complex and symbolically richer rituals and their desire to perform them.[19] Their remarks reflect the ambiguity of the position of Freemasonry with respect to the main Protestant denominations in Great Britain – an ambiguity which, from the beginning of the eighteenth century, has been inherent in British Masonic religious self-awareness and is frequently felt by Freemasons themselves.[20] It is this tension between *Protestant religiousness* and *Masonic religion* which makes a High Church clergyman, belonging to the "much higher" Degrees, a little uneasy – in his religious self-awareness, it must be emphasized, not his conscience, for he very often tries to present his own religious situation as if it were partaking of Protestant religion and Masonic religiousness in equal shares.

At last, the question may be asked which was first formulated by Durkheim and repeated innumerable times since: ". . . What society is it that has . . . made [i.e. produced] the basis of religion?"[21] *Historically*, the question has no sense at all, needless to say, and the answer will be "none". At the same time, it might be possible to reformulate it in such a way that all associations with and references to any concrete, historically existing society would be cancelled. This is done by constructing a totally abstract idea of society, an ideal which, after having assumed its symbolic form, would become the model for the social organization of any particular religion. But even then it would not be impossible to imagine the whole picture the other way around, reversing the flow of causation, and ask the following question: "What religion is it that has provided the symbolic basis for its *own* social organization?"[22] Nobody, indeed, would seriously suggest that it is the society of King Solomon's Israel that provided Freemasonry with the "model" for its social organization. Nor could it be said of any medieval corporation of working Masons, for even if we accept the hypothesis of their being the immediate predecessors of the speculative Freemasons, we will then have to admit that the former, in its social form, followed the model which was as neutral and immaterial to the organization of their actual professional activity as it was neutral and immaterial to the actual professional (i.e., priestly) activity of their successors.[23]

Astonishingly enough, however much the social forms of the religious institutions built up around a form of organized priestly ritual may have changed, essential features of the latter have remained almost unaltered during the five millennia or more of recorded human history. It is the character of the ritual that determines the way it structures itself socially, not the other way round. In Freemasonry the Ritual, due to its relatively reduced form, might be seen as reproducing some essential features of priestly organizations which in other religions have been blurred and overlaid, in the process of their development, by more complex organizational structures and superstructures.

Notes

1 David Pocock, *Social Anthropology*, London and New York, 1961, p. 89.

2 And, ironically enough, was not Max Weber saying exactly this when he stated (in *The Protestant Ethics and the Spirit of Capitalism*, New York, 1930) that, in a certain type of religion, as in the bud of a flower, one can recognize an "ideal" but definite type of society?

3 "Social" here means that which belongs to, or figures in, a given society taken as a whole. So, for instance, when we speak of the social status of a priest, it is implied that priests possess a certain place in the structure of society (English society of the eighteenth century, or French society today, etc.). Whereas "societal" is a term relating to the position of a person or group of people who are not included in any given social hierarchy and whose status is not recognized by society in general. So, for instance, the Deputy Grand Warden is a societal, not social, status.

4 I would like to stress here, that in the Masonic *societal* context, Gentleman was, in the eighteenth century, *a profession*, appearing side by side with that of carpenter or book-keeper, while in the context of the whole of English society of the eighteenth century, it was a *social status*.

5 M. S. Herries, 1948, pp. 109–12.

6 The Lodge in Mayfair is not an ordinary one in the sense that to get there some of its members commute from as far afield as Bromley and Gillingham.

7 *Idem*, p. 18.

8 "Whatever role divine interference may or may not play in the creation of faith – and it is not the business of the scientist to pronounce upon such matters one way or the other – it is primarily, at least, out of the context of concrete acts of religious observance, that religious conviction emerges on the human plane". Clifford Geertz, *The Interpretation of Cultures*, London, 1975 (C. Geertz, 1975), p. 112–13.

9 Geertz's interesting opinion is that when a Bororo Indian says, "I am a parakeet," or when a Christian says "I am a sinner", we indeed ought not to describe it in terms of beliefs, convictions or thoughts as we understand these words in a non-religious context. He writes: ". . . In the religious [perspective], our Bororo is 'really' a 'parakeet', and given the proper *ritual context* might well 'mate' with other 'parakeets' – with metaphysical ones, like himself." *Idem*, p. 121.

10 In calling religion "a social *phenomenon*" I mean that it is perceived by its own members not only as related to society in general, but as being a society in particular. This, of course, does not mean that all religions can be considered as social phenomena in this limited sense. Nor does this social phenomenality form a part or condition of definition of religion in general, but it applies nevertheless to any religious context formed by any known religions or religious sects of the Judaeo-Christian complex (including Islam).

11 So, in the final analysis, what Max Weber conceptualizes as "the Protestant Ethos" is his very secondary reflection on Protestantism's own secondary awareness of itself as based on Christian beliefs, not on rituals. For Weber's own mode of reflection was as Protestant as that of its object of conceptualization.

12 In all probability this accounts for the fact that so few Catholic priests and theologians are Masons.

367

13 I am abandoning the phenomenological principle here and adopting a strictly etic tone!

14 Even such a staunch partisan of "Three Degrees Craft Masonry" as J. G. Findel (1869, p. 11) writes: "In Freemasonry, the fundamental idea is that of a *General Priesthood* capable of voluntary action . . ."

15 This sits uneasily with what has been said before about the actual occupational composition of the Craft, for it requires a lot of free time. Ideally, it is persons of the so-called "free professions" who are best suited to the profession of Master Mason. W. Preston writes (1804, pp. 22–3): ". . . all the intricate parts of the science . . . are only intended for persons who may have *leisure and opportunity*. . . . To persons, however, whose early years have been dedicated to literary pursuits, or whose circumstances and situations of life render them *independent*, the offices of the lodge ought principally to be restricted. The industrious *tradesman* proves himself a valuable member of society . . . but the nature of his *profession* will not admit of that leisure which is necessary to qualify him to become an *expert* Mason."

16 In point of historical fact, Freemasonry as a purely priestly corporation fits perfectly the religio-sociological scheme of Max Weber, particularly when he deals with the division of labour as an essential aspect of the Protestant ethos. But to say that Freemasonry in Great Britain was a way to accommodate those who were dissatisfied with radical Protestantism while unwilling to become Catholic would be far beyond the mark; for that purpose the Anglican Church would have been an acceptable solution. I would rather conjecture that it is the spontaneous pressure of the Protestant ethos that generated in a religiously oriented individual a division between belief and ritual. See: *From Max Weber*, ed. by H. H. Gerth and C. Wright, Oxford University Press, 1946, [M. Weber, 1946 (1915)], p. 271.

17 Which eventually gave way to the modern fashionable problem of choice *between* religions.

18 This could have hardly any statistical value, but out of nineteen members of the same Lodge only two told me that they had been particularly interested in performing the Ritual at the time of their admission as Apprentices.

19 So to the rather pertinent remark of Dewar's that Freemasonry gives one "quality of life", I would have added, speaking of the Higher Degrees in particular, "quality of religion".

20 The situation of the French, Portuguese or Spanish Freemasons seems to be much easier, for they were plainly and overtly anti-Catholic. The Italian Freemasons are all too pragmatic and do not care much about their "objective" religious position, whereas poor Russian Freemasons of old were too preoccupied with social changes and cultural progress to think about their relation to the Russian Orthodox Church at all.

21 Emile Durkheim, *The Elementary Forms of the Religious Life*, trans. by J. Swain, Free Press of Glencoe, 1961. [E. Durkheim, 1961 (1912)], p. 56.

22 Provided, of course, that we deal with societies (or cultures) where religion has its own social structure different from that of society as a whole.

23 Let me remind the reader that priestly ritual is only that ritual which can be performed by the members of a specialized professional contingent of sacrificers, and which includes the ritual of initiation of new priests.

APPENDIX B

An Interlude: A Little About Masonic Favours

It is a situation in which it very soon becomes impossible to refuse to do a favour. To put it precisely, one is desperate: to put it still more precisely, one is very happy.

Franz Kafka, *The Castle*[1]

The subject at first glance seems to be too banal to be treated seriously. Yet what we deal with in the above passage from Kafka smells of curious self-cultivation, or, to put it "still more precisely", of a kind of philosophical pragmatism bordering on a refined self-indulgence. Not being altogether alien to the world of Masonic intricacies (many of his friends were Masons), Kafka could not help feeling that when it happens (and God knows it happens often enough) that one really finds oneself in a position to do a favour, the temptation to do it is almost overwhelming. And one does it for reasons which are far more complex than those of pure altruism, intellectual curiosity, self-interest, or a simple *quid pro quo*. For, when someone is in such a position, he may feel very strongly that it is up to him to decide how far the limits of his own individual power of choice can be stretched – and these should not be confused with the limits of one man's power over another. Such a person may think: "I will do it because there exists a space here for manoeuvre – a space where such a favour *can* be done", and his decision then would not necessarily involve a clash of individual desire with public duty.[2]

I do not know whether the celebrated Protestant preacher and Grand Chaplain of the Grand Lodge, Dr Dodd, had any hope that his prominent position among Masons would save him from the gallows when he forged a cheque in the name of his patron Lord Chesterfield. A posse of notables, including Samuel Johnson, endeavoured in vain to prevent his execution.[3] Nor did being a Mason help another criminal, Kenneth Noy, when he grasped the hand of the Detective Chief Superintendent with the Mason's grip, imploring him to set him free.[4] And a notorious murderer, F. H. Seddon, obviously hoped for a favourable response from the judge, who was a highly placed Mason, when he made the "sign of distress" to him during the cross-examination: of course it, too, was to no avail.[5] These cases demonstrate that there need not be, and indeed *should* not be, any clash between a Mason's fulfilment of his Masonic obligations to his fellows and the fulfilment of his social obligation to obey the law. The priorities are clearly set out in the numerous instructions to Masons on their relations to society. But in real life, of course, since even Masons are not perfect, these priorities have, on occasion, been reversed.

But do not imagine that when a favour is done or refused it is always a case of a simple and unequivocal "yes" or "no". A real favour often operates within a set of parameters formed by very many points of ambiguity, each of which is "no, but . . .", or "yes, given that . . ." which temper the impulse, determine its direction, and provide the mode of its expression. The *causes célèbres* of Masonic favours, so well trodden in both Masonic and anti-Masonic literature, occupy the broadest possible spectrum: from an American officer, rescued during the War of Independence by a Red Indian Mason from torture and death, and the hundreds of prisoners of war who were Masons helped by Masons on the enemy side,[6] to the alleged (though far from proven) "lucrative contracts" given to Masonic builders by the Masonic Councillors in the London Borough of Hackney.[7] On the surface, there is nothing dubious or ambiguous in these examples which, from practically any Masonic point of view might be regarded as instances of proper and correct Masonic behaviour. That is why I would prefer to look from a different angle at the range of Masonic favours and I will analyse four quite different examples. However, before doing this, I will make an attempt to define what I think a real Masonic favour is.

Firstly, to do someone such a favour may mean to indulge in doing something which is not entirely or not always proper and permissible even Masonically. And, secondly, to do someone this favour would necessarily mean making a small sacrifice, giving up some of your advantage for the sake of another who begs the favour. But the more this is so, the more you want to do the favour, and paradoxically, the fact of your wanting it makes you, in your own eyes, somewhat morally wanting. Your motives are suspect, even contaminated by a certain pride. Let us take, for example, such an apparently morally ambiguous situation as the following episode from the American War of Independence.

An American officer and a Mason, Colonel McKenstry, was taken prisoner by the Indians who were preparing to put him to a cruel death. In despair, he gave the Masonic sign of distress, which was noticed by a British officer, who was both a fellow Mason and a Red Indian, who immediately intervened and spared his life. Alexei Selianinoff, a well-known right-wing Russian journalist, an anti-Semite and anti-Mason, comments on this case: "This is a flagrant breach of the military oath of allegiance. The fact that Freemasonry is above the army means corruption of the officers' corps and treason on the part of individual officers."[8] So it is not surprising that the behaviour of the British officer in this case was unambiguously wrong and amounted to treachery. What is surprising is the commentary on the same episode by the prominent Masonic author John Fellows. He writes:

While this transaction reflects honour upon this officer as a *Mason*, it at the same time leaves an indelible stain upon his character as a *man*, which equally attaches to his *King* and *government*. What! employ savages as auxiliaries in war, and then stand by and look coolly on, while they amuse themselves in . . . *scalping* their prisoners, unless the latter can give the talismanic signal, and pronounce the *Shibboleth* of Masonry?[9]

This is not simply an outpouring of moral indignation, for Fellows knew that to save one person partially is better than to save none impartially. Yet he desperately wants his beloved Brotherhood to stop being exclusive and partial in their social dealings while continuing to be doctrinally secret and highly elitist. In other words, he desires to eliminate ambiguity from the idea of Masonry, not realizing that, like the inhabitants of Kafka's castle, Masons cannot do without that minimum of ethical and metaphysical manoeuvring, without which there can be no space for individual freedom of judgement within a voluntary organization of any kind, if it wants to remain voluntary.

When the young Robert Burns was reproached by a lady for his excessive drinking in Masonic company, he responded quite seriously: "Don't upbraid me, Madam – if I don't drink with them they won't thank me for my company."[10] He was no drunkard, and by that time had already become aware of his worsening state of health. So, while liking his tipple very much (nobody of his company would have denied that), he nevertheless indulged in drinking with his Masonic friends as a favour, mainly to please them and despite the fact that his inability to refuse also made him apprehensive.[11]

Another episode, related to the same period, is far more exotic Masonically. It remains unknown whether, indeed, certain inmates of a prison in London had expressed their ardent desire to be initiated, or whether the initiative had come from their visitors who, aware that there was no clause in the Constitutions specifically forbidding Masons to gather in *due form* in a prison, decided to do just that. Preston writes:

. . . On the 19th of November, 1783, information was given to the Grand Lodge, that two brethren under sanction of the Royal Military Lodge at Woolwich, which claimed the privilege of an *Itinerant Lodge*[12] had lately held an *irregular meeting in the King's Bench Prison*, and had there unwarrantably initiated sundry persons into Masonry. The Grand Lodge ... ordered the said Lodge to be erased from the list and determined that it was inconsistent with the principles of the Masonry to hold any lodge for the purpose of making, passing, or raising Masons, in any prison, or place of confinement.[13]

What happened was that a couple of officers, both Masons, happened to be visiting some of their friends in prison. (There could be no fewer than three, or the meeting would have been referred to as "non-existent", and not as "irregular".) It is highly likely that they brought some port or claret with them. After having become slightly (or heavily) inebriated, they might then have offered to initiate some other inmates of the same prison who had expressed an interest, or they might have been asked to do this – in either case it was evidently "for company's sake". What undoubtedly underlay the situation, however, was that slight feeling of ambivalence: to do something that was neither permitted, nor forbidden, neither necessary nor superfluous, but definitely a bit of a lark.[14]

The Masonic historians have treated this case with due condescension and rightly so – it was a small favour, after all. But there is, by contrast, an example of a Masonic favour that greatly transcends in importance, and in the scale of its consequences, not only all Masonic favours past, present and, dare I say, future, but, in its impact both on modern history and on the individual destinies of the persons involved, far exceeds any other favour carried out within the space of the last three centuries.

The story begins in 1914, before the beginning of the First World War, when one of the leading Socialists of the day, Vandervelde – a Belgian and one of the leaders of the Second International – went to St Petersburg for talks with his Russian colleagues, Bolsheviks and Mensheviks, about the necessity of working out a common strategy for the approaching conflict. However, as everyone remarked at the time, though Vandervelde talked a lot, it was not as much to the Russian Socialists as to the leading Russian Masons, and in particular to Maxim Kovalevsky, the chief instigator of the Masonic renaissance in Russia.[15] Back in Belgium, Vandervelde sent a telegram to his colleagues in the Russian broad left, urging them to join the French and Belgian Socialists in their struggle against German imperialism. Lenin and the Bolsheviks refused point blank, some of the Mensheviks hesitated, and some of them supported the war wholeheartedly. What, however, is of supreme importance is that the absolute majority of politically active Russian Masons supported the war against Germany, and supported it not because they considered such support consistent or even compatible with their political or moral ideals or, least of all, with their Masonic conscience, but because their French Brethren in the Lodge *Grand Orient* (and some in the English *Grand Lodge*) had implored them to do so. They requested it from Russian Masons as the *greatest possible favour* one Mason could do for another. So the Russian Masons, as a favour, swore their full allegiance to a cause which very many of them felt to be morally dubious, some felt to be totally unacceptable politically, and quite a few knew to be entirely contrary to the very spirit of Masonry.

Later on, in the spring of 1917, when the situation on both front lines, Russian–German and French–German, had gone from bad to worse, and the majority of Russian politicians. from all camps felt that there could be only one way out, to wit: a separate peace with Germany (the disintegration of the Russian Army had already begun), two French-men came to the then Prime Minister and Commander in Chief of the Armed Services, Kerensky, who was a Mason. One of them was Albert Thomas, the Minister of Armaments and a Mason of the thirtieth Degree, and the other Marcel Cachin, a radical socialist and Mason who later became General Secretary of the French Communist Party. When Colonel Poradedov, Kerensky's bodyguard, entered the room where they were conferring without knocking, he saw Thomas kneeling before Kerensky begging him hysterically not to leave France at the hour of disaster, while Cachin, overcome by weeping, hid his face in his handker-chief.[16] It must have been crystal clear to Kerensky and his ten Ministers (nine of them Freemasons) that the only thing Masonic about the favour they would be doing by continuing the war was the oath he had person-ally given to the French Lodge Grand Orient that whatever line they took regarding the war he would follow it, for none of them identified his political position at that time with any of the Masonic *ideals*.[17] So the third Provisional Government, in the penultimate stage of its inglori-ous and short-lived history, while realizing that for Russia the war was irrevocably lost, prolonged their involvement for another three months at the cost of approximately a quarter of a million lives. Yet several of them could not help feeling, even in those desperate circumstances, a certain Masonic satisfaction at the thought that although their efforts had been doomed to failure from the very start, they had nevertheless persisted in them till the last moment. I heard one of their younger contemporaries, D.L.,[18] say: "In those days of confusion and despair, my

Masonic friend T. [I suspect it was Foreign Minister Mikhail Ivanovich Teretshenko] and I were secretly glorying in being against popular opinion, in being against ourselves, and even in behaving contrary to common sense, in continuing to help the French Masons against Germany.''

But this shows how hopelessly present-oriented French Masonry had become, and how Russian Freemasonry was, almost from the beginning, doomed to defeat by following the French and not the British example. When, in the beginning of the twentieth century, Maxim Kovalevsky and some of his friends started the third (and, I am afraid, probably the last) revival of Freemasonry in Russia, and the first new Russian Lodges were warranted by the French Grand Lodges, their proclaimed aim was social and political *par excellence*. And this, almost immediately, led them objectively towards confrontation with the basic principles of Masonry itself. The Masonic ideal of universal peace, though it somehow managed to survive the reality of Russian–German war during the first two years, fell apart when the leading Russian Masons found themselves contemplating the prospect, however remote, of political power. Let us look at a small pocket prayerbook, very poorly, and secretly, published in 1915 by a *Military Lodge* for the use of half-literate Russian soldiers. We read: ''Don't kill the German Brothers, don't shoot at them; pretend to do it, if necessary, and try to miss the target.'' And only a year and a half later, one of the most influential Ministers in the Provisional Government wrote: ''All our, I still dare say, benevolent influence, all our chances of establishing a fair and just power in our half-ruined country, depends on our determination to bring our war with Germany to its victorious conclusion.'' That could hardly have been achieved by shooting in the air. And, finally, when confronted with the inevitability of revolution in Petrograd, in September–October 1917, the Masons in the Army, and some even in provisional government, forsook their own previous strategy based on doing their final favour to the French Masons, and became allies of the Bolsheviks in the Petrograd Council. How right Kovalevsky was when he said in 1914 that ''once politically involved, Freemasonry would inevitably become the worst case of political opportunism''.

The British Masons have been better students of history. Having learnt well their first lesson of political non-involvement during the Jacobite conspiracies of the beginning of the eighteenth century, they abstained, without the slightest hesitation, from any involvement in the anti-Catholic riots of Lord George Gordon in 1780, despite traditional Catholic hatred of Masons, and survived two of the worst political crises

– the American and French Revolutions. They have been abstaining ever since.

Notes

1 Trans. by W. & E. Muir, Penguin Books, London, 1957, p. 252.

2 Peter K., a policeman, Freemason, and Methodist, said: "I have never regarded myself as a bare instrument of law, or a tool in God's hands. Even being a policeman on duty, I remain a person with freedom of judgement and decision – as a religious person I mean." To which Peter Lionel, a teacher, responded: "The Freemasons are people with a highly developed sense of *individual irresponsibility*. That is what their individualism is about."

3 See in G. Oliver, 1847, pp. 241–3.

4 "The Crooked Midas", *Daily Mail*, 4 July 1986.

5 See in F. L. Pick and G. Norman Knight, 1983, pp. 123–4.

6 J.M. refers to an episode very popular in the middle of the eighteenth century: "Instances are said to have frequently occurred during land battles and naval engagements of the *sign* of Masonry being the means of saving life ... In the battle of Dettingen, 1745, one of the King's Guards having his horse killed under him ... was unable to extricate himself. When an English dragoon galloped to him, and was about to deprive him of his life: but the French soldier having the *sign* ... the dragoon not only saved his life, but freed him from this dangerous situation." J.M. (R.W.M.). *A Winter with Robert Burns (1786–7)*. Edinburgh, 1846. (J.M. 1846) pp. 159–60.

7 From the article by G. Parry, *The Guardian*, 8 April 1987.

8 A. Selianinoff, *The Secret Power of Masonry* (in Russian). St Petersburg, 1911 (A. Selianinoff, 1911), p. 27.

9 J. Fellows, *Mysteries*, 1866, p. v.

10 J.M. 1846, p. 127. Though G. Oliver, while commenting on the drinking habits of Dr Th. Manningham, writes that "... the only alternative a gentleman had in these days, at a dinner or tavern party, was to get drunk, or give mortal offence to his entertainer" (1855, p. 74), he was obviously aware (as was Dr Manningham himself) that even in those bucolic days excessive drinking was the main cause of the Masons' bad moral reputation.

11 "Some [in Edinburgh]", says the same author, "*became* Masons in order to meet Burns. The boy Walter Scott was then too young for initiation: 'Yet ...' said the matured Sir Walter, 'I ... would have given the world to, know him ...'" J.M., 1846, p. 32.

12 "Itinerant" means attached to a regiment and, therefore, moving with the latter. Not all Military Lodges were itinerant.

13 W. Preston, 1804, pp. 294–5. The case in question is of great interest for, as one could see it, the Grand Lodge did not, then, forbid Lodges in prisons in general, but only those met for the purpose of Initiation.

14 M. S. Margulies, a young Russian lawyer and (at that time) revolutionary, was initiated into the first three Degrees (at least) of the French *Grand Orient* in the famous Kresty (the Crosses) Prison in St Petersburg, in 1906. N. N. Berberova,

Liudi i Lozhi (in Russian): *Russkie Masony 20ze stoletia* (Russian Freemasons of the Twentieth Century), Russica Publishers, New York, 1986), N. Berberova, 1986), p. 19. His Initiation in prison was no favour at all; it does not have the ambiguity of a classical Masonic favour, however, for it was not only intended, but indeed ordered to be performed by the Council of *Grand Orient.*

15 Brushing aside the legend that Freemasonry was introduced into Russia under (or even by) Peter the Great, we may assign its beginning to a Captain John Phillips who was appointed Provincial Grand Master of Russia and Prussia in 1731. His successor, General James Keith (in the Russian service) was appointed by the Grand Lodge of England in 1740. Later, the English Rite of Three Degrees was established in St Petersburg and Moscow by Ivan Yelagin, who became Grand Master in 1772. The 1780s saw the predominance of the German, and particularly the Swedish ("Strict Observance") Masonry. Masons in general flourished under Catherine the Great, though some of them were arrested for their "revolutionary" (in fact no more than literary and educational) activity. Paul I suppressed, but did not totally prohibit, Masonry and his son Alexander I, himself a Mason, after some hesitation, permitted it once more in 1803. At the beginning of the nineteenth century the number of Lodges of all kinds in Russia was 200 to 210, and their influence on the cultural, political, and even religious life (though mostly in towns) was very significant. In 1822 Alexander I forbade all secret societies. The Masons played a very important role in Decembrist circles, and after 1825 Masonry of all varieties was totally forbidden. Till the end of the nineteenth century all known Russian Masons were members of foreign Lodges, mainly French. The re-emergence of Masonry in Russia is connected with one of these "foreign" Masons, Maxim Kovalevsky, who established in 1906 the first of several Lodges under the jurisdiction of the Grand Orient. Around 1910 the first Russian Lodges were inaugurated, which owed almost nothing to the personality and initiative of Kovalesky and were far more socially and politically oriented. J. F. Clarke, "Freemasonry in Russia" in *The Modern Encyclopaedia of Russian and Soviet History*, Vol. 15. pp. 14–18. Nathan Smith, "Masonic Movement in Russia after 1905", *idem*, Vol. 21, pp. 128–33.

16 N. Berberova, 1986, pp. 34–5.

17 Unlike their French Brethren who, at that time and later, definitely identified the Masonic ideals with the political ideals and aims of radical socialism.

18 A Russian Mason, all his life after the Revolution living in California. He is about a hundred now.

APPENDIX C

The Scheme Showing the Relationship between Five Parts of the Manual

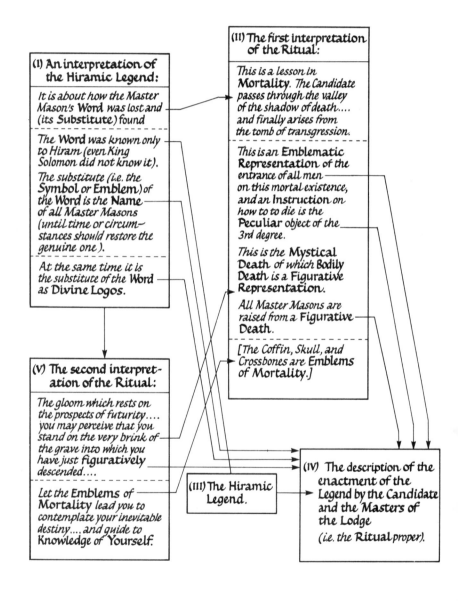

(II) The first interpretation of the Ritual:

This is a lesson in **Mortality**. *The Candidate passes through the valley of the shadow of death.... and finally arises from the tomb of transgression.*

This is an **Emblematic Representation** of the entrance of all men on this mortal existence, and an **Instruction** on how to to die is the **Peculiar** object of the 3rd degree.

This is the **Mystical Death** of which **Bodily Death** is a **Figurative Representation**.

All Master Masons are raised from a **Figurative Death**.

[*The Coffin, Skull, and Crossbones are* **Emblems** *of Mortality.*]

(I) An interpretation of the Hiramic Legend:

It is about how the Master Mason's Word was lost and (its **Substitute**) found

The **Word** was known only to Hiram (even King Solomon did not know it).

The substitute (i.e. the **Symbol** or **Emblem**) of the Word is the **Name** of all Master Masons (until time or circumstances should restore the genuine one).

At the same time it is the substitute of the **Word** as **Divine Logos**.

(V) The second interpretation of the Ritual:

The gloom which rests on the prospects of futurity.... you may perceive that you stand on the very brink of the grave into which you have just **figuratively** *descended....*

Let the **Emblems** *of* **Mortality** *lead you to contemplate your inevitable destiny.... and guide to Knowledge of Yourself.*

(III) The Hiramic Legend.

(IV) The description of the enactment of the Legend by the Candidate and the Masters of the Lodge (i.e. the **Ritual** *proper*).

INDEX